A2 Level for **Edexcel**

# Applied **ICT**

Series editor: K. Mary Reid

www.heinemann.co.uk
✓ Free online support
✓ Useful weblinks
✓ 24 hour online ordering

01865 888058

**Heinemann**

*Inspiring generations*

Heinemann Educational Publishers
Halley Court, Jordan Hill, Oxford OX2 8EJ
Part of Harcourt Education

Heinemann is the registered trademark of
Harcourt Education Limited

© Jenny Lawson, Alan Jarvis, Peter Blundell,
Andrew Smith and Richard McGill 2006

First published 2006

10 09 08 07 06
10 9 8 7 6 5 4 3 2 1

British Library Cataloguing in Publication Data is available
from the British Library on request.

10-digit ISBN: 0 435462 15 6
13-digit ISBN: 978 0 435462 15 4

Edited by David Kershaw
Typeset by Planman

Original illustrations © Harcourt Education Limited, 2006
Printed in the UK by Scotprint
Cover photo © Getty / The Image Bank
Picture research by Jemma Street

# Contents

### Unit 14 — Programming — 301

## Web resources

The following materials are available from the Heinemann website (www.heinemann.co.uk/vocational). Click on **IT & Office Technology**, click on **GCE** and select **Free Resources**. The password is **A2ICTEdexcel**

### Unit 13 — Web management — 385

**Standard ways of working**

# Acknowledgements

Every effort has been made to contact copyright holders of material reproduced in this book. Any omissions will be rectified in subsequent printings if notice is given to the publishers.

The authors and publisher would like to thank all organisations and individuals who granted permission to reproduce materials.

Page 1: Charles Mann / Corbis.

Page 53: Cameron / Corbis.

Page 85: Corbis.

Page 99: Alan Smith.

Page 102: 3do.com.

Page 105: 3do.com.

Page 106: Alan Smith.

Pages 109–110: Gareth Boden.

Page 111: Alan Smith (*both*).

Page 135: Yuriko Nakao / Reuters / Corbis.

Page 171: NHS Direct.

Page 201: Getty Images / PhotoDisc.

Page 257: Allana Wesley White / Corbis.

Page 301: Getty Images / PhotoDisc.

Page 385: Richard Levine / Alamy.

Page 389: FastHosts.co.uk.

Page 390: The Phact Zone.

Page 394: Network Solutions.

Page 395: Network Solutions.

Page 396: LogMeIn.

Page 400: Google.

Page 410: World Wide Web Consortium.

Page 411: Yahoo!.

Page 412: Edexcel.

Page 414: WatchFire (*left*); Usable.net (*right*).

Page 421: South Ayrshire Council.

Page 425: Lyris Technologies Inc.

Page 426: Yahoo! (*left*); Travel Mood (*right*).

Page 427: Apple (*left*); PhotoBox (*right*).

All Microsoft product screenshots reproduced with permission from Microsoft Corporation.

## Websites

There are links to relevant websites in this book. In order to ensure that the links are up to date, that the links work, and that the sites are not inadvertently linked to sites that could be considered offensive, we have made the links available on the Heinemann website at www.heinemann.co.uk/hotlinks. When you access the site the express code is 2156P.

Tel: 01865 888058
www.heinemann.co.uk

# Introduction

This is one in a series of three volumes that support the Edexcel qualifications in Applied Information and Communication Technology for GCE.

The books are organised as follows:

* AS (Single Award), which covers Units 1 to 3
* AS (Double Award), which covers Units 1 to 6
* A2 (Single and Double Award), which covers Units 7 to 14.

## A Level (Single Award)

This book covers the five units that are offered at A2 Level for the A Level (Single Award):

* Unit 7: Using Database Software
* Unit 8: Managing ICT projects
* Unit 10: Using multimedia software
* Unit 11: Using spreadsheet software
* Unit 12: Customising applications

If you have already taken the AS (Single Award) then you can complete the A Level (Single Award) by studying three further units. These should be selected as follows:

* Units 7 and 8
* One unit chosen from Units 10, 11 and 12

## A Level (Double Award)

This book covers the five units that are offered at A2 Level for the A Level (Single Award) – see above. In addition, it covers three further units that are offered at A2 Level in the A Level (Double Award):

* Unit 9: Communications and Networks
* Unit 13: Web management
* Unit 14: Programming

Unit 13 can be downloaded from the Heinemann website. Go to www.heinemann. co.uk/vocational. Click on **IT & Office Technology**, click on **GCE** and select **Free Resources**. The password is **A2ICTEdexcel**

If you have already taken the AS (Double Award) then you can complete the A Level (Double Award) by studying six further units. These should be selected as follows:

✳ Units 7, 8 and 9
✳ three units chosen from Units 10 to 14

## Standard Ways of Working

'Standard Ways of Working' runs as a common theme through all the units. This topic is covered in the two AS level volumes, and you are advised to remind yourself of what you are expected to demonstrate. You can also download this section from the Heinemann website. Go to www.heinemann.co.uk/vocational, click on **IT & Office Technology**, click on **GCE** and click on **Free Resources**.

## Assessment

Your achievements at A2 Level on this qualification will be assessed through portfolios of evidence and examinations. Portfolios will be assessed internally and the examinations will be assessed externally.

For the Single Award, Unit 7 will be assessed externally by the examination board.

For the Double Award, Units 7 and 9 will be assessed externally by the examination board.

For Unit 7 you will be set a database assignment to complete over no more than 25 hours under supervision. For Unit 9 you will be set a networking assignment to complete over no more than 10 hours under supervision.

All other units will be assessed internally. You will be expected to construct an e-portfolio for each unit. Further guidance on this is given in each unit.

## Further information

You can find further information about these qualifications at the Edexcel website (via www.heinemann.co.uk/hotlinks, express code 2156P, where you will find other links to useful sites). Remember to search for GCE Applied ICT. You can download the complete specification, which gives full details of all the units, both AS and A2, and how they are assessed. This document is over 300 pages long.

We hope you enjoy your studies and wish you every success.

K Mary Reid
April 2006

# Using database software

**Unit 7**

During the AS course, while completing *Unit 2: The digital economy*, you used database software to organise and interrogate structured information and to produce reports. You saw how large organisations rely on databases to manage their information and to provide them with fast and flexible access to this data. You looked at examples of transactional websites which use databases to store product, customer and sales information. You learnt, at first hand, how database queries can be used to analyse information and identify trends.

In this user-focused unit, you will develop these skills further. You will learn about data modelling and how best to design databases.

This compulsory unit contains 9 elements:

7.1 Database applications

7.2 Functional specification

7.3 Database development

7.4 Data modelling

7.5 Creating a relational database structure

7.6 Validation techniques

7.7 The user interface

7.8 Testing

7.9 ICT skills

Your task for this unit is to use relational databases to build working database systems capable of storing large quantities of data and of handling both routine and one-off requests for information.

To help others to use your databases, you will design and implement user interfaces that make it easier to enter data and extract information. At the same time, you will make sure that any use of your database does not adversely affect the overall security and integrity of the database.

If you are taking the Double Award, you may choose to study *Unit 12: Customising applications* at the same time as this unit. If you plan to take *Unit 13: Web management*, you will benefit from having studied this unit first so that you can appreciate how and why database integration has become a key feature on most websites. This unit may also prove useful for applying some of the project management techniques covered in *Unit 8: Managing ICT projects*.

The ICT skills of Section 7.9 will be developed while working through this unit; refer to Table 7.5 on page 50. The standard ways of working (see the Introduction) should be adopted in this unit – and in all other units.

## Resources required in this unit

✳ You will use a DBMS to create a relational database. Only a fully functional RDBMS capable of supporting one-to-many relationships is to be used; Edexcel's website provides an up-to-date list of acceptable software and you should check to make sure that your RDBMS is approved by Edexcel. Microsoft Access and Lotus Approach are two such examples.

> **Key terms**
>
> *DBMS* stands for database management software. *RDBMS* stands for relational database management software.

Carrying out other research will help you to understand better how databases are used – for example, contacting organisations and discussing their use of databases. It is important that you also acquire experience of live, large-scale database systems.

You need to appreciate the volume of data handled, the different views of the data they provide to each type of user, and the way in which data is imported from and exported to other software applications.

## How you will be assessed

This user-focused unit is externally assessed. Edexcel will publish, on its website, instructions of how you will be examined in advance of the date of your examination. This will also specify the formats that will be acceptable.

You will be set practical computer-based activities to be completed under supervision and within a set time of 10 hours. The tasks set by Edexcel will require you to design, implement and test a relational database system to meet a given set of functional requirements and for a specific purpose. During the production of this database system, you should actively seek and respond to feedback from others. However, the final database solution must be entirely your own work.

Some of the data to be stored in your database will be supplied to you as a CSV file; this means that you will not be faced with sourcing huge amounts of data nor keying it into the computer.

Figure 7.1 shows how you identify the type of file that you are importing.

> **Key terms**
>
> *CSV* stands for comma separated variable. This format of file can be imported into most database management software packages.

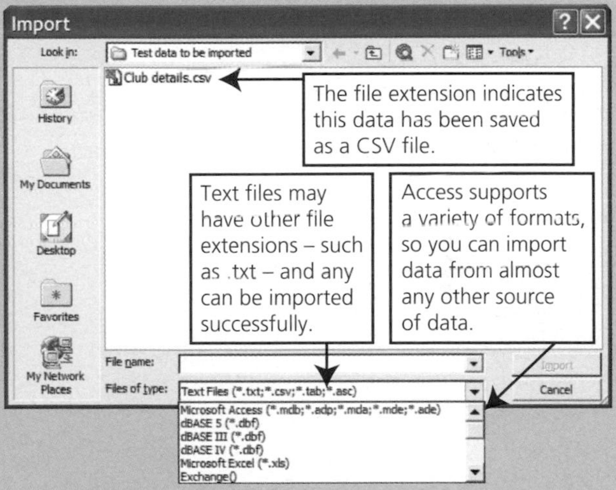

FIGURE 7.1 *Importing a CSV file*

## How high can you aim?

The knowledge and skills developed in this user-focused unit will be particularly relevant to those who plan to use advanced ICT skills on a daily basis. You should therefore aim to raise your skill levels to the point where you are confident in your use of ICT at work or at school/college for personal, social and work-related purposes.

## Ready to start?

This unit builds on the database knowledge and skills you acquired in *Unit 2: The digital economy*. Before you start, read back through your notes for that unit and refresh your memory.

This unit should take you 60 hours to complete. Why not keep a log of your time?

# 7.1 Database applications

In this section the focus moves on from the day-to-day operation of databases that you studied in *Unit 2: The digital economy*.

## Think it over...

In small groups, discuss the databases that you studied during your AS course.

Here, you will look at databases used in commerce, education and manufacturing. The purpose of this change of focus is to give you lots of ideas for your own database, when you are ready to develop it.

While studying these various database application areas, make a point of concentrating on design issues:

✱ What is the underlying database structure? What data is recorded? How are the data items grouped into records?

✱ How good is the user interface? Is it user-friendly? Does it make allowances for users with special requirements?

✱ What measures have been used to protect the quality of the data? How easy would it be to enter invalid, nonsense data?

✱ What types and forms of output are in evidence? How clear are the screen reports? How useful are the printed reports?

✱ What methods are used to extract information? Can you trace where the data originates?

You will learn more about these issues as you progress through this unit.

## Theory into practice

1 For one of the databases that you studied for Unit 2, make brief notes on its structure, the user interface, the measures taken to protect the quality of the data, the types and forms of output, and the methods used to extract data.

2 Working in small groups, present to each other the databases studied in Unit 2.

3 Look for similarities between these databases. In what ways did they differ?

## CASE STUDY

BestBank offers personal banking services to the general public. Each customer is allocated a personal user identification number, and then an account number for each account held with BestBank – e.g. a current (cheque) account, a savings account, and various credit cards. Transactions on an account include monies paid into an account (such as over-the-counter cash and cheques), BACS transfers (e.g. a person's salary paid directly into a bank account by the employer) and outgoings (such as standing orders, direct debit payments and cheques). Customers are notified when statements are available online and can print a hardcopy of a statement (Figure 7.2).

### Your **BestBankCard statement**

| | |
|---|---|
| statement date | 1 October 2005 to 30 October 2005 |
| card | BestBankCard |
| card number | 4627 5804 2093 6831 |

Anything you don't understand or want to query about your transactions?

get help ▶

| Date | Description | Amount |
|---|---|---|
| | OPENING BALANCE | £-13.88 |
| 15 Oct 2005 | THE GAMEKEEPERS BASINGSTOKE GB | £19.45 DR |
| 18 Oct 2005 | BP HORNBILL CONNEC BRACKNELL GB | £42.43 DR |
| 18 Oct 2005 | SAINSBURY'S S/MKT BAGSHOT RD GB | £35.47 DR |
| 21 Oct 2005 | AMAZON.CO.UK Amazon.co.uk GB | £19.36 DR |
| 25 Oct 2005 | WHITE ELEPHANT NORTHAMPTON GB | £17.10 DR |
| | Closing balance | £119.93 DR |
| | Minimum payment | £5.00 |

FIGURE 7.2 *Bank hardcopy statement*

Customers can also view recent transactions (Figure 7.3) at anytime.

1 Looking at the statement shown in Figure 7.2, identify the data that relates to the customer and that will appear, unchanged, on every statement. What data might the customer have to enter to gain access to this statement?

2 Looking at the list of recent transactions (Figure 7.3), identify what data is held for each purchase made. Which data fields are calculated? Explain how they are calculated.

3 Explain why is important for BestBank to issue each customer with a unique customer number as well as separate account numbers for each account held with the bank.

4 How can the customer number that the user enters be validated?

5 How can the information relating to one customer be kept confidential from other customers who may be online at the same time?

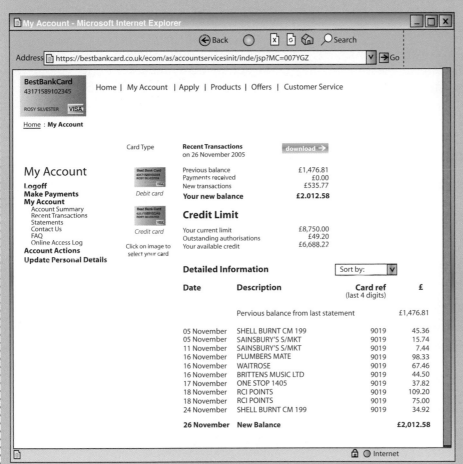

FIGURE 7.3 *Online recent transactions*

## Databases used in commerce

Commerce covers all organisations involved in buying and selling goods and services, plus service industries such as banking.

Think it over...

In small groups, list at least 10 organisations in the area of commerce. Group these in any way that you think makes sense. Compare your lists with other groups.

## Databases used in education

Education embraces schools, colleges and universities – and other organisations such as the government departments who determine the curriculum, and the examination boards who examine and assess candidates.

In the examination field of education, examination boards hold data about centres and centres hold information about candidates.

**Think it over...**

What information, to do with examination entries, might a centre hold about its students?

### CASE STUDY

Sunnersbury Sixth Form College keeps a database of all students, including details of where they studied before joining the college and where they went to after leaving college: work or university.

1  An analysis of the types of schools that feed into the college, and the eventual destination of each student, is to be included in the annual report. What format might best be used for this information?

2  Find out what information your school or college keeps on you. How is this information used?

3  How can the rights of each student to privacy be guaranteed when they complete a form to say where they went to, after leaving college?

## Databases used in manufacturing

Manufacturing is an aspect of industry that involves taking raw products and processing these in some way to create a new product that can then be sold.

**Think it over...**

In small groups, list examples of manufacturing industries' use of databases. Compare your list with those of other groups.

### CASE STUDY

BettaBottles Ltd manufactures glass bottles of all shapes and sizes. Glass is melted in a furnace and molten glass is poured in a continuous stream through a chute into a waiting mould. At intervals, a guillotine 'cuts' the glass flow and, at the same time, the moulds move on one place. Thus each mould is filled with a precise volume of glass. This automated process is computer controlled.

Further down the production line, once the glass in each bottle has set, each bottle is tapped to make sure it is strong enough. Broken bottles fall back into a trough and the remnants are fed back to the furnace. These over-light bottles trigger a slower guillotining.

Even further down the production line, each bottle that passes the tap test is weighed to make sure it is not too heavy. The over-heavy bottles are pushed into the trough and recycled to the furnace. Over-heavy bottles trigger a faster guillotining.

A database holds the data that specifies how much molten glass is needed for particular moulds – for different customers – and the initial guillotining pace.

1  The factory area is hot and smoky. How can the computer which controls this production process be best protected? What interface will suit such hazardous conditions?

2  The management team require data about the number of bottles produced each day, for each client, and what profit is being made on each job. How might this data be provided?

## 7.2 Functional specification

Databases tend to be complex data structures, needing careful design and thorough testing of the database that has been built.

In this unit, as with any software development (Figure 7.4), you will follow a process of structured development (Sections 7.3–7.7) and will then test your database (Section 7.8).

The first step in the process – the top box in Figure 7.4 – is to investigate the needs of the client (called **requirements analysis**) and to produce a **functional specification**. This should identify the purpose of the database:

✻ What task(s) must the database perform?

✻ What information must it supply?

✻ In what format must the information be supplied?

✻ To whom will the information be supplied?

✻ How and from where will the data be input into the database?

✻ What processing is required?

✻ What level of security is needed?

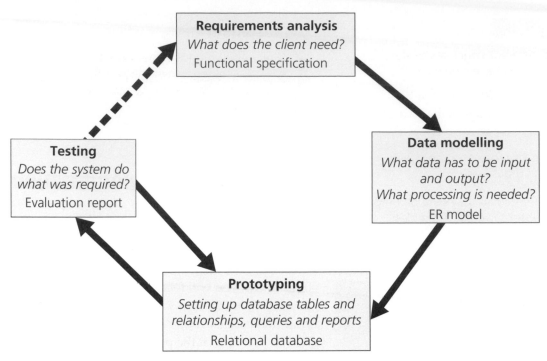

**FIGURE 7.4** *System lifecycle*

The specification provides details of what the database should do, and it can be used as a benchmark when testing it (see page 48 for details of database testing techniques). The specification also provides the basis on which the design and implementation of the system rest.

The next section looks at the development process in more detail.

1 Name the four main stages of developing a database.

2 Explain the term 'requirements analysis'.

3 What is a functional specification? What purpose does it serve?

## Theory into practice

1 For HolidayHomes'R'Us, or some other organisation, list the tasks that the database must perform. Present this information as part of a functional specification report.

2 Prepare a presentation to show to Hazel (or the owner of your own chosen organisation) to explain how you will make sure the information in the database is kept secure.

## Assessment activity

1 You will be provided with information about the needs of a client. Read this information carefully and make notes on important aspects of the problem.

2 Identify what tasks your database has to perform.

3 List the information it must supply.

4 Establish the format in which the information must be supplied.

5 Make notes on to whom the information will be supplied.

6 Establish how and where the data will be input into the database.

7 Identify what processing is required.

8 Establish what level of security is needed.

## Assessment hint

✓ Save your notes as a word-processed document. Then, as your database development progresses, you can use this document to check that you have met all the requirements you anticipated at the outset.

# 7.3 Database development

Having written a **functional specification** – and having had it approved by the client – it is time to begin work on the design stage of the database development.

## Designing a database

This involves three distinct activities: analysis, design and implementation, as discussed below.

### Analysing data requirements

Using the information gleaned from the client, it is important to analyse the **data requirements** of the system. This involves identifying the inputs and outputs, and what processing is needed to turn the inputs into outputs.

## CASE STUDY

The HolidayHomes'R'Us agency collects information from home owners and those wanting to buy or rent a home. These are the inputs to the system.

When someone is interested in buying or renting a home, Hazel produces a shortlist of available properties. This is an output of the system.

The processing that takes place involves filtering the database to find suitable properties (e.g. within a price range, within one part of the country and being available on given dates).

1 For Holidayhomes'R'Us, or some other organisation, focus on the data requirements of the system. Extend your functional specification to include information about the inputs and outputs of the system and any processing that takes place.

2 Prepare a presentation to show to Hazel (or the owner of your own organisation) to explain what reports the database system will offer.

## Designing a data model

Having analysed the data requirements, the next step is to produce a **data model**. This is not the database itself, but documentation that describes the design of the database and, hence, how it will be built. There are data modelling conventions that you should follow, and these are explained in Section 7.4, which shows how to set up a data model.

## Implementing the design

The final stage is to translate the data model into a physical database using appropriate database software. This stage is explained in Section 7.5.

### Think it over...

What other types of modelling are there?

### Prototyping

It is important to study the data requirements carefully and to model the data precisely so that it then becomes easy to create a working database.

At all stages, it is also important to build in checkpoints, and to go back to the client for approval. Is the database going to provide the client with what he or she wants?

Often, a **prototype** will be created which indicates the data structure that is planned, and the queries (Section 7.5) and reports (Section 7.7) that will be provided.

### Key terms

A *prototype* is a scaled-down version of the final product, showing the navigational routes through a system and an idea of the functionality that is planned.

A prototype can provide the client with something tangible that he or she can look at, rather than a report describing what the end product will be. The team working on the development of a database, from inception to final testing, should be able to work from complex documentation, but the user could hardly be expected to understand the conventions that are used or to make sense of what is proposed. A prototype provides a visual guide to what is planned and should be immediately understood by the client.

### Validation

The development of a database also includes the writing of data entry and validation functions (Section 7.6) that are needed to make the database robust, but this may be postponed until most of the input forms and output reports have been developed.

### Key terms

*Robust:* a system is robust if it is difficult for the user to cause it to crash.

### User interface

This unit concentrates on the development of a user interface, which involves setting up menus (Section 7.7) as a navigational aid to the user. The prototype should show the main routes for a user and how to perform the most common tasks: set up a new record, amend a record, make a booking, print a report and so on.

### Testing

Testing (Section 7.8) is discussed last in this unit, but it can start as soon as the first prototype has been developed.

### Think it over...

Discuss with others in your group the benefits of starting testing as soon as each new form, query or report has been developed.

## Documentation

In real-life projects, the three steps – analysis, modelling (or design) and implementation – may be undertaken by three different people or teams of people. The documentation that each person or team of people produces, and which becomes the documentation the next person/team works from, is therefore crucial.

## Knowledge check

1 Describe the stages involved in developing a database.

2 Explain the purpose of a prototype.

3 Why is it important to maintain communication with the client during the development of a database?

4 Why is it important to document each stage of development?

## Assessment activity

1 Study the material supplied for your assessment task and the notes that you have made so far. Analyse the data requirements of the task.

2 Identify the inputs and outputs, and what processing is required to turn the inputs into outputs.

## Assessment hint

✓ Check that you fully understand what you have to do.

# 7.4 Data modelling

Modelling is an important part of problem-solving.

* When you use numbers and equations – in maths classes – to present rules and to solve problems, this is also an example of modelling.

* In *Unit 3: The knowledge worker*, you used spreadsheets to model real-life processes or situations and to solve 'what-if' problems.

* Architects use drawings and 3D models (e.g. of a building) to plan what a structure will look like when it is built.

Modelling provides an abstract version of a real thing and involves its own terminology.

## Think it over…

Discuss these terms: entity, attribute, instance, relationship, key.

Which have you heard of before? Do you know any alternative names for them?

In this section, the focus is on entity-relationship modelling to represent the data in a given scenario.

## Entity-relationship models

Entity-relationship models (ER models) have three components:

* entities
* attributes
* relationships.

These are shown in an ERD, as shown in Figure 7.5 (on page 13).

## Key terms

*ERD* stands for entity-relationship diagram.

Before trying to 'read' the ERD, you need to understand its component parts.

### Entities

## Key terms

An *entity* is something (a person, a thing, a concept) in the real world that is to be represented in a database.

In an ERD, each entity is represented by a rectangular box and its name is written in capital letters.

Each entity will be represented physically as a **table** within the database – each row of the table holds the data for each **instance** of the entity in the model (called a **record**) and each column represents an **attribute** (called a **field**) of that entity.

As you will see later, identifying the attributes for an entity – and thinking carefully about how the entities may be linked by relationships – may result in another entity being created and attributes being shared differently among them. To start with, though, the 'method' is simply to list each attribute that you think belongs to an entity.

## Attributes

### Key terms

An *attribute* is a data item that describes an entity that is considered important enough to be stored in a database.

Attributes are assigned to an entity and given a name: this name will become the **field name** in the database. Lower case is used for field names to make them meaningful, and an underscore may be used to link words within them.

Each field in the database is assigned a data type which describes the content of the field, determines how it will be stored, what processing might be done on it and how it might be displayed. When you come to the point of creating the relational database (Section 7.5), you will need to think carefully about what data types are most appropriate for a particular attribute. For now, just list them!

## Relationships

One of the most powerful features – and essential constructions – in a relational database is the facility to form links between the tables. These allow you, while interrogating the database, to glean data from more than one table at a time. These links represent relationships between the entities.

### Key terms

A *relationship* links two entities via their attributes.

The **degree of a relationship** can be one-to-one, many-to-one, one-to-many (or many-to-many) and many-to-many (Figure 7.5).

On the ERD, the 'many' part of the relationship can be shown by the 'crow's feet' – when you create the database using DBMS software, the end of the line that represents the 'many' end is often labelled with an infinity symbol ($\infty$).

The bad news is that most database models cannot accommodate many-to-many relationships! The good news is that there is a standard way of

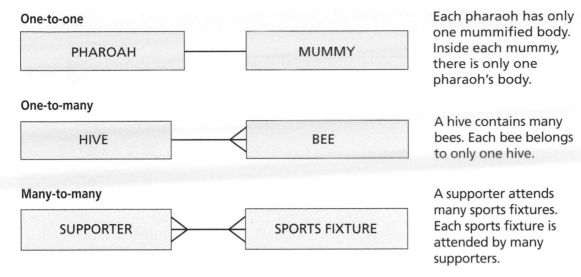

| One-to-one | | Each pharaoh has only one mummified body. Inside each mummy, there is only one pharaoh's body. |

PHAROAH — MUMMY

| One-to-many | | A hive contains many bees. Each bee belongs to only one hive. |

HIVE — BEE

| Many-to-many | | A supporter attends many sports fixtures. Each sports fixture is attended by many supporters. |

SUPPORTER — SPORTS FIXTURE

**FIGURE 7.5** *Degrees of relationship between entities*

resolving them in the relational database model: you create a *third* entity set to act as a link, and the relationships are *always* one-to-many from the original entity to the link entity (Figure 7.6).

Notice that the supporter is a person, the attendance can be visualised as a ticket (a thing) and the sports fixture is an event. Often, finding the third entity involves thinking about what people are doing and how this is documented.

### Theory into practice

1   Construct an ERD model showing the entities and the relationship between them for the HolidayHomes'R'Us database, or for another organisation you have been studying.

2   Show how you have used a third entity to eliminate a many-to-many situation.

## Normalisation

Having decided on the entities for a database system so that no many-to-many relationships remain, the next step is to assign the attributes to the most appropriate entity. Creating a table which lists all the attributes and has one column per entity may help you to see what belongs where (see Table 7.1).

Notice that some attributes seem to 'belong' to more than one entity. In deciding how to group attributes with each entity, ask yourself which attributes are essential to describe the entity. It is important to list all the data items so that the system – when you create it – contains all the necessary information.

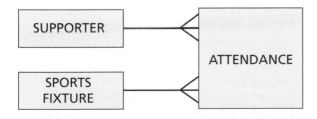

SUPPORTER

SPORTS FIXTURE

ATTENDANCE

Each supporter attends many sports fixtures

Each sports fixture is attended by many supporters

**FIGURE 7.6** *Introducing a third entity to cope with a many-to-many relationship*

| ATTRIBUTE | SUPPORTER | ATTENDANCE | SPORTS FIXTURE |
|---|---|---|---|
| Name | ✓ | | |
| Ticket number | ✓ | ✓ | |
| Date of fixture | | ✓ | ✓ |
| Home sports team | | | ✓ |
| Away sports team | | | ✓ |
| Venue | | ✓ | ✓ |
| Kick-off time | | | ✓ |

TABLE 7.1 *Assigning attributes to entities*

### Theory into practice

Supporters tend to support just one sports team, and sports teams have a whole season of fixtures.

1 Produce a copy of Table 7.1 of your own to include a column for the entity SPORTS_CLUB.

2 Think about other entities that might be important (e.g. 'is a season ticket holder of').

3 Extend your copy of Table 7.1 further to include the data items for all your entities.

4 Compare your 'solution' with others in your group. Add data items to your own table so that it is as comprehensive as possible.

You might think that Table 7.2 is a sensible way of recording Chris's planned attendance.

This is fine for a report or for a confirmation to be sent to each supporter. However, this format will not work within a relational database. For the data to 'work', it has to be normalised.

### Key terms

*Normalisation* involves checking that there is no unnecessary duplicated data; it maximises the efficiency of a database.

You may start with a database design that happens not to be normalised and then 'test it' to see what needs to be changed to make it

### CASE STUDY

Chris is a season ticket holder and supports Rainham Rangers. Each year she is sent a letter asking her to say which games she would like to attend. She tries to attend all the home games and as many away games as she can.

1 Check your extended version of Table 7.1. Make sure it has sufficient information for the letter to be sent to a supporter like Chris.

2 For football, or some other sport or event that involves several activities (such as the Proms at the Royal Albert Hall or the tennis

at Wimbledon), find out what data might be sent to advertise the events. Check that your extended version of Table 7.1 includes appropriate attributes.

3 Look at a ticket for an event such as a football match or the showing of a play. What information is given? Check your version of Table 7.1 again.

4 Compare your list of attributes with others in your group. Finalise your own list using feedback from others.

| NAME | CLUB SUPPORTED | MATCH DATE | OPPONENT | H/A? | MATCH VENUE | SEAT |
|------|----------------|------------|----------|------|-------------|------|
| Chris Collins | Rainham Rangers | 14/8/05 | Team A | H | Rainham Road | F45 |
| | | 21/8/05 | Team B | A | Venue B | DNA |
| | | 28/8/05 | Team C | H | Rainham Road | F45 |
| | | 4/9/05 | Team D | A | Venue D | |
| | | 11/9/05 | Team E | H | Rainham Road | F45 |
| | | Next date... | | | | |
| Next supporter | Team A | | | | | |
| | | | | | | |
| | | | | | | |
| Next supporter | Team B | | | | | |

**TABLE 7.2** *Repeating elements*

normalised. So, normalisation may be thought of as a process to determine which attributes belong with each entity – as demonstrated here.

As your database design skills improve, you should automatically design normalised databases – and then normalisation represents a series of tests that you do to make sure that your initial design really is normalised.

There are three degrees of normalisation: first, second and third normal form (called 1NF, 2NF and 3NF).

## First normal form

In first normal form, there may only be one table holding all the data – sometimes in a quite complex way. The process of normalisation results in more tables, but each one is very simple.

In Table 7.2, for each supporter, there two attributes (name and club supported) and then five attributes that are repeated (Match date, Opponent, H/A, Match venue and Seat). This can be written as:

```
Name, Club_Supported, Match_date,
Opponent, H/A, Match_Venue, Seat
```

The overscore means that these attributes are repeated.

The first stage of normalisation removes the repeating element problem by including the name of the supporter and the club supported in each row (Table 7.3).

It may seem that copying data into what would have been blanks or spaces will take up more room and make the database less efficient, but the next two stages of the normalisation process reduce the amount of data that has to be stored.

The data no longer has repeating groups and each row of the table, or 'record', can be written as:

```
Name, Club_Supported, Match_date,
Opponent, H/A, Match_Venue, Seat
```

| NAME | CLUB SUPPORTED | MATCH DATE | OPPONENT | H/A | MATCH VENUE | SEAT |
|---|---|---|---|---|---|---|
| Chris Collins | Rainham Rangers | 14/8/05 | Team A | H | Rainham Road | F45 |
| Chris Collins | Rainham Rangers | 21/8/05 | Team B | A | Venue B | DNA |
| Chris Collins | Rainham Rangers | 28/8/05 | Team C | H | Rainham Road | F45 |
| Chris Collins | Rainham Rangers | 4/9/05 | Team D | A | Venue D | |
| Chris Collins | Rainham Rangers | 11/9/05 | Team E | H | Rainham Road | F45 |
| Next supporter | Team A | | | | | |

TABLE 7.3 *Repeating elements*

Some of these attributes describe the supporter; others describe a match the supporter might attend; and others describe the club that is supported. The next stage of normalisation identifies the entities and redistributes the attributes so that they are more sensibly grouped.

**Think it over...**

Refer back to your completed Table 7.1. Does it include all the data items, and do your ticks show which ones relate to which entities?

## Second normal form

For second normal form, the attributes need to be grouped into separate tables, one for each entity.

For the football data, the entities could be:

* SUPPORTER
* CLUB
* FIXTURE
* ATTENDANCE

Having decided on your entities, you can then begin to group the attributes more sensibly, as shown in Figure 7.7.

This is a good time to choose the attribute names more carefully so that they are more meaningful within the entity. Notice that the underscore is used instead of a space, because if this database is to be used on the WWW, spaces within names can cause problems.

For each entity there will be a table. Each attribute within that entity will be allocated a single column (called a **field**), and then each row of the table is used for a single instance of the entity (called a **record**). To visualise the database, you may find it easier to draw the separate tables

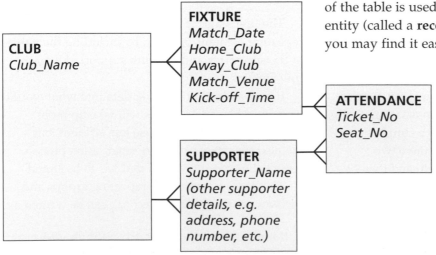

FIGURE 7.7 *Football data ERD*

and to invent some sample data to populate the tables. Later, you might use this sample data to test your database, when you have set it up on your computer. The data needed for testing is discussed on page 48.

discussed on page 48.

> ## Theory into practice
>
> Review your database design:
>
> 1 Check that separating the data has not resulted in your 'losing' some information.
>
> 2 Can you still tell which match the supporter is to attend?
>
> 3 Which table tells you which seat a supporter will sit in?

Including links between the tables of data involves identifying, or setting up, **key attributes**, and hence identifying the **non-key attributes**. This takes the design closer to second normal form (2NF).

> ## Key terms
>
> A table is in *2NF* if and only if it is already in 1NF, and every non-key attribute is *fully* dependent on the primary key.

So, reaching the second normal form involves the identification of **primary keys**, and then assigning the rest of the attributes to those keys in a special way.

> ## Key terms
>
> A *primary key* is an attribute that uniquely identifies the record.

In Table 7.3, the Name field identifies who the supporter is. But, because there could be more than one supporter called 'Chris Collins', it cannot uniquely identify the supporter. Instead, it is usual to assign a unique reference to each supporter.

Similarly, there could be two clubs with the same name – or very similar names – so a club number might be assigned.

Some way of uniquely identifying a fixture is also needed. The date and the location of the home team's pitch might seem enough, but some fixtures may be played at a venue that 'belongs' to neither club, so a fixture reference may be a better solution.

The data might then look like this:

**SUPPORTER**: Supporter_No, Supporter_ Name, {contact details}

**CLUB**: Club_No, Club_Name, Home_Ground_ Venue, {other data, e.g. telephone number, web address}

**FIXTURE**: Match_No, Match_Date, Home_Club_ No, Away_Club_No, Venue_Club_No, Kick-off_Time

**ATTENDANCE**: Ticket_No, Seat_No

The underscored attribute names are the keys.

Notice that the FIXTURE table refers to Home_Club_No, Away_Club_No and Venue_Club_No. These three attributes all hold the Club_No (as in the CLUB table) for the clubs involved in a match. These three attributes are called **foreign keys**, and serve to link the FIXTURE table to the CLUB table. (Foreign keys are explained in more detail on page 26.)

Figure 7.8 shows the distribution of attributes within the four entities SUPPORTER, CLUB, FIXTURE and ATTENDANCE. It also shows the primary keys (in bold) and the foreign keys (in italic).

If you decide that a single attribute cannot uniquely identify an instance of an entity, you could select two or more attributes and use these as joint keys. However, this is poor practice and can lead to all sorts of problems. So, instead, decide to set up an extra field to use as a primary key. Since its value is irrelevant, you can let the database software choose it automatically (as shown in Figure 7.20 on page 26).

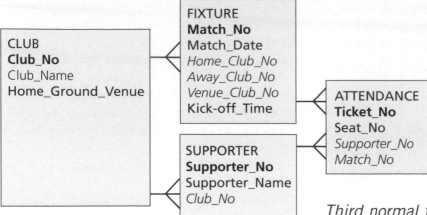

**FIGURE 7.8** *Football data ERD with keys identified*

There is no single correct solution to the design of a database. Your solution may have more entities or fewer entities. You may have different attributes. You will most probably have chosen different names for the attributes and, perhaps also, for the entities.

## Third normal form

A database in 2NF can be set up using database management software. It will work so it is not essential to refine the design to 3NF. However, to minimise the amount of data held within the database tables – and to produce a more elegant solution – you should consider your design one last time, to make sure it cannot be improved.

The non-key attributes should all be independent of each other. This may already be the case, which means you have nothing extra to do.

One example of data items that might not be independent can be found in contact details. The 'normal' way of storing a contact address is to include the full address. However, if you know the postcode and the house number, in theory, the remainder of the address is 'known' – provided you have access to a database which identifies addresses according to this crucial data.

Many databases incorporate the address data – so, when completing a form, you just have to enter your postcode and then confirm the full address from an offered list. The benefits of this are twofold:

* The person completing the form does not have to enter so much data. This saves time.

* The amount of data being entered is reduced, and this reduces the chances of error. So accuracy is assured.

In the football data, it may be that the Match_No could include the date of the match. If this is the case, there might be no reason to have the attribute Match_Date.

## Theory into practice

Review your database design to check whether it needs some amendments to make it 3NF.

## Knowledge check

1  Explain these terms: entity, attribute, relationship.

2  What is the difference between each normal form?

3  Why should data be normalised?

## CASE STUDY

Karen Hall runs a cycle repair business. She wants more accurate reports on the repairs that are carried out. At present, the details of her customers are on paper, kept in box files in her office. These paper records are easily misfiled and frequently out of order. Sometimes they are mislaid or simply lost. Karen has bought a new computer and wants a database created so that she can store details of her customers, cycles to be repaired and the charges for her customers.

1  For what entities might tables be created?

2  What relationships exist? What type are they?

3  What data could be recorded in each entity table?

4  Propose an ERD with fields for each table and identify the key fields and foreign keys.

## Assessment activity

1  For your assessment scenario, determine the entities needed and draw up an initial ERD.

2  If there are any many-to-many relationships, resolve these by creating a link entity.

3  Decide on the tables you will need. List them, giving their attributes and underlining the names of the attributes that form primary keys.

## Assessment hint

✓  Check that you have used the correct conventions on your ERD.

# 7.5  Creating a relational database structure

In this section you will use database software to build physical representations of data models. Software such as Microsoft Access – like other approved RDBMS – provides all the functions that you will need.

The first step is to create a new database.

### How to... create a new database

1  Open Microsoft Access. The dialogue box appears as shown in Figure 7.9. Decide where you want your database to be stored. If need be, create a new folder for it.

2  Decide on a filename for your database. Call it **Football** (or something that is more meaningful for you), and click on **Create**.

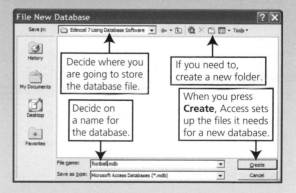

FIGURE 7.9  *Opening the Microsoft Access dialogue box*

# Database tables

The next stage is to set up the database tables, one table per entity.

In relational databases, entities are represented as tables: each row represents a single instance of the entity and is called a **record**; and each column is a **field**, used to store the values of an attribute for each record within the table.

In Access, you have the choice of viewing the data within a table (**Worksheet view**, as in Figure 7.32 on page 30), or the design of the fields within that table (**Design view**, as in Figure 7.12 on page 21). You can toggle between the two views so that you can see the effect of changes to the design on the data; and if you are not happy with how the data looks, you can toggle back to Design view. This toggling option is not so important when setting up tables but will prove invaluable when setting up queries (page 28) and producing reports (page 42).

When setting up a table, refer to your diagram of the overall design of the database you are planning to create. Much of the information that you need will appear on your diagram. Eventually, when you have set up all the tables,

the fields within them, and the links between them, Access can be used to print an electronic version of this table (Figure 7.10).

The next subsection covers the data types and formats that you need to assign to each field. There are also other details you might enter at this stage, as listed in the **Field Properties** box (Figure 7.12). However, much of this can wait – and what these entries can hold and their uses are covered later in this unit.

When you have completed entering as much information about your fields as you can at this stage, you need to identify the primary key field. This is explained in more detail on pages 25 and 26. The key field is identified by a key icon (Figure 7.12).

If you try to close or save the table without identifying a key field, Access will prompt you to do so and will offer to set up an extra attribute as the key field; it is better to have determined this yourself before saving the table.

Now save the table using a meaningful name. Prefix the name with **Tbl** so that, later, you can identify this table as the one you created rather than one created as a result of a query; this is explained further on page 28.

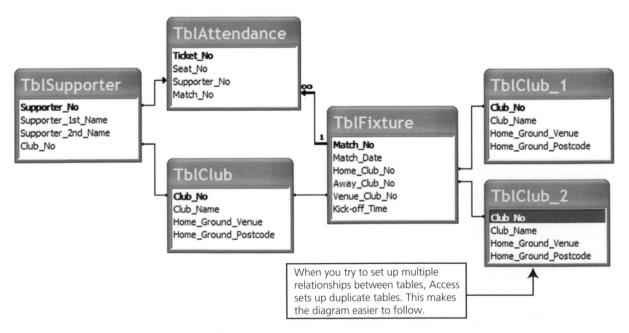

**FIGURE 7.10** *ERD produced within Access*

1 Having created a new database, you will then be presented with a dialogue box (Figure 7.11).

2 Click on the **New** button. A smaller dialogue box will open.

3 Notice that there are several options for entering data. This section focuses on Design view, but you might like to experiment with using the other methods too. So, for now, choose Design view (also shown in Figure 7.11).

4 Within Design view (Figure 7.12), you can start entering the fields.

When you create a new database, the first step is to set up your tables. Access offers the three 'normal' methods, but...

... if you press **New**...

... two other options become available to you: importing a table or by linking.

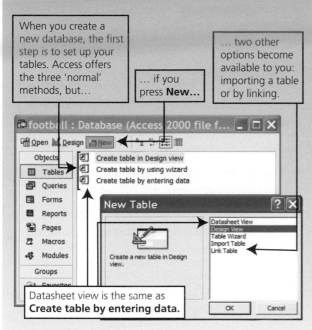

Datasheet view is the same as **Create table by entering data.**

FIGURE 7.11 *Creating a new table in Access*

The default name for a table is Table1. When you save the table, choose something more meaningful. If you precede the name with Tbl it will be even clearer, later, how this table was created.

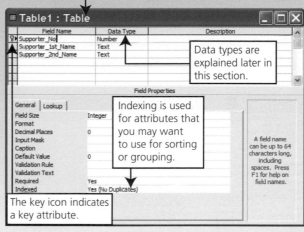

Data types are explained later in this section.

Indexing is used for attributes that you may want to use for sorting or grouping.

A field name can be up to 64 characters long, including spaces. Press F1 for help on field names.

The key icon indicates a key attribute.

FIGURE 7.12 *Design view choice*

# Data types and formats

For each field, a data type (which controls how it is stored) and a data format (which controls how it appears on paper or on the screen) need to be specified.

There are two main data types:

\* text

\* number.

However, databases can also contain non-textual data, such as sounds and pictures.

Both Text and Number data types are used in the SUPPORTER table (Figure 7.12).

Most fields contain either text or a number, and there are many options for storing and displaying this data.

For both text and number, there are lots of options so that the user's requirements can be met. Figure 7.13 shows the range of options for numeric data types, and Figure 7.14 shows the range of formats for display purposes.

FIGURE 7.13 *Number data type options*

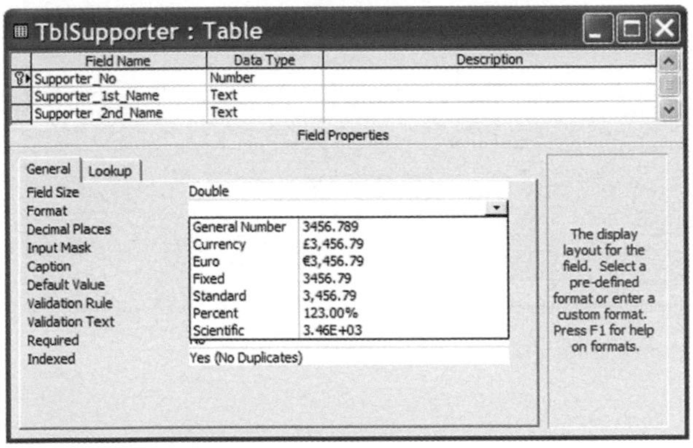

FIGURE 7.14 *Number data formats*

## Textual data

**Text** data types can be categorised further:

✳ limited length

✳ unlimited length

✳ memo.

Figure 7.19 on page 25 shows a text field, defined with length 50, reduced from the default length of 255. Since the width of the column in Datasheet view is initially decided by the field length, it makes sense to choose a length that is long enough, but not overlong. In Datasheet view, you can reduce the width of the field that is visible; it does not change the length of the field that is stored and will not save any space – it just hides the tail end of these fields.

If you change your mind about the field length and try to reduce it after you have entered some data, you will be warned that making this change might result in a loss of data; the fields already entered will be truncated and extraneous characters lost.

**Think it over...**

Which of your data fields will contain textual data? What length of text might be stored in a particular field?

## Numeric data

**Number** data types serve many uses:

✳ a single bit – called a **Boolean data type** – may be used to represent on/off, yes/no

✳ various numbers of bits may be used to represent, for example, **integers** or **floating point** numbers.

Numbers are also used to store dates, times and currencies. These are formatted in special ways:

✳ **Dates** can be presented in many different formats (e.g. dd/mm/yy, dd month).

✳ **Time** can be in the 12-hour or 24-hour clock and may include seconds too, as in hh:mm:ss.

✳ **Currencies** are displayed with the currency symbol immediately before the amount of money – e.g. for pounds (£xxx), or for dollars ($yyy).

It is also possible to make the system create the next number using a special data type called an **AutoNumber** (as shown in Figure 7.15). This is useful for data such as invoice numbers which need to run consecutively.

Because a number is stored according to the data type you select and using a fixed number of bits, there has to be a compromise between the range of numbers that can be stored and the accuracy with which they can be stored. If you need to store numbers that are very large or very small, with many significant numbers, you need to choose the data type carefully.

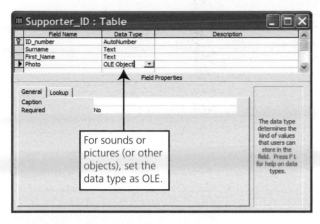

For sounds or pictures (or other objects), set the data type as OLE.

**FIGURE 7.15** *OLE object data type*

## Theory into practice

You are now ready to start setting up your tables.

1 Choose suitable data types for the fields in your tables, thinking carefully about the range of values that might need to be stored.

2 Choose suitable formats for each field, thinking carefully about how you might want them to appear in reports.

3 Print out a copy of the design of each table for documentation purposes.

## Sounds and pictures

Nowadays, data is not simply words and numbers. As the cost of storage has dropped and the technology involved in capturing sounds and images has improved, databases can now contain richer forms of data, such as sounds and pictures:

❋ **Sounds** can be recorded using a microphone and stored on your hard drive in the same way as any other data. Sourcing the sounds and editing them so that the data is exactly how you want it, is covered in Section 9 of *Unit 10: Using multimedia software*.

## Think it over...

Discuss situations where sounds might be stored within a database.

❋ **Pictures** – still or moving images – can also be stored within a database table. You may have completed AS *Unit 6: Computer artwork* and feel confident about creating your own images. Or you can use images that are supplied for you. In real life, the client would supply all the objects that are to go in the database.

## Think it over...

Discuss situations where pictures might be stored within a database.

The data type needed for sound and pictures is **OLE Object** (Figure 7.15).

## Key terms

An *OLE object* is something like a Microsoft Excel spreadsheet, a Microsoft Word document, graphics, sounds or other binary data which is linked to or embedded in an Access table.

If the source (sound or picture) may change over time (called **dynamic**) and you want the most up-to-date version to appear in the database, then a link to the source is needed. If the original will never change (called **static**), you can simply embed the OLE within the database.

When you embed an object into your document, if you activate it, the application that was used to create it will automatically open. Similarly, when you create a link, the file extension of the chosen file will determine which application will be needed to open the file.

It is therefore important to make sure that the file type is one that is supported by the RDMS you are using. If not, you will have to convert the file type, loading it into one application and using Save As to save it in a different format.

## How to... embed a sound or image file

1. Set up the field data type as an OLE object.

2. From Worksheet view, right-clicking on the field offers the option to **Insert Object** (Figure 7.16).

3. Decide whether you are going to create a new sound/image file or use one that you prepared earlier. Click on the radio button to show your choice (Figure 7.17).

4. If you are creating a new object, select the type and click on **OK**. A window will open inviting you to create the new object (Figure 7.18).

5. If you have stored the object already and have clicked the **Create from File** radio button, browse for your file.

6. If you want a dynamic link, tick the box marked **Link**. Then, rather than embedding the file within the database, you create a link to the file and, consequently, to the most up-to-date version of the data.

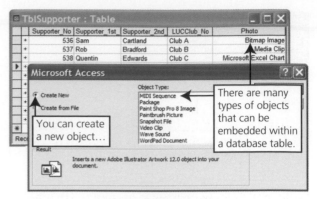

There are many types of objects that can be embedded within a database table.

You can create a new object...

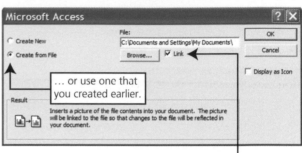

... or use one that you created earlier.

If you click the Link box, a link will be created to the file rather than the file being embedded, This is so the data can be kept up to date.

**FIGURE 7.17** *The variety of object types supported by Access*

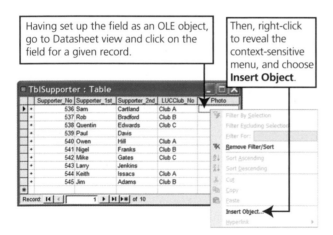

Having set up the field as an OLE object, go to Datasheet view and click on the field for a given record.

Then, right-click to reveal the context-sensitive menu, and choose **Insert Object**.

**FIGURE 7.16** *Embedding an object into an OLE field*

## Theory into practice

1. Set up a database table to record information about a recording artist. Include at least one field to hold a sound extract from one of his or her tracks.

2. Set up a database table for a dating agency. For each person who is seeking a partner, include a photo and a short audio file in which he or she describes him or herself.

**FIGURE 7.18** *Creating a new bitmap image to embed within a database table*

## Data organisation and indexing

Often, the records of data are needed in a particular order. To do this, the data must be sorted.

**Think it over...**

Think about which fields in your database design might need to be sorted. On your design diagram, highlight these fields.

Sorting can be a time-consuming process. If the sorting has to be done when you print a report, the time this takes can become noticeable and unacceptably long. However, if you know you will want to view or print data in a particular order based on a particular field, that field can be indexed, and this speeds up the printing process, at the time of printing.

Indexing a field (as shown in Figure 7.19) results in another table being set up to keep track of the data within the field. This indexed table is created automatically by the software; you need not worry about it. Then, when the data is needed in order, the index table is used to present it in the correct order – very quickly. Keeping the index table up to date is an overhead that is not so noticeable when you are updating the database.

Figure 7.19 shows how the field containing the surname of a supporter can be indexed, allowing duplicates. If the index is set up not to allow duplicates, the first time you try to enter the details of a supporter who shares the same surname with a supporter whose details are already on the database, the data entry will be rejected. This is one way of validating the data; other methods are discussed in greater detail in Section 7.6.

You can index more than one field, according to your output needs. You can then group data so that the layout of your reports is as helpful to the reader as possible. (See page 44 for more details about grouping.) However, you should avoid indexing every field. Otherwise, apart from wasting precious space, the overhead in maintaining the indexes might become more noticeable.

Note, though, that it is not possible to index all fields (e.g. you cannot index an OLE object field). If you need to present your sounds/pictures in some order, you would need to set up an additional field describing the picture or sound and index that field.

It is quite likely you will want to print a list of supporters in alphabetical order of their surname. If so, index this field.

Because it is most likely that supporters will share the same surname, choose the **Yes (Duplicates OK)** option.

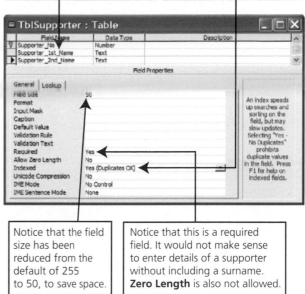

Notice that the field size has been reduced from the default of 255 to 50, to save space.

Notice that this is a required field. It would not make sense to enter details of a supporter without including a surname. **Zero Length** is also not allowed.

**FIGURE 7.19** *Indexing fields to allow for quicker sorting*

**Theory into practice**

1 For each table within your database design, review the field properties.

2 Make sure that the field size is large enough, but not too large for text fields.

3 Make sure that fields that cannot be omitted are set as **Required**, and that **Zero Length** is not allowed.

4 Index the fields that you plan to use for sorting.

## Primary and foreign keys

Keys are used to create relationships between tables. A link between a field in one table and a matching field in another table is possible, provided the two fields share the same properties – i.e. data type.

### Primary keys

Each of your tables should already have a primary key; Access does not allow you to save a table without one!

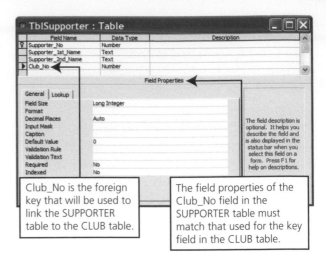
**Key terms**

A *primary key* is a field (or group of fields) that uniquely identifies a data record (i.e. one row in a database table).

Apart from uniquely identifying each record within a table, the primary keys provide a way of pointing from one table to another – i.e. of linking them.

## How to... set up a primary key

1 Position the cursor on the field that you want to make the primary key.

2 Right-click to reveal the context-sensitive menu (Figure 7.20).

3 Select **Primary Key**.

4 The key icon will appear next to the key field, on the left-hand side.

**FIGURE 7.21** *Setting up a foreign key to match a primary key*

**Key terms**

A *foreign key* is a field (or field combination) in one table whose value is required to match those of the primary key in another table.

The data type of the foreign key and the primary key that it points to must be identical. Otherwise, the data could be stored in a different way and no match would be found.

It is therefore important to decide on the data type of the primary keys, and to make a note of these. Then, when setting the data type of the foreign key, you can copy the details.

Notice, in Figure 7.20, the field properties for Club_No in the CLUB table.

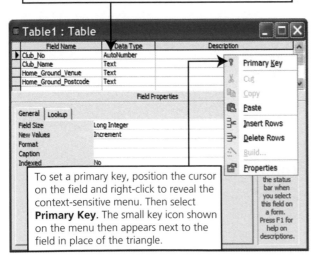

If the numbering of the clubs has no special significance, let the database software number them automatically.

To set a primary key, position the cursor on the field and right-click to reveal the context-sensitive menu. Then select **Primary Key**. The small key icon shown on the menu then appears next to the field in place of the triangle.

**FIGURE 7.20** *Setting up a primary key*

## Foreign keys

Figure 7.21 shows how the foreign key, Club_No in the SUPPORTER table, is set up to match the primary key, Club_No, in the CLUB table.

## Theory into practice

1 Review the data types and field properties of your key fields.

2 Check the data type and field properties of all foreign keys. Make sure they match the primary keys to which they are to be linked.

## Integrity of data

When setting up the relationship (see page 27), there are options as to how a change to data is allowed to impact on other data to which it is connected. This is called **referential integrity**.

There are situations where, if one record is updated or deleted, then any other record linked to it should also be updated/deleted. This 'domino' effect is called **cascading** (Figure 7.22).

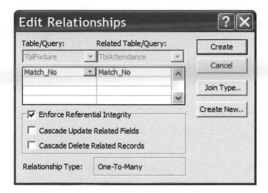

FIGURE 7.22 *Referential integrity*

**Think it over...**

In your database design, consider every foreign key and the primary key to which it is to be linked. How is the data in these two tables related? If you delete the record in one, should the matching record in the other be deleted also?

## Relationships

Relationships between the tables within a relational database are created as links or **joins**. The join properties fall into one of three types: one-to-one, one-to-many or many-to-one. As explained on page 13, relational databases cannot support many-to-many relationships. If you have two entities linked in this way, you need to create a third entity to slip between the other two to solve this problem.

The ERD in Figure 7.8 (on page 18) shows that the relationship is one-to-many from FIXTURE to ATTENDANCE. So, of the three join properties on offer in Figure 7.27, the middle option is the one to choose. Although this refers to 'only those records from TblAttendance where the joined fields are equal', there are many more tickets for matches than there are matches.

Confirmation that the relation is one-to-many in the correct direction can be achieved by looking at the ERD created by the software (Figure 7.26).

**How to... set up a relationship between two tables**

1. Click on the **Relationship** icon on the main toolbar (Figure 7.23). If you have not yet set up any relationships, the **Show table** (Figure 7.24) dialogue box appears. If you have already set up some relationships they will appear, but if you right-click, you can select more tables to create more links (Figure 7.25).

2. Select the two tables that you plan to link (for example, FIXTURE and ATTENDANCE as shown in Figure 7.26).

3. Click on the foreign key and drag the cursor to the primary key. A link will be drawn in place and the **Join Properties** dialogue box will open (Figure 7.27).

4. Decide on the join properties and click on **OK**.

5. Decide what level of referential integrity you require, if any, and then click on **Create** (see Figure 7.22).

6. Check that the link appears between the two tables, as required.

FIGURE 7.23 *The main Access toolbar*

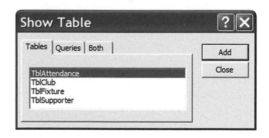

FIGURE 7.24 *Selecting the tables for a relationship*

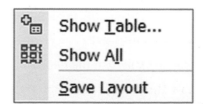

FIGURE 7.25 *Selecting extra tables for a link*

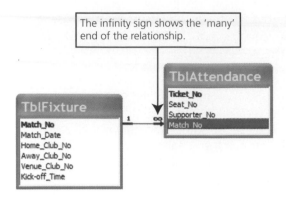

The infinity sign shows the 'many' end of the relationship.

**TblAttendance**
Ticket_No
Seat_No
Supporter_No
Match_No

**TblFixture**
Match_No
Match_Date
Home_Club_No
Away_Club_No
Venue_Club_No
Kick-off_Time

FIGURE 7.26 *The one-to-many relationship between FIXTURE and ATTENDANCE*

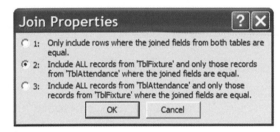

FIGURE 7.27 *Join properties*

### Theory into practice

1   Create the links between the tables in your database. For each one, decide the join properties and what level of integrity you require.

2   Print a diagram showing all the links between your tables (similar to that shown in Figure 7.10 on page 20).

## Queries

Much of the work in setting up a database is the initial design of the tables and the inputting of data. The next stage is to think about how to make the database provide the answers to questions you want to ask.

The simplest questions rely on data from just one table:

✱ What is the home ground of club P?

✱ Who is playing against Team Q in the match on data R?

✱ What time is the kick-off for the match between clubs X and Y on data Z?

To answer these questions, you could print a report of the data from just one table and scan the report to find the answer.

More complex questions need data from more than one table:

✱ Which club does supporter X support?

✱ Which matches has supporter X booked to see?

✱ How many supporters have bought tickets for match Y?

You could scan one table to find part of the answer, but you would then need to refer to another table to find the complete answer.

These more complex questions can be answered using the database software, by setting up a query. The query produces a new table, combining relevant data from the other tables.

The fields that form the columns of this new table are selected by you during the setup of the query. This would be the field that you are testing to match a particular criteria, as well as other fields that you want to appear in the answer to your query.

The rows of the table contain the data for any records that match the criteria you have specified.

To distinguish tables that are set up as a result of a query, use a prefix such as **Qry** before the meaningful name that you choose for the query.

### How to... set up a query

1   Click on the **Queries** tab (Figure 7.28).

2   Click on **Create query by using wizard**.

3   Select a table that contains fields that are important for your query.

4   Click on **>** to select the fields that you want from this table. Click on **>>** if you want all the fields.

5   If you need data from another table, repeat steps 3 and 4 (Figure 7.29).

6   When you have selected all the fields you need, click on **Next**.

7   In the next dialogue box (Figure 7.30), select **Detail**, then click on **Next**.

8   In the final dialogue box, decide on a name for your query (Figure 7.31).

The query set up in Figures 7.28–7.31 provides sufficient data in a single table to answer the question: *Which club does a supporter support?*

The field names for the fields in the new table are generated according to the original tables and may be prefixed with the table number to avoid confusion (Figure 7.32).

Figure 7.33 shows the Design view of this query. Notice that the table name and field name are displayed on separate rows in the lower section of the screen.

You could decide to set up a query without the wizard. In this case, you would be presented with a blank Design view, and you would then select the tables and fields.

Click on the **Queries** tab and then on **Create query by using wizard**.

You could set up a query using Design view, but it is easier to let the wizard do most of the work.

For each table involved in your query, choose which fields you want to appear in the answer to your query.

Use the **>** key to select one field at a time.

Click on **>>** is you want all fields.

Notice that you can choose from more than one table.

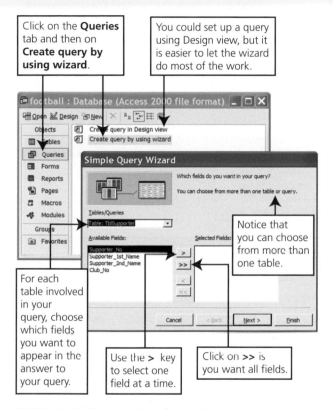

**FIGURE 7.28** *Query wizard: step 1*

Having selected the fields from the first table, select the second table.

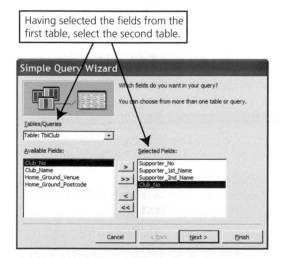

**FIGURE 7.29** *Query wizard: step 2*

If you choose **Summary**, you will be presented with the **Summary options**, and can automate the calculation of summary data like totals and averages.

Choose **Detail** to create one row per matching data instance.

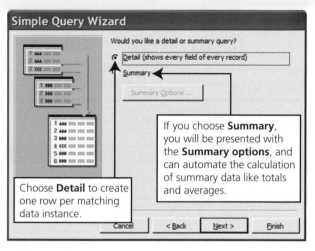

**FIGURE 7.30** *Query wizard: step 3*

The default name for the query table is created from the first table from which you selected fields. Rather than accept this, choose a name that is more meaningful for your query. Prefix the name with '**Qry**' so you know how the table is generated.

To see the table that is generated straightaway, accept the default setting to **Open the query to view information**.

If you want to change anything, you can always go back through the wizard before the table is created.

If you know you want to customise the query straightaway, click on **Modify the query design**.

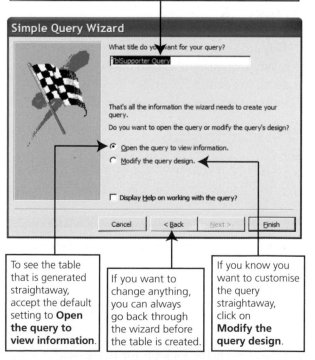

**FIGURE 7.31** *Query wizard: step 4*

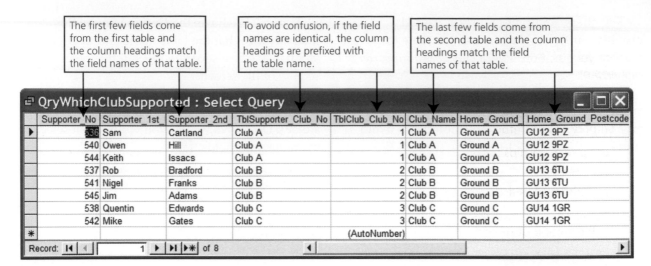

FIGURE 7.32 *The query table*

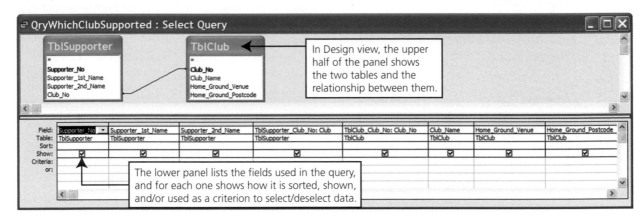

FIGURE 7.33 *Design view of a query*

Having set up a basic query, it can be refined to select only certain data. This is considered in detail in Section 7.7 under the heading 'Complex searches'. And, having identified the right data, the information needs to be presented to the user. This is also covered in Section 7.7 under the heading 'Producing reports'.

## Knowledge check

1 Explain these terms: data type, data format, AutoNumber, primary key, foreign key, cascading, join.

2 How are entities represented in a relational database?

3 In a relational database, what does each column of a table represent?

4 In a relational database, what does each row of a table represent?

5 What is the difference between Worksheet view and Design view?

6 Give examples of data types for numeric data.

7 Explain why objects might be embedded within a field, while other objects are linked rather than embedded.

8 Why is it important to consider referential integrity?

9 What types of relationships are supported by database management software?

10 Explain how to set up a query.

# 7.6 Validation techniques

Data entering a database needs to be correct. Otherwise, any output from the database could be flawed, and decisions taken based on that information could have disastrous consequences.

Data entry happens through the **user interface**; this is covered in greater detail in Section 7.7. Incorrect data needs to be trapped and rejected, and the user told what is wrong so that the data can be re-entered, correctly this time. Section 7.7 focuses on the messages that might be given to the user when data is rejected. Here, the focus is on trapping the incorrect data.

Data can be incorrect for one of two reasons. The data may be:

* valid – i.e. reasonable – but untrue, or

* invalid – i.e. unreasonable and not at all suitable.

**Validation techniques**, of which there are many, can be used to check that the data is reasonable and that its entry will not have dire consequences on the system (e.g. cause it to crash).

Each validation technique focuses on a different aspect of the data (e.g. its data type or its length). Validation can be built into the design for each field of data (Figure 7.34).

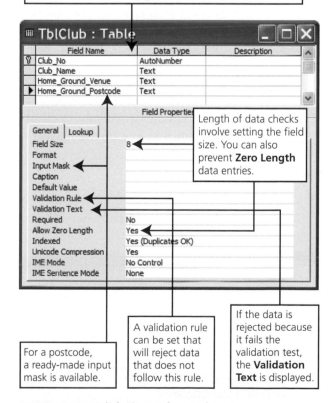

You should set the validation rules for each field that needs them. But not all fields can be validated sensibly. Here the Club_No is automatically generated, so it will be valid!

Length of data checks involve setting the field size. You can also prevent **Zero Length** data entries.

For a postcode, a ready-made input mask is available.

A validation rule can be set that will reject data that does not follow this rule.

If the data is rejected because it fails the validation test, the **Validation Text** is displayed.

**FIGURE 7.34** *Validation rules and text*

However, since none of the validation checks can confirm that the data is correct, in addition, you need also to carry out **verification** – some form of comparing the incoming data with another source of the same data that is, hopefully, already known to be true. This, too, can be built into the design of each field – for example, using lookup tables (page 34). Or you can include a final question to the data entry clerk – at the end of the input form (page 39) – asking for confirmation that the data that has been entered is correct. This is to encourage the data entry clerk to review all the entries and to compare them with any source documents, before pressing the **Save** or **Submit** button.

For this unit, you need to build in a range of checks and show that you have made every effort to prevent incorrect data entering your database. Any checks you choose to include will depend on the data:

* A **presence check** uses the data entered to locate a record that should already be held in the database. This check is used when updating a database, and you need to be sure a record is available to be updated.
* A **range check** rejects data outside a valid range of values.
* A **file lookup check** matches the data entered to a record within a file and presents that information to the data entry clerk for verification.

* A **list check** compares the data entered against a list of acceptable values that are already saved within the database.
* A **format (picture) check** checks the characters entered against a **mask** which specifies the data type of individual characters within a data item.
* A **length of data check** limits the number of characters that can be entered.

Each of these checks might be appropriate for some fields and not appropriate for others. This section now explains which to use, and when.

## Presence check

A presence check is important when you are updating the details on a database. Suppose that a record already exists with all the relevant data: a unique reference number and other textual details.

* The data that is being entered may be used to amend the database, and has to match the unique reference number before the update can happen.
* The data being entered may result in the deletion of some data. It is therefore essential that the correct record is identified.

For example, if you enter an account number, the computer could check that it is an active account number. However, this only checks that there is a match, not necessarily a correct match. It is better to use other techniques, such as the file lookup check discussed below, which involves the data entry clerk verifying the entry is a correct match (i.e. matches the correct customer).

**Think it over…**

Think about other examples where you might check that a data entry is valid, just by comparing it with data that is already on the database.

*Hint*: Think about closing the account of a customer – the account must be open before it can be closed!

A presence check cannot be used when data is being entered for the first time (e.g. when entering details for a new bank account to be opened). In this situation, each data item should be validated individually as appropriate, and then the complete form verified before the data is saved.

Presence checks can be done using the file lookup check (see below).

# Range check

**Key terms**

A *range check* rejects data outside a valid range of values.

Most numerical data can be identified as having to fall within a certain range of values.

* Valid data is within range.
* **Boundary data** is valid but at the extremes of the data range.
* Invalid data is outside the range.

For example, the dates of birth of students in a school are determined by the age range for that school: 5–7 years for an infant school, 11–18 years for a secondary school and so on. It is important to work out which date of birth is the earliest valid date, and which date of birth is the latest valid date; these are the boundary values.

**Think it over…**

Think about the valid dates of birth for all the people in your class. Who is the oldest? Who is the youngest?

When setting up test data (see page 48), it is important to include examples of valid and invalid data – and boundary values in particular – to make sure that any range check has been set up correctly. Figure 7.35 shows how a range check can be set up.

You could key in the range unaided, but an **Expression Builder** – a sort of wizard – is available to help you. This includes many built-in functions, such as **IsDate** and **DatePart**.

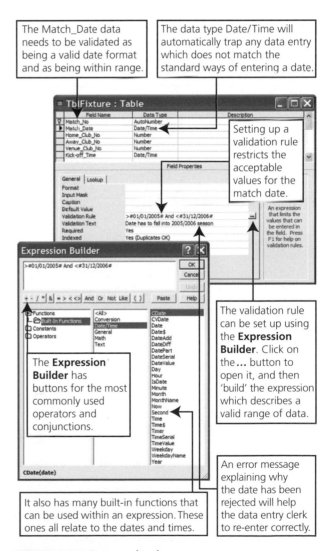

The Match_Date data needs to be validated as being a valid date format and as being within range.

The data type Date/Time will automatically trap any data entry which does not match the standard ways of entering a date.

Setting up a validation rule restricts the acceptable values for the match date.

An expression that limits the values that can be entered in the field. Press F1 for help on validation rules.

The validation rule can be set up using the **Expression Builder**. Click on the **…** button to open it, and then 'build' the expression which describes a valid range of data.

The **Expression Builder** has buttons for the most commonly used operators and conjunctions.

It also has many built-in functions that can be used within an expression. These ones all relate to the dates and times.

An error message explaining why the date has been rejected will help the data entry clerk to re-enter correctly.

**FIGURE 7.35** *Range check*

Note that after you have entered data, if you change your mind about a validation rule, the system will warn you that data integrity is in doubt (Figure 7.36). The system offers to check all the data entered so far, and this can take time to complete. So make sure you have set up all the validation rules correctly, before the majority of data has been input.

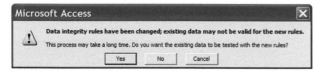

FIGURE 7.36 *Changing a validation rule can affect the integrity of data*

## File lookup check

In the SUPPORTER table, one field contains the Club_No of the club that the supporter supports. The source of this data – on a paper form completed by the supporter – is more likely to be the name of the club, so to turn this into a number – called **encoding the data** – creates extra work and the possibility of entering incorrect data. If, instead, this data field is set up as a lookup field, then the data entry clerk would be choosing from an acceptable list of clubs and looking for a match on a name.

This involves a change of the data type originally set up for this table. However, provided you have not already entered lots of data, the software is quite forgiving.

When you are developing a relational database, you need to think about validation techniques early on – because they affect the data types that you will decide to use.

Also, you will find that if you change your mind about a data type, and if that field has been used in setting up a relationship, you will need to delete the relationship (Figure 7.37) and set it up again. This all takes time, so it is important to think ahead!

Figure 7.38 shows how this can be achieved. Notice that you have choices about what type of lookup table you can use:

* You can link to another table, and the wizard will set up the relationship for you. This is useful when the other table will be kept up to date (called a dynamic table) and the data entry clerk needs to be able to select from the most up-to-date data.

* You can enter the values yourself. This is usually only a sensible option if there are very few values to assign to some codes and they will never change.

FIGURE 7.37 *Error message when trying to change the data type of a field set up in a relationship*

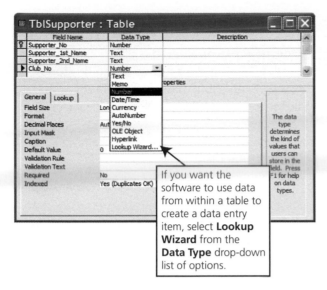

If you want the software to use data from within a table to create a data entry item, select **Lookup Wizard** from the **Data Type** drop-down list of options.

**FIGURE 7.38** *Using the Lookup wizard*

## How to... use the Lookup wizard

Figure 7.39 shows the steps in using the Lookup wizard to look up the values in a table.

1 Click the radio button to say you want to link to a table.

2 Select the table. This could be a query table and hence could use data from more than one original table.

3 Select the data items that you need: the key column and the data that will be 'looked up' using that key.

4 Choose a sensible name for the lookup column.

5 Click on **Yes** so that the link will be set up automatically between your data table and the one being used for the lookup.

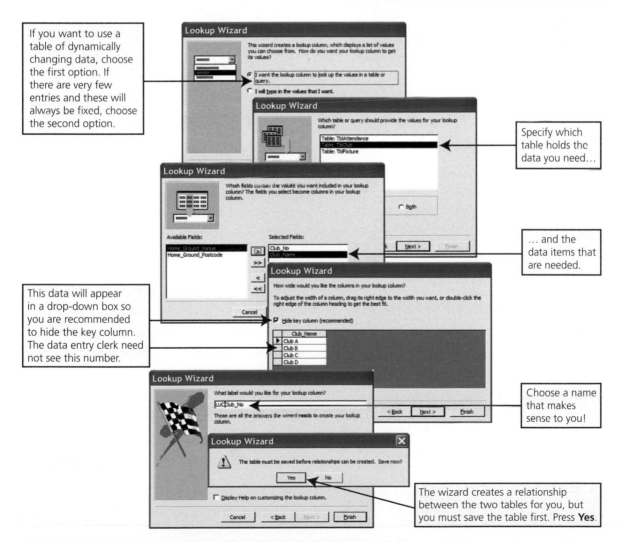

If you want to use a table of dynamically changing data, choose the first option. If there are very few entries and these will always be fixed, choose the second option.

Specify which table holds the data you need…

… and the data items that are needed.

This data will appear in a drop-down box so you are recommended to hide the key column. The data entry clerk need not see this number.

Choose a name that makes sense to you!

The wizard creates a relationship between the two tables for you, but you must save the table first. Press **Yes**.

**FIGURE 7.39** *Using the Lookup wizard to look up values in a table*

## List check

A list check compares the data entered against a list of acceptable values. To help the data entry clerk, these values can be set up (using the Table Lookup feature) so that the clerk is offered the acceptable values and simply selects one of them.

**Think it over...**

Under what circumstances might you key in a list of acceptable values?

## Format (picture) check

**Key terms**

A *format (picture) check* checks the characters entered against a mask that specifies the data type of individual characters within a data item.

For some fields the data may fall into a standard pattern, such as a postcode or a telephone number. For these fields, a mask can be set up to validate the string of characters that is entered.

Figure 7.40 shows how a postcode might be validated using the **Input Mask Wizard**.

If you need to set up your own mask, you can do so using characters, as shown in Table 7.4.

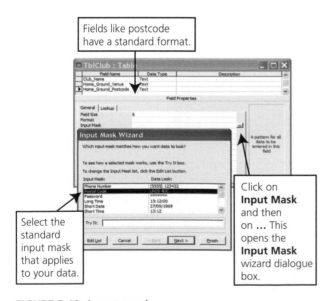

Fields like postcode have a standard format.

Select the standard input mask that applies to your data.

Click on **Input Mask** and then on **...** This opens the **Input Mask** wizard dialogue box.

**FIGURE 7.40** *Input masks*

For many of them, there is a 'required' version and an 'optional' version. Also, for the decimal placeholder, the actual character used depends on the settings in the **Regional Settings Properties** dialogue box in the Windows **Control Panel**.

**Theory into practice**

1 Identify a field in your database that needs one of the standard masks. Apply that mask and check that you understand the characters that have been generated.

2 Identify another field in your database that needs a mask for validation purposes, but for which the standard one is not suitable. Write the mask using the codes used in Table 7.4 (on page 37).

3 Test your masks and find out what error messages are displayed if you enter something which is invalid. How helpful are the error messages?

## Length of data check

**Key terms**

A *length of data check* limits the number of characters that can be entered.

The maximum number of characters allowed is the number set in the field length; two examples can be seen in the screenshots in this unit:

* Figure 7.19 on page 25 shows a text field with a field length reduced from the default value of 255 to 50 characters

* Figure 7.34 on page 31 shows a postcode field specified as 8 characters.

The minimum number of characters is zero, unless you have chosen **No** for the **Allow Zero Length** field (see Figure 7.34 again).

If the data entry clerk keys more than the allowed number of characters – or tries to skip the field when **Zero Length** is not allowed – an error message is displayed automatically.

| CHARACTER | REQUIRED/ OPTIONAL | MASK INTERPRETATION |
|---|---|---|
| 0 | R | Digit (0–9); plus [+] and minus [–] signs not allowed |
| 9 | O | Digit or space; plus and minus signs not allowed |
| # | O | Digit or space; spaces are displayed as blanks while in Edit mode, but blanks are removed when data is saved; plus and minus signs allowed |
| L | R | Letter (A–Z) |
| ? | O | Letter (A–Z) |
| A | R | Letter or digit |
| a | O | Letter or digit |
| & | R | Any character or a space |
| C | O | Any character or a space |
| . , : ; - / | | Decimal placeholder and thousand, date and time separators |
| < | | Causes all characters to be converted to lower case |
| > | | Causes all characters to be converted to upper case |
| ! | | Causes the input mask to display from right to left, rather than from left to right. Characters typed into the mask always fill it from left to right. You can include the exclamation point anywhere in the input mask |
| \ | | Causes the character that follows to be displayed as the literal character (for example, \A is displayed as just A) |

TABLE 7.4 *Mask characters*

## Theory into practice

1  Check all fields in your database and make sure you have defined sensible lengths for them.

2  Try entering data that is overlong. What error message is displayed? How helpful is this?

3  Try entering no data into a field for which **Zero Length** is not permitted. What happens?

The error messages that are displayed when the data entry clerk makes a mistake need to be helpful enough so that, when the clerk tries to re-enter the data, he or she knows what is expected. This important feature of the user interface is discussed in Section 7.7.

## Knowledge check

1  Explain the difference between these terms: validation and verification.

2  Give an example of when it would be appropriate to use a presence check.

3  What are boundary values?

4  What is the purpose of a file lookup check?

5  What is a list check?

6  What is a mask? How is it used to perform a format check? Give two examples of characters that might be used in a mask: one for a required entry and another for an optional entry.

7  Why might you use a length of data check?

# 7.7 The user interface

While developing a database, you might enter data directly into a table. You might then perform queries or print reports, directly using the functions available through the RDBMS. Your client, though, need not be exposed to the 'background' workings of the database.

When you have finished testing the database and are ready to pass it your client, you must make sure the client can use the database.

Clients rarely need to understand the finer details of the RDBMS. Instead, you need to create an interface – called the **HCI** – that will offer the features they expect and that will present the results they want to see.

This section looks at how to design and implement a user-friendly HCI to help others to enter data into your database and to extract information from it.

## Designing a user-friendly HCI

What appears on the screen is an important aspect of the user interface. It guides the user as to what needs to be input, so your attention will focus on designing **screen input forms**.

The user may make mistakes during entry and will need to be guided towards making correct entries. You need to consider what helpful **error messages** you might present to make your database as user-friendly as possible.

The user interface also includes the formatting of **reports** that may appear on-screen and/or as hard copy.

Finally, to make interrogation of the database as simple as possible for the user, you should consider providing **menus** to aid navigation through the system. This will incorporate buttons that offer options such as searches, report production and exiting the system.

In designing the HCI, you should follow some basic guidelines.

You should aim to present the user with a **logical view** of the data. This means following as closely as possible what the user may be used to seeing in manual documents (e.g. application forms).

You should aim to make all the forms similar. This is the same as aiming for a '**house style**' in a suite of documentation; familiarity with one form will help the user to learn how to input data to the next one. This can be achieved by having a standard layout (e.g. the same type of information in the header section of each form).

To make data entry as easy as possible, and therefore less of an obstacle course for the user, set up the forms so that the user can decide an order of input, and hop about if he or she wants to, but make a **tabbed order** that matches a sensible order of input.

It will help the user if you give meaningful feedback when mistakes are made and offer options rather than expecting the user to remember what happens next in a process.

## Screen input forms

Creating an on-screen form is straightforward. A wizard is provided that takes you through the steps involved (Figure 7.41).

The design of your screen should include facilities to help the user to enter data as quickly and as accurately as possible.

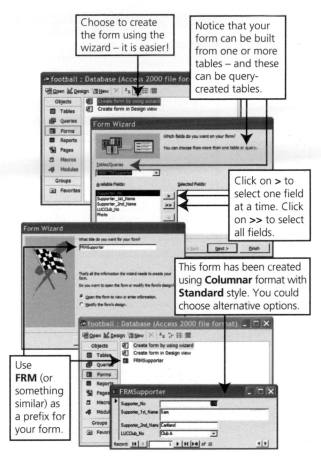

Choose to create the form using the wizard – it is easier!

Notice that your form can be built from one or more tables – and these can be query-created tables.

Click on **>** to select one field at a time. Click on **>>** to select all fields.

This form has been created using **Columnar** format with **Standard** style. You could choose alternative options.

Use **FRM** (or something similar) as a prefix for your form.

**FIGURE 7.41** *Creating a form using the Form wizard*

### The structure of a form

Figure 7.42 shows the Design view of a form. Notice the three sections of the form:

✳ The **Form Header** should contain one or more label fields to show the purpose of the form. It may include a button to allow the user to **Quit** this form.

✳ The **Detail** section shows the labels and the text boxes in which the data appears. If you complete the **Caption** field for a field, the caption appears as its label. Otherwise, the field name is used, which might not be quite as user-friendly, not least because you may have used underscore characters to create a continuous string of characters.

✳ The **Form Footer** could contain buttons offering options such as **Save this record**.

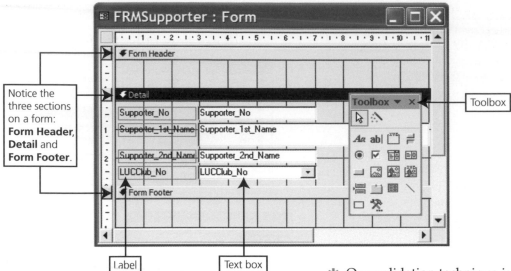

Notice the three sections on a form: **Form Header**, **Detail** and **Form Footer**.

Label

Text box

Toolbox

**FIGURE 7.42** *The Design view of an on-screen form*

## Form controls

Everything on a form is called a **control**; these are created using the **toolbox** (Figure 7.43).

### Key terms

A *control* is an item on a form (or report) such as a label, text box or button.

You are expected to create forms for your user and to include within them appropriate controls:

✱ An **input mask** may be defined for a field partly to guide the user during input but, mainly, as a validation technique. This is explained in detail on page 36.

✱ One validation technique is to use file lookup (page 34). When the user is inputting data to a field that relies on file lookup, the options are presented as a **drop-down list**. You might also enter all the values – if these are limited and fixed.

✱ If a field could contain one of a number of options, each of these options can be made available using either **check boxes** (for YES and NO options) or **radio buttons** (also called **option buttons**) which could be used to choose from several options (e.g. the colour of a car). A **combo box** allows more than one option to be selected from those offered.

✱ **Command buttons** provide a one-click route to a particular function. For example, there may be an option to 'print this page' or to be given more information, or to exit the database. For the command button to do something, you will need to create a macro; how to do this is explained on page 46.

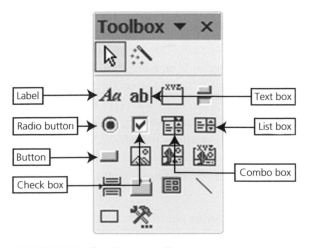

Label

Radio button

Button

Check box

Text box

List box

Combo box

**FIGURE 7.43** *The Form toolbox*

### How to... create a control on a form

1 Click on the feature within the toolbox, e.g. the option button (or radio button) feature.

2 The cursor changes to a cross bar. Click the cursor where you want the control to be, and drag it to create a rectangle.

3 The control is given a default name, such as Label4 or Option8. Change this to something more meaningful.

Each control has properties (Figure 7.44) which define what is to appear and how. If you click on a control to select it and then right-click, a context-sensitive menu will offer **Properties** as an option. Choose this to view – and alter – the properties of a control, including its name (Figure 7.45).

## Help

Even if your form is brilliantly designed, there will be users who don't know what to do or who are confused during the process of inputting data.

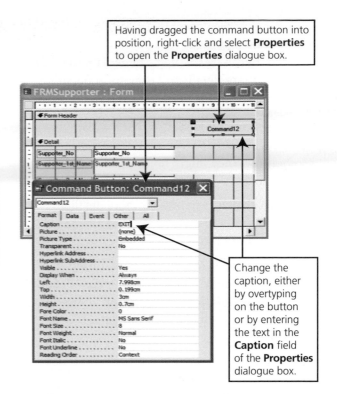

Having dragged the command button into position, right-click and select **Properties** to open the **Properties** dialogue box.

Change the caption, either by overtyping on the button or by entering the text in the **Caption** field of the **Properties** dialogue box.

**FIGURE 7.45** *Renaming a command button*

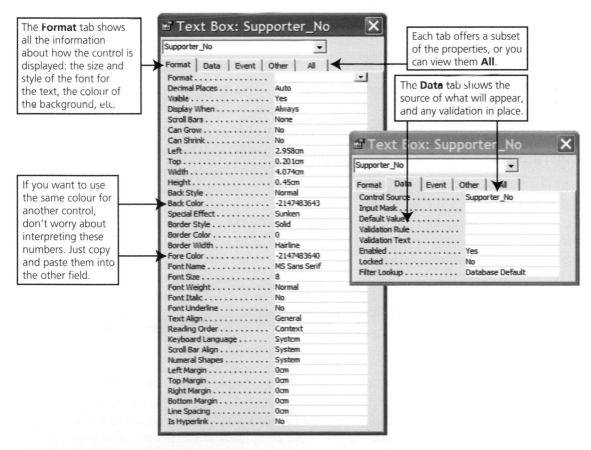

The **Format** tab shows all the information about how the control is displayed: the size and style of the font for the text, the colour of the background, etc.

Each tab offers a subset of the properties, or you can view them **All**.

The **Data** tab shows the source of what will appear, and any validation in place.

If you want to use the same colour for another control, don't worry about interpreting these numbers. Just copy and paste them into the other field.

**FIGURE 7.44** *The properties of a control*

You can help these users by including **instructions** that make it clear what data is expected, **help screens** that can explain the process in more detail, and easy-to-understand **error messages** if they enter invalid data:

✳ **Instructions** are best placed at the start of a form, perhaps as part of the header – otherwise, they might not be read until it is too late!

✳ A **help screen** may present more detailed information and may be made available using a command button.

✳ **Error messages** can be included during the design of a field. Figure 7.35 on page 33 shows how the **Validation Text** field can be used to guide the user to enter a valid date.

# Producing reports

The output from a database will be a report, either on-screen or on hardcopy (i.e. on paper). You will need to use the presentation and formatting features of the software to generate these reports so that they provide meaningful information for the user.

The wizard for producing a report is very similar to that used to create a form.

As with forms, you can use data from more than one table. These tables need to be linked, and the simplest way is to create a query drawing data from both tables; see page 43 for more information on creating queries.

The Design view of a report shows a header section, the detail and a footer (as in Figure 7.42 on page 40). The data appearing in the Detail section will most likely be sorted and, perhaps, on more than one field, so the option exists to group data. Grouping, and using group headers and footers, is explained on page 44.

## Using titles and layout

It is important, especially in printed reports, that the report header information identifies the report, and that other information printed in the page headers and page footers on subsequent pages helps the reader.

✳ What does the report tell the reader? What is its content? This information may appear at the start of the report and might be repeated at the top of every subsequent page.

✳ On what date is the report printed, and how current is the data? For example, a report for the salespeople to show how close they are to hitting sales targets may state: 'Sales for the period June–Sept 2005, as of 31 July.'

✳ If there are several pages, each page ought to be numbered. This might appear in the footer of each page and can be generated automatically by the software.

✳ At the end of the report, there may be totals or a summary.

The layout of the report, especially for grouped reports, should aid the reader. Plenty of white space is necessary, as is the correct alignment of data in columns (Figure 7.46).

## Calculations

A report may present details, line by line, but to make the report useful, totals may also be needed. These may be grand totals at the end of a report or running sums through the body of the report.

Access provides functions to help you to calculate totals, averages and other statistical data. These can be built using the **Expression Builder** (see Figure 7.35 on page 33).

## Complex searches

More complex searches involve selecting only certain records, not all of them. The criteria

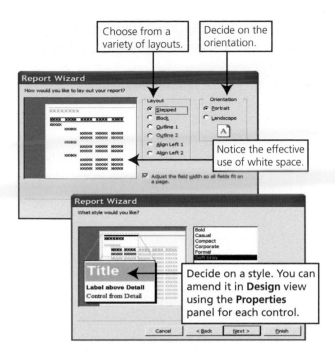

Choose from a variety of layouts.

Decide on the orientation.

Notice the effective use of white space.

Decide on a style. You can amend it in **Design** view using the **Properties** panel for each control.

**FIGURE 7.46** *The layout and style options for a report*

for selecting – or rejecting records – have to be specified. You may:

* require a perfect match of one field with a set value

* expect several fields to match given values

* accept data that falls within a certain range or that matches one of several values.

All these can be specified using the QBE system.

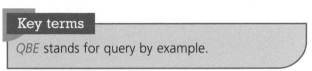

### Key terms

*QBE* stands for query by example.

Figure 7.47 shows examples of the ways criteria can be set up.

The **Expression Builder** (shown in Figure 7.35 on page 33) is available to help you to set up more complex criteria.

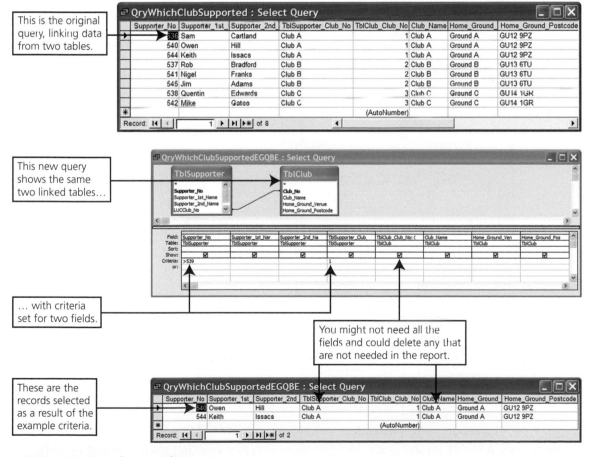

This is the original query, linking data from two tables.

This new query shows the same two linked tables…

… with criteria set for two fields.

You might not need all the fields and could delete any that are not needed in the report.

These are the records selected as a result of the example criteria.

**FIGURE 7.47** *Complex searches*

You may want a match with a value input by the user. This is called a **parameter search** and involves setting up a **crosstab query**.

Like most features available in Access, you must follow a process to achieve an effect. For each software product, this can vary slightly and it is important that you become familiar with your own RDBMS software.

## Grouped reports

If you decide to sort data on a single field, the details of the report could be in that order. If you sort on two or more fields, you can also present the report in that order, but it becomes more readable when you group the data.

### How to... create a grouped report

1 Click on the **Reports** tab (it is the next one down from **Forms**; see Figure 7.41 on page 39).

2 Click on **Create report by using wizard**.

3 Choose the tables and, from them, the fields that you want to include in the report. (This is the same process as that used for creating a form.)

4 Decide on any grouping (the upper dialogue box in Figure 7.48).

5 Decide the fields for sorting (the middle dialogue box in Figure 7.48).

6 Opt for **Summary Options** if you want to.

7 Decide the layout and orientation, and the style (Figure 7.46 on page 43).

8 Choose a name for your report.

9 Click on **Finish** so that your report will be generated automatically (as in Figure 7.49).

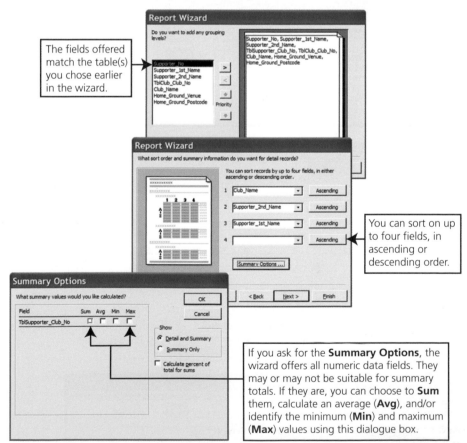

The fields offered match the table(s) you chose earlier in the wizard.

You can sort on up to four fields, in ascending or descending order.

If you ask for the **Summary Options**, the wizard offers all numeric data fields. They may or may not be suitable for summary totals. If they are, you can choose to **Sum** them, calculate an average (**Avg**), and/or identify the minimum (**Min**) and maximum (**Max**) values using this dialogue box.

**FIGURE 7.48** *Setting up grouping*

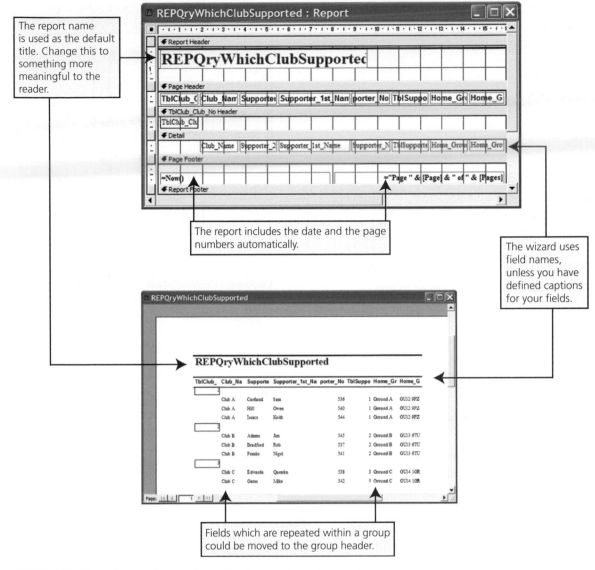

The report name is used as the default title. Change this to something more meaningful to the reader.

The report includes the date and the page numbers automatically.

The wizard uses field names, unless you have defined captions for your fields.

Fields which are repeated within a group could be moved to the group header.

**FIGURE 7.49** *Two views of an automatically produced report*

## Macros

Most of the functions on a RDBMS are achieved using wizards and setting up tables and the fields within them, designing forms, creating queries and producing reports.

The next 'layer' of sophistication involves setting up macros. Command buttons will not do anything unless you assign them with a macro, according to an **event**.

Every form that you design ought to have an **EXIT** button that takes the user back, probably to the main menu screen. Since the user probably arrived at this form by clicking on a button on the main menu, to return to the main menu you need only make the form window close. This is equivalent to clicking on the **X** icon in the top right-hand corner of each open window.

The command button can be created by clicking on the icon in the toolbox and dragging it into position. Figure 7.45 on page 41 shows the button being renamed **EXIT**. Figure 7.50 then shows the stages of building the macro. If you want to assign more macros to the same button – e.g. if the user double-clicks – go through the same process again (steps 1–4 of the **How to...** panel opposite). A button can have lots of different events attached to it, not just one.

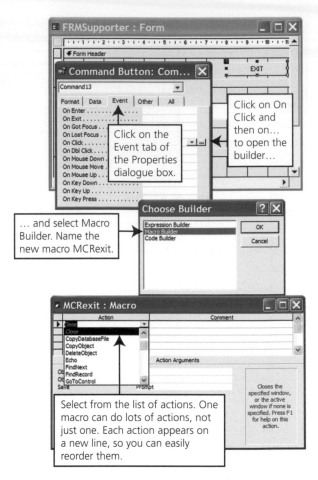

**FIGURE 7.50** *Assigning a macro to an EXIT button*

### How to... assign a macro to an EXIT button

1 In the **Properties** box for the button, click on **Event** and then select the event you want to assign. Most buttons are clicked to make something happen, so choose **On Click** first, and click on the three dots.

2 There are three builders; select **Macro Builder**.

3 You will be asked to choose a name for the macro. Pick a meaningful name prefixed with **MCR** (e.g. **MCRexit**).

4 The builder then offers a selection of actions that can be used to write the macro. Select **Close** and save the macro.

5 **Save** the form and then open it again in Datasheet view. Test the button by clicking on it. It should close the form!

## Menus

You need to set up a menu system which will take the user from a start-up screen to whichever form is needed for data entry, or to an on-screen report. From each form or report you also need to create the navigation back to the menu, and this is usually via an **EXIT** or **BACK** button.

Figure 7.51 shows a sample menu system and the macro for taking the user to a form from this menu. The action for that command button is to open the form in a separate window. (Then, when that window is closed, on exit, the menu will reappear.)

Note that you can set up all the command buttons without having to assign a macro to any one of them. They will just do nothing if clicked! This is useful when creating a prototype. You can show the client what you intend, without actually having to develop all the screen forms and the functionality associated with those forms (e.g. validation routines). Note, though, that to build a macro to open a form, for example, the form has to be created already.

### Knowledge check

1  What does HCI stand for?

2  Explain these terms: house style, tabbed order, wizard.

3  Distinguish between a form header and a form footer.

4  What is a control?

5  What is an input mask? Give an example.

6  What is the difference between an option button and a command button?

7  Why is it important to include helpful error messages?

8  What is a parameter search?

9  What is white space?

10  How is a macro used in database software?

11  Give two examples of events that might prompt an action in a macro.

12  Explain how menus can be useful when creating a prototype.

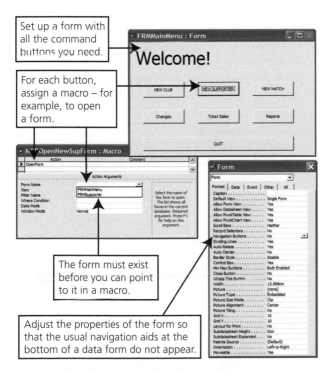

**FIGURE 7.51** *A menu system*

Set up a form with all the command buttons you need.

For each button, assign a macro – for example, to open a form.

The form must exist before you can point to it in a macro.

Adjust the properties of the form so that the usual navigation aids at the bottom of a data form do not appear.

## Assessment activity

1  For your assessment database, create a user interface to make it easy for someone else to use it.

2  According to the instructions supplied, create a screen input form. Incorporate appropriate form controls.

3  Incorporate helpful error messages for fields that involve validation rules.

4  Generate extra Help information as appropriate, and make it available via an on-screen button.

5  Generate reports as necessary, incorporating sorting and grouping so that the information is presented in as useful a way as possible.

6  Set up a menu system, using macros to take the user from one screen to the next.

# 7.8  Testing

Testing is an essential part of any development process. To test the end product, you need to know what it was you were trying to produce. The functional specification documents the aims of the database, and it is against this that any testing should be done.

You should ask yourself these questions:

* Does the solution meet all the requirements of the functional specification?

* Are all the menus working properly?

* Do your validation checks prevent unacceptable data from being entered?

* Can the database cope with normal, extreme and abnormal data?

* Is the output from the database complete, accurate and in the required format?

* Are other people able to use it without your help?

## Prototyping

You do not need to wait until the database development has been completed to start the testing process. Instead, prototypes can be produced and the testing of these completed before further development work is done.

Each prototype should be thoroughly tested to make sure it works as required, before further development is contemplated. This ensures that you progress from one working situation to the next. It makes testing easier, because you can focus only on the most recently developed functions. If anything does not work, you know it is due to something you have just changed.

## Test data

It is important that you select or create test data that will properly test every aspect of the database

design and implementation. There are two ways of thinking about test data:

* During data entry to a field, for some data, one of a range of values is expected. The terms normal data (or valid data), extreme data (or boundary data) and abnormal data (or invalid data) were introduced on page 33. It is important to include all three types in your test data.

* During normal use of your database, the user will interact via the HCI. Because the user has the option to decide what to do next, there are a multitude of events that could happen, in any order. **Event testing** is therefore an essential part of testing your system.

**Key terms**

An *event* is, for example, a mouse click: something that the user does to interact with a system.

In creating sample data, you need only create enough to test your system. However, within that data, you need a variety of values to cover all possible inputs.

Figure 7.52 shows that a very limited number of supporters belong to very few clubs and the fixtures arranged between these clubs.

If the system works for this data, it ought also to work for the complete system with all clubs, all supporters, all fixtures and all ticket sales.

**Think it over...**

Suppose you have tested a system using very limited numbers of data records. Under what circumstances might a system fail when you enter all the data?

You then need to simulate normal usage of your system and plan a variety of sequences of events that the user may initiate.

## Test plan

It is important to plan how you will test your database. As well as inventing test data which tests that your validation will trap all possible errors, you must anticipate every user event.

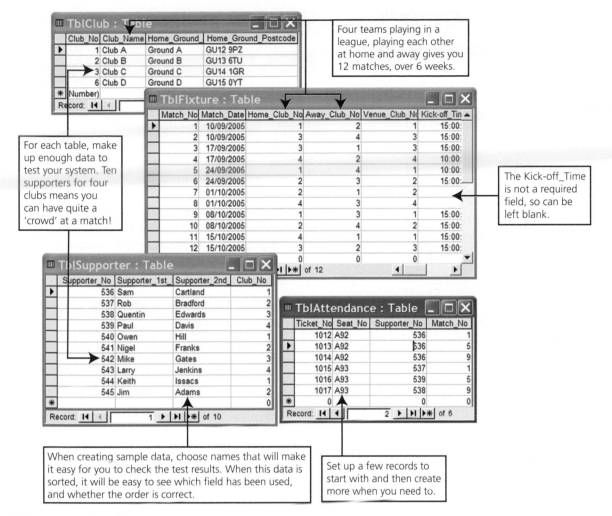

Four teams playing in a league, playing each other at home and away gives you 12 matches, over 6 weeks.

For each table, make up enough data to test your system. Ten supporters for four clubs means you can have quite a 'crowd' at a match!

The Kick-off_Time is not a required field, so can be left blank.

When creating sample data, choose names that will make it easy for you to check the test results. When this data is sorted, it will be easy to see which field has been used, and whether the order is correct.

Set up a few records to start with and then create more when you need to.

FIGURE 7.52 *Sample test data*

What will happen if the user right-clicks here, or double-clicks there, or takes this route through, instead of the route you normally follow?

For example, what would happen if the user tried to update the record of a supporter who was not already on the system? What would happen if the client tried to delete a record that had already been deleted?

Since there are many routes through a system, listing these routes systematically and then following them will ensure that there are no problems when the user starts to use the system for real.

### Theory into practice

1 Design some sample test data, using as few records as possible, but enough to demonstrate the features of your system.

2 Find out how you can import larger volumes of data into your database tables.

3 Devise a test plan that incorporates event testing. Carry it through and make notes on what happens.

4 List any parts of your system that do not seem to work as planned. Decide how you might fix these bugs.

## Evaluation techniques

It is difficult to take an objective view of the work you have done, so it helps to ask others to test your system and to provide you with feedback.

You can request feedback at each stage of the process, as each new prototype is released.

You should then act on the comments made, building in corrections to the next stage.

If you are producing a database for a client, the client will want to test the system and pass it before paying you for the time you have spent on developing it. The client may ask him or herself different questions in deciding whether the system is acceptable, such as:

✱ Is the system easy to use?

✱ Is the output appropriate?

## Theory into practice

1 Evaluate your work. Make notes.

2 What went well?

3 What did not go as planned?

4 How might you do things differently next time round?

## Knowledge check

1 Differentiate between valid, invalid and boundary data.

2 What is prototyping?

3 Why is it important to have a test plan, and to follow it through?

## Assessment activity

1 For your assessment database, devise a test plan.

2 Carry out thorough testing of your assessment database, and make notes of your findings.

3 If time allows, fix the faults that you find. If not, make notes as to how you would hope to correct the faults.

## Assessment hint

✓ If you test your database during the developmental stage, there should be few remaining faults when you arrive at this formal testing point. However, you still need to complete a full test and make sure the system works as expected.

# 7.9 ICT skills

You will be using database software to produce relational databases and will need to have acquired skills in particular tasks.

Table 7.5 lists the tasks that you must be able to do prior to completing this unit.

You will also create screen data-entry forms, and these need to be of a certain standard. Table 7.6 lists the features.

### I CAN...

Construct tables to represent entities

Define the fields in each table to represent attributes

Define appropriate data types and formats

Define primary keys

Create relationships between tables

Define searches and sorts (single and multiple fields and tables)

Use relational logic in searches

Import data from and export data to other databases and applications

Use macros to automate common tasks

Use wizards effectively

TABLE 7.5 *Database tasks*

### MY DATA ENTRY FORMS...

Enable the entry of data into single and multiple tables

Have appropriate entry-form field lengths

Provide clear labelling of entry form fields

Provide instruction fields where necessary

Include validation checks on field entries as appropriate

Enable the selection and entry of data from built-in lists (constructed from other tables)

Include calculation (formula) fields

Make use of automated number fields (counter fields)

Use date and time fields

TABLE 7.6 *Standards for database forms*

You will create database reports, and these need to meet the standards shown in Table 7.7.

| MY DATABASE REPORTS... |
| --- |
| Have suitable headers and footers |
| Have an appropriate format and layout |
| Have sorted data grouping |
| Include calculations and total fields |
| Include specified queries |

TABLE 7.7 *Standards for database reports*

## Theory into practice

1 Review Table 7.5. Make sure you are confident in all these tasks, to the point of being able to show someone else how to do them.

2 For any knowledge 'gaps' you may have in Table 7.5, ask a friend to help you. Offer to help others who have gaps in areas where you have confidence.

3 Review Table 7.6. Refine any forms that fall short of perfect!

4 Review Table 7.7. Take a critical look at your reports and those of your friends. Make improvements according to the feedback obtained.

## Knowledge check

1 Choose ten technical terms that relate to databases and write a definition for each one.

2 Compare your definitions with others in your group and refine them.

3 Collate the definitions to produce a glossary. (If you are clever about how the data is collected, this could be a very easy activity.)

4 Identify any terms that have been omitted and work with others to complete the missing definitions and thus produce a comprehensive glossary.

## Assessment activity

1 For your assessment database, check that you have demonstrated the skills expected of you.

2 Annotate your work to explain what you have done, and how.

## Assessment hint

✓ Look back through all the printouts you have produced – evidence of your skills should be easy to find. You can annotate your printouts by hand.

## UNIT ASSESSMENT

1 Guidance for assessment is provided throughout this unit in the *Assessment hint* features. Read back through this chapter to remind yourself of the skills you have developed since starting on this unit.

2 Check the contents of your portfolio to make sure that you have included evidence of all your ICT skills and all documentation required.

# Managing ICT projects

As a result of the work you have done for your A2 course you will already have considerable experience of planning and carrying out small-scale projects. You will know, therefore, how difficult it can be to juggle resources and to make effective use of your time. Imagine how much more difficult it is to manage a project when there are large numbers of people, lots of resources and a lot of money involved! Deciding who has to do what and when, keeping track of progress and reporting to senior management, requires much expertise on behalf of the project manager. Perhaps not surprisingly, therefore, a large number of projects, particularly in ICT, do not meet their objectives fully. Some fail spectacularly!

It is widely recognised that a successful project manager requires specialist knowledge and skills. This unit introduces you to some of the formal project management tools and methods a project manager can take advantage of, and it will give you the opportunity to use specialist software to plan and monitor your own projects.

This compulsory unit contains 12 elements:

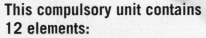

8.1   Examples of projects

8.2   Stakeholders

8.3   Project proposal

8.4   Definition of scope

8.5   Project organisation

8.6   Phases of a project

8.7   Project planning

8.8   Project execution

8.9   Deliverables

8.10  Reviews

8.11  Close down and end of project review

8.12  ICT skills

# Unit 8 Introduction

This unit puts into practice the theory of project management. During your course of study for the unit, you will set up and run a small-scale software project. For this, you will draw on the knowledge and skills you learn throughout your A2 course to plan for and produce this software. You should already have skills in at least two different software applications and some experience of the processes involved in software design and implementation.

Although budgeting is an important factor in any project, this unit does not consider finance. However, you will need to identify other resource requirements, such as people skills, equipment and time. Even though this project is not a team activity, it will involve working closely with others. People skills and good communications are key to successful project management.

The evaluation of your work for this unit will take the form of an end-of-project review. During this review, all project stakeholders will assess the success of your project and your performance as a project manager.

This is a user-focused unit. The knowledge and skills developed in this unit are particularly relevant to those who use ICT on a daily basis at work or at school/college for personal, social and work-related purposes.

This unit builds on the work done throughout your course. It assumes that you have some experience of developing a software product, possibly though your work on *Unit 7: Using database software*.

## Resources required in this unit

You will need printing facilities, sufficient individual storage space, Internet access (broadband) and a Windows XP operating system (or equivalent). You will also require software to fulfil the following functions:

* project management (e.g. Microsoft Project)
* word processing (e.g. Microsoft Word, OpenOffice Writer)
* presentation (e.g. Microsoft PowerPoint, OpenOffice Impress).

## How you will be assessed

To meet the assessment requirements for this unit you will:

* research and produce a proposal for a new software product
* produce a detailed project plan and use it to monitor and communicate progress
* keep detailed project management records
* design and produce the deliverables in line with the project plan
* evaluate the project and your own performance, using the end-of-project review.

You will produce an e-portfolio for this unit, which should include the following:

* A **project proposal**, with evidence of how you presented this to senior management, and a project definition document that senior management has approved.
* A **project plan** covering all the key phases of the project. This should also include evidence of your use of the plan to monitor and communicate progress throughout the project.
* **Evidence** of your performance as a project manager, showing how you communicated with stakeholders, acted on feedback, provided accurate information and ran meetings.
* The **software product** – plus any other specified deliverables – that you produce as outcomes of the project. This should also include evidence showing how the production of the product correlated with the schedule specified in the plan.
* An **evaluation** – using feedback from the end-of-project review – assessing the success of the project, and of the effectiveness of the project management methods you used and of your own performance.

## How high can you aim?

The final section of the unit tells you what to do and how to do this to gain the highest marks possible.

# 8.1 Examples of projects

Unlike many ICT activities, a project is not a never-ending process: the support and maintenance required for a PC's hardware, for example, is *not* a project – both processes are ongoing. Projects have a well defined start and a well defined end. A project often runs for a set period of time during which it should achieve a specific goal. A project will often also involve a number of different people.

Various factors go together to make a project successful or otherwise. These factors include detailed planning, the efficient use of resources and effective communication. This unit explains how you, as project manager, can best use these factors to make your project a success.

To help you get to grips with the idea of project management, the following case studies present real-world projects, both large and small.

## CASE STUDY

The Niaz family want to build their own house. First, they buy a plot of land on which to build the house and then decide on their requirements, such as the number of bedrooms they need and the size of the garage. Next, they employ an architect to design the house. When the house has been designed, the work passes to a builder. The builder employs trades people to undertake various tasks on his behalf: to lay the bricks, install the plumbing and central heating, and to plaster the walls (see Figure 8.1). The project finishes when the builder completes the house and the Niaz family moves in.

1    Of the various people involved in this project, who do you think would be in the best position to act as the project manager? Give your reasons.

2    What must the manager do to ensure that the project runs as smoothly as possible?

FIGURE 8.1 *A project to build a house*

## CASE STUDY

Alice decides she would like to change how her living room looks. She decides on the new colours, layout and furniture then buys the paint and wallpaper and does the work herself.

1    Alice is acting as her own project manager. What planning would she have to undertake to make sure she did the job as quickly and efficiently as possible?

2    When would Alice be able to say that this project had been completed?

Adrian decides to apply to university. First, he must decide on his personal requirements. These may include the subjects he wants to study, the size and type of university, whether he wants to live at home or move away, and how good the exam results will be that he expects to achieve at college. Adrian then researches which courses at which universities would meet his needs.

1    Adrian is his own project manager. Who or what could help him to decide which universities to apply to?

2    When might Adrian consider that his project has been completed?

## Common characteristics

All projects have three things in common:

* they have an overall objective
* they aim to change something
* they have an end where, if they have been successful, the objective has been met.

Most projects involve the following people but, as you saw in the case studies above, in a small project, these roles may be undertaken by one person.

* The customer, who benefits from a successful project.
* The designer, who turns the customer's needs into something realisable.
* The constructor, who does the work.
* The project manager, who plans, manages and monitors the work.

### Think it over...

Consider again the case studies of building a house, decorating a room and applying to university. What are the start, change and end activities? Who is the customer, designer and constructor?

## Critical success factors

At the start of your project you should define what success should look like. Success may include any of the factors that are important to the people involved in the project.

### Functional

The functional factors state what the project must achieve. For example, an ICT project might contain a list of possible features to be incorporated into a piece of software. A critical success factor in this example might be for the software to contain all priority-one (**mandatory**) features, 90 per cent of priority-two (**important**) features and 75 per cent of priority-three (**desirable**) features.

### Key terms

*Mandatory* features are those things the project must do. *Important* features are those things the project should do, if at all possible. *Desirable* features are those things the project should do if to achieve these features does not overstrain the available resources.

### Timescale

All projects have a timescale that will include the end date. A software project, for example, may need to be ready before the Christmas selling peak, by an external date for legal reasons or to support a new product launch.

### Resources

A project's resources include people, their effort and money. For any project, there may be a limit on how many people can be involved, how much effort they can put in, and a fixed cost which the project must not exceed.

### Ease of use

Software which full-time, trained users will operate should be full of features. Powerful functions should be available with just a few clicks or key presses. Software intended for casual users, perhaps customers of a business using the Internet, should be easy to use. Rather than being powerful, functions should be very simple and with much user guidance.

### Performance

Most software should meet minimum performance requirements that depend upon the user's needs. For example, the functions in a PC game may be required to work in much less than a second, whereas the time it takes to run a large organisation's monthly payroll may be several hours.

## Reasons why some projects fail

Newcomers to computers often think that the most likely cause of failure in an ICT project is technical. In the early days of computers, the 1960s to the 1980s, this was undoubtedly true. Many people then had visions beyond what the available technology could deliver. Today, however, very few professional ICT projects fail for technical reasons. There still are many failures, though, for the following reasons.

### The project does not meet the customer's needs

There are many reasons why a project may not meet the customer's needs. For example, the customer's requirements may not have been stated clearly at the start of the project. Alternatively, the customer's needs may change during the course of a project. These changed requirements might be passed on incorrectly to you or not passed on at all. Occasionally the customer may change during a project, and the new customer has different ideas about what is required.

### The project is more complex than expected

Project managers are often put under pressure at the start of a project – they might be expected

---

## CASE STUDY

Brian Gilbert, the newly-appointed Chief Executive of the engineering company Fix-It, decided to replace all the company's ICT systems. Brian wanted to buy in a large, ready-made business package. Were he to do this, Fix-It would be the first in their industry to use such software. The main benefit of the package would be to allow Fix-It to meet a new business need: to take on work on a commercial basis on behalf of companies outside Fix-It's own group.

Because none of Brian's ICT staff had experience of this package, Fix-It transferred these employees elsewhere within the group. Brian then brought in expensive consultants from Woffle & Spendalot to configure and implement the package.

Unfortunately, things went wrong. Brian moved on to run a bigger business, and his replacement, Richard Wood, had a different business focus. Under Richard, Fix-It were now just to serve group companies. Two years late and many millions over budget, Fix-It finally put the new system in place.

Worse was to come: some of the software didn't work and Fix-It now had no skilled ICT staff to look into the problems just before the annual business peak. Where the software did work, some of the staff couldn't use it properly. All this had a major effect on the customer service for the whole group – it lost Fix-It many more millions of pounds.

1   What research should Brian have undertaken before he bought in the ready-made business package?

2   Who is the customer for the new software package? Do the customer's needs change throughout the life of the project?

Mohamed works as a project manager for a software company, Dynamic Solutions. A potential client, Global Logistics, approaches him for a quote for a payroll system for their 40,000 employees. Based on previous work for similar-sized companies, Dynamic Solutions provide a price and a timescale.

After Dynamic Solutions has won the contract, Mohamed finds that Global Logistics has the most complex set of work rules he has ever seen. For example, for many Global Logistics staff, the system must pay meal allowances based on the local clock time, local meal rates and in local currencies. Henry in Harare, for instance, is paid less (in Zimbabwe dollars) than Nazim in New York (in US dollars) because of the difference in the cost of living in each country. This means the new system will have to track the location of 10,000 employees daily as they fly round the world.

1   What factors made this system more complex than it first appeared?

2   Was there anything Mohamed should have done before he gave Global Logistics a price and a timescale?

to say how long the project will take and how much it will cost before it is clear what the project has to do.

## The project grows as it goes along

While you are trying to establish the software's detailed requirements, the customer may add many more minor features to the original request. Even though these features will bring few extra benefits, they might incur a large increase in timescale and cost to build and deliver. This situation is likely to arise when an organisation has little focus on costs. It is also likely to arise when an external software builder is paid on a per-day basis rather than on a fixed price for delivery basis.

The senior management of We Deliver – a mail-order sales company – wanted a new system built quickly and cheaply to meet their expanding business needs. Abdul, a project manager in the ICT department, proposed to senior management that they should use an application generation package – a software package that has most of the functions already built-in. The senior management agreed to this package, even though it would limit their flexibility in screen and report design.

In earlier projects, the main customer for this software, Ben (the head of the sales department) was used to specifying precisely how each screen and report should look. Ben insisted that he should still be able to do this. Abdul and his ICT team, therefore, were forced to spend much time and effort changing the screens and reports produced by the package so that they looked exactly as Ben wanted.

The result of this was that the project took even longer and cost even more than if Abdul had built the system in a traditional manner. Ben was also unhappy, because Abdul did not do exactly as Ben wanted.

1   What should have been done before the project was started to avoid all this extra time and effort?

2   Can you think of any further examples of cost-cutting that, in the end, proved costlier than they should because they had to be changed or adapted?

At its most complex, a supplier or group of suppliers may provide a broad solution that includes hardware, standard software and specially developed software. The supplier may have responsibility for system specification and may have to put in place or roll out the solution. They may have to develop and deliver specific training. They may have to maintain the system for its lifetime. For a large government project, such a project might be worth a hundred million pounds.

While the supplier wants a satisfied customer, they want to make money out of the contract even more. You should be aware of this possible conflict of interest for the supplier.

## Knowledge check

1 Who might be the stakeholders in a project?

2 What role would each of these stakeholders play?

## Think it over...

You are the project manager for a new library system at your school or college. Who are your stakeholders? What do you think they will want from the new system? What roles would you expect each stakeholder to play?

## Assessment activity

1 For each of the two project proposals you outlined at the end of Section 8.1, decide who the project stakeholders would be.

2 For each project, now try to decide who would fulfil each of the following roles: customer, designer, constructor, project manager.

## Assessment hint

✓ Make each stakeholder's role as clear as possible. Have a different person act for each role, even if in practice several of the roles could be combined in one person.

# 8.3 Project proposal

## What the project is about

The starting point for any project is either a problem that needs solving or a bright idea: someone identifies a need or an opportunity that may be worth pursuing.

A project should start with a thorough study of this initial idea. From this study will come the project proposal.

## What it will deliver

The initial study must make clear what the new or changed ICT system will deliver. It should answer, *but not in detail*, the following questions:

* What data will the system need to capture?

* What sort of displays and reports will it have?

* What processing will there be?

* What hardware is needed?

* What standard software is needed?

## The benefits it will bring and any potential risks

The benefits of the new system could include one or more of the following:

* better customer service

* lower costs

* increased revenue

* greater staff productivity

* better management decision-making

* compliance with legislation

* better safety and security.

For example, a new sales order system could improve customer service through:

* a faster order processing time

* better stock-checking

* better visibility to the customers of the status of their orders.

At this stage it is difficult to quantify the benefits. However, the study must make it clear how the benefits will arise from what will be delivered.

The study should also outline any potential risks the new system may present. For example, there may be a risk in that the staff are reluctant to learn how to use the new software. In the case of the new sales order system, customers may initially dislike having to change from a system they have become accustomed to. The benefits of the new system must be weighed against the risks. If the benefits outweigh the risks, then it may be decided to continue with the proposal.

## Impact on personnel and practices

Few computer systems are simply automated versions of existing manual processes. When designing a new system, a good systems analyst will take the opportunity to exploit the computer's strengths compared with those of a clerk who is currently doing the job by hand. As is now well known, computers are very speedy and accurate at searching, sorting, reporting and displaying.

The management, therefore, will often take the opportunity to change existing working practices when a new computer system is to be introduced. These changed working practices could affect the staff for the following reasons:

* The work becomes harder and, hence, too difficult.

* Alternatively, the work becomes easier and, hence, there is pressure to reduce their pay.

* Skills built up over the years become redundant.

* The staff need training to learn how to use the new system.

In extreme cases, the new system can reduce the workload so much that some staff are no longer required. This may mean redundancy, retraining or redeployment.

## Functional requirements

The system designer does not have a free hand in the design of the solution. There may be many constraints, and the study should state these. These constraints may include:

* links to other systems

* ease of use

* user skill levels

* response times or performance

* volume of use

* technical needs, such as which type of hardware or software to use

* compliance with certain predetermined standards

* the system's users may be in different places or even anywhere in the world.

## Who will use the product or service?

The study should make clear who will use each part of the system. These people could be, for example, one or more of:

* the organisation's customers

* the organisation's staff, as a small or large part of their job

* the management team.

Who will use the system may have a big effect on the system's design. For example, customers cannot be trained to use the new system, so the customer user interface must be kept very simple. The organisation's clerical staff, on the other hand, will want powerful functions so that they can do their job quickly and effectively. A lot may be invested in their training.

The study should also make it clear which user will do what. For example, the designer may plan that the sales department will capture the data that the finance department will then use. This system would not work, however, if both departments demanded the right to enter all the data as only their department's data was correct and timely. The situation would be even worse if neither department agreed to put the data in.

## How long will it take?

Projects almost always take at least as much time as they are allowed to take, and they often take much longer! The study will state the minimum amount of time the project should take, given sensible staffing levels. If a project estimate is 12 **person-months**, for example, then a reasonable

time period for an average of two people working on the project might be six calendar months.

## When must it be finished?

If there is an absolute deadline, then the study should state this. For example, a financial system might need to be in place and working effectively by a specified date, say April 1st. A sales system could be needed well before the Christmas sales peak, and an academic system before the start of the new academic year.

A deadline stated in the terms 'As soon as possible' is usually only acceptable if the new system is a response to an urgent competitive threat. Deadlines such as this often increase costs and deliver a poor-quality system. Senior management should be discouraged from making a quick decision to have a too-early delivery date.

## What resources will be needed?

The study should say what ICT skills are needed, both when and for how long. It should also identify what ICT resources will be needed beyond those that are normally available. For example, the system might need its own dedicated test system or specialised **prototype** versions of the production hardware.

> **Key terms**
>
> A *person-month* is the amount of time a person can be expected to work during one calendar month. Unlike a calendar month, therefore, a person-month does not include weekends, bank holidays and nights. It is a measure of effort, not duration, and is sometimes called a man-month.

> **Key terms**
>
> A *prototype* is a model or mock-up built, quickly and cheaply, to resemble the finished product. This is usually done so that the proposed system can be tested and so that the customer can have an idea of what the final system will look like.

> **Think it over...**
>
> A project scheduled to take six calendar months starts with two people in the team. The estimated person-months for the project, therefore, is twelve. The project team, however, grows to include four people. Can the calendar months for this project now be adjusted accordingly?
>
> *Hint:* A project scheduled to take 12 person-months cannot feasibly be completed in one calendar month, even if 12 people are allocated to work on it.

The customer will want to know what resources they must provide. They will also need to make time available to work with the system designers to develop, review and sign off the specification. They will similarly have to provide staff to test the system once the ICT department has handed it over to them to make sure it meets their needs. They will have to train their staff in how to use the new system. They may also need to reload data or configure the system in some way.

# Who else will be involved?

A large and complex system will affect people well beyond the confines of the organisation. For example, a manufacturing organisation will deal with outside suppliers, customers of their products, transport firms and so on, some of whom may be overseas. The study must state to what degree and at what stage these other people will be involved.

# Ways of tackling the project, including recommendations

Getting senior management approval is not a foregone conclusion. In your role as project manager, to obtain senior management approval, you need to be:

* a good communicator
* able to impart complex information in a jargon-free way
* willing to compromise if necessary
* confident and determined enough to hold out for what you believe is really important.

Your project proposal may contain several options. Some of your alternative proposals might be:

* very expensive, lengthy to implement, risky, but they meet everyone's needs
* reasonably priced, with a good **business case**, and they meet all the mandatory and many of the desirable needs
* cheap, quick, but they only address part of the problem with a poor solution.

You can present your project proposal on paper, electronically or verbally, or any combination of these. You will learn later on how to organise formal meetings and how to communicate complex technical information to a non-specialist audience.

## Knowledge check

1 What benefits might a project proposal identify?

2 What impact might an ICT project have on personnel and work practices?

3 Who might be the users of an ICT project?

4 Explain what these terms mean: functional requirements, person-month, prototype, business case.

## Assessment activity

1 Decide which, if any, of your two outline projects could be expanded to form the project you would like to undertake for this unit. If you are not sure which one to develop or if you feel neither will work for you, discuss this with your tutor or fellow students so that you can reach a decision as to what form your project will take.

2 Work on your draft proposal. Use the headings in this section to structure your draft and to ensure you include all you should ('What the project is about', 'What it will deliver', 'The benefits it will bring and any potential risks', and so on).

3 When you are happy with your outline proposal, you will need approval to go ahead with it. Discuss gaining approval for your project with your tutor.

## Assessment hint

✓ Discuss how to go about gaining approval with your tutor, both before you start writing your proposal and when you have it in draft form. Make sure that you understand what each of the stakeholders will look for from your proposal.

# 8.4 Definition of scope

Once you have approval to go ahead with your project, you must make sure that everyone involved knows exactly what the project aims to achieve. They must also know by when, by whom and how the project will be achieved. In other words, you must set out the **scope** of your project.

> **Key terms**
>
> The *scope* of a project is what the project aims to achieve.

The project proposal or study contained your initial ideas. Your project scope builds on this. You must produce a document that sets out, or defines, the details of the project and that includes a measure against which to judge your project's performance.

The rest of this section explains what you should include in the **definition** of your project's scope.

> **Key terms**
>
> A *definition* is a document that explains clearly a project's scope: who will be involved, the benefits that should arise from undertaking the project, its success criteria and so on.

## Reason for undertaking the project

You must define clearly what your project aims to achieve, and why. This should have been established in your project proposal. You must now expand on this so that the reasons for undertaking the project are apparent to all concerned.

## Expected benefits to the organisation

You should now be in a position to explain in detail the benefits of your project to the organisation. You should identify the net benefits: the financial benefits to be gained *after* you have deducted the cost it took to build your system. You might also identify any changes in annual ICT costs from implementing your project.

## Objectives of the project

This is a statement of what the project aims to achieve. For example, a project might have as an objective to increase the amount of Internet sales to at least $x$ per cent. The benefit of this to the organisation might be to reduce the cost of sales by $y$ per cent and to reduce sales staff by $z$ per cent.

## Key success criteria

ICT staff often measure a project's success in three ways. They ask – was it delivered:

* to the specification?
* on time?
* within budget?

Senior management consider a project to be a success if it delivers the expected benefits to the organisation. The users consider the project a success if it enables them do their jobs better than before. The stakeholders should have a common view of what constitutes success, and this should be recorded in the definition.

> **Think it over…**
>
> From whose point of view might the following project outcomes be considered a success (ICT staff, senior management, users or stakeholders)?
>
> The project:
>
> 1 cost less than the budgeted £200,000
>
> 2 was delivered and up and running by the estimated project completion date
>
> 3 contained fewer than 10 bugs in the first month of running
>
> 4 reduced the cost to handle an order by 5 per cent
>
> 5 has enabled all existing staff to use the new system effectively following training.

## Constraints

The project definition should state any known obstacles, or constraints, that may make the project difficult to achieve. For example:

* **Financial** – no major investment may be allowed until the next year.

* **ICT staff** – the skills needed for this project may not be available. The necessary staff would have to be trained or recruited.

* **ICT equipment** – the project may require specialised hardware or software. This may have to be developed, bought in or installed before the project can proceed very far.

* **Business** – the project may be needed to support the launch of a new product or service. It must therefore be complete in some form in time for that launch.

* **Legislation** – the project may be required if the organisation is to conform to new laws. Again, the project must be completed in time for the new legislation.

* **Competition** – the project may provide a competitive advantage or may be a reply to a competitive threat. Here, a part or phased solution delivered quickly is preferable to no solution at all.

* **User resources** – the users may be unavailable for training during the peak business season.

## Areas of risk

All projects face risks. You should consider them, and what you might reasonably do both to prevent them happening and if they do happen. There are many types of risk, not least of which is the business itself. The nature of the business may, for example, change during the life of a project. While you might not have known this when you wrote the project definition, these changes will cause the definition to change.

The following are some examples of business changes that could affect a project:

* the chief executive announces a change in business strategy

* there is a takeover or merger

* there is a radical reorganisation of the business's structure

* the senior manager who is the driving force behind the project moves on.

The ICT itself could also form a risk. Typical ICT risks include:

* the reliability of the new hardware or software

* the availability of staff with the right business and technical skills at the right time

* the integration of different technologies.

Most stakeholders understand that to add a big new function to a project is likely to increase the cost and to lengthen the timescales. This is known as **scope creep** (see Figure 8.3). The stakeholders,

FIGURE 8.3 *Scope creep in a car*

however, often do not see small changes in this way. You must, therefore, control these small changes and make sure you understand fully their potential impact.

The implementation of the project itself may similarly be a risk (Figure 8.4). For example, it is not a good idea to introduce a new system just prior to an expected peak in business activity. Relatively minor problems within the project could lead to major risks for the business.

### Think it over...

Look back at the Fix-It case study given earlier in this unit (page 58). Imagine you are on the steering committee for this project.

1 What risks might you expect the definition to identify?

2 For each of these risks, what could be done to reduce their effects?

## Project roadmap

The project roadmap is a rough estimate of what will be delivered and when. It also sets out the order in which the parts of the system will be delivered.

The customer will often want those parts of the system delivered first that give the most benefit. The ICT team, on the other hand, will often want to adopt the lowest cost approach. For example, they may want to build all the data capture programs first so that they can use these to set up their test data. Your role as project manager is to produce a roadmap that everyone is happy with. This will often mean a compromise.

FIGURE 8.4 *Implementation timing*

## Resource requirements

The resources involved in a project include people, materials, equipment and time. The most critical resources in any project are usually people and their time. The definition should identify the skills required and over what period of time. For example, a project might require a systems analyst full-time for three months, January to March, followed by two days a week from April until the project is due to come to an end in July.

In the definition for a small project, you may be able to **personalise** or name the specific people who will be involved; in a large project you may just refer to analyst-1 or programmer-3.

### Key terms

You *personalise* a project plan when you allocate project tasks to specific people.

A project may require equipment and materials. There may be servers, PCs and printers to buy and install, and the project may involve new network equipment and the installation of cabling. There may also be a need for special stationery. The definition should identify all these resources.

## Project stakeholders

The stakeholders are the people involved in a project. They are the people:

* whom the project team are doing the project for
* who do the work to make the project happen
* whom the project affects.

## Interim review points

Most projects are divided into several parts, often called **phases**. There is usually an interim review point after each phase. At this review, the stakeholders look back on what has just been done. What the project manager and stakeholders learn from this review should improve what is done in the next phases.

**Key terms**

A *phase* is a subproject within a project. Phases make projects easier to manage.

These phases may be business-led: they could be determined by the most urgent priorities, and then the next, and so on. They could be determined by geography: first, put the project in place for the southern region, then the central region, and so on. They can also be determined by the organisation itself: first, put the project in place for sales, then for finance, and so on.

The phases may be ICT-led. The first phase may be analysis, the second phase design, the third coding and unit testing, and the fourth the ICT system and customer testing. You will learn more about ICT phases in Section 8.6.

## Project deliverables

**Key terms**

A *deliverable* is a product or service that a project endeavours to produce.

Clear objectives are crucial, and many of the stakeholders will judge the success of a project on how closely it has met its objectives. The objectives should be specific and measurable.

That a project should be delivered *on time* is one objective. A specific measurable objective may be that the project produces all its deliverables by July. This objective would remove all doubt as to what 'on time' means.

Another objective is that a project should be delivered *within budget*. A specific measurable objective is that, up to the time a project is delivered to the customers, it will cost less than £200,000. This objective makes it clear what the budget is. It also makes it clear that the budget does not include any ongoing support costs or any later additional features.

You will learn more about deliverables in Section 8.9.

## Quality criteria for deliverables

A deliverable will often have **quality criteria** it must meet. For a delivered software system, the quality criteria may include:

* how well it meets the definition
* how few bugs there are
* how easy it is to use.

**Key terms**

*Quality criteria* are the predetermined standards a deliverable must conform to.

## Target completion date

A target completion date should be set for each part of a project. This helps to keep track of how well a project is going.

There is often an external target date for the project as a whole, and this may be a fixed date. For example, if a project needs to end in time for the start of the 2012 Olympics, then it would be no good to deliver it in 2013. Alternatively, extra costs may be incurred if a project does not get finished when it is expected to finish. For example, a delay in constructing a football stadium may cost the builders £1 million per day.

Sometimes the progress on a project is unavoidably delayed. This may be because of:

✳ illness

✳ an increase in the work needed

✳ changed priorities.

The project manager and the stakeholders must make the decision whether to put back the target completion date or to increase the work rate to catch up and deliver to the original date.

# 8.5 Project organisation

Many projects involve a group of people who work together to deliver the project. Some of these people may use the results of the project. At the start of the project you must establish the ground rules for communicating with and reporting to these people.

This section outlines how you should set up and use the procedures for:

✳ your project folder

✳ information protection

✳ communication

✳ reports

✳ reviews.

## Project folder

The project folder stores the master copy of all the documents involved in a project. This is often held electronically. The server that supports most of the project staff's work is a good place to keep this.

For a small project, the project folder may be a hard copy held in a ring binder.

## Protecting information from accidental damage

You should decide how to protect your project information. There should be at least one backup copy of all electronic data. This may be held off-site. If appropriate, you can set rules for who should be allowed to read this data and who can update it. You may also put in place a system of checks that must be followed before anyone can update the data.

When the master copy is held on paper, you should consider the number, location and update frequency of copies of that data.

## Communicating with stakeholders

Another of the project manager's responsibilities is to make sure there is good communication between everyone involved. This does not mean that all communication must go through the project manager. However, the manager should organise meetings or reports to make sure everyone knows what is going on in those areas of the project that affect them. You should consider your audience when you communicate.

## Reporting on progress

There are two sorts of reports. First, you receive reports *from* those doing the work. These people will tell you what they have done, what they still have left to do and any problems or delays they have had or are facing. In a formal project, they may report to you on **person-hours** spent, person-hours remaining, elapsed time remaining and the percentage of completion. These reports may be produced daily, weekly or fortnightly.

You will also send reports *to* the stakeholders. One of your major tasks is to put together all the information you receive. On the basis of this information you can report to the stakeholders on how well the project as a whole is going, on any major problems you face and how likely the project will be ready as expected. This reporting will be anything from weekly to monthly.

## Holding reviews

As project manager, you may call review meetings at key points during the project. The aim of reviews is to let everyone know what is going on and what is expected of him or her. They may also consider the problems the project must overcome if it is to succeed. These reviews are often undertaken:

* at the start of a phase of a project
* at the end of a project phase (see Section 8.6)
* after a major change to the project scope
* after a major delay
* a few months after project implementation.

The last review listed above is called a **post-implementation review** (see Section 8.11).

From this review you establish what went well and what went badly, so that you can learn what to do better the next time.

**Knowledge check**

1 What is held in a project folder?

2 How can you protect a project folder from accidental damage?

3 When might you hold a project review?

## Assessment activity

1 For your assessment project, set up an area on your PC or server where you can store your project folder safely.

2 Put in place a system to protect your folder from accidental damage, establish the rules for who can have access to your folder and set up a procedure for backing it up.

3 Decide what sort of information each of your stakeholders will require either at progress review meetings or in written reports. Remember, you will receive reports *from* people as well as give reports *to* people yourself. Make sure you are clear what these reports should contain.

4 Finally, work out when you should call review meetings. For each meeting you plan, make sure the aims of the meeting are clearly defined.

## Assessment hint

✓ You should not only do each of these assessment activities well, but also document what you have done. For example, as well as holding and recording timely review meetings, you should document the aims both before and after each meeting, and how successful it was in meeting those aims.

# 8.6 Phases of a project

Detailed planning is critical to the success of any project. You must establish what things are required if the project is to be successful. You then draw up and maintain the project plan.

During your A2 course you will already have learnt about those things involved in designing and producing software products, such as relational databases and complex spreadsheet models. This knowledge will help you to divide projects into phases, such as analysis, design, build, test, document and handover. Depending on your project, you may combine these phases or split them. For example, if your project involved using bought-in, already-written software, then you would probably not have any design or prototype phases.

This section discusses how to break each phase down into a number of activities. For each activity you should estimate how much time you will need. You should also identify any other events each activity depends on for its completion.

## Analysis

The analysis phase is about finding out what the customer wants. It may include recording what the customer does now, what he or she wants to do once the new system is in place and any performance needs.

The four main activities of this phase are:

* interviewing the customer

* analysing the customer's requirements

* producing a definition

* producing a business case.

The end result of this phase is usually:

* a definition saying what the new system must do

* a business case for going ahead with the new system, giving the potential costs and benefits.

## Initial design

The plan for the design phase turns the customer's requirements into a potential computer solution. The design phase often involves five major activities. To:

* produce an overall design
* design an input system
* design an output system
* design a processing system
* produce design documentation.

Alternatively, the plan for design may be based on the planned system's functions – for example, create, update, delete, display. It could also be based on the system's users – for example, sales, marketing and finance.

## Prototyping and formative testing

This phase is sometimes known as **build and test**. Prototyping (building something that resembles the real thing) comes from engineering, where a prototype is often built before the construction of an assembly line that will produce many copies of the final product.

A prototype does not usually have the **robustness** and **validity-checking features** that are built into the final system. A prototype is often thrown away because it can be more costly to add in this robustness rather than to start again.

> **Key terms**
>
> *Robustness:* strength or endurance; *validity-checking features:* features built into a system to ensure that it functions as expected. These are often to check that the input to a system appears correct.

The aim of formative testing is to find the errors in the program code while the program is still under test.

The main activities of formative testing include:

* building the code
* producing the test data.

Then repeatedly:

* testing the program
* getting user feedback
* fixing the problems.

During the formative testing phase there are often lots of **dependencies**. You may, for example, want to use data-creation programs to produce test data for update, report or delete programs. There may also be people dependencies: one developer cannot start full-time on a required program until he or she has finished the previous one.

> **Key terms**
>
> A *dependency* is something that must be done before a task in a project can be started.

Despite all this, the formative testing phase is often the easiest phase to plan. Although there are lots of activities, it is relatively easy to estimate the time each one should take from the expected size and complexity of each module or program activity. Big modules will each take longer to build or test than a small one. It is also relatively easy to track how this phase is progressing as you can add up the progress of the many small activities involved.

## Summative testing

Summative testing is also known as system testing. During this phase the developer makes sure that all the parts of the system fit together as they should. The difference between formative testing and summative testing is that summative testing is done at the end of the development phase rather than during it.

Summative testing activities involve preparing test data then repeatedly:

* running tests
* producing error reports
* analysing reports
* fixing errors.

This is often the most difficult phase to plan. The time it takes depends on the quality of the system delivered for testing and how good the developers are at finding and fixing errors. There are usually a great many dependencies. For example, the later part of a test cannot be run because there has been an error in an earlier part of the test.

## Documentation

Your software development environment or your local rules may specify the documentation you should include. If a document is classified as optional and you decide not to include it, then you should record why you chose not to do so.

If your rules do not specify what documentation will be needed, then your project definition should say what documents you and your team will produce.

Typically, you should document the following:

* the business and technical requirements
* the design of each of the system's functions: *what* each piece does
* the design of the logical and physical data
* *how* each piece of the system fulfils its function.

You should plan to write most of the documentation before, during or immediately after you have built the part of the system to which it refers. However, towards the end of the project, you should plan the important activities involved in producing the final copies of all documentation. This documentation should include all the changes that have taken place during development. All these pieces of documentation should be consistent. They should also agree with what the final, delivered system does.

Once these final versions are complete, you should put in place a change control process: any requested changes to the project should be agreed, documented and planned before any work takes place as a result of them.

## Handover to the customer

The size of this phase will vary, depending on the project. It may involve the following activities:

* customer testing and acceptance
* customer training
* the production of customer manuals
* customer equipment installation
* data movement from the old to the new system
* parallel running of the old and the new system
* a gradual or 'big-bang' switch to the new system
* the switch-off of the old system.

**Think it over...**

For a project that involves bought-in software rolled out to a large number of users, how big do you think the handover phase would be, in comparison with the other phases in the project? How big would the handover phase be in a project that had developed a system for a small number of experienced users?

**Knowledge check**

1 What are the four main activities of the analysis phase?

2 What are the five main activities of the initial design phase?

3 Explain the difference between formative and summative testing.

4 What activities might the customer handover involve?

## Assessment activity

1 For your assessment project, work out clearly what you hope to establish in the analysis phase. Then produce a definition of what the new system must do and provide a business case for the system.

2 Plan the design phase, taking into account all your customer's requirements.

3 Decide how you will test your system. Specify both the formative and summative testing you intend to undertake. You may also need to build a prototype. Outline how you will achieve this.

4 Establish what documentation you should produce, for whom and when. Set aside a time towards the end of your project when you will aim to complete the final documentation.

5 Plan the handover phase: what will this involve? Who will it involve? How long will it take?

## Assessment hint

✓ When you design and build a system, it often seems important to get on with the work rather than plan it. However, as this unit is about project management, for your assessment it is more important to demonstrate that you have planned correctly.

# 8.7 Project planning

Every computer project should have a plan. A good plan is one that is both easy to read and to maintain. For a very simple project, you may produce the plan with word-processing or spreadsheet software. For larger projects, you should use project management software to help you produce detailed plans. These plans should show:

* the phases
* the activities
* the start and end dates
* the dependencies

* the resources
* the key dates
* the risks.

## Phases of the project

In Section 8.6 you learnt about some of the possible phases for a standard design, build and implement ICT project. If your project is different from this (for example, installing or upgrading a network), then you may modify these phases as needed.

## Activities to be carried out in each phase

Section 8.6 also showed you some of the activities for a standard ICT project. You should add activities as appropriate. As you work through the project, you should break the later activities down into more detail – but should avoid going into unnecessary detail.

## Start date and end date for each activity

The start date for each activity can give you an indication of how well your project is going overall – i.e. if one activity is running late, this may have a knock-on effect on the start date of the next activity. The main value of an activity's start date is to use the resources available to calculate an activity's end date.

An activity's end date tells you where you should be now in relation to the whole project. If as many activities were completed before their end dates as after their end dates, then you are

FIGURE 8.5 *Christmas shopping project plan*

probably on track. If there are no outstanding activities with an end date before today's date, then your project is probably still on track.

## Dependencies

In a complex project, the management of the dependencies is one of the biggest project tasks. Project management software, however, makes this much easier. Some dependencies are obvious, such as the completion of the design before the coding can start. Others are less obvious. For example, before starting customer training, a great many activities should have been completed, such as:

* obtaining a training room
* installing training equipment
* preparing training manuals
* preparing training courses
* training the trainer
* having enough of the system working to an acceptable standard.

### Theory into practice

You estimate that your Christmas shopping will take 20 person-hours, with a start date of 1 November and end date of 24 December. It probably doesn't matter if you haven't started shopping until 15 November or if you have only bought one present by 1 December. However, if it is still not started by 23 December, then you will not complete on time if your estimate was correct (see Figure 8.5).

## Resources required for each activity

For each activity you should estimate:

* how many hours or days of effort it will take to do the job

* the minimum time it should take to complete

* the skills needed for the job.

For example, you might estimate that an activity will take 40 person-hours. However, because this activity involves other people, it might not be practical to complete it in less than 10 working days.

Once you have a draft plan and an idea of who will be working with you, you should personalise the plan. This is so you can know who will do what. For a simple project, who does what may be obvious, and your plan can include this from the start.

## Dates of key milestones

Your plan should include **milestones** so that, should you re-plan your project in any way, you can still make sure your overall plan is on schedule.

### Key terms

A *milestone* is a date, external to the project, by which certain activities must be finished.

### Theory into practice

A milestone in your buying Christmas presents project is the last posting date for overseas: you must buy and send presents to overseas friends before this milestone.

## Risk management

Risks were discussed in Section 8.4. You should identify potential risks and work out their effects on the plan, should they occur. You should then decide how to minimise the effects of that risk if it were to happen. Identifying and planning for risks is known as **risk management**. Even though you cannot

expect to anticipate every risk your project may face (some risks will inevitably remain unforeseen), you can anticipate those that are likely to occur. The typical risks most projects face are activities that:

* are delayed because a team member is ill

* are more complex than planned

* take longer than expected

* are missing

* are of low quality and therefore have to be done again.

One way you can manage risks is by adding in **contingencies**. Should an anticipated risk occur, you can implement your contingency plan to minimise the effects of the risk. The number of contingencies should reduce as the project nears completion.

Some risks may affect the whole project, especially if:

* the requirements change

* the project's funding is reduced.

### Key terms

A *contingency* is an activity you add to a plan to allow for as yet unknown work.

### Think it over...

What practical measures (contingencies) can you put in place when devising your plan to accommodate potential risks? Why should the number of contingencies in a project reduce as the project nears completion?

## Charts

Project management software, such as Microsoft Project, is invaluable for larger projects. What this software does is to help you manage the administration of your project. You can often use the software-charting facilities this software includes to produce graphical representations of your plans.

Project management software has the following features:

* it can create a task

* it can store information about a task, such as who is assigned to, how long it will take, how it is to be done, whether it depends on other tasks and so on

* it updates task information as your project changes

* it generates plans based on the tasks

* it publishes charts and reports to help you manage the project and to present information to stakeholders.

### Theory into practice

Find out what project management software you have available. Using its online help, the Internet or books, gain a broad understanding of how it could help you in your project.

Now think of a simple personal project, such as buying a present, arranging a meeting or party, or planning a holiday. Use this software to produce a project plan for your chosen project. Change part of the plan (for example, some of the dates), and use the software to produce a revised plan.

Two of the charts project management software can produce are Gantt charts and PERT charts:

* A **Gantt chart** is a graphical representation of how long tasks should take (see Figure 8.6).

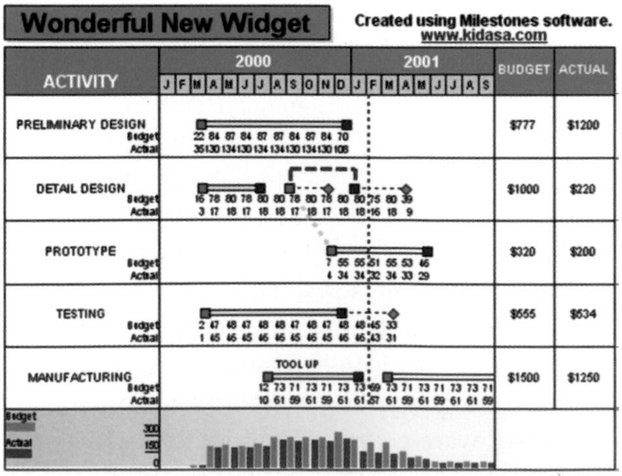

FIGURE 8.6 *A Gantt chart*

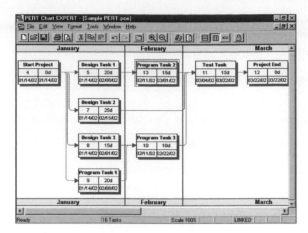

FIGURE 8.7 *A PERT chart*

* A **PERT (Program Evaluation and Review Technique) chart** (see Figure 8.7) shows the dependencies between tasks. It depicts the task, its duration and dependency information.

Each chart starts with a node where the first task begins. If more than one task begins at the same time, they all start from the same node. A named line represents each task. The line may also include the task duration and who will do it. At the other end of the task line is another node. This shows the start of any dependent tasks or any waiting time between tasks.

### How to... create a project plan

Start with a list of all the tasks in your project or this phase.

For each task you will need to decide:

1 What elapsed time will it take?

2 How much effort is required?

3 Are any specialised skills needed?

4 What tasks must be completed before this starts and what tasks cannot start until this is complete? (Dependencies.)

Enter these into your project planning software. The result of this will be a plan with no limit on the resources used. Then you should add in how much effort can be spent on your project each day, week or month. This will give you a more realistic plan. You should then review the dependencies and tasks again because failure to notice a dependency and missing tasks are the two most likely causes of project overruns.

## Project plans

Far from being fixed in time, the project plan is an ever-changing document. It is likely to change many times during the course of a project. You should check progress against your plan at regular intervals. After each progress review, you should modify and update the plan so that it is always current. Your plan should show accurately:

* what work has been done
* what work still needs to be done
* what potential problems need to be addressed.

The plan provides a snapshot of the project at a particular point in time. You or anyone else looking at it should be able to see the current state of the project at a glance.

## Project history

You should keep a history of your project so that you and others can understand how well the project is going. A project history is also a way for you to improve your planning skills for future projects. You should keep a set of **baseline plans** from the start of each phase and from other key events. You can then build up a complete project history over the entire life of the project.

The project history is a valuable input into the post-implementation review (see Section 8.11).

### Knowledge check

1. What should be included in every project plan?
2. What sort of risks might affect a project?
3. What do Gantt and PERT charts show?
4. Explain the following terms: dependency, milestone, contingency, baseline plan.

### Assessment activity

As far as you can, for the following activities, use project management software to produce graphical representations of your plans.

1. Finalise the phases in your assessment project and the activities that should occur in those phases.

2. Establish any project dependencies you may have, work out the resources required for each activity and fix the dates for the key milestones.

3. Try to identify any potential risks your project may face and add contingency plans to cater for these risks, should they occur.

4. Keep a history of your project. Include in this the agreed baseline plans so that you can use your project history as an input when you evaluate the overall success of your project.

### Assessment hint

✓ This assessment is about project management software, so try to show your skill in using many parts of the software. Make sure that you clearly show your use of appropriate phases, dependencies and risks.

# 8.8 Project execution

The first task in any project is to draw up an outline plan. Once you have approval from the stakeholders for this, you can start to run the project in line with the plan.

There are many different techniques for managing an ICT project. The processes needed for a multi-year government project involving hundreds of staff are much more complex than two people working part-time for a couple of months to improve part of the ICT at their college. The techniques described here are appropriate for projects lasting 3–100 person-months.

You might review project progress on a weekly basis with team members and suppliers. If problems develop, you might increase this review period with the person responsible daily until the problem is fixed. The project manager might meet with senior management on a monthly basis if progress is satisfactory. Senior management might call for a weekly written report, however, if major problems arise.

To manage a project well, you should measure progress against the plan and identify any potential problems. Even the best made plans can go wrong!

You should be aware of what can go wrong in a project:

* a change in user requirements
* missing pieces of equipment
* illness
* the project is simply too complex or ambitious.

You must decide how much deviation from the plan is acceptable before you tell senior management that there is a problem. You should strike a balance. You need not let them know of every minor problem you can fix on your own. However, you should not keep them in the dark when a major problem or delay occurs.

## 8.9 Deliverables

The output of a project is a set of deliverables – for example, the final version of the developed software or the installed equipment. Interim deliverables often have an ICT focus, such as the software's specifications. Many activities (such as 'interview customers' or 'evaluate possible design solutions') do not directly produce a deliverable.

Early in the project you should identify the customer deliverables (the software products, documentation, user training and equipment, and so on). You need to manage these from both a customer and ICT perspective. For example, the customer will want to know when a complete new system can be introduced into their Kingston shop and their Slough factory. They will not be concerned about exactly which software modules Kingston will use, or which ICT equipment Slough needs.

## Software products

The initial plan may simply indicate the functions of the new system. However, the baseline plan at the start of the build phase should show all the activities involved in this phase. The customer does not want to know about hundreds of meaningless ICT activity names. You should summarise this information into functions or groups of functions that the customer understands. So, for the Kingston shop, you might have a till or point-of-sale function, a stock control function and a shop management reporting function.

## Documentation

Each project phase is likely to have documentation that records the output of that phase. The analysis phase, for example, has a document that analyses the business problem. It may also have a business case document. The build and test phases have lots of documents that describe what is built.

The final phase delivers most or all of the documentation the user needs to run and support the system. You should make sure your

**FIGURE 8.8** *Documentation*

project plan has activities to produce and review all this documentation. Do not underestimate how long this documentation takes to produce (Figure 8.8).

## User training

Most ICT projects are complex, so the user will need training before he or she can use the system fully. The development team may have to train the users. Even if the user takes the responsibility for training, the project team should produce training materials or train the trainers. Your plan should show these activities, even if you do not have the direct responsibility for training delivery.

### Think it over...

You are about to implement the new system for your school or college library. What training will you need to deliver, and to whom?

## Equipment

You may need to buy in extra equipment for the users, which will require installation and testing. If this equipment is specialised, you may need to manage the supplier's software or hardware development.

Your plan should include a schedule that tells the customers what equipment will be delivered, when and to whom. You should write this in terms the customer can understand. So you should write, for example, 'Point-of-sale hardware delivered to Kingston shop' rather than '5 model 684B-3 and 1 model 8500 server to site KIN02'.

### Knowledge check

1 Explain the difference between customer and interim deliverables.

2 What different types of project documentation must be produced?

## Assessment activity

You should now design and produce your software product in accordance with your project plan. Your product should include:

* all the deliverables agreed between yourself and your customer

* all the necessary documentation the customer and/or the users will require

* provision for training (whether you undertake this or not)

* a list of any extra equipment the customer will need, plus a schedule that explains when this will be delivered and to whom.

You will also need to incorporate reviews into this product development phase. These are covered in the next section.

## Assessment hint

✓ As well as producing all these deliverables and other items, you should record when they were produced and who they were produced for.

# 8.10 Reviews

A good way to check that your project is going well and is likely to succeed is to hold an independent review. Someone who has no day-to-day involvement with your project is the best person to carry out this review. This reviewer usually feeds back his or her findings to you, as the project manager, and also to senior management.

You should identify suitable people and persuade them to act as reviewers for your project. The following are some characteristics they should have:

* credibility with senior management
* knowledge of similar types of project to your own
* project management experience.

### Think it over...

Who would be the best people you could invite to act as the independent reviewers for your new school or college library system?

You should make full use of your independent reviewers' knowledge and expertise.

Formal management reviews also take place from time to time during the life of a project. The dates for these are usually agreed at the start of the project. You should list them in the project definition. In the business world, you should not forget that senior management has the power to order work on a project to stop or change direction at any time.

At a formal management review, you should prepare and present the following information:

* A summary of the project's aims and objectives.
* The purpose of the review. Is it to mark the end of a phase, or is it a special review called because of problems or because things have changed?
* What you have achieved since the last review.
* The current state of the project.
* Your plans for the rest of the project, with an emphasis on the next phase.

* The issues now facing the project.
* The decisions you want this management review to make.
* A request for senior management's continued support for the project and for their continuing commitment to the resources required for the rest of the project.

You should also prepare answers for any questions you think they may ask. Senior management will expect you to have your own views on any issues facing the project, even though they might not expect you to make a decision on them.

### Knowledge check

1 Explain the differences between an independent review and a formal management review.

2 What information should you present to a formal management review?

### Assessment activity

While you are executing the product development phase, you will need to hold reviews so that you can check your product will meet fully the customer's requirements.

1 Build in at least one independent review. Be prepared to act on the feedback you receive from the person who has agreed to undertake this independent review.

2 Agree dates for formal management reviews. Make sure you have carefully prepared all the information senior management may require at these reviews, and that you have answers to any questions they may ask you.

### Assessment hint

✓ You should record feedback from the independent reviewer, together with any action that you take as a result of this feedback. You should also record senior management's questions and any answers that you give to these.

# 8.11 Close down and end of project review

## Completing the project

Sometimes projects simply refuse to come to an end. This is usually down to poor planning. There could be several reasons for this:

* The customer continues to demand minor enhancements to meet what he or she regards as the agreed definition. Should this occur, it is best to regard this as a form of project maintenance rather than as part of the project itself.

* You want to keep your team busy until your next project or job is ready to start.

* Your project may still have funding which you will lose if the project is closed down.

Your project plan should specify the dates for formal close down and the end of project review. The project definition should be used as a yardstick to measure the project's achievement.

## End of project review

The end of project review is sometimes called the post-implementation review. Its purpose is to identify and document the successes of your project. It also records those things that didn't go so well; this is to make sure they do not happen in your next project. Either you or an independent reviewer (see Section 8.10) will set up and run this meeting.

The organiser of this meeting should make sure that:

* all stakeholders or their representatives come to the meeting so that there is a balance of views

* all attendees voice their opinions

* the meeting covers all aspects of the project

* someone takes accurate notes on the discussion

* there is a written summary of the main points.

You should use this opportunity to gather information about your own performance and to identify further development needs. You should make a list of the lessons you have learnt.

**Assessment activity**

Evaluate the success of your project and of your own performance in managing your project. Use the feedback you receive from the post-implementation review to undertake this evaluation.

**Assessment hint**

✓ Your project management might be a great success, even if the delivered software products fail to work or are not completed. For your review of this unit, focus on the successes, or otherwise, of the project management rather than the delivered software product.

# 8.12 ICT skills

In order to manage projects efficiently, you should be able to use ICT for various management tasks.

## Producing and maintaining a project plan

For large or complex projects, you will use project-planning software. This has the facilities to produce Gantt and PERT charts. It will also produce reports of activities, resource needs and dependencies. You should also use this software for your practical work for this unit. This will develop the project skills you should demonstrate to your assessor.

For small, simple projects, you may plan your project manually or with support from a word processor or spreadsheet.

## Creating and managing a shared work area

Each project should have a secure, shared work area or folder in which you keep the master copy of all your documents. You should manage these documents and control who has access to them.

## Presenting information to stakeholders

Each stakeholder has different information needs. The developers need to know about technical and design decisions. Senior management will not want the technical detail, but will want to know the impact the project will have on the organisation. You should make sure you present each type of information appropriately.

To present written reports, you will need to use a word processor. You may also use a spreadsheet to produce progress charts or graphs. If you have to make a formal presentation, then you will use presentation software. You are likely to use emails to distribute the information to the stakeholders. You may also set up and maintain a website to display the project's progress and its status.

## UNIT ASSESSMENT

For this unit you will research and produce a proposal for a new software product, present this proposal to senior management and draw up a project definition that defines the scope of the project once this has been agreed (assessment evidence a).

You will produce a detailed project plan and use it to monitor and communicate progress throughout the project (assessment evidence b).

You will keep detailed records showing how you managed the project (assessment evidence c).

You will design and produce the software product and other deliverables specified in the project definition in accordance with the project plan (assessment evidence d).

You will evaluate the project and you own performance, incorporating feedback from the end of project review (assessment evidence e).

Your e-portfolio for this unit should include a project proposal, with evidence of how you presented it to senior management, and a project definition document that has been approved by senior management.

It should also include a project plan covering all the key phases of the project, plus evidence of your use of the plan to monitor and communicate progress throughout the project.

It should contain evidence of your performance as a project manager, showing how you communicated with stakeholders, acted upon feedback, provided accurate information and ran meetings.

It should include details of the software product – plus any other specified deliverables – that you produced as outcomes of the project. It should contain evidence showing how the production of the product correlated with the schedule specified in the plan.

Finally, your e-portfolio should contain an evaluation – using feedback from the end of project review – assessing the success of your project, the effectiveness of the project management methods you used and of your own performance.

# Communications and networks

In today's information society, computer networks are essential if organisations and individuals are to access information, irrespective of where they are located in the world. Computer networks also allow us to make efficient use of hardware and software resources, and they permit us to communicate in a way that is more effective than ever before.

This compulsory unit contains 9 elements:

9.1   Benefits of networks

9.2   Types of networks

9.3   Network architectures

9.4   Network topologies

9.5   Components of a network

9.6   Network addressing and protocols

9.7   Connectivity

9.8   Network design

9.9   Network management

9.10  ICT skills

By studying this unit and completing the assessment you will acquire a sound knowledge of network architectures, topologies and components, as well as of the protocols and standards that govern the way various hardware devices communicate with one another on a network.

You will draw on this knowledge to help you devise effective network solutions, producing detailed designs that are clearly presented and easy to understand. Throughout this unit you will learn about the benefits of networks, as well as the risks associated with them. You will find out what managing a network involves and put into practice some routine network management tasks.

Users cannot be expected to know or to understand specialist network terminology or to have an in-depth knowledge of management issues. You must provide professional, unbiased advice to clients and present complex concepts in easy-to-understand, non-technical language.

## What you need to learn

This unit covers a wide range of technologies in use in today's networked society. In particular, you will have to consider:

* the impact network systems have on ICT users
* the technological limitations of networks
* how a system can be extended or modified should the demands placed on the system change
* the impact of the system's design on the customers and the technicians
* the equipment required to operate the system
* the speed of the system
* the legal implications of the data stored or transmitted on the network
* the costs of installing and maintaining the system.

Your work for this unit will culminate in the design and presentation of a network solution to meet the needs of a specified client.

## Resources required for this unit

You will need printing facilities and sufficient individual storage space for your files. The computer system must use the Windows XP operating system or equivalent and be loaded with the relevant applications:

* network design (e.g. Network Notepad, Microsoft Visio, Cisco Config Maker)
* word processing (e.g. Microsoft Word, Open Office suite)
* presentation (e.g. Microsoft PowerPoint, Open Office suite)
* spreadsheet (e.g. Microsoft Excel, Open Office suite).

## How you will be assessed

This module is externally assessed. To make sure that you are successful, you must read the specifications for the assessment carefully and plan your work for the assignment in advance. Working under supervision you will produce and justify a network design solution to meet a given functional specification for a specified scenario. You have 10 hours in which to complete this work.

You will download the scenario and any other material from a designated location. You will need access to network design software (such as Network Notepad) as well as word-processing, spreadsheet and presentation software for the duration of the examination.

The network design and any other documents you are asked to produce must be submitted in digital format as read-only files using prescribed file formats. Further details will be supplied with the task sheet issued for each examination. At the end of the examination you will upload your work to a specified location.

# 9.1 Benefits of networks

Because people have become so accustomed to using computer networks, many people take them for granted and often do not understand what a network is. Computer networks emerged in the 1960s when it was found that separate computers could be linked together so that they could share resources and swap information with each other. These early networks relied on cable of some form to connect one computer with another, but wireless technologies (such as Wi-Fi and Bluetooth) have, in many cases, now made cabling redundant.

> **Theory into practice**
>
> Perhaps the most famous network of all is the Internet. Using the Internet itself and your school or college library, find out how the Internet has developed to become a network that now spans the entire world.

Computer networks have the following benefits:

* networked computers (called workstations) can share the same software and hardware (such as printers, hard drives and servers)

* information can be transmitted quickly and effectively between computers, which means that people can communicate with each other across the world

* businesses can be run more efficiently because workers are no longer tied to the office but can work from home or from wherever they are needed, and at times to suit themselves and their work

* improved reliability, because a network can provide a centrally managed backup and security system, as well as a wide range of user support.

But, as with all technology, computer networks do present certain risks:

* **security implications** – the dangers of unauthorised access to data

* **reliability** – the system may fail

* **network dependency** – organisations that use networks come to depend on them to perform all their tasks

* **the installation of the wrong system** – money and effort are wasted if an incorrect network is installed.

## Efficient use of hardware and software resources

Before the development of networks, a computer system was simply a collection of independent computers. Each computer had its own applications software, did its own processing, stored and backed up its own data and undertook its own printing. This meant there was often a great deal of duplication of computing resources.

Connecting different computer systems together via a network means an organisation can manage its resources more efficiently:

* **a reduction in hardware costs** – because expensive components can be shared

* **an improvement in data storage** – a network can supply greater storage capacity than a standalone computer system

* **greater fault tolerance** – one part of the system can provide a 'fall back' service for another part of the system should that system fail or be in high demand

* **an increase in processing power** – a network system can share out the management of complex computations.

### Theory into practice

Computer animation studios often employ 'cluster' or 'grid' network systems so that the system's processing power is shared between the different animators.

Using the Internet, search for **cluster** and **grid** network systems.

1  Who else uses these systems?

2  What operating systems are required for these networks?

## Information sharing

Before the advent of networks, if data had to be copied from one computer to another, it had to be copied on to some form of removable storage device first (such as a floppy disk). This system often lead to data reliability problems – by the time the data had been copied on to another computer, the original data on the first computer might have been changed in some way.

Now that all the computers in an organisation can be linked together, data can be stored in one location but can still remain accessible to all those who need to use it. This data is therefore managed centrally, which improves its quality and reliability.

## Effective communication

While most networks are used for central data storage and for their processing power, they are also employed as a means of communication. Email, for example, first became available in 1973 and, within a few years, it became the most extensively used network communication system.

Other common network communication systems include:

* chat and messenger services
* news groups and bulletin boards
* video conferencing
* Internet web pages
* voiceover **IP** telecommunications (VoIP).

## Support for group, collaborative and flexible working

Because of the many communication systems now available, workers no longer need to be tied to the workplace. Workers can now access their network:

* on the move
* at home
* at different workplaces from their own.

Workers can connect to their organisation's network via the Internet, the organisation's intranet, email, etc., from almost any location in the world.

## Productivity gains

Network systems offer companies and other organisations many opportunities to increase their **productivity**. For example, networks can:

* reduce the unnecessary and expensive duplication of certain tasks (e.g. the entry of the same data by different departments within an organisation)
* keep track of project timescales because all involved are managed centrally
* automate repetitive tasks (e.g. the creation of personalised mail shots)
* increase the speed of communication and commerce because the 'paper trail' that once relied on the post and couriers can now exist electronically.

## Central management

You have already seen how one of the benefits of networks is the central management of data and access to the system. Centrally organised backup and security systems ensure the whole system is managed to the same standard.

A good example of a productivity gain concerns you and this qualification. There was a time in the not too distant past when your tutor had to go through the following process when you started your course:

1 Collect a student's record card.

2 Copy all the details from student's record card on to the qualification centre's enrolment form.

3 Keep a copy this form for him or herself and submit a copy to the examination office at the qualification centre.

4 The centre's examination office sends the form to the local examining body's office.

5 The examination body's office enters the data into its computer by scanning or keying in the information. It then updates this information (e.g. allocates the student a candidate number, etc.).

6 The examination body sends the updated information to the centre's examination office.

7 The centre's examination office sends the updated information to the tutor for checking. If there are any errors, the tutor completes an amendment form.

8 The tutor keeps a copy of this amendment form and submits a copy to the centre's examination office.

9 The centre's examination office sends the form to the local examining body's office.

10 The examining body's office enters the data by scanning or keying in the information...

As you can see, this was a time consuming process and was very prone to error.

1 What sort of networking arrangements could be put in place to reduce the number of errors and to increase the productivity of this enrolment process?

2 Visit Edexcel's website (go to www.heinemann.co.uk/hotlinks, insert the express code 2156P and click on this unit) to find out how students are now enrolled for examinations.

Most organisations employ a network manager whose main job is to ensure the network operates as efficiently and effectively as possible. If an organisation does not employ such a person or has no procedures to manage its system centrally, the following network problems may occur:

* if data is not backed up at individual workstations or by certain departments as frequently as it should be, the whole network may lose essential data when there is a system failure

* extra hardware or software is added to the system on a random basis so that, when the whole system is integrated, there are compatibility problems

* different security measures on different parts of the system eventually lead to an unwanted intrusion, which then affects the entire system

* a lack of centralised user support means that employees may miss out on the assistance they need to operate the system effectively.

## Controlling and monitoring access to the system

Many organisations' networks handle sensitive data – data they do not want unauthorised people or rival organisations to see. Who is allowed to view or change this data, therefore, must be carefully controlled:

* the network manager should make sure that sensitive data is password-protected so only authorised personnel may view or change it

* similarly, there are strict controls as to who can use what (e.g. only certain employees may use the cheque printer in finance)

* employees' communications with the outside world are monitored carefully to ensure they are not passing on company secrets to rival agencies or organisations

* all access to the Internet is work-related – employees must not waste company time surfing the Internet for personal reasons or visit sites deemed inappropriate.

## Cost savings

There are many ways a network can reduce costs:

* **efficiency** savings – a network allows employees to use their time more efficiently

* savings in **hardware and software costs** – there is no need to purchase duplicate devices or duplicate software packages

* **downtime** savings – a network can supply backup systems that come online when other parts of the system fail.

Against these savings, however, must be set the additional costs networks incur (e.g. for extra administrative staff and for setting up the network in the first place).

## Security implications

As a result of the growth of network systems and, hence, of global communications, organisations and individuals now have to contend with the issue of security:

* preventing criminals and hackers from gaining unauthorised access to the system

* ensuring that communications are encrypted to prevent the theft of the information the communications contain

* protecting the system from attacks by **viruses**, **worms** or by the insertion of **Trojans**

* monitoring and controlling employees' and/or customers' access to the organisation's resources.

## Reliability

Because of their dependency on networks, many organisations would be seriously affected if there was a network failure. Networks, however, rarely go down because their operating systems are generally very reliable.

The major causes of system failure, therefore, are as follows:

* the network is very busy and cannot cope with all the demands placed on it (a common problem with mobile telecommunication systems)

* a line has been cut accidentally by building work or by road repairs

* someone has unplugged the connection

* an essential server has failed and the fail-over system has not yet come online.

A system's reliability can be improved by the following measures:

* Ensuring the system can manage a greater load than normal. This will enable the system to cope with occasional peaks but not with prolonged periods of excessive use.

* Installing extra communication lines to improve the system's ability to cope with accidental damage.

* Supplying additional servers and other devices so that the workload is shared. When one device fails, another can be called upon to take its place.

## Critical dependency

Could you manage without the Internet or email? The chances are that your life now depends on these two methods of communication to such an extent that their loss would have a profound impact on your ability to work and to communicate. If this is the case for yourself, imagine the impact on an organisation should these methods of communication fail:

* a loss of business
* a loss of good faith and trust in the organisation's customers
* a loss in income
* decreased productivity.

All these things will have a detrimental effect on the organisation.

## Purchase, set-up and maintenance costs

Sections 9.8 and 9.9 explore in detail the purchase, set up and maintenance of computer networks. The case study below is offered, however, so that you can begin to explore those things involved in setting up a computer network.

> ### Knowledge check
>
> 1 What are the benefits of networks?
>
> 2 How can a network increase productivity?
>
> 3 In communicating with each other, how does a network help?

### Assessment activity

Look at the network in your centre and identify what the critical dependencies are. Ensure you have identified the security implications, issues with reliability (who does this affect and the risk to business) and comment on how the system is used to facilitate work, communication and productivity.

## CASE STUDY

Widgets R Us is a medium-size international company with factories in the USA, Australasia and Europe. For the last 20 years, each factory has been run as a separate company, with its own network, server and email system.

As Widgets R Us must now adapt itself to meet the needs of the growing global economy, senior management have decided to appoint a centralised 'network systems' manager. This person will have the responsibility for integrating all the company's systems – in particular, for setting up a common email server to improve communications with existing customers and to help in the management of new, large customers.

1 What problems might the company encounter when the new system is finally connected?

2 What new security threats will the company have to overcome?

3 How will the new system improve the reliability of the company's existing system?

# 9.2 Types of networks

There are many types of network systems, and one way of categorising them is by the geographical areas they cover. This section describes the characteristics, properties and uses of the following types of networks:

* personal area networks (PANs)
* local area networks (LANs)
* wide area networks (WANs)
* metropolitan area networks (MANs).

To fulfil the requirements for this unit, you must be able to select the most appropriate type of network for a given situation/organisation and be able to justify your choice.

## Personal area networks (PANs)

Personal area networks (PANs) are a recent development in network technology, and they have the advantage that 'wires' are not needed to connect the devices on the network – PANs are wireless. PANs rely on **Bluetooth** technology and, in some cases, **Wi-Fi** technology.

**Key terms**

*Wi-Fi* Short for **wi**reless **fi**delity. Wi-Fi devices connect over distances of up to 30 m (98 ft) using radio signals.

Bluetooth is an ultra-high-frequency wireless communication system that allows devices within approximately 10 m (33 ft) of each other to communicate. While the speed and power of Bluetooth are lower than conventional wired systems, Bluetooth's 'wirelessness' makes it the most suitable connection medium for certain situations.

For example, since it is now no longer legal to drive while operating a handheld mobile phone, Bluetooth makes it possible to connect wirelessly to a mobile phone via a headset. This means the driver does not have to hold the phone when conducting a call. Some **PDAs** also offer wireless connection via a headset.

**Key terms**

*PDA* stands for Personal Digital Assistant. PDAs are handheld computers that often include a Bluetooth or Wi-Fi connection, and some even incorporate a mobile phone.

Bluetooth and PAN networks enable:

* close-proximity file sharing
* the connection of a small device so that an Internet connection can be shared
* keyless car-locking systems
* wireless keyboards, mice and other input devices.

**Theory into practice**

Find out what other devices use Bluetooth technology. Visit the Bluetooth website (go to www.heinemann.co.uk/hotlinks, insert the express code 2156P and click on this unit) and create a table that lists Bluetooth-enabled devices. Include in your table the reasons you think these devices work more efficiently or better using a Bluetooth connection.

## Local area networks (LANs)

The LAN (local area network) is the cornerstone of all network systems. Over the last 30 or so years, LAN networks have become more complex, but the following are typical examples of LANs:

* A LAN can be as small as two home computers connected together, sharing access to the Internet (the wire between the computers is the LAN).
* In a large organisation, a LAN in one building may serve over 500 different computers.

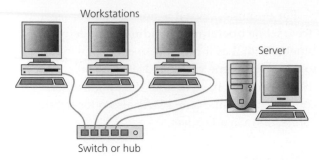

Workstations

Server

Switch or hub

FIGURE 9.1 *An example of a LAN*

* Individual LANs can be positioned in each of an organisation's different sites. Even though these LANs are some considerable distance apart, the interconnection between them is such that members of the organisation at one site cannot detect the interconnection between them and their colleagues at other sites across the globe.

LANs (see Figure 9.1) serve a variety of purposes:

* the sharing of a common resource, such as the Internet or a file storage system

* the provision of a standardised method of communication

* the management of the computer system by one central team

* data-processing at one central point

* entertainment – the sharing of video and audio images or shared resources for online gaming.

Most LANs are connect by a copper cabling system called Cat 5 (category 5). Some, however, are connected with coaxial or fibre-optic cable, while yet others use wireless technologies.

LANs are explored in detail in Section 9.5.

**Theory into practice**

In all probability your school or college network system is a LAN. Find out how the system is connected. Does it employ wireless technology? Are there any fibre-optic connections?

## Wide area networks (WANs)

WANs (wide area networks) (see Figure 9.2) connect individual LANs. For example:

* the LANs of a large company that are located in different sites in one country or region, or across the world

* the LANs of organisations that share a common interest, such as government departments.

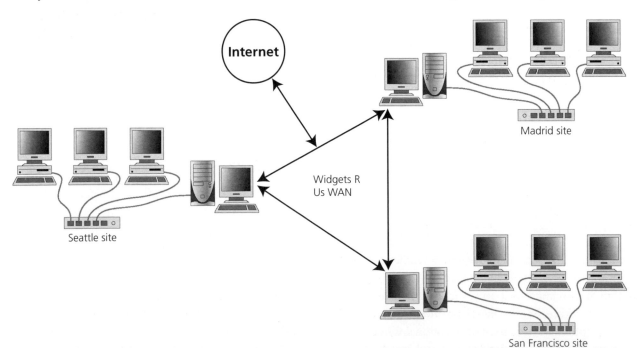

Internet

Madrid site

Widgets R Us WAN

Seattle site

San Francisco site

FIGURE 9.2 *An example of a WAN*

The size of a WAN depends on the size of the organisation using it. If your local college is spread across different sites in your town or city, it may have a small WAN so that all these sites can communicate with each other. A national retailer, on the other hand, will have a large WAN so that all its outlets can communicate with each other and with headquarters.

## Metropolitan area networks (MANs)

A MAN (metropolitan area network) is a hybrid between a WAN and a LAN. MANs (see Figure 9.3) are specially designed networks that allow the organisations connected to them to share a common service. For example, in the City of London, a MAN links all the banks, traders and stockbrokers to the Stock Exchange – the common service by which all these organisations manage their finances.

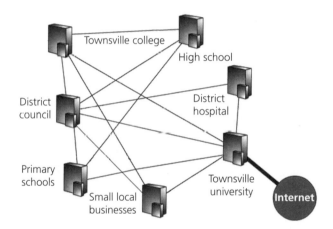

**FIGURE 9.3** *An example of a MAN*

## What is the most appropriate network?

The biggest challenge in designing a system is to select the most appropriate type of network for the circumstances. While PANs, LANs, WANs and MANs appear to have clearly defined uses, there are occasions when it may not be evident which type of network to employ. For example, would a large LAN or MAN be better as a WAN? It is up to the network designer to resolve these uncertainties before he or she begins work on the network.

### Theory into practice

Generally speaking, what would be the most appropriate networks for the following situations: PAN, WAN, LAN or MAN?

1   A small home network.

2   A network between the offices of a town council situated at different locations in the town.

3   A big-city theatre-ticket agency that has many branches scattered across the city.

4   A government department that has branches across the UK.

5   An international charity that has offices in countries throughout the world.

### Knowledge check

1   What type of network is a WAN?

2   Where is a MAN commonly used?

3   Who uses LAN technology?

### Assessment activity

Create a comparison chart for PAN, LAN, WAN and MAN. What are the benefits, purpose and limitations?

### Assessment hint

✓ In your response, appreciate that the use of a system such as a PAN is entirely different from a WAN.

## 9.3 Network architectures

A network must be designed so that it connects the various components of that network together in the most efficient way possible. The design of a network is known as its **architecture**. Just like a building, a network must be planned before it is constructed, and this plan should show the

**functional relationships** between the different components of the network. There are two major network architectures:

* peer-to-peer
* client-server.

## Peer-to-peer

A peer-to-peer network is a network of equals – each computer on the system is equal to all the other computers on the system. In a peer-to-peer network, therefore, there is no central control point. This is a simple type of network that allows individual computers to join or leave the network without detriment to the other computers on the system.

Peer-to-peer networks (see Figure 9.4) are found in many situations:

* the private network you may create at home to share your Internet connection
* online games
* in companies with fewer than 10 computers.

The main advantage of peer-to-peer systems is their simplicity: they are easy to install, operate and manage. However, they cannot be expanded beyond about 20 individual computers.

While most peer-to-peer systems are networks of equals, there are occasions when

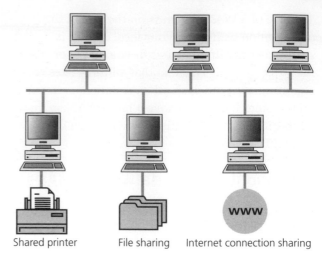

Shared printer    File sharing    Internet connection sharing

**FIGURE 9.4** *An example of a peer-based network*

one computer performs a function for all the other computers on the system. This often occurs with file sharing. Should all the computers on the system need access to the same files, a server can be added to the network to distribute and store the files.

## Client-server

Unlike peer-to-peer systems, client-server systems have a central control and management point (see Figure 9.5). This means that a great many functions can be removed from the individual computers on the system, to be managed instead by the central control point – functions such as file sharing, printing, backup, Internet access, email and so on. Because these services are handled centrally by powerful devices, a considerably larger number of

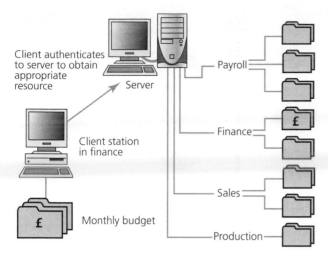

Client authenticates to server to obtain appropriate resource

Server

Client station in finance

£ Monthly budget

Payroll

Finance £

Sales

Production

**FIGURE 9.5** *Client-server systems*

computers can be added to a client-server network than to a peer-to-peer network without straining the network's resources.

There are many different examples of client-server systems:

* a web server accessed by many customers

* online gaming systems

* file servers in workplaces or educational institutions that are accessed via Windows Explorer

* MSM and other chat/communication systems

* web radio.

On a client-server network, therefore, are different systems and devices for the clients and the servers.

The client's side of the network often comprises:

* a limited amount of software, but this software must provide network or Internet access

* a lower-specification computer system than the server.

The server's side of the network often comprises:

* a **network operating system** (or one that supports multiple connections and processes)

* a high-specification computer system (multiple processors, a large memory, large hard drives, etc.)

* a good-quality network/Internet connection so that it can cope with the anticipated workload.

Many network operating systems are available, such as the various versions of Linux, Novell Netware, and Windows Server 2000 and 2003.

### Theory into practice

Which would be the better system for the following situations: peer-to-peer or client-server? Give the reasons for your choice.

1 A small community centre with 15 computers.

2 A large corporation with over 200 computers.

3 A web company, such as eBay.

### Knowledge check

1 Gamers may use what type of network architecture?

2 Corporations using the Internet prefer to use what type of network architecture?

## Assessment activity

With the permission of your tutor, conduct research on common gaming systems and how they use different methods to allow 'gamers' to communicate, play each other and record their successes.

## Assessment hint

✓ These systems use a wide range of technologies to enable small- to large-scale game clans, as well as Internet-based 'online experiences'.

## 9.4 Network topologies

A network's **topology** describes the way it has been structured. This will include such things as the connections between the different hardware devices, the networking software employed, the measures in place to keep the system secure and so on.

The network's topology is the shape of the entire system – both **physically** and **logically**. A network's topology dictates the way the system will operate, its speed, efficiency and the services it will offer.

> ### Key terms
>
> The *logical topology* of a network is the 'network on paper' – the design and planning phase. This is often shown by a simple diagram. A network's *physical topology* is the finalised structure: the wiring, the devices that will be used, the software that will be installed and so on.

In this section you will explore five common topologies:

* bus
* star
* tree
* ring
* mesh.

### Bus

Bus networks (see Figure 9.6) are very simple. A bus network – just like the public means of transport – comprises the cabling connecting a series of computers along which all the data can flow. Because bus networks are straightforward, they are used in many network systems, such as **Ethernet**. It is very likely that the system you have at home or at your school or college is connected by a bus network.

One great advantage of bus networks is that they can be expanded easily: extra devices can be

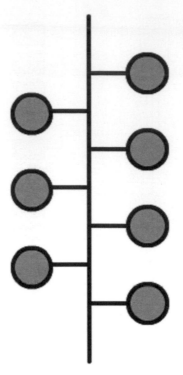

FIGURE 9.6 *A bus network*

added to the system simply by connecting them to the central cable.

> ### Key terms
>
> *Ethernet* A bus network technology devised in the late 1970s, considered to be a 'best effort' system, which is designed to cope with lost network traffic.

Because all the computers on a bus network are linked via one cable, these networks employ a device called a **switch** (see Figure 9.7). A switch can create mini-circuits within the main circuit so that data sent from one computer arrives at the correct destination. Switches thus improve the speed and reliability of bus topologies, but problems still remain. Even though switches try to route data to the correct destination, data collisions can still occur.

Data collisions (see Figure 9.8) happen when two devices are trying to send data across the same line at the same time. Each device must

FIGURE 9.7 *A switch*

therefore wait for the line to clear before it can resend, but collisions may still occur.

To overcome this problem, the **CSMA/CD** system was developed. This system employs five rules:

* check if a local line has any traffic on it

* if there is no traffic, then send the data

* wait for the recipient of the data to send an acknowledgement

* if there is no acknowledgement, wait for a random period of time

* then go back to step one and resend the data.

---

**Key terms**

*CSMA/CD* stands for Carrier Sense Multiple Access/Collision Detection.

---

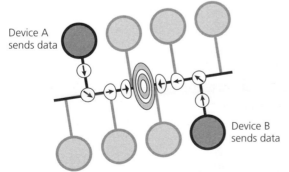

Device A sends data

Device B sends data

As both devices have sent data at the same time a collision occurs

FIGURE 9.8 *Collision detection*

CSMA/CD splits a network into very small sections, which means that collisions only occur in a small area and thus have less of an impact on the whole network.

This system is often referred to as the 'back-off algorithm', and it is applied to all the devices on a system. CSMA/CD (or the back-off algorithm) means that, unless a network is extremely busy, repeat attempts to send data are usually successful.

CSMA/CD has improved the speed and security of bus topologies (on older bus topologies, everyone on the network could see the traffic from all the other users on the network). With switched networks, conversations between devices are private.

Bus topologies are used in many settings, and you may find your school or college employs one using RJ45 connections (see Section 9.5). If you have broadband at home, this similarly may employ a bus topology, via coaxial cable (the same type of cable that connects your TV aerial).

Bus topologies have many advantages. They are:

* easy to extend

* easy to manage

* simple and, therefore, adaptable.

But, even with switches, they can have the following disadvantages:

* the loss of data through collisions

* inefficient data transportation.

## Star

Star topologies (see Figure 9.9) are radically different from bus topologies. Star topologies have a central node, called a **hub**. This hub is like the centre of a bicycle wheel. Data travels from one device in the system to this hub, where it is routed to the receiving device.

Star topologies can be extended through the addition of extra hubs at the ends of the network (the ends of the 'spokes' in the wheel). However, while one of the strengths of star topologies is their ability to grow, in practice, should a hub fail, this will have an impact on the entire system.

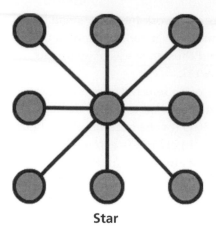

**Star**

**FIGURE 9.9** *Star topology*

Many star systems are, in fact, based on bus topologies (see Figure 9.10). This is the case with Ethernet – each spoke in the star is like a segment of a bus topology, as is each hub.

**Theory into practice**

Which system does your school or college network employ – bus or star? What devices are used to ensure that the network runs smoothly?

## Tree

A tree, or a hierarchal, system is a star network but with the hub at the top rather than in the middle (see Figure 9.11). A tree network, therefore, often reflects the structure of an organisation – central control is at the top, and from this central point extend all the different branches of the organisation.

The main benefit of a tree topology is the same as that for a star (its capability for growth)

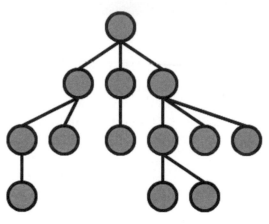

**FIGURE 9.11** *A tree network*

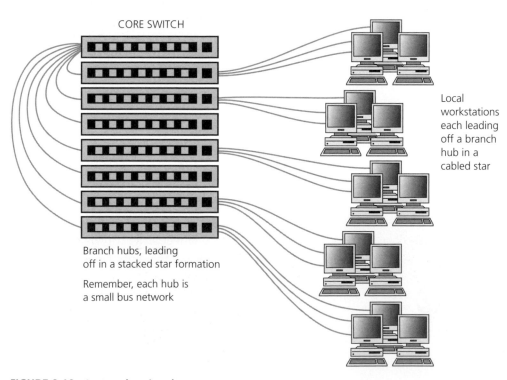

CORE SWITCH

Branch hubs, leading off in a stacked star formation

Remember, each hub is a small bus network

Local workstations each leading off a branch hub in a cabled star

**FIGURE 9.10** *A star that is a bus*

but, like the star, should the hub fail, this will have an impact on the entire system.

## Ring

A ring topology (see Figure 9.12) is like a game of pass the parcel – data is sent around the ring from one computer to another. While ring topologies guarantee equality of access to all the computers on the network, the devices on the system must contend with each other for network space.

To overcome this contention for space, ring topologies employ a special **datagram** called a **token**. When a device on the system has this token, it is allowed to send data. While all the devices on the system can receive data as it is passed round, only the device currently holding the token is able to send data.

### Key terms

A *datagram* is a special message that transports data from one device on a network to another.

Rings can be joined together, and systems can comprise multiple, 'concentric' rings. While the main advantage of ring topologies is their fairness, their disadvantages include the following:

* the speed of communication is limited
* they are not very adaptable

* big talkers (devices such as servers, etc.) and 'bursty' devices (big talkers but for a short period of time only) are not given the extra speed they may need.

## Mesh

In a mesh topology (see Figure 9.13), every device on the network is connected to every other device on the network. While meshes are expensive to build, their multiple connections can handle a high volume of traffic and, in the event of one line failing, the system will continue to operate through the other lines. For these reasons, mesh topologies are primarily employed on WANs, where reliability is of the utmost importance.

The core of a mesh topology is the router – a device that ensures data sent from one part of the system reaches the correct destination.

### Think it over…

In a group of four or five people, discuss the advantages and disadvantages of the different topologies described in this section. When you have finished, write up your results as a table, one column listing the advantages and the other the disadvantages.

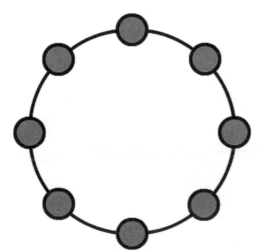

**FIGURE 9.12** *Ring topology*

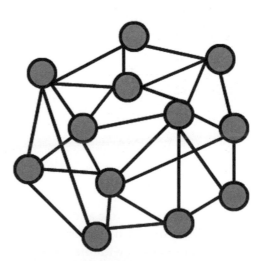

**FIGURE 9.13** *Mesh topology*

## Assessment activity

Create a comparison chart for mesh, ring, star, bus and tree topologies. In what systems are they commonly used, and what are their benefits and potential weaknesses?

## Assessment hint

✓ Some of the topologies lend themselves to WAN use and others LAN.

# 9.5 Components of a network

So far in this unit we have considered different network structures. This section looks at the devices that enable computers to access networks, as well as those devices that allow communication between LANs and WANs. These devices include the following:

* network interface card (NIC)
* modem
* server
* repeater and hub
* bridge and switch
* multi-station access unit (MAU)
* router
* gateway.

This section also considers the role and functions of a **network operating system**, and how this system interacts with the clients on a network. Finally, it discusses the types

and properties of transmission media used to connect devices together:

* unshielded twisted-pair (UTP) wire
* shielded twisted-pair (STP) wire
* coaxial cable
* fibre-optic cable
* radio and microwave
* infrared.

## Network interface card (NIC)

A network interface card (NIC) is a device found on workstations or servers (see Figure 9.14). Its sole purpose is to connect the workstation or server to the network. The type of card employed depends on the network topology and the transmission media. For example, there are unshielded twisted pair NICs that automatically detect the network's speed, wireless NICs, Bluetooth NICs and so on. Without an NIC, a device cannot connect to a LAN, wireless network or broadband Internet system.

All NICs have a unique ID number – its **MAC** address (see Section 9.6) – which enables a network to identify the correct device to send data to.

### Key terms

MAC stands for Media Access Control.

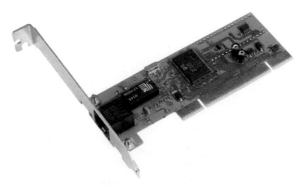

**FIGURE 9.14** *An NIC*

To see the MAC address of your computer:

1. On the **Start** menu, click on **Run**.

2. In the **Open** box, enter **cmd** (see Figure 9.15).

3. Now enter the command **ipconfig/all**. The MAC address and other details of your computer's network card will be displayed (see Figure 9.16).

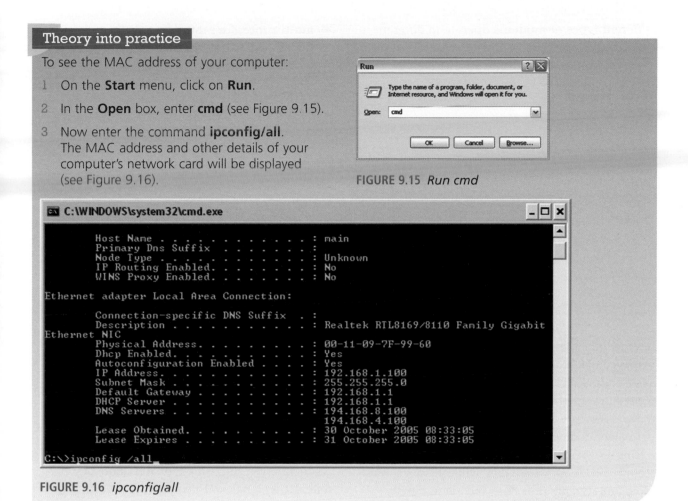

FIGURE 9.15 *Run cmd*

**C:\WINDOWS\system32\cmd.exe**

```
        Host Name . . . . . . . . . . . . : main
        Primary Dns Suffix  . . . . . . . :
        Node Type . . . . . . . . . . . . : Unknown
        IP Routing Enabled. . . . . . . . : No
        WINS Proxy Enabled. . . . . . . . : No

Ethernet adapter Local Area Connection:

        Connection-specific DNS Suffix  . :
        Description . . . . . . . . . . . : Realtek RTL8169/8110 Family Gigabit
Ethernet NIC
        Physical Address. . . . . . . . . : 00-11-09-7F-99-60
        Dhcp Enabled. . . . . . . . . . . : Yes
        Autoconfiguration Enabled . . . . : Yes
        IP Address. . . . . . . . . . . . : 192.168.1.100
        Subnet Mask . . . . . . . . . . . : 255.255.255.0
        Default Gateway . . . . . . . . . : 192.168.1.1
        DHCP Server . . . . . . . . . . . : 192.168.1.1
        DNS Servers . . . . . . . . . . . : 194.168.8.100
                                            194.168.4.100
        Lease Obtained. . . . . . . . . . : 30 October 2005 08:33:05
        Lease Expires . . . . . . . . . . : 31 October 2005 08:33:05

C:\>ipconfig /all
```

FIGURE 9.16 *ipconfig/all*

## Modem

A modem enables communication between a network and a computer via a landline telephone. The word 'modem' is a shortened form of the phrase MODulator, DEModulator. This phrase reflects the communication task that modems perform (see Figure 9.17):

✱ First, the sending computer's modem (modem A) dials the phone number of the receiving computer's modem (modem B).

✱ The receiving computer's modem (B) answers and acknowledges the call.

✱ In response to the data sent to modem B from modem A, modem B sends the required data to modem A. Telephone lines carry an analogue voice signal, but computers work in binary code. Modem A therefore converts (**modulates**)

the binary code to analogue and transmits this data via the telephone line to modem B.

✱ Modem B accepts the modulated transmission and converts (**demodulates**) this into a binary code.

✱ Modem B modulates a reply to modem A, and this loop continues until one of the computers is disconnected.

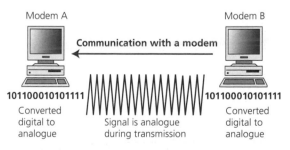

FIGURE 9.17 *Communication between two computers using a modem*

Different types of modems operate in different ways, but all modems offer both **asynchronous** and **synchronous** communication.

Internet transmissions are synchronised: timed and managed blocks of data are sent from one device to another device via the receiving device's Internet service provider. Modems offer asynchronous transmission to remote systems that require a permanent 'immediate' connection. This may be a critical system which is found in some building security products, where they will contact a control-room and feed all video, fire and alarm signals.

## Server

A server is a specialist computer system designed to offer a dedicated service to a network's clients and devices. There are many types of servers:

* web
* email
* print
* file
* security or firewall
* network addressing
* chat, discussion and conference
* game management and so on.

Most servers require a higher hardware specification than ordinary computer systems:

* **more memory** – perhaps in excess of 2 Gb
* a **large hard drive system**, which may be in a **RAID** array to cope with failures

* **multi-processor motherboards** to cope with the extra demands placed on them.

Servers must have their own operating systems, which are discussed later in this section.

## Repeater and hub

As their name suggests, **repeaters** boost or reiterate a signal sent through a network. They were commonly used to extend the reach of a network's cabling beyond the normal range for that cabling – they boosted the signal so that it could be sent further down the cable (cabling is discussed in detail later in this section). This has long been considered unacceptable practice:

* fibre-optic cable has now largely removed the need to use repeaters because it can transmit data at greater speeds and at greater distances than earlier forms of cabling
* the noise (unacceptable background interference) generated when a signal is boosted interferes with high-speed network connections.

A **hub** is a multi-port repeater. This device has many connections that repeat the incoming signals to all outgoing **ports**.

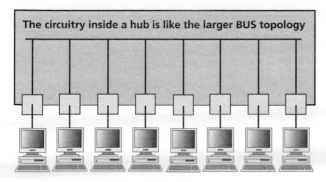

**FIGURE 9.18** *A hub in operation*

Hubs (see Figure 9.18) are used in Ethernet bus topologies, but they have certain disadvantages:

* as the data is broadcast (i.e. repeated) to all outgoing ports, there a great deal of traffic and therefore a greater risk of collision

* there is no security on the system as all users can see all the traffic

* the system's speed and the bandwidths it can cope with are severely affected by the amount of traffic in the system.

Wireless access points (see Figure 9.19) are also hubs. The devices on a network may therefore be connected together via cabling, via a wireless medium or by a combination of both.

## Bridge and switch

**Bridges** are used to connect different parts of a network together. They are similar to repeaters in that they receive data and send this on further into the network but, unlike repeaters which

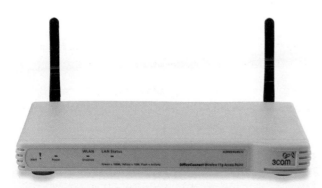

**FIGURE 9.19** *Wireless access points*

simply boost and then send on data, bridges filter the data so that only those messages required by another segment of the network are sent to that segment.

A **switch** is a complex array of bridges. Switches route data to the correct receiving devices via mini-networks (circuits). This speeds up the communication rate of the entire network because only those devices which require certain data receive it. Switches can be installed on a LAN for the following reasons. To:

* Increase the speed of network connections.

* Improve the security of the network. The network can be divided into **VLANs** by the addition of switches.

* Control large systems. A core switch is often required to manage all the other switches on a system.

> **Key terms**
>
> *VLAN* stands for Virtual Local Area Network. A VLAN is created when a LAN is divided into smaller areas, often for security reasons.

Switches come in a variety of specifications. These range from very small switches with four ports to commercial switches with 48 ports.

Because switches create mini-networks between communicating devices on the system, they increase the network's bandwidth, thus improving security and reducing the number of collisions. To do this, switches store the MAC addresses of all the devices attached to their ports so that they can forward data to the correct address.

## Multi-station access unit (MAU)

You saw in Section 9.4 how ring topologies employ tokens to manage the traffic on the network. To achieve this, the network uses a MAU; the MAU (see Figure 9.20) is to token ring networks what the switch is to the Ethernet bus topology.

FIGURE 9.20 *A MAU*

## Router

Whereas a bridge connects network segments, a router connects multiple networks (see Figure 9.21). Routers, therefore:

* connect networks to the Internet
* connect networks to a WAN
* forward traffic coming into a network to the correct destination
* direct outgoing traffic.

A large network may have many switches but only one router, which must be capable of handling all the traffic on the network.

Routers can control access to the system, can provide firewalls and can manage the connections between different sections of a LAN. Most routers must be programmed so that they can recognise the different devices connected to a network.

## Gateway

A gateway is a device on a network that acts as an entrance point to another network. This point is often referred to as the 'way out' so, naturally,

this point is also the way in. A gateway may therefore be:

* a router
* a switch with routing capabilities
* a firewall
* a proxy server.

Most large networks will have many gateways so that, should one fail, the others can be used. To set up this fail-safe system, a routing technology called HSRP (Hot Standby Routing Protocol) is employed (see Figure 9.22).

## Network operating system

A network operating system will have different functions for different organisations. A network operating system (unlike the client operating system used on Windows XP, etc.) requires its own dedicated computer system, called a **server**.

Common network operating systems include:

* Windows 2000 and 2003
* Linux in its various forms
* Unix.

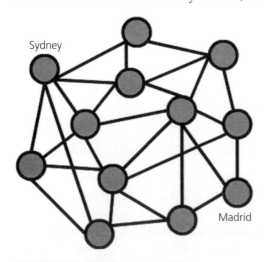

FIGURE 9.21 *Router connections*

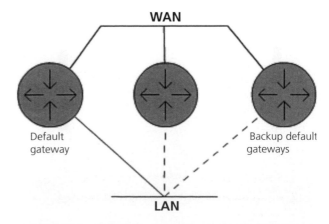

FIGURE 9.22 *HSRP for managing default gateways*

Via the server, the network operating system provides services that are accessed by other computers and users on the system. The services offered by network operating systems vary enormously:

* **web servers**, to provide e-commerce and information portals
* **file servers**, to share common resources
* **database servers**, to manage large quantities of information
* **print servers**, to manage the network's printers
* **domain name(ing) servers** (**DNS**), to keep a log of all web addresses and IP addresses
* **firewalls**, to control the network's security and to protect the entire system from unwanted intrusion
* **proxy servers**, to regulate access to the Internet
* **content management systems**, to control which websites may be visited
* **dynamic host configuration protocol** (**DHCP**) **servers** (used by many organisations and Internet service providers), to ensure client computers have addresses that will enable these computers to access the network or Internet
* **mail servers**, to manage email.

The list continues. All these services are available using Windows 2000/2003, Linux and Unix. The network manager will configure the system so that it best meets the organisation's needs.

## Unshielded twisted-pair (UTP) wire

Unshielded twisted-pair (UTP) is the most popular type of cable for use on educational and commercial networks throughout the world. UTP and STP (shielded twisted pair) cable were developed in the 1980s in response to changes in telephone technology. UTP and STP are used for several reasons:

* they are **low cost** in comparison with fibre-optic and coaxial cabling
* they are **versatile** – they can be adapted to many uses
* they can be **adapted** to accommodate changing speeds and standards.

UTP comes in long lengths. These lengths comprise eight cables contained within an outer jacket (see Figure 9.23). These eight cables are arranged as coloured pairs:

* orange/orange with a white stripe
* green/green with a white stripe
* blue/blue with a white stripe
* brown/brown with a white stripe.

Each cable generates a small magnetic field that interferes with the neighbouring cable. The cables in each pair are twisted around each other to produce the effect of **cancellation** (hence the term 'twisted pair'). Each pair (of which there are four) is then twisted around the other pairs.

### Theory into practice

Setting up a server is not difficult – in fact, you can run one from your own home computer without placing any unreasonable demands on your system.

The Linux community believes that small is good, and therefore an operating system called DSL has been developed that will run in less than 50 MB of storage (small enough to fit on a memory stick).

You can download a copy of this small version of the Linux operation system from www.heinemann.co.uk/hotlinks (insert the express code 2156P and click on this unit). The download includes instructions in the readme file on how to start the operating system while running Windows.

Follow the instructions and you will be able to set up a simple web server.

## Key terms

*Cancellation* When a signal travels down a conductor an electric field is created, which interferes with any wires close by. Twisting pairs of wires, to an extent, cancels this effect.

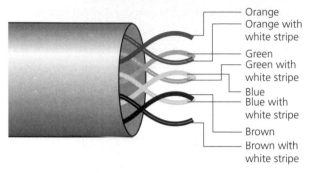

- Orange
- Orange with white stripe
- Green
- Green with white stripe
- Blue
- Blue with white stripe
- Brown
- Brown with white stripe

FIGURE 9.23 *Unshielded twisted pair cable*

UTP is very susceptible to external interference. If it is not protected from external sources of interference, such as power cables, the data sent along the cable may be corrupted. To overcome this problem the more expensive STP cable can be used. This operates on the same principles as UTP, but it has an extra foil wrapping around the cables to protect it from interference.

UTP cable comes in different categories, depending on where it will be used. Current LAN standards include Categories 5, 5e, 6 and 7. Categories 1, 2, 3, and 4 (these categories include coaxial cable) are no longer used for LANs but are used for WANs because WANs between buildings often require only slow connections. The categories relate to the quality of the cable, its connectors and the speeds at which data can be sent reliably via that category of cable (see Table 9.1).

For Category 6 and 7 cable, all the termination (wiring) is done at the factory or with specialist equipment. Category 5e cable is normally terminated with an RJ45 plug or socket (see Figure 9.24), and this can be achieved easily with low-cost equipment.

## Key terms

*Integrated Services Digital Network (ISDN)* is a digital telephone line that can share voice and data communications. *Mbps* stands for megabits per second.

| CATEGORY | MAXIMUM DATA RATE IN MBPS (MEGABITS PER SECOND) | USUAL APPLICATION |
|---|---|---|
| 1 | Less than 1 | Voice cabling. Used for an **ISDN (Integrated Services Digital Network)** |
| 2 | 4 | IBM token ring |
| 3 | 16 | The original category for use on Ethernet systems |
| 4 | 20 | No longer used |
| 5 | 10 | Still in use in small office and home networks and in some old networks |
| 5e | 100–1,000 | The ideal LAN cabling standard. Will handle a guaranteed 1,000 **Mbps** in ideal cabling circumstances |
| 6 | 1,000 | The higher quality of this cable means it can manage continuous high data rates |
| 7 | 1,000 and above | Still under development in some commercial applications |

TABLE 9.1 *UTP categories*

## How to... create UTP cable with RJ45 connectors

1 Cut category-5 cable to the correct length.

2 Use a cyclops tool to strip off the outer jacket.

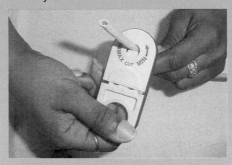

3 Untangle the wires.

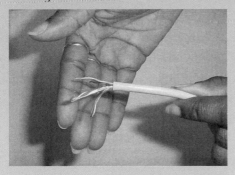

4 Organise the wires according to your required wiring standard.

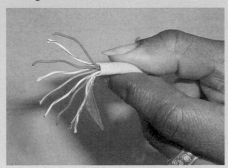

5 Straighten the wires, making sure you keep them in order.

6 Cut the stripped wires to 12 mm.

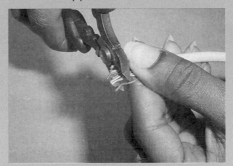

7 Insert the wires into the RJ45 (making sure you keep them in order) until all eight cables reach the end of the connector and the jacket is also inside the connector.

8 Use a termination (crimp) tool to seal the connection.

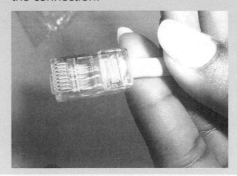

9 Repeat steps 2–8 for the opposite end of the cable.

10 Use a cable tester to ensure that you have a valid cable.

FIGURE 9.24 *An RJ45 connector*

Preparing cable is not a complex process and, with some practice, you may find you become very proficient at this.

## Shielded twisted-pair (STP) wire

As mentioned in the previous section, STP (shielded twisted-pair) cable is very similar to UTP cable. The use of, and wiring rules for, STP cable, therefore, are the same as for UTP cable. There are, however, some exceptions:

* STP cable is less susceptible to external electrical interference than UTP cable because this cable has layers of foil cladding round the pairs of cable and round the cable as a whole

* because of this cladding, STP cable is more expensive

* the communication offered by this cable is more reliable.

## Coaxial cable

Coaxial cable (see Figure 9.25) was used extensively during the late 1980s and early 1990s but has now largely been replaced by UTP. However, coaxial is making a comeback because it is often employed by some home broadband/ADSL services, and it has always been used with terrestrial TV rooftop aerials.

Coaxial cable is so named because it has a copper core surrounded by a plastic sheaf that is surrounded by a copper braid. The inner cable transmits the data and the outer cable acts as a ground (an earth).

The advantages of coaxial cable are as follows:

* it can run up to 185 m (607 ft) before the signal becomes weak and unreliable

* it can handle high-bandwidth signals, such as multiple video channels (i.e. television)

* it is flexible and reliable.

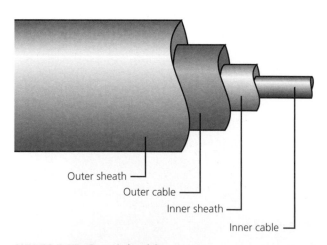

Outer sheath
Outer cable
Inner sheath
Inner cable

FIGURE 9.25 *Coaxial cable*

The disadvantages of coaxial cable are as follows:

* it is susceptible to external interference
* it is costly to install because the higher-quality cable costs more to produce
* it is less adaptable than its UTP counterpart.

In networking, a connector called a BNC (Bayonet Neil-Concelman) is used to join coaxial cable to older Ethernet T-shaped connectors (see Figure 9.26).

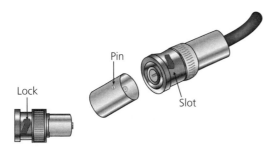

FIGURE 9.26 *A BNC connector*

## Fibre-optic cable

Both coaxial and UTP rely on electricity to transmit data down a copper cable. Fibre-optic cable, on the other hand, uses light to transmit data and, as a result, data can be transmitted at greater speeds and over greater distances than via coaxial or UTP cable.

If light travels in a straight line, how does fibre-optic cable, which bends, manage to transmit light?

A light-emitting diode (LED) or laser sends data down a fibre-optic cable in the form of light impulses (see Figure 9.27). Because this cable is made of many strands of fine glass, as the light travels down the cable it is reflected internally from one strand of glass to another. Some of the light, however, will be lost as it is absorbed by the cable's outer coating. Every time some light

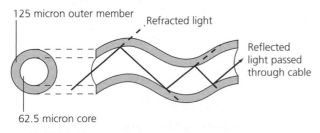

FIGURE 9.27 *How light travels down a fibre*

is lost, the overall signal becomes weaker, but a signal can travel up to 3 km (1.9 miles) before it becomes too weak to carry data. On most LANs, the cable run is normally less than 285 m (935 ft), which means a signal can carry data at a rate of one gigabit per second.

Two types of cable are in common use:

* **single-mode**, which is 8 **microns** in diameter
* **multi-mode**, which is 125 microns in diameter (with an inner core of 62.5 microns).

### Key terms

A *micron* is a thousandth of a millimetre.

Fibre-optic cable is surrounded by Kevlar fibre – an ultra-strong resin used in the manufacture of bullet-proof clothing. This makes the cable strong – an important factor when you consider that the cable has to be bent to fit into ducts.

Fibre-optic cable is more costly than its copper counterparts, and the termination of the cable has to be done under exacting and clean conditions. Different systems use different connectors, but SC and ST are the most commonly used (see Figure 9.28).

Single-mode fibre-optic cable (see Figure 9.29) is thin (8 microns), and uses a Class-3 laser to send the data. This small width reduces the angle of reflection and thus minimises refraction and signal loss. A Class-3 laser is dangerous – the light it emits is outside the visible spectrum. If you accidentally look into a Class-3 enabled fibre-optic cable, you will not see any light but will burn the cells at the back of your eye. This will cause a permanent blind spot in your vision.

FIGURE 9.28 *SC and ST connectors*

Single mode fibre offers less refraction

FIGURE 9.29 *Single-mode fibre*

**Think it over...**

Create a table listing the different types of cabling discussed in this section. Make notes about the advantages and disadvantages of each type, and indicate situations where one type of cable should be used in preference to the others.

## Radio and microwave

Many network systems now use radio and microwave transmission technology:

* **Bluetooth**, which has a range of 10 m (33 ft) and speeds of less than 1 Mbps

* **Wi-Fi**, which has a range of up to 100 m (330 ft) and speeds of over 100 Mbps

* **mobile telecommunications**, which have a range of up to 2 km (1.2 miles) from a suitable base station

* **commercial microwave**, which covers distance of over 50 km (31 miles).

Microwaves are super-high-frequency radio waves that are capable of transmitting data. While powerful microwaves are employed in the kitchen to cook food (powerful microwaves cause substances to oscillate, which generates heat), home and personal microwave devices (such as Wi-Fi and Bluetooth) are not as powerful and are thus harmless.

**Think it over...**

Wireless technology continues to expand. Search the Internet for examples of devices that have 'gone wireless'. Can you think of any other devices that would benefit from wireless technology?

Wireless network cards and access points are based on **IEEE** Standard 802.11.

**Key terms**

The *IEEE* is the Institute of Electrical and Electronics Engineers. This is an American organisation that sets standards in the fields of electrical and electronic engineering.

Within this standard there are four signal specifications: 802.11, 802.11a, 802.11b and 802.11.g. Each signal operates at a different frequency and speed:

* 802.11a operates at speeds of up to 6 megabits per second.

* 802.11b is the signal commonly used for home, school, college or small-business networks. This can operate at up to 11 megabits per second.

* 802.11g operates in the 2.4 GHz range (like Bluetooth) but, with its greater power, can offer up to 104 megabits per second.

Wireless adaptors use both **spread-spectrum** and **narrowband** transmission techniques.

**Key terms**

*Spread-spectrum* signals use a wide range of frequencies and broadcasting techniques; *narrowband* signals have a limited frequency range.

Wireless LANs (see Figure 9.30) have the following benefits:

* the network's range can be extended into areas where it may be too costly or impractical to run a cable

* users can logon to the system without the need for a wall socket

* portable network centres can be established.

When implementing a wireless network, the network's geographical spread must be

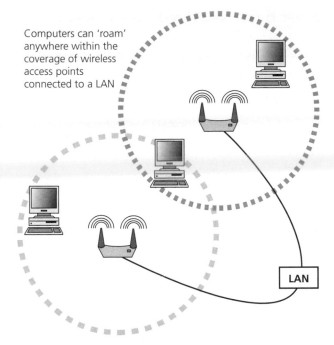

Computers can 'roam' anywhere within the coverage of wireless access points connected to a LAN

FIGURE 9.30 *Wireless coverage*

considered: the devices on the system must be able to span the distances between them.

Wireless networking is achieved through the use of two pieces of equipment:

* A **wireless adaptor** – a network card that transmits radio signals. Computers connected to the network can communicate directly with each other on a peer-to-peer basis.

* A **wireless access point** (WAP) (also called a **wireless bridge**). This is a network hub connected by UTP or fibre-optic cable to the main network. A WAP shares and distributes network communications.

Bluetooth is an ultra-high-frequency, spread-spectrum signal with a wavelength of over 2.4 GHz. Bluetooth is used for short-range networking and, so far, the benefits of Bluetooth have been a follows:

* mobile phones can now send and receive pictures and documents on a one-to-one basis

* laptop computers can be connected together on a small, peer-based network

* the connection of PDAs (personal digital assistants) to computers or mobile phones without the need for cables or software.

## Infrared

On the spectrum, infrared is the light between the visible and microwave. It has been used for over 30 years as a method of sending simple signals, such as those sent by a television remote control. Infrared is short range, so the transmitting device must be pointed towards the receiving device to make a connection.

Because it has only a short range, infrared is used for:

* file transfer between laptop computers

* mobile phone to PDA data transfer.

Infrared can manage a bandwidth of up to 4 megabits per second.

### Knowledge check

1 What devices are used to connect a computer to a network?

2 What are the cable and connector types used to connect a computer to a network?

3 How does light travel around corners?

### Assessment activity

Many devices and communication systems are used in networking systems. Which technologies are commonly used in a WAN, and which are used in a LAN? Why do you think this is?

### Assessment hint

✓ WANs have to consider distance, Internet work communication and speed, whereas a LAN has speed, flexibility and short, local distances.

# 9.6 Network addressing and protocols

## The importance of protocols

A computer network is a collection of hardware devices run by various software. This hardware and software may have been manufactured by different companies but, when connected together, it must operate as one system – the different parts of the system must be able to communicate with each other. So that communication can take place between these different devices, the devices on a system employ **protocols**.

Protocols, therefore, are the means by which network devices communicate with each other. Without protocols, it would not be possible to transmit data from one device to another or from one network to another.

## OSI seven-layer model

Because of this wide variety of computer hardware and software, the **International Standards Organisation (ISO)** established the OSI (Open Systems Interconnection) model so that different systems can communicate effectively with each other. For example, the OSI model makes it possible for a Windows-based system to visit a website based on a Linux system.

> **Key terms**
>
> The *International Standards Organisation (ISO)* sets standards for a wide range of areas, not just computing.

The OSI model has seven layers, each layer representing a different part of the communication process.

### Layer 7 (application software)

This layer downloads data via the system's communication applications, such as a web browser and email.

### Layer 6 (presentation)

This layer translates the incoming data into a form users can understand. The form this data takes depends on the format of the data. For example:

* **HTML** text for web page documents
* **SWF** (shockwave format) for website flash media
* **doc.** for Word documents
* **jpg.** (Joint Photographic Experts Group) for images
* **MP3** (Multimedia Players Engineers Group, format 3) for audio media.

### Layer 5 (session)

The communication session is managed by a hardware device driver, and each separate communication is achieved through the commands contained in a **sockets library**. In Windows, sessions are managed by a **DLL** called WSOCK32.

> **Key terms**
>
> A *DLL* (a Dynamic Link Library) is a file containing set of commands that controls a device or service.

The DLL allows the user to open different browser, chat and email windows simultaneously, without any conflicts in the data being transmitted – a technique exploited by illegal file-sharing applications.

### Layer 4 (transport)

The transport layer looks after the system's security, via such devices as firewalls. It is also the layer that prioritises the data. Data prioritisation is essential when using **VoIP (Voice over Internet Protocol)** because this protocol needs a greater share of the bandwidth.

> **Key terms**
>
> *VoIP (Voice over Internet Protocol)* Allows the user to make telephone calls using a broadband Internet connection instead of a regular phone line.

Protocols such as TCP (Transmission Control Protocol) and UDP (User Datagram Protocol) operate at this layer (these are discussed in depth later in this section). Each network communication channel in this layer is called a port.

## Layer 3 (network)

The server's or workstation's logical address is managed in this layer. The most common protocol for managing this address is TCP/IP (Transmission Control Protocol/Internet Protocol) (see below). The server's or workstation's network card is allocated a unique IP address (e.g. 10.189.12.3).

Routing (the movement of data between networks) takes place at this layer. This is achieved via routers and via some specialist layer-3 switches.

## Layer 2 (data link)

On a LAN, the data link layer contains the physical address (the Media Access Control (MAC) address) that is used to identify each device on the network. This address is usually hardwired into a chip on the network card. Some WANs have similar addressing systems, but these are often simpler than those found on LANs.

The data link layer also holds network cards and Ethernet switches, as well as specialist WAN connections.

## Layer 1 (physical)

Layer 1 principally comprises the media, cables or wireless infrastructures. This layer transmits and encodes data bits. Older systems may have such devices as hubs and repeaters. The wireless access point operates at this level, but it is controlled on layer 2.

### Theory into practice

You will be able to see parts of the OSI model in operation on your own system if you look at some of your computer's settings.

1 From the **Start** menu, select **Run** and enter **cmd**.

2 Enter the command **ipconfig/all**. The layer-2 and layer-3 addresses will be listed.

## TCP/IP four-layer model

The TCP/IP (Transmission Control Protocol/Internet Protocol) model is similar to the OSI model but, instead of seven layers, it has four. However, whereas the OSI model is not generally used to build networks, the TCP/IP model is, possibly because the Internet is based on this model. Both models are similar in that they use layers to distinguish tasks and have very similar transport and network layers (see Figure 9.31).

In this model, the terms **socket** and **port** are used to describe the communication routes.

### Application layer

In the TCP/IP model, the application layer contains the OSI presentation layer and session layer. This layer manages all the processes involved in user interaction. It determines how data will be presented and controls the session.

### Transport layer

There are two transport layer protocols. Transmission Control Protocol (TCP) ensures that information is received as it was sent, whereas User Datagram Protocol (UDP) does not perform such a check (see later in this section).

### Internet layer

Because the TCP/IP model is based on the Internet, this layer is commonly referred to as the Internet layer. All upper and lower layer communications travel through IP as they are passed through the TCP/IP protocol suite.

| OSI MODEL | TCP/IP MODEL |
|---|---|
| 1 Application | Application |
| 2 Presentation | |
| 3 Session | |
| 4 Transport | Transport |
| 3 Network | Internet |
| 2 Data link | Data flow (or network access layer) |
| 1 Physical | |

FIGURE 9.31 *The OSI and TCP/IP models compared*

### *Data flow or network access layer*

In the TCP/IP model, the data link and physical layers of the OSI are normally grouped together. This is so that the TCP/IP can use the different systems installed on other networks to manage data flow and access.

## Physical addressing

Physical addressing ensures that all the devices connected to a network can be identified. Different networks have different physical addressing systems, however, and this is one of the reasons why the TCP/IP model uses the addressing systems of the devices attached to the network rather than creating its own.

Because each device on the network can be identified individually, the Network Administrator does not have to intervene to locate a device. There are also no conflicts with any other devices on the system or with devices connected to the system (now that PDAs, mobile phones and laptops are often connected to computer systems, this later point is essential).

The physical address can be likened to a National Insurance number – there may be many Jacob Smiths but there is only one with the National Insurance number NQ213171Z. This number is unique to Jacob.

LANs use MAC (Media Access Control) addresses. This is a 48-bit address ($2^{48}$ = 281,474,976,710,656 possibilities), and each address is coded into the network card or fabric of the switching or routing device. The address is split into two parts: the **OUI** number and the device's own unique number (see Figure 9.32).

**Key terms**

*OUI* stands for Organisationally Unique Identifier. This is the part of the MAC address that identifies the device's manufacturer.

**Theory into practice**

You can use the **ipconfig/all** command to see your computer's MAC address. Try keying in **arp –a**. This should bring up any devices your computer has been communicating with recently.

Other systems employ their own physical addressing schemes. On WANs, for example, ISDN uses phone numbers (which is not surprising for ISDN), and Frame Relay DLCIs (Data Link Control Identifiers).

**Key terms**

*Frame Relay* An efficient data transmission technique using a relay of frames to one or many destinations from one or many end-points. A cheaper 'always on' connection than DSL or cable.

## Logical addressing

MAC addresses are permanent: they are assigned to a device during its manufacture. Logical addresses, on the other hand, can be assigned automatically to a device when it accesses a network. This enables the network to create and manage an addressing system of its own.

Logical addressing is achieved through IP (Internet Protocol), which operates at layer 3 of the OSI model. Logical (or IP) addresses are allocated to devices according to the network's management policy. Some IP addresses are permanent whereas others can be changed depending on the circumstances.

One addressing protocol is IPv4. This is a 32-bit protocol which means that, for any given LAN or WAN, $2^{32}$ (or 4,294,967,296) IP addresses are available. For a corporate LAN or for your network at home, 4,294,967,296 addresses are more than enough. However, there are

| | | | | | | | | | | | |
|---|---|---|---|---|---|---|---|---|---|---|---|
| C | 1 | 5 | C | 0 | 9 | 9 | C | 1 | 5 | C | 0 |
| 1100 | 0001 | 0101 | 1100 | 0000 | 1001 | 1001 | 1100 | 0001 | 0101 | 1100 | 0000 |
| The first three bytes are the Organisational Unique Identifier, which is issued by the IEEE to the manufacturer | | | | | | The last three bytes are the unique code, which is managed and issued to the NIC (or other networking device) by the manufacturer | | | | | |

FIGURE 9.32 *MAC address structure*

| Octet 1 | Octet 2 | Octet 3 | Octet 4 |
|---|---|---|---|
| 1 0 1 1 1 0 1 0 | 1 1 0 1 0 1 1 1 | 1 0 1 1 1 0 0 1 | 1 1 1 0 1 0 0 1 |
| 186 | 215 | 185 | 233 |

**FIGURE 9.33** *Octets*

circumstances when the range of IPv4 addresses available may be problematic:

* Internet service providers (ISPs) have to issue a unique IP address to every user. This problem has become especially acute now there has been an explosion in the numbers of broadband and modem Internet users.

* Modern telecommunications and media communications companies need IP addresses for each device accessing their systems. This means an IP address is needed for each cable or satellite television connection, for each mobile phone that is WAP enabled and for systems that use VoIP.

* The Internet is a complex WAN structure, and all networking devices that directly face the Internet require an IP address. This is the area where the availability of IP addresses is rapidly diminishing, and so the allocation of addresses is now tightly controlled.

Unlike MAC addresses, IP addresses are easy to understand because the 32-bit address structure is divided into four 8-bit portions called **octets** (a byte of information) (see Figure 9.33). As the 32-bit address is separated into four octets, each with 8 bits, the range of the octet is $2^8$, which is from 0 to 255 (see Figure 9.34).

The resulting address is in dotted decimal notation, and each of the four numbers is no greater than 255. This is done so that IP addresses are easy to remember.

Because there are 32 bits in an address, the bits in an address can be divided into identifying classes.

Binary value

| 128 | 64 | 32 | 16 | 8 | 4 | 2 | 1 |
|---|---|---|---|---|---|---|---|
| 0 | 0 | 0 | 0 | 0 | 0 | 0 | 0 |
| 1 | 1 | 1 | 1 | 1 | 1 | 1 | 1 |

Result = 0
Result = 225

**FIGURE 9.34** *Range of an octet*

In the IPv4 standard there are five classes, each one based on the most significant bit in the IP address.

Each class in an IP address ensures that there is a specification for:

* the number of hosts per network

* the number of networks available for each class

* the method of identification for each IP address.

When looking at Table 9.2 (page 118), you can see that octet 1 identifies the class of IP address. This means there are many IP addresses in each class, which can be seen in Table 9.3. 32-bit IP addresses allow for five classes of address, of which A–C is useable by network administrators, D is a specialist class for different network technologies, and E is simply experimental.

**Theory into practice**

What classes are the following addresses?

1  101.0.0.0      4  191.0.0.0

2  129.0.0.0      5  193.0.0.0

3  123.0.0.0      6  1.0.0.0

## Connection-oriented systems

Moving data across a network is easier said than done, primarily because, when we send data, we have to break it down into **packets**, trust the system to direct these packets to the correct device and then reassemble the data on receipt.

**TCP** is the protocol used to manage the transfer of data. TCP ensures each packet of data leaves in a controlled sequence and that the receiving device reassembles the data in the same sequence it was sent in.

| CLASS | MOST SIGNIFICANT BIT(S) | NUMBER RANGE FOR OCTET 1 | OCTET 1 | OCTET 2 | OCTET 3 | OCTET 4 | TOTAL AVAILABLE NETWORKS | TOTAL AVAILABLE HOSTS ON EACH NETWORK |
|---|---|---|---|---|---|---|---|---|
| A | 0 | 0–127 | Network | Host | Host | Host | 128 | 16,777,214 |
| B | 10 | 128–191 | Network | Network | Host | Host | 16,384 | 65,534 |
| C | 110 | 192–223 | Network | Network | Network | Host | 2,097,152 | 254 |
| D | 1110 | 224–239 | There is no host or network portion | | | | | |
| E | 1111 | 240–255 | Class D is for multicast and unicast addresses Class E is experimental and therefore is not useable | | | | | |

TABLE 9.2 *IPv4 classes*

| CLASS | | | |
|---|---|---|---|
| A | B | C | D |
| 1.0.2.1 | 128.14.21.19 | 192.168.0.1 | 224.0.0.5 |
| 10.5.45.99 | 172.16.12.14 | 195.100.0.0 | |
| 69.0.224.255 | 191.90.254.2 | 223.255.255.254 | |
| 126.4.0.0 | 160.10.0.4 | | |
| 99.1.1.2 | | | |
| 100.100.100.100 | | | |

TABLE 9.3 *IP addresses*

**Key terms**

*TCP* stands for Transmission Control Protocol.

When a packet is sent across a network, it is **encapsulated** with information at OSI layers 4, 3 and 2 (all of which have equivalent layers in the TCP/IP model) (see Figure 9.35 on page 119):

* at layer 4, source and destination, sequence and port number are sent

* at layer 3, source and destination IP address are sent

* at layer 2, source and destination MAC addresses are sent.

**Key terms**

To *encapsulate* means to wrap in or to enclose.

**Theory into practice**

There are many free applications that enable you to look at the content of the data packets entering and leaving your computer. If you are interested, go to www.heinemann.co.uk/hotlinks, insert the express code 2156P and click on the link to download the guide to 'packet sniffing'. This explains how to download and install a suitable 'packet sniffing' application.

As you can see from Figure 9.35, TCP creates a sequence number that clearly identifies the order in which the packet came. You will also notice an **ACK** (an acknowledgement), which is a reply to say that the packet has been received safely.

If a packet is lost, TCP will send an ACK which asks for more. This ensures that data is transferred reliably and is reassembled correctly.

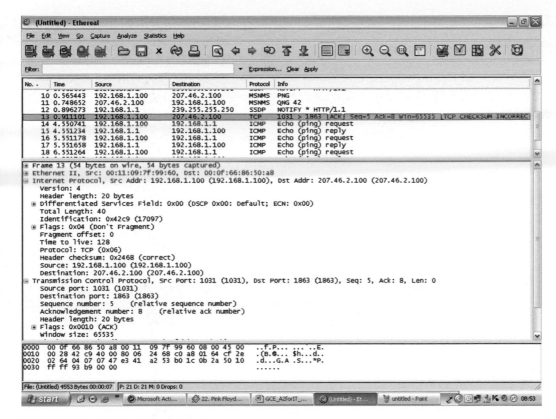

FIGURE 9.35 *TCP packet contents*

TCP (like UDP; see the next section) uses port numbers to identify the channel (or stream) on which the data will travel. Typical TCP/UDP ports are shown in Table 9.4.

## Connectionless systems

When data is transmitted using TCP, the sending and receiving devices remain connected for the duration of the transmission. UDP (User Datagram Protocol), on the other hand, is connectionless. Whereas TCP:

* tries to ensure that all the data gets through

* requires the data to be re-sent if there is a data loss

| PORT NUMBER | NAME | ABBREVIATION |
|---|---|---|
| 21 | File Transfer Protocol | FTP |
| 25 | Simple Mail Transport Protocol | SMTP |
| 53 | Domain Naming System | DNS |
| 80 | Hyper Text Transport Protocol | HTTP |
| 119 | Post Office Protocol (v3) | POP3 |
| 443 | Secure Sockets Layer (Hyper Text Transport Protocol Secure) | SSL/HTTPS |
| 666 | The port used by doom for its network/Internet gaming option | Doom 3 |

TABLE 9.4 *TCP and UDP ports*

* requires the data to be reassembled successfully at the destination

UDP:

* will send the data without the need for an acknowledgement

* will handle the data as received and will not react to a minor data loss.

The main advantage of UDP lies in its delivery of traffic that is sensitive to delay:

* VoIP (Voice over Internet Protocol) telecommunications

* video streaming, such as web casts or digital television images

* audio streaming, such as podcasts (iPod), streamcasts (WinAmp) and web radio

* the routing protocol, where Internet devices exchange information with each other to ensure the networks can communicate.

As you can see from Figure 9.36, the UDP packets sent while listening to a web radio station are medium sized (approximately 700 bytes). If any of these packets are lost on the way to the web radio player and are not replaced, the transmission will become jittery. This often happens when the network connection is busy.

## Assessment activity

Create a table, with layers 2, 3 and 4 of the OSI model. Which protocols and addresses operate at these layers, and what is their purpose?

## Assessment hint

✓ Each layer is completely different as the technology used changes.

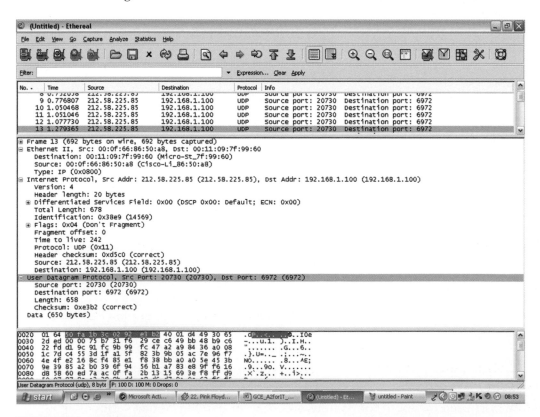

FIGURE 9.36 UDP packet

# 9.7 Connectivity

There are many factors you must take into consideration when you connect two or more networks together, either locally or over a great distance. In particular, you should consider:

* packet routing
* the security implications
* the hardware and software requirements
* the impact on performance
* compatibility.

## Packet routing

As was explained earlier in this unit, a router is a device that connects two or more networks together. It is thus a system for ensuring that only the intended traffic travels across the divide between each network. On most systems, a router is in fact simply a high-speed inter-network switching device.

Routers use routing protocols to communicate with each other. These protocols advertise which network each router is connected to and the other networks each router is aware of.

When a router receives an update from an adjacent router, it will add this information to a database called a **routing table**. While updates come through from other routers, the routing table remains valid. If, however, a device is disconnected or a line is lost and the updates stop, a router will wait for a while (this is called a **hold down**). If no updates arrive after this waiting period, the non-communicating router and its connected networks are removed from the routing table.

## Security implications

As soon as one network is connected to another there is a security risk, particularly when you connect to the Internet, which is a network of interconnected networks. To ensure your network (and other networks connected to your system) is protected, the following are needed at the network's edge:

* A **firewall** that controls the entry and exit of all traffic, as defined by the system's rules. These rules will deem some traffic suitable and other traffic unsuitable. The rules will allow traffic to enter a device on the internal network only if that device initiated the communication.

* **Access control** to filter unwanted traffic. This stops potentially sensitive data from leaving the system unless this has been sanctioned (agreed). Access control has the added benefit of reducing the quantity of data moving between networks, which increases the bandwidth available for the essential traffic.

All devices (servers and workstations) must have an up-to-date anti-virus application to ensure viruses and Trojans do not enter the system.

## Hardware and software requirements

The connectivity between networks is managed by:

* switches
* routers
* and, sometimes, by proxy servers or firewalls.

A network needs the correct hardware and software if it is to perform properly. Speed is a particularly important consideration. Every device connected to a network adds **latency** (delay) to the system because the data passing through a device has to be processed. This processing creates minute delays, which can affect the quality of the network's service if they happen too frequently.

The bandwidth of a connection can limit the speed of the communication. A hub, for example, which is a multi-port repeater, is very detrimental to the speed and efficiency of a network. Too many devices connected to a wireless access point will similarly hinder a system's performance.

When specifying an inter-networking device, the speed of the processor and motherboard must be taken into consideration, as should the switches, routers and servers on commercial networks. It is no good having the best bandwidth if the router cannot handle the volume of traffic on the network.

The software will also have an impact on the system's speed and performance. Software adds to the processing burden, so the more features the software has, the slower the device may become. Most home routers, for example, use a simple web interface that requires the minimum amount of processing (see Figure 9.37). Useful software features, such as a graphical user interface, only slow down a system's performance.

## Impact on performance

A great deal of this section has considered how the different ways of connecting networks together can affect a network's performance. When you are connecting different systems together, you must consider the following:

* The switch, router or server's **processing abilities** – can it handle the work allocated to it?

* **Latency** – are too many devices involved in processing the network's traffic?

* The **firewall rules** – are these detrimental to the network's performance?

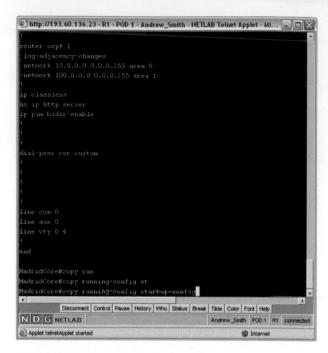

**FIGURE 9.37** *A router text interface*

* The **access control techniques** – are these causing the traffic to slow down? Do they lead to the loss of essential traffic?

* The bandwidth – is it suitable for the network?

* The **volume of traffic** sent and received – if this accounts, on average, for over 50 per cent of the bandwidth, the line is unreliable.

* If the service is **shared** (e.g. a wireless access point), are there bandwidth problems?

## Compatibility

The OSI and TCP/IP models have resolved many compatibility problems because all manufacturers must now ensure their systems will communicate to these standards. The only area where compatibility problems may still exist is at the physical layer (layer 1). The devices at this layer *must* work with the same technologies, otherwise no communication will take place. For example:

* Most LANs communicate using Ethernet, which means you must have Ethernet network cards that can be connected to a suitable switch.

* Many remote WAN connections in the UK still use ISDN. You will therefore need equipment that is compatible with this type of connection.

* Wireless networks have three standards (802.11a, b and g). Standard 'b' can only see 'b', 'g' can be configured to work with both 'a' and 'b', and 'a' is a separate standard. This can make for compatibility problems if there are many different devices on the system.

### Assessment activity

What types of routers (and manufacturers of routers) are available? Complete research and compare the products. Ensure you have considered the scale of networks supported by the different routers.

### Assessment hint

✓ Routers will support the connection of LANs through to the management of the core Internet.

# 9.8 Network design

For a network to operate effectively and efficiently, it must first be designed thoroughly. While it is unlikely you will be called upon to design an entire network from scratch, you may be required to amend an existing network and to suggest improvements in the light of developments in network technology. This section considers those factors you should take into account when undertaking network design.

## Number of users

You must establish not only how many users the system will have but also how the system will be used. For example, your school or college may have 3,000 students – all of them network users – but only 500 computers on the system. It would not be appropriate, therefore, to design a system to handle 3,000 users. Instead, you should consider the 500 computers.

When addressing the number of users on a system, you should consider the following questions:

* How many devices are going to need access to the network and in which locations?

* What percentage of use will be *inside* the network?

* What percentage of use will be *outside* the network (e.g. on the Internet)?

* Is every device going to be used all the time?

* Are there any peak times when most of the users will be on the system?

Your network design should address each of these questions, and you should add 20 per cent above the maximum to all your answers. This extra will allow for system growth and it will also ensure that the system can cope adequately with the highest possible demand, without any effect on its performance.

## Size and geographical spread

Networks are not neat and tidy things: most networks are spread over considerable distances, and they often include large sites, small sites, remote sites and home users. Many systems grow according to the nature of the organisation that owns them – over time, additional networks join the original network as new departments are created and new businesses are acquired.

Networks, therefore, come in all shapes and sizes:

* a small company on one site

* a large multinational organisation with sites in many countries, and many different regions in each of those countries

* retail organisations that have many sites, all connected to a central core

* Internet service providers whose users are spread across the world

* educational establishments, which tend to have a high volume of users

* online retailers whose customers connect directly to their networks.

## Layout of buildings

The layout of the building will affect the type of cabling that can be used. You must consider, for example, the reach required of the cable. UTP/STP can only extend 100 m (330 ft), and the cabling may have to be routed above the ceiling or under the floor. Fibre-optic cable, on the other hand, has a reach of up to 3 km (1.9 miles).

You must also take into account interference, which affects UTP and STP cable, but not fibre-optic cable. Wireless media will be affected by interference, if it is pronounced.

You may have to create a cabinet called an **MDF** (Main Distribution Frame, or Facility). This will contain the core of the system. To extend the system's reach, **IDFs** (Intermediate Distribution Frames, or Facilities) may be added as required.

Whatever the layout of the building, you will be presented with many challenges.

## Required functionality

### Key terms

*Required functionality:* what the network will be required to do.

Before beginning the design for a new network, a network designer must take into account the following considerations:

* What will the network be used for?

* What might the network be used for in the future?

While future gazing may seem far fetched, over the last ten years (with the advent of IP television and IP telephony), many new networks have been designed to include provision for audio and video streaming.

(Both IP television and IP telephony are now in common use on many systems.)

Different technologies place different demands on bandwidth. This may simply be a matter of a service that requires more bandwidth than others (a busy web or mail server, for example) or a communication that needs a higher traffic priority.

As you saw earlier in this unit, UDP (User Datagram Protocol) is time sensitive. To enable the speedy transmission of UDP traffic, you can include rules at layer 4 of the OSI model so that:

* voice and video traffic will always get through

* data and network management traffic will wait their turn.

## Future plans

Your network is not going to remain the same and, as discussed previously, you may have to anticipate how the network will be used in the future. As this is a technically impossible task, the best way to make sure you have designed a network appropriately is to ensure it is **scalable**.

### Key terms

A *scalable* network is one that can be extended easily or that is capable of growth.

To be scalable, a network must be able to meet the following requirements:

* its traffic and use can grow by up to 20 per cent before there is a need to buy more equipment

* between 50 and 100 per cent more equipment can be installed before the system must be subdivided

* the network is designed in such a way that more systems can be added to it without affecting its performance

* its addressing system can survive any planned changes.

## The existing system

When adding to an existing system, you should ensure you include in your design the existing network's equipment, infrastructure and software. This network was created at considerable expense, and it is probably still able to offer excellent service:

* The extended system could incorporate the existing equipment, which might still be capable of providing an effective service.
* The existing system could be redesigned in such a way to make maximum use of its resources.
* Extra sites could be added to the existing system, which will then remain central to the redesigned network.

## Current capacity required

A system's capacity is not simply a matter of the number of users on the system but also the way the new system will be used. Some services will place greater demands on the network than others. You therefore have to consider:

* the traffic load on specific lines
* the workload expected of the servers
* the popularity of external services
* traffic-sensitive services, such as VoIP and IPTV.

Manufacturers supply **benchmarking data** with their devices. This data should specify the device's quality and uses. You should use this data to ensure your network design offers the best possible service.

## System expectations

As network technology has improved, the expectations people have of networks have similarly increased. In particular, network users now expect a system to have acceptable response times, to be reliable and to be secure.

### Response time

The response time a system is capable of depends on a combination of:

* the bandwidth required for each workstation
* the bandwidth of all shared services
* the latency of the devices on the system.

An old but valid idea is the **coffee-break syndrome**. If the wait time for a response is long enough for someone to think about getting up to have a cup of coffee, the delay is not acceptable.

### Reliability

Networks themselves seldom fail. When faults do occur, these are usually on servers (which are complex systems) and on communication systems where there are many demands for a service. To ensure system reliability, the following measures can be taken:

* the communication lines can be set up so that they share the load – should one then fail, another will take its place
* servers can be mirrored – they can be configured in such a way that one server can take over the work of another server should it fail.

### Security

Security breaches can cost organisations incalculable amounts of money. The following are measures organisations can take to protect their systems from attack:

* the installation of the latest anti-virus (and Trojan) software, as well as the latest operating system **patches**
* firewalls
* security policies and system structures to detect and evade intrusion.

> **Key terms**
>
> *Patch* (in this context) – an additional item of software, created to fix an error or security flaw in an application or operating system.

## Budget

The customers for a network will have a limited amount of money they can spend on the new system, and it is likely they will give the contract for the design of the new system to the consultant or company that submits the lowest tender (the consultant or company that, of all those asked to submit a price for the job, offers to do it for the least amount of money). Network designers, therefore, have to win over not only the network manager but also the financial managers.

Before beginning work on a new network, the designer must establish:

* the scope of the project (i.e. what is required of the network, any limitations that must be taken into consideration, etc.)
* the available budget
* what the customer expects to get for their money.

Whether the new network is for a system at home, for a small business or for a large multinational corporation, the pricing considerations are the same. The costs of:

* the cabling (UTP and/or fibre-optic) and wireless access (if any)
* specialist network cards
* the switches, routers and servers required
* workstation hardware and software
* virus management
* server software licences
* the line to the Internet
* installation and configuration.

### Theory into practice

Using various websites, find the prices for:

1  a Cisco 3700 series switch
2  a Cisco 2800 series router
3  a Windows 2003 server licence
4  the corporate licence for a well-known anti-virus application.

## Legislation and standards

Designers must ensure that their proposed networks comply with certain laws, standards and regulations:

* The TIA (Telecommunications Industry Association) standards for the installation of fibre-optic and UTP cable require that cables should work to a high standard and should be free from interference.
* The government regulations that apply to the installation of electric cables also apply to the installation of computer network cables.
* Under the provisions of the Health and Safety at Work Act 1974, the installation of a network must be accomplished in a safe manner. This Act stipulates that anyone responsible for unsafe practices or procedures is liable to criminal prosecution.

## Creating a network design

There are many software applications you can use to design computer networks:

* Microsoft Visio
* Cisco ConfigMaker
* Smart Draw
* any art/design software packages that contain network icons.

Whichever software you use, you must produce detailed designs that show the structure of the network:

* the position of the network devices and any other equipment
* the means of connection (cable, media or wireless)
* IP addresses.

You must also specify such details as:

* collision detection/segmentation
* the network operating system and other software
* the protocols.

Look carefully at Figure 9.38. This is a plan (not to scale) of a single-storey factory recently acquired by Widgets R Us. This factory will connect to the Internet and to the company's other sites in Madrid, Seattle and San Francisco. You have been contracted to design and cost the implementation of the network cabling structure, the protocol design and server acquisition.

Seven rooms are labelled on the plan:

1 Reception will need three computers, one for the switchboard and two to provide an interactive multimedia display of the range of products developed by Widgets R Us.

2 The sales and marketing team will need at least 10 computers and there must be room for growth.

3 The factory management area will have seven computers.

4 Financial management and personnel need 30 computers and capacity for growth.

5 Customer support and after-sales services will need 10 computers and capacity for growth.

6 Factory maintenance will have two workstations for equipment management.

7 The web developers and ICT team currently use 30 workstations. They will be responsible for the corporate servers, which will be housed in a small air-conditioned room.

There must be a firewall to control access to the system and a router to provide external connectivity.

As the designer, you are expected to take the following considerations into account:

1 Redraw the factory plan showing the MDF and any IDFs. This redrawn plan will be submitted for approval to the finance director, who is in charge of ICT procurement.

2 You should show the cable runs for areas 2, 3, 4, 5, 6 and 7 from the **POP** (and any MDFs/IDFs, following the TIA cabling standards).

3 Indicate how many UTP outlets will be required for each room on the plan.

4 The server room will have three servers and must have a 1 Gbit connection.

5 You are restricted in what you can do in areas 6 and 7 because the factory employs large machinery that will interfere with all copper and wireless systems.

6 The IP addressing scheme must allow for expansion.

7 The POP will have an 8 Mbit leased line to the Internet.

8 Add 25 per cent to all your cabling to allow for growth. Widgets R Us is an up-and-coming company that expects to expand over the next five years.

9 Provide a spreadsheet that details the cost of all the cabling, all the equipment, the workstations, the lease and the server licences.

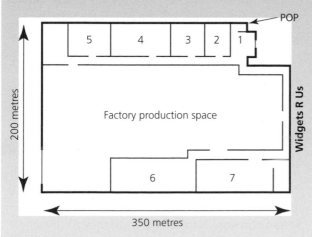

**FIGURE 9.38** *Widgets R Us factory plan*

**Knowledge check**

1 How do legislation and standards affect the implementation of a network?

2 What factors affect the design of a network?

## Assessment activity

What current standards affect the implantation of cabling in a new network? How will this affect the cost of the network and the long-term benefits?

## Assessment hint

✓ Consider the wiring standards and legislation that has an impact on 'how and where' cables can be installed.

# 9.9 Network management

Computer networks are complex systems, and many companies and organisations rely on them to carry out their business or to operate effectively. Once a network is up and running, therefore, it must be managed to ensure it functions smoothly and without interruption.

## System configuration

The system will have been configured before it was brought online. Once it is in operation, further configuration will be necessary when:

✱ a new server is added

✱ an upgrade is taking place

✱ a new network (or network segment) is joined to the system

✱ a minor modification is made to improve the network's performance.

Before any major changes are made to a network, they should be tested on a device external to the system to make sure they will have the predicted effects. It is also wise to create a **roll-back** position so that, if the network, server or workstation reacts unfavourably to the updated system configuration, the original system can be restored quickly.

## User support and management

Customers may need support in two ways: reassurance that their network is capable of meeting their needs, and technical help should things go wrong.

Should a customer feel ill at ease with a new network, as the network's designer there are a few things you should bear in mind:

✱ The customer may rely on the network to carry our his or her work. The customer, therefore, should be handled patiently and given time to understand how the network functions.

✱ The customer will be competent in his or her own field of work – a field of work in which you may have little expertise. Your role is to ensure the network serves the customer and his or her work. Do not, therefore, bamboozle the customer with computer talk – listen carefully to what he or she says and frame your answers in a language the customer can understand.

Technically, you can offer customers support in many ways:

✱ monitoring their user of the network to ensure they can access the resources they require

✱ over-the-phone assistance to help resolve minor problems

✱ visits in person to solve difficult problems

✱ the immediate replacement of any components that may be faulty.

## Usage monitoring

As organisations are becoming more conscious of their network users' behaviour, they are beginning to gauge usage levels. This is often for billing purposes but sometimes it is to check whether someone is on the Internet too much or is using illegal file shares.

While there may be a 'big brother' aspect to usage monitoring, this technology can also establish bandwidth use and can provide useful information on peak flow times where a decision must be made to increase the bandwidth accordingly.

## Fault detection

On many systems, the network manager monitors the behaviour of remote devices on the network to make sure they are performing as expected. In this way, the network manager can ascertain:

* the status and performance of the devices on the system

* by tracking a device's performance, whether a fault is about to occur

* whether any devices are not functioning.

## Backup and security procedures

Backing up and restoring disks and data are some of a network manager's most important tasks. Depending on the size, type and nature of the organisation, the network manager should complete at least one backup per day.

Some systems employ incremental backups where only the changed data is stored; others use differential backups where, on selected days, different data is stored.

To determine a system's backup requirements, you should establish:

* the exact quantity of data that will need backing up

* the appropriate backup media

* the frequency of backups

* where the backup will be stored off site.

While we would like to back up and recover all the information on a network, there is some data that is not critical to the running of the organisation, such as system logs and applications that can be reinstalled, etc.

The backup media used (tape, DVD-RW or CD-RW) should be capable of holding the required volume of information, and backups should be arranged according to how often the data is changed.

If an organisation's data is continuously updated, backups will be made every eight hours. Most companies, however, perform a complete backup every night and, for security reasons, this backup is stored in an offsite location.

The backup procedure is based on what is critical to the running of the system:

* How quickly data that has been deleted or altered can be recovered.

* How soon a 'downed' server can be restarted.

* How soon a damaged or stolen server can be replaced and the data accessed.

On most server systems, storage is managed by a **RAID** (Redundant Array of Independent Disks). This is a 'live' backup mechanism where multiple hard disks store the same data copies. If one of these hard drives fails, the system can be rebuilt from the backup copies and can continue operating while a new hard drive is installed.

Systems such as RAID and mirroring provide companies with quicker recovery times. RAID allows data to be recovered from 'duplicated' hard drives. Mirroring requires a second, duplicate server that operates at the same time as the primary server.

The cost of backup and recovery is based on how critical the network is to an organisation's operations. An office-cleaning company, for example, could manage for 48 hours without its computers. A city bank, on the other hand, would struggle after five minutes of computer loss.

A security loss has much the same impact on an organisation as a data loss. To make a system secure, therefore, a network manager must ensure the following:

* If the users have email access, that the system is protected from viruses.

* The network is safe from external attacks. Connections to the Internet or a WAN are weak points in any network.

* Unauthorised users do not have access to sensitive data.

* Regular backups so that the system can be recovered if any part fails.

* User access to system resources is managed carefully, and that there are regular audits of who may access what.

* The system is tested regularly to check for potential faults.

* All system devices have the latest patches so that their vulnerability is kept to the minimum.

## Contingency planning

Human or technical disasters can beset any organisation. For example, if there was a fire, what are the recovery techniques? How quickly could the network be restored? How quickly could the data be recovered? How soon could a business restart trading?

For some government departments and service organisations, the answer to these questions should be 'immediately' – lives may depend on the solution. If there is a computer system failure in a hospital, someone may die as a result of the communication and service loss.

A contingency plan will attempt to cover all eventualities. It will include methods to recover from a disaster and will outline what length of delay is acceptable. It may also set out the following:

* data-recovery techniques

* the minimum server, WAN and Internet requirements to get the system up and running

* the minimum number of workstations required to reopen operations

* any new software needed

* the maximum acceptable turnaround time

* the technicians/consultants who must be called in.

## Strategic long-term planning

There should be a strategy in place to deal with any changes that may occur to the network. This strategy should address the following questions:

* By how much will the network have grown in five and ten years' time?

* What financial resources will be needed to cope with this growth?

* Will any new services be needed?

* What new protocols may be used?

* How might the company change?

* Will the network be required to perform any new tasks?

## Software licensing

Like books, films and CDs, software is copyrighted. This means it is illegal to copy – even in part or by accident – software without the copyright owner's permission.

People or organisations that infringe the copyright laws may be liable to all or any of the following:

* a considerable fine

* the cost of the software licences that should have been bought in the first place

* the legal costs of the prosecution proceedings

* the confiscation of all the equipment deemed to have been used in the infringement of the copyright.

This means that, if an employee was caught copying an item of software that was worth £250, his or her employer may be liable to pay £10,000 in costs by the time the court case has been heard.

Most software manufacturers work closely with **FAST** (the Federation Against Software Theft) to ensure that software theft is kept to a minimum. Now that Internet access is commonplace, on installation, most applications will send a specially formulated message to a web server managed by the software's manufacturer. Unless you know how to stop this message, the manufacturer will then know if the software has been pirated. There are increasing reports of the police and legal representatives visiting unsuspecting individuals who believe that no one knows their software is 'dodgy'.

Unlike books and other published material, you are not allowed to copy even one part of a software application. Using parts of others' software is a legal minefield and can have the same consequences as if you had been selling dodgy copies of the entire software on your local market.

The only way you can legally copy software is for backup purposes. An example of this is when you purchase a new application or system and make a copy of the software's installation disk(s) so that you can store the original(s) in a fireproof safe. This is accepted good practice.

So that individuals and organisations obtain the best deal for their needs, most software manufacturers offer a wide range of licence agreements:

* **Individual**: for one user or one computer only. Copying the software on to another computer system may invalidate the licence and/or may incur criminal prosecution.

* **Concurrent**: for a user who has more than one computer but who only uses one at a time (e.g. a home computer, an office computer and a laptop). Concurrent licences are more expensive than individual licences.

* **Site/campus**: for all the different offices of one specific organisation (e.g. for all the regional branches of a national company or for the different sites of one school or college).

* **Corporate**: for an entire organisation, including all its sites.

* **Freeware**: there are many definitions of this type of licence. The word 'freeware' suggests this software is free, but you cannot distribute it or sell copies of it without making a payment to the owner.

* **Shareware**: shareware is like freeware, but if you use it regularly or intend to use it for commercial gain, you will have to pay a fee to its creator. The difference between freeware and shareware is a grey area because it is up to the software's creator to decide which term to use.

* **Open source**: these licences are agreed individually between the software manufacturer and the licence holder. Under the terms of such licences, the holder may have the manufacturer's permission to edit or reconfigure the software.

* **Educational**: some software manufacturers offer reduced licence fees for educational establishments and for some charities. The purpose of this reduced fee is often to encourage people to buy copies of the software for their own use at home.

* **Student**: students can sometimes buy older versions of software at a reduced cost. Often, these deals do not include manuals or support.

## Code of practice

Most large organisations and educational institutions have a code of practice all users – from the office junior to the chief executive – must sign. When they sign this code of practice, the users make an agreement with the organisation to abide by the rules contained within it. If they infringe these rules, the users may be liable to a punishment (including dismissal).

A code of practice should clearly state the following:

* what is considered acceptable use (e.g. which work can be carried out on the network and whether personal work is acceptable or unacceptable)
* any software licensing restrictions
* whether users can or cannot install software on the system, including their own
* how the Computer Misuse Act 1990 and the Data Protection Act 1998 affect the ways the system may be used
* software copyright laws
* whether the network is monitored and whether email is checked
* the consequences of any breach of the code of practice
* what is considered unacceptable use of external systems, such as the Internet
* what behaviour is unacceptable.

Many organisations will not allow users access to their systems unless they sign the code of practice. Some organisations enforce this agreement with annual reaffirmations. As society develops, so does our use of information technology, and what may be acceptable practice now may become unacceptable in the future.

### Theory into practice

In a group of four or five people, look at the working practices of your school or college. Consider carefully:

1 How you could draft out a networking code of practice.

2 What terms would be included in this code.

3 What practices are 'acceptable'.

4 How you could define 'unacceptable' practices.

5 What the consequences of breaching this code would be.

6 Whom the code must apply to.

## User training

Nearly all users will need training, at different levels and for a wide range of reasons. Like all forms of education, training is often an ongoing process. In almost all places where a network has been installed, user training may be necessary for the following reasons:

* the system is modified or upgraded, or new software is installed
* the users require new skills to complete a task or to fulfil their responsibilities
* a user has basic ICT skills
* users must gain a thorough understanding of the system so that they can supervise others' use of the network.

It is likely that the users will not understand the technicalities of network systems, so the trainer should:

* adopt a professional attitude
* remain courteous and patient, even when a user says something that sounds absurd
* instruct in such a way that the users learn from their own experience of operating the system.

### Theory into practice

What commercial training courses do the educational establishments in you area offer? If you cannot find any, search the Internet to see what range is available.

## Legislation

A network manager should be aware of four areas of legislation that affect the use of computer systems:

* the Computer Misuse Act 1990
* the Data Protection Act 1998
* copyright legislation
* the Freedom of Information Act 2000.

### The Computer Misuse Act 1990

You learnt about the Computer Misuse Act 1990 during your AS course (see *AS Level for Edexcel*

*Applied ICT*, pages 10 and 255). As was noted earlier in this section, the code of practice should include information on how this Act affects users' access to the system.

## The Data Protection Act 1998

Again, you learnt about the Data Protection Act 1998 during your AS course (see *AS Level for Edexcel Applied ICT*, pages 8 and 62). As with the Computer Misuse Act 1990, users should be made aware of the implications of this Act in the code of practice.

## Copyright legislation

You saw earlier in this section how there are different types of software licence, depending on the user's requirements. The network manager should be aware of other ways in which copyright might be infringed:

* Copyright extends to anything an author, photographer, designer, etc., has created that may be copied. Scanned images, e-books or electronic manuscripts cannot, therefore, be broadcast on a system without the creator's permission.

* Music, films and other forms of entertainment may similarly not be broadcast without the originator's permission.

## Freedom of Information Act 2000

The Freedom of Information Act covers the following areas:

* All the electronic documents an organisation may hold.

* Spreadsheets containing financial data, surveys or statistics.

* Any retained email communications.

* Internal (intranet) web pages, bulletin boards or chat logs.

* Any memos or meeting minutes.

* A wide range of non-electronic storage systems (while this may not be the direct responsibility of the network manager, you have to be aware of this provision).

**Theory into practice**

Visit the Information Commissioner's Office's website (go to www.heinemann.co.uk/hotlinks, insert the express code 2156P and click on this unit) and decide how the Freedom of Information Act affects your school or college and the awarding body for your qualification.

**Knowledge check**

1  Why must you consider the needs of the user?

2  What impact does legislation have on the management of a network/computer system?

**Assessment activity**

How do the needs of the user and Acts like Freedom of Information and Data Protection create issues for the management of a network?

**Assessment hint**

✓ Consider the restraints these issues place on the deployment of data and services.

# 9.10  ICT skills

There are a number of ICT skills you will need to complete this unit. You will need to

* use network design software and standard network symbols

* use a file exchange program such as FTP or HTTP to transmit and receive data

* prepare files for electronic transfer by converting them to a suitable format and compressing them if necessary

* use the Internet to locate, select and retrieve electronic information.

## UNIT ASSESSMENT

This module is externally assessed. You will work from a brief that has been set by the awarding body. In this external assessment, you will be:

Asked to produce network designs for specific clients or purposes.

Expected to use network design software and standard network symbols to carry out these activities.

Expected to download the examination materials for this unit from, and upload your work to, a location specified by your tutor. In order to do so, you will need to be able to send and receive files across the Internet.

Asked to convert files to a compressed format.

Expected to carry out research into specific topics. You must therefore be able to use the Internet to locate, select and electronically retrieve stored information effectively.

# Using multimedia software

Advances in digital technology have transformed the way people all over the world live and learn and, in particular, how they communicate with each other. The growing sophistication of the methods of communication – via email, the Internet and mobile phones – and the development of web software (such as Internet browsers) and presentation software (such as Microsoft PowerPoint) – has led to an increased used of multimedia. This combination – of two or more media types such as text, graphics and video – provides an ideal communication medium for those wanting to make the maximum impact on an audience. Multimedia is therefore widely used throughout the world in business, education, industry and leisure.

This optional unit contains 14 elements:

10.1   Applications of multimedia

10.2   Functional specification

10.3   Product design

10.4   Navigation

10.5   Graphical design

10.6   Interactivity design

10.7   Image capture and manipulation

10.8   Video

10.9   Sound

10.10  Animation

10.11  User interface

10.12  Testing

10.13  Distribution

10.14  Evaluation

You will already have gained experience of some of the ICT tools and techniques needed to develop a multimedia product. This unit provides an opportunity for you to increase your understanding of the features and possibilities of these and other tools, so that you can combine them to produce well-designed multimedia products that communicate your ideas effectively. You will design, develop and test an interactive multimedia product for a specified target audience. First, though, you will determine the functional requirements of the product so that you are clear of your aims and objectives in developing the product.

Throughout the developmental process, you will carry out **formative evaluation** and testing of the product. You will spend some time reviewing the work of fellow students and, in return, they will review your work. You and they will learn the importance of seeking and making use of feedback from others. When you have completed the development, you will carry out a **summative evaluation** of your work. This self-assessment of your current skill level should indicate what else you need to know or be able to do in order to further enhance your ability to produce interactive multimedia products.

> ### Key terms
>
> *Formative evaluation:* if you learn from the evaluation and it then helps you to improve your work, it is called formative. Evaluation carried out during the development allows time for you to implement change and produce a better end product.
>
> *Summative evaluation* looks back over what you have done; it may help you to do better on the next project, but it is too late to make changes to this one.
>
> For example, a chef tasting a dish while preparing it, and adjusting the seasoning as a consequence, is carrying out formative evaluation. The diners, after they have finished eating, may express the results with a summative evaluation: 'that was delicious!'

This user-focused unit builds on the knowledge and skills related to producing on-screen publications that you acquired in *Unit 1: The Information Age* and *Unit 5: Web development*. Production of a multimedia product could be used as the focus for *Unit 8: Managing ICT projects*.

The standard ways of working should be adopted in this unit – and in all other units.

## Resources required in this unit

You will be creating multimedia products and will need specialist equipment for this purpose:

* digital camera, scanner, tape recorder
* video camera (digital or webcam).

You will need printing facilities and sufficient individual storage space for your files. The computer system must use the Windows XP operating system or equivalent and be loaded with the relevant applications, such as office, web-authoring, graphic and animation software. You will need access to the Internet to carry out research – for example, to visit the Edexcel site and to check the details of the specification for this unit.

The most important piece of software will be fully featured multimedia authoring software. Your portfolio of work must be constructed so that its contents can be accessed using 5th generation, or equivalent, web browsers, such as Microsoft Internet Explorer version 5 or Netscape version 5, and be in a format appropriate for viewing at a resolution of 1024 × 768 pixels.

Your portfolio must be submitted in one of the approved file formats specified by Edexcel and, at the end of the designated examination period, you will be expected to transfer your work to a location specified by your tutor (as instructed by Edexcel). The computer system that your centre uses will therefore need to support the formats specified and have the facility to upload folders of your work to the required location.

When researching the Internet, you might visit sites recommended in the specification: go to www.heinemann.co.uk/hotlinks, insert the express code 2156P and click on this unit. These provide examples of multimedia products.

## How you will be assessed

This user-focused unit is internally assessed. Most of the marks available for this unit are for practical, hands-on activities, involving the development of a fully working interactive multimedia product. So, although you need to learn the terminology and understand the concepts, your final marks will depend mostly on the quality of your multimedia product.

The product must have a clear purpose and you are advised to choose one that will be sufficiently complex in nature to challenge your expertise and encourage you to develop new skills and techniques en route to producing a fully functional solution. It is important that you choose a product which provides sufficient scope for you to be able to demonstrate your ability to design and produce interactive multimedia products. A collection of small unrelated tasks would not be appropriate. However, suitable products, as suggested by Edexcel in their specification of this qualification, may be an e-learning package, a computer game, an interactive information point, a jukebox or a web promotion.

You will produce an e-portfolio as evidence of your design, production and evaluation of a multimedia product, one that meets a given set of functional requirements specified by your client or your tutor. The portfolio will include several sections:

* The *functional specification* will describe the purpose, audience and context for the multimedia product and explain what it is required to do.

* To show the solution that you propose to develop, your portfolio will include an *initial design* that satisfies the functional requirements. It will consider all aspects of multimedia design, combining multimedia components (both ready made and original) to convey information.

* To provide *evidence of prototyping*, and how you have used it to improve and refine the design, you should include selected intermediate non-working versions of the prototype, showing how the multimedia product was developed and refined. You might also include notes on feedback obtained, plus your formative test results, and the changes that were made as a result of this.

* To show that you have produced a fully working multimedia product, your portfolio will include a *run-time version of the product*, with supporting 'getting started with…' instructions for users.

* Your portfolio must include evidence of both *formative and summative testing and evaluation*. Your evaluation will assess the multimedia product and your own performance and current skill level.

## How high can you aim?

The knowledge and skills developed in this user-focused unit will be particularly relevant to those who plan to use advanced ICT skills on a daily basis. You should therefore aim to raise your skill levels to the point where you are confident in your use of ICT at work or at school/college for personal, social and work-related purposes.

It is not essential that you undertake work experience. However, you may benefit from learning about industry practices in relation to the design and production of multimedia products, such as information points, web promotions, e-learning packages, games, etc. In addition, a number of software producers, such as Macromedia, run online design workshops and seminars which you might find useful.

It might also help you to examine examples of multimedia products online such as subject tutorials, a revision site with a quiz-style assessment and/or an e-book.

Studying an e-learning site may be beneficial in developing your understanding of how an interactive multimedia product could be used to enhance communication.

## Ready to start?

This unit builds on the database knowledge and skills you acquired in *Unit 1: The Information Age*. Before you start, read back through your notes for that unit and refresh your knowledge.

This unit should take you 60 hours to complete. Why not keep a log of your time?

# 10.1 Applications of multimedia

Multimedia products serve to communicate a message from the author to his or her audience. How well that message is communicated is a measure of the writing and artistic skills of the author, but much also depends on the ability to use multimedia tools in the creation of the product.

As an experienced author of at least one multimedia product – your e-book for Unit 1 – you already have an appreciation of the process of developing a multimedia product.

In this unit you will identify and learn to use more advanced multimedia tools and techniques. You will then apply these skills in the creation of useful multimedia products.

So that you are familiar with what can be done, and can recognise both good and bad practice, it will be important that you explore the use of multimedia in a variety of contexts, as discussed in this section.

### Theory into practice

1   Look back at the e-book you created for Unit 1. Read through your documentation to refresh your mind on the processes you followed.

2   Share access to your e-book with others in your group. Compare the features that each of you used during the development process.

3   Identify other sources of multimedia in your school or college, and arrange a time to view them.

## Education and training

In schools, many courses are supported by television programmes and other multimedia products.

### CASE STUDY

Kate is studying Spanish at a local adult education centre. She goes every Thursday for two hours, and joins a class of 13 other students. The recommended book for the course includes a CD with spoken tracts which match the material presented in the course book. She is also advised to record TV programmes from the Learning Zone. These show Spanish being spoken in everyday situations.

1   How else might Kate learn Spanish? What material is available on the Internet to help students on language courses?

2   Identify the media that are used: paper-based, oral on tape cassette and/or DVD.

3   What other courses are supported by multimedia products? Compare your findings with others in your group.

For some people, attending an educational centre for a course is not feasible. Instead, they rely on **e-learning** courses as offered by local libraries or online.

As the technology available within schools and colleges improves, e-learning options in a school/college framework are also becoming the norm.

Currently, there are limitations as to how much multimedia can be built into e-learning products. This is due to improving but still relatively slow communications links to the Internet.

So, while improvements in technology – image capture, animation, video and sound recording – allow the development of multimedia products, their successful distribution is, as yet, limited to CDs and other more traditional media. For more discussion on the distribution of multimedia products, see Section 10.13.

The manufacturers of the more sophisticated software products offer training via online workshops. Screengrabs show what the user might expect to see on-screen – and clever animation brings the topic to life.

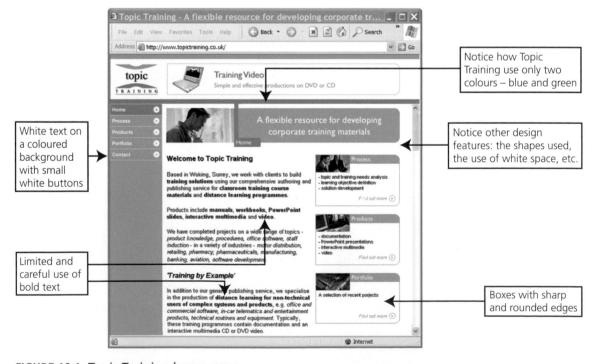

**FIGURE 10.1** *Topic Training home page*

**Think it over…**

What are the benefits of a multimedia presentation? In what situations is a TV programme better than a book, for learning purposes?

## Entertainment

The world of entertainment was transformed when silent movies were replaced by the talkies. There have been similar transformations since the introduction of DVD. No longer do film buffs need to go to the cinema to see their favourite actors on screen. Home cinema systems with wide screens provide a new way of entertaining the family. The DVD offers extras too: extra material about the film and sometimes even the option to look at stills and outtakes.

**Think it over…**

Think of other ways in which multimedia has affected the entertainment world.

## Marketing and advertising

Marketing involves planning how to launch a product and bring it to the attention of potential buyers.

Advertising is the process of putting forward information about a product or service so that its availability is known to potential buyers.

So an advertising campaign would most probably form part of a marketing plan.

Advertisements may appear on hoardings, in newspaper and magazines, on electronic billboards (e.g. at railway stations) or digitally via websites, email attachments or CDs. The advertisements seen on television, at the cinema or online all aim to make the best use of the media. And this is another example where multimedia comes into play.

## Teleconferencing

Teleconferencing utilises communications technology to the full so that people can have a meeting without actually travelling to the same location.

Conference calls allow two or more people to take part in a telephone conversation.

Messenger and chat-room facilities allow two or more people to 'talk' to each other by text messages.

If audio links and webcam links are also activated, the same group of people can have a mini-conference.

For organisations which regularly need their staff to 'meet' without incurring huge travel costs, specialist equipment can be set up in a meeting room at each venue where staff are sited. A camera can be trained on individuals or a group of people at each venue. Screens can then show what is being captured at each of the other sites. Audio links (microphones for each person attending the meeting and for the speakers at each venue) allow a soundtrack to run parallel to what people are seeing.

## Publishing

Nowadays, many publishers supply material on CD-ROM as well as on paper. Some, like manufacturers of software, have abandoned the paper-based product (e.g. a manual) and supply only on CD.

One advantage of CDs as a medium is that the data is held electronically, so it is possible to search the data.

## Interactive television

Interactive TV (iTV) is the latest development in broadcasting. It is any television equipped with a 'return path' so that information can flow from the viewer to the broadcaster as well as the normal broadcaster-to-viewer route. It offers the viewer the chance to make decisions and to send information via the iTV link.

ITV offers a number of benefits:

* **Interactive programmes** invite the viewer's participation in quizzes (like *Test the Nation*) and offer voting opportunities (as in *The Big Read*).

* **T-commerce** allows the viewer to place an order online, without picking up the telephone and talking to someone.

**Key terms**

*T-commerce* is commerce via your TV.

As with any new technology, caution suggests there are potential downsides. Any information that the viewer volunteers, and what is being watched, can be monitored. For some, this may be seen as an invasion of privacy.

**Click-stream analysis** can build a profile of the viewer. This information is valuable and is a marketable item.

The viewer's **telegraphics** tell potential advertisers how he or she reacts to advertising material and can provide a route for direct marketing efforts.

With iTV, a host of other technologies are emerging:

* **EPG (electronic programming guide)** allows a viewer to select interactively his or her television programming. Applications are being devised to enhance the viewer's enjoyment: dynamic video selection; recording options; summaries of shows; details of crew members; setting personal viewing programmes.

* **ETV (enhanced television)** is a type of iTV technology that allows HTML data to be sent along with an analogue signal. This is displayed as an overlay on the TV screen.

* **HDTV (high-definition television)** uses a digital format for the transmission and reception of TV signals and therefore provides a higher-quality signal resolution.

* **Hypervideo** is a type of iTVC in which digital video clips are embedded within hotspots and markings, in links to the WWW or to other movie/media formats.

* **Multi-camera angle (individualised TV)** allows viewers to control the camera angle during live events, choose which commercials they would want to watch and to control, for example, how

a story might end. What the viewers are offered is then based on their earlier choices.

* **PVR (personal video recording)** is a combination of software and data service that lets the viewer interactively select programme choices from a guide, and to be reminded when he or she is about to view a show – or to record them automatically for later viewing.

* **SYNCTV (synchronised TV)** involves the simultaneous broadcast of an Internet application directly related to a programme the viewer is watching. So, while watching the programme, the viewer can take part in a poll and learn background information on the programme.

**Theory into practice**

1  Research the Internet for the latest news on interactive TV technologies.

2  What is a walled garden? How might this option prove useful?

3  Find out what is meant by spy TV. How much of a threat do you see this to your privacy? Discuss this with others in your group.

## Product demonstration

Nowadays, in the queue at the post office, you are quite likely to see a multimedia presentation. While waiting patiently for your turn, you are a captive audience.

These presentations tend to explain products and services in a continuous loop. The length of the loop should be longer than the time any individual might be expected to wait in the queue!

**Think it over…**

Where else have you seen multimedia presentations trying to sell products to passers-by?

Compile a list of the types of products that tend to be promoted in this way.

# 10.2 Functional specification

A functional specification puts into writing what is needed of a product. It explains what you are aiming to achieve:

* What is the purpose of the multimedia product?

* What information must it supply? What content will you be providing?

* How will that content be presented?

* How will the product be used? In what context? And by whom?

* How will you judge the effectiveness of your solution?

## The functional specification report

The functional specification report presents written documentation of the proposed product. Much of it will be presented in a standard report style, with single paragraphs allocated to answer specific questions:

* What is the purpose of the product?

* In what context will the product be used?

### Purpose

Most communications serve one primary purpose – to inform. The main reason you are planning to develop a multimedia product is to provide evidence of your ICT skills in doing so, and hence meeting the requirements of this qualification. That aside, when writing the functional specification, you need to identify the purpose of the product.

In the real world, unless a product has a purpose and one that a market will recognise

The team at Topic Training create training and learning materials and incorporate multimedia wherever it adds value to the product.

Part of the process used is to analyse topics and training needs, so as to establish project specifications. This requires access to the systems and products involved, and consultation with client experts and users. The CEO explains:

*A key aspect is to establish defined learning levels for the retention of knowledge and the performance of skills after training.*

*Typically, we use worked examples at these defined learning levels and then require the learner to practise these examples, or*

*equivalents at the same learning levels, to reinforce knowledge and build skills.*

*Test pieces and quizzes, once again at defined learning levels, can then be used to gauge learning.*

1. For one of your two ideas for multimedia products, read over your notes. Develop these so that you have briefly described the purpose of the product, the context and the intended audience.

2. Do the same for your other idea. Make sure that you have outlined what the product will do. You may not have a clear picture of exactly what it will do, but write as much as you can specify at this stage.

and hence guarantee sales, the resources needed to invest in the development of the product are unlikely to be made available.

Your product does not need to be viable, but multimedia product designers do need to think clearly about the viability of their products:

* What use would it be to anyone?

* Who, in particular, might want to use the product?

* How many people might want to use it?

* What benefit(s) would they enjoy from using the product?

* Would someone be willing to pay to use it?

* Would someone else be willing to pay for it, to provide for others to use?

Only if you are sure – or almost sure – that the product is viable, should you go ahead with the development.

In writing about the purpose of your product, you might include sentences like these:

* This product offers users…

* This product is ideal for people who…

* This product can save you time by…

* This product will help you to…

Think of some more ways of promoting a multimedia product.

## Context

Whatever the media you decide to combine in your product, the content you write or source, and how you manage the user interface, must be suitable for the intended audience and the context in which it will be viewed:

* Is your multimedia product to be viewed by the passing public?

* Will it be presented to a captive audience?

* Will the viewers have any choice over what is viewed, or will it be dictated to them?

The context determines much of the structural design of your product, but also how you will present the information. In short, the product must meet the needs of an intended audience according to the context in which it will be viewed.

Suppose you decide to develop an e-learning package about road safety to be viewed in the classroom by the whole class. If your intended audience is 5–7-year-olds, the product should have a completely different look and feel about it when compared with a similar product intended for 12–18-year-olds:

* The language that you use has to match the reading age of your intended audience. This includes the terminology used as well as the length of sentences and how these are structured.

* The images used must be familiar to the intended age group.

* The message must be relevant to the experiences of the audience.

* The impact of the product must be good enough to hold the viewers' attention.

**Think it over...**

What techniques could you use to hold the attention of a 5-year-old viewer?

As well as the presentation of material, the actual content would also vary according to the age of the intended audience:

* For a 5-year-old, a road safety product could talk about holding the hand of the parent, not running out into traffic and so on.

* For a 12-year-old, the product might explain how a pelican crossing works. This would not be relevant for a 5-year-old; he or she wouldn't be expected to be crossing alone and, in any event, might not be able to reach the crossing controls.

The tone that would be used would also be different. A 5-year-old may need a gentler tone, but you could perhaps afford to be quite dictatorial when addressing a 12-year-old.

The terminology used, and how this is put together, though, is the most important difference between age groups. Words that make sense to a 12-year-old might not be suitable for a 5-year-old. For example, you could refer to 'select your preferred option from this list' when explaining how your product works to a 12-year-old. For the 5-year-old, you might rephrase this as 'pick what you want to do'. There are arguments in favour of writing as simply as

possible for all readers, but you should still notice a difference in content for the broad age groups.

**Think it over...**

Read through your notes on your two product ideas. Might any of the terms related to your multimedia product be too difficult for a child to understand? Consider simpler ways of explaining what the product does.

**Theory into practice**

1 Search the Internet for e-learning packages with a target audience of primary-aged children (e.g. to improve their spelling). The BBC Schools site offers 'Spelling with the Spellits', but you may find other examples. Bookmark some of these sites.

2 For one particular e-learning package, look at the words and images used. How much information is displayed on one screen at a time? How does the learner move from one screen to the next?

3 Find a site (like the BBC site) that includes information for parents. Look to see how the content for parents is written differently – perhaps in a smaller font, with longer sentences, and more text to a page.

4 Search the Internet for a similar e-learning package, aimed specifically at adults. Notice what is done differently.

## Using the functional specification as a tool

The functional specification tends to be written at the start of a project. However, things change. So it makes sense to review it and amend it as time passes. Also, as the dialogue between you and your client continues, you may understand more fully what it is that the product must do, and be able to specify these requirements more exactly.

The functional specification should identify what you plan to develop. However, it will also – by default – specify the **scope** of your project (i.e. the boundaries of the product) and, hence, what it will not do!

One important benefit of having a functional specification to refer to is that, while you are developing the product, you need never lose sight of your goals. And when you have completed the development, you have a yardstick to measure the end product against.

# 10.3 Product design

As with any product, the end product can only be as good as the original design. The more time and thought you put into what you intend to do, the better you will be able to use your time sensibly during development, and the better your product could be as a result of this efficient use of your resources.

This section considers what is expected of a designer and looks at some of the issues faced by a designer.

## The role of the designer

In a real-life project, as the designer, you would be responsible for thinking through how to meet the functional specification requirement. The functional specification may well have been written by someone else, and you may have little or no access to the client for further clarification.

You will be faced with making a number of decisions. However, as with any problem, there is usually 'more than one way to skin a cat'. Consequently, you are advised to experiment with alternative designs before finally deciding which one to choose.

Some of the decisions you will be making are discussed in this section:

✱ How should you structure the product?

✱ How will the user navigate through the product?

✱ What are the component parts of your multimedia product?

Others are discussed in later sections:

✱ The graphical design – your choice of layout and presentation, and how to achieve consistency – is discussed in Section 10.5 (page 160).

✳ The level of interactivity and design issues related to the user interface are discussed in Section 10.6 (page 170).

Because an iterative approach to design (see page 154) is recommended, testing is also part of the designer's role. This section introduces the concept of prototyping (page 154) and then Section 10.12 (page 195) looks at the topic in greater detail.

Finally, as designer, you must prepare some documentation; this is covered on pages 152–4.

## How should you structure the product?

The structure of a product depends very much on the type of product and how you propose to present it to the user:

✳ A product based on a slide show presentation can be **linear** in structure (i.e. a sequence of slides). There may be slides that offer the viewer a choice of routes from then on. The structure then becomes more complicated and very similar to a website structure.

✳ A product based on a website can be **hierarchical** in structure. One screen may offer routes to a number of other screens, and these, eventually, can lead back to the home page.

✳ A product based on a book, like this one, may have a contents page which points to the main sections of the product. There may then be cross-references within the text of the product

which lead wherever the viewer wants to go. This may be called a **matrix** (or **mesh** or **network**) structure.

Figure 10.2 on page 149 shows all three structures.

Having decided on the overall structure of your product, you will need to consider the structure from the user's point of view.

## How will the user navigate through the product?

How the user navigates through your product depends very much on its structure:

✳ Within a linear sequence of slides, for example, the navigation may be achieved through Back and Forward buttons. On the opening screen, you might have a 'Start the presentation' button. On the penultimate slide, you might have a 'Finish' button which leads to the final screen, where the viewer is thanked for taking part.

✳ Within a hierarchical structure, you might have a **nav bar** which lists the main sections of the product. You might also have Forward and Back buttons so that the viewer can retrace his or her footsteps.

### Key terms

*Nav bar* is short for navigation bar.

*(a) Linear*                              *(b) Hierarchical*

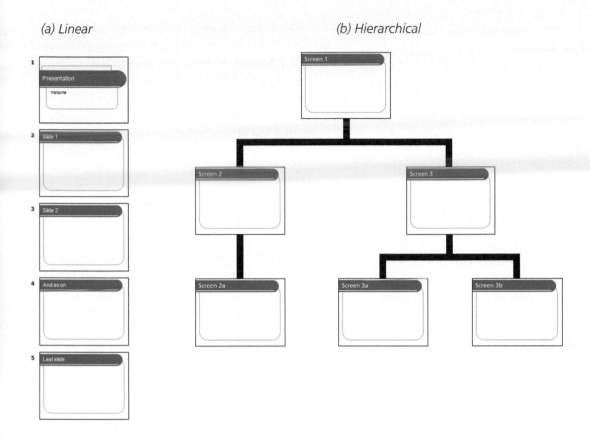

*(c) Matrix/mesh/network*

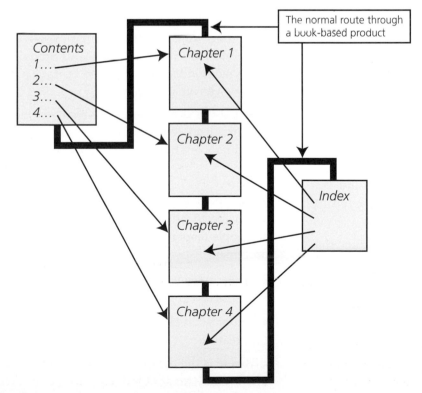

The normal route through a book-based product

**FIGURE 10.2** *The structure of a product*

* Within a matrix structure, you might have a nav bar for the underlying hierarchical structure, supported by links coded in a special way (using **command buttons** or **hyperlinks**) which take the viewer off the beaten track.

How you might allow the client to navigate through your product is considered in more detail in Section 10.4 (see page 155). You will have to decide what is best, and to specify exactly how this is to be achieved. As suggested in Section 10.4 (page 156), you might specify the navigation using a diagram showing the sequencing of events and how they are linked together.

## What are the component parts of your multimedia product?

Because you are producing a multimedia product, you will be involved in pulling together and combining material of a variety of media types. One of the most important design decisions is: 'What multimedia components will you include?'

* **Images** and how you might capture and manipulate them are discussed in Section 10.7 (page 175).

* **Video** may well feature in your product; this is discussed in Section 10.8 (page 182).

* You are unlikely to have a product that has no **sound** at all. How you might record or source the soundtrack is the topic of Section 10.9, starting on page 186.

* **Animation** can bring your product to life and involves the latest ICT tools. These are introduced in Section 10.10 (page 190).

You will design an **interface** through which interactivity between the user and your product will be achieved. Section 10.11 (page 194) focuses on this aspect of the development of your multimedia product.

Within the product, there will be component parts that are identifiable:

* In a product based on a slide show presentation, each separate slide is a component. A sequence of slides (e.g. to explain something at the start of the show) might also be thought of as a component.

* In a product based on a website, each web page is a component. Within each page there may be objects, such as text, images, sound, video clips and animations. Each of these is also a component.

### CASE STUDY

For the ICE system, the design team at Topic Training developed a DVD which involved the capture of video sequences, the recording of a voiceover, the integration of library footage, plus a music track.

1 Check your functional specification for information about what your product needs in the way of video footage, voiceover, music, etc.

2 List the component parts that you plan to incorporate.

The components need to be identified in the design specification and full details given so that the people responsible know how to develop each component:

* Where does the component fit into the overall product?

* Under what circumstances is the component to feature?

* Where is the component to be sourced? Is it ready made? Or does it need to be created anew?

For each component, you also need to identify the various media that are to be incorporated: still images, animations, video and sound. These topics are covered in Sections 10.7–10.10 and, once you have studied how to incorporate these options, as a designer, you need to decide exactly which ones to include and how to combine them to create the best (i.e. the most effective) way of communicating the message of your product.

## Theory into practice

1 For the multimedia product that you have decided to develop, decide how you will structure the product. Draw a diagram to explain the structure.

2 Identify the component parts of the product. List these and categorise them according to type: text, images, sound, video clips or animation.

3 Specify the source of each component.

4 Sketch the navigation through your product.

## Design issues

You then need to think about conventional design issues:

✱ What graphical design will you apply?

✱ How will you lay out the material?

✱ What method(s) of presentation will you use?

These aspects of graphical design are covered in Section 10.5 (page 160).

You will also need to consider how the user will interface with the product:

✱ What level of interactivity is needed?

✱ How will you design the user interface?

Section 10.6 (page 170) looks at the interactivity design, and Section 10.11 (page 194) focuses on the user interface.

Although all the design decisions are made by the designer, it usually falls to members of the production team to implement the design. So the design documentation has to specify exactly what is needed in sufficient detail for someone else to carry through your ideas.

In any design, there are some issues that are generic and some that are specific to the type of product.

Two generic issues that apply to all products that include an element of publication are consistency and the related issue of house style. It is important to establish some consistency within your product:

✱ You might decide that it is necessary to set up a **template** for a web page if your product is to be presented online.

✱ You might devise a **house style** for any documentation that is supplied with the product.

## Key terms

A *template* shows the basic layout of a document such as a web page. With web-authoring software, if you change the template, all pages based on that template are updated automatically.

## Key terms

A *house style* specifies any requirements of documents which represent an organisation. This includes sizing and positioning of logos, static information that needs to be included (like company registration details), which font is to be used, acceptable colours and so on.

When producing multimedia products, because there are so many different media, one specific issue relates to **file formats**.

There are many different file formats, each one developed for a purpose. Often you will have a choice, and it will be important to make the right choice. You will need to consider a number of issues:

✱ Does the format suit the media mix that you have in mind?

✱ Will the quality be good enough?

✱ Will the file size be too large for your purposes?

✱ Is the format supported both by the development software and the software on which the client will view the product?

You also need to think carefully about the format of the final product. During development, the production team will be making amendments to the files and will need access to them. Once the product is finished and ready for distribution, you will not want to allow the users the freedom to alter the product in any way.

This issue of restricting access to files to protect them is considered in detail in Section 10.13 (page 197).

## Design documentation

While the functional specification might be mostly written paragraphs of explanation, design documentation tends to be more diagrammatical, or presented in tables. The functional specification may be read by the client, and so will be written with this non-technical reader in mind.

The design specification, though, is written for a technical audience and is intended as a reference by those who have to implement the design. They do not want to have to wade through a long text so, the more succinctly you present your ideas, the better:

* **Flowcharts** can be used to show the logic of a product.

* **Storyboards** are visual scripts but can also be used to show the graphical design plans.

* A **prototype** might show the planned navigation and a sample of the level of user interaction.

* **Stills** – or mock-ups – might be used to show what is planned in a video sequence.

* **Wire frames** may be used to show the planned interaction within any one screen or slide.

* **Sample screens** or slides might be produced to show the graphical design and intended layout.

How you present your ideas depends very much on the product.

If you are planning to develop an **e-learning package**, this might involve your developing a number of slides using a presentation package such as PowerPoint.

To convey what your product will offer, you could produce some hand-drawn slides; a diagram to show how these might be linked is illustrated in Figure 10.3. (Navigation is considered in Section 10.4 on page 155.)

If you are planning a computer game or a film, you might use a **storyboard** to show the stages of the game/film (Figure 10.4).

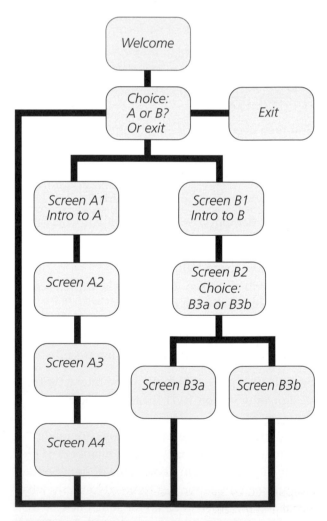

**FIGURE 10.3** *Sample navigation diagram*

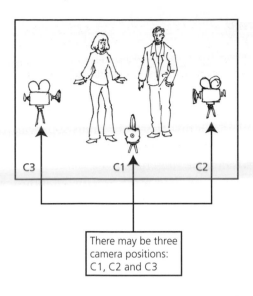

FIGURE 10.4 *Sample storyboard*

Because a storyboard is a visual script, it should make it easier for the director and cameraman to 'see' the shots before executing them. This is used for movies, commercials and animation, to save time and money.

If you are planning an interactive information point, you would need to clearly show the information that you intend to offer and how the user will interact with the product.

You might show sample screens showing the points at which the input would be expected. You could develop **wire frames** to illustrate the logic of your product (as shown in Figure 10.5).

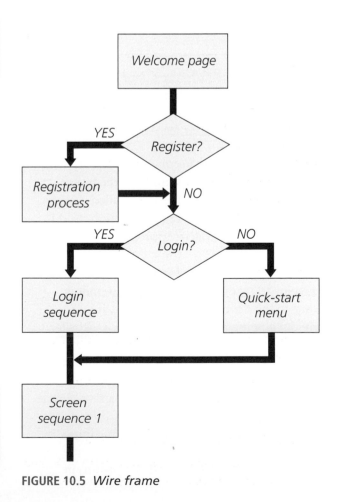

FIGURE 10.5 *Wire frame*

A wire frame shows the logic of a product: how the various sequences of screens are linked together. It would be supported with documentation showing what is to appear on the screens.

Because the functional specification is a report, it cannot include, for example, a prototype of the product. Instead, if you do develop an early prototype, you might include some sample screens to show what the user of the product may see, and what output might be expected.

You should include enough detail in your design documentation to have a measure of what is expected when you are testing the product.

You will need to devise a test plan and some sample interactions so that you can check the product works. Testing is considered in more detail in Section 10.12 (page 195).

## Iterative design

The more expert you become in applying multimedia tools and techniques, the better you will become at producing detailed designs. However, at this early stage, you might find it easier to use an iterative approach to software development.

This approach suits products that are developed using authoring software that is kind to the developer. For example, if you are developing a product based on a website, and are using Dreamweaver to create the web pages, you can set up an initial template which illustrates your design decisions regarding house style. You can then develop a few sample pages and show these to the client. If they are not happy, you can revise the design simply by amending the template.

The sample pages are called a **prototype**.

With prototyping in this way – obtaining approval at each stage – each prototype then brings you that much closer to a final, fully functional solution and helps to clarify in your mind exactly what the product needs to do.

Another benefit of the iterative approach, and creating prototypes at each stage, is that you can test the product during development. You can:

* check that it is functional, as far as it goes, and works as expected

* check for ease of use

* test for robustness

* test users' response/reaction to the product.

Prototyping therefore enables you to interweave design, implementation and testing, rather than each of these being a distinct one-off stage of development.

**Knowledge check**

1  What is the job of a designer?

2  Explain these terms: linear, hierarchical, matrix.

3  Explain these terms: nav bar, command button, hyperlink.

4  Give four examples of the components of a multimedia product.

5  What is the purpose of a template? How does it help to improve the consistency of a product?

6  What is a house style?

7  What issues relate to the many choices of file format?

8  What is a storyboard?

9  What is the function of a wire frame?

10  What is a prototype? How can prototyping help in the design of a product?

# 10.4 Navigation

One of the first decisions you need to make, having decided on the overall structure of the product, is how the navigation will work.

## Navigational structures

This course deals with two basic forms of navigational structure: hierarchical and linear. (Matrix structures can also be used, but are not needed for you to pass this course.) Which you decide to use will depend on the product being developed.

Figure 10.6 shows a typical **linear navigational structure** used in an e-learning

package. There is only one route from each component to the next; and there is a definite sequence that you want the viewer to follow. This structure may be necessary, for example, in an e-learning package where the learner has to be taught about one topic before he or she can begin to understand the next topic. Within one topic, the reader may be expected to work through the material, one slide/screen/page at a time, and click on Next when he or she is ready to move on. There may be some material that has to be read and understood before an example can be understood. In order to check learning, some questions may be posed and answers accepted and marked. Finally, there

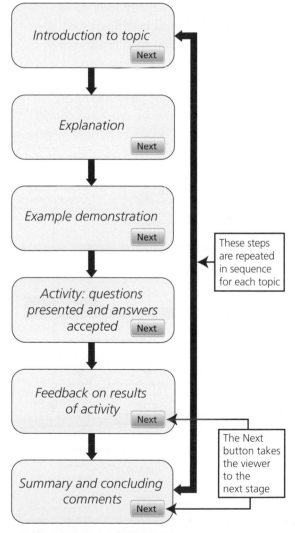

**FIGURE 10.6** *Flowchart of a linear structure within an e-learning package*

may be some feedback and a summary of the learning achieved in that topic. The reader can then move on to the next topic.

Figure 10.7 shows a typical **hierarchical navigational structure** for a product that is presented via a website. There is more than one route out of one component (and into any component). The viewer therefore has more choice of routes through the product. This may be suitable if the product is showing the viewer a number of things and it doesn't matter how the viewer wanders around the material.

Notice that it is possible to have a linear sequence within a hierarchical structure.

The structure can become even more complicated if the product demands such versatility, but you should be able to spot the basic two types within that: linear and hierarchical.

For example, an e-book has a hierarchical structure and, within that, there are linear sequences; there may also be cross-references within the text. This is because, in theory, you

might expect the viewer to start at page 1 and work through systematically until he or she reaches the end. However, there may be situations where a reader wants to refer back, to jump forward, or dip into the book, just as you would a 'normal' book. To help such a reader, you might provide a contents page and an index, and bookmarks (Figure 10.8). The software used to read the e-book will also provide ways of moving through the book: **Forward** and **Back** buttons and a way to jump to a particular page (as explained further in the next subsection).

## Specifying navigation

The decision making about the navigation through a product should be established at the design stage, and it should be specified in the design documentation using diagrams.

For a simple linear sequence, you could show the navigation as a **flowchart** (as seen in Figure 10.6).

A site map lists the sequences of screens that appear on a site.

Within the main sections there are subsections.

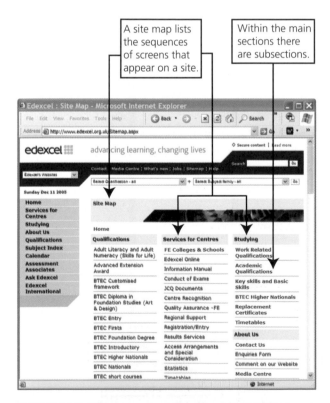

**FIGURE 10.7** *Site map showing the hierarchical structure of a website*

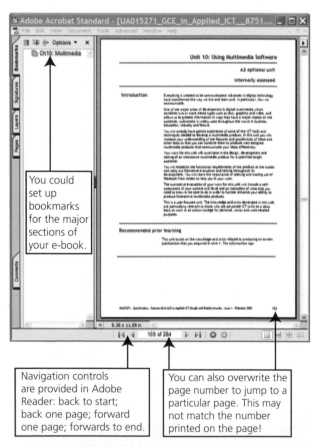

You could set up bookmarks for the major sections of your e-book.

Navigation controls are provided in Adobe Reader: back to start; back one page; forward one page; forwards to end.

You can also overwrite the page number to jump to a particular page. This may not match the number printed on the page!

**FIGURE 10.8** *Navigating an e-book*

For example, if the method of presenting the multimedia product is via a website, a **site map** (as shown in Figure 10.7) could be used to specify the way a visitor can visit the pages within the site. Each box on the diagram represents a web page on the site, but could equally represent a sequence of screens.

### Key terms

A *site map* lists all the pages in a website diagrammatically and shows how they are interlinked.

If you are creating an e-book, a **page plan** (Figure 10.9) could show where material will be, and could show the links from one page to another – e.g. from the contents page to new sections, as shown in Figure 10.2(c) on page 149. The page plan is important for publications that need to fit within a certain extent.

### Key terms

The *extent* of a book is the number of pages – including prelims (at the start of the book) and endmatter (at the end of the book).

### Think it over…

In what other ways might you illustrate the navigation for your product?

## Navigation devices

The navigation devices depend on the product.

## Presentations

If you are developing a product that comprises of a sequence of slides and are using software such as PowerPoint, you have to provide the user with a way of making progress through the presentation.

This navigation will most likely be achieved using **command buttons**:

### Key terms

A *command button* is a control on a form or slide that is linked to a macro so that, if clicked (triggered by an event), an action happens.

* A **Next** button which they click on to reveal the next slide is the simplest option.

* You may also offer the option for the user to retrace his or her footsteps. For this, a **Back** button may be needed.

* You ought also to provide a **Quit** button so that the user can abandon the product at any time, if he or she so wishes.

### Think it over…

What other wording on buttons might you expect to see on a presentation? What wording might you use on your buttons?

PowerPoint calls command buttons 'action buttons' and offers a range of the standard ones with icons that should be immediately recognisable. Figure 10.10 shows a sample screen with two action buttons in place. These buttons should appear in the same positions on each screen so that the viewer becomes used to the layout.

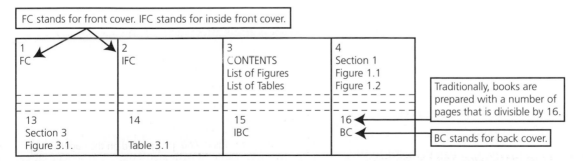

FC stands for front cover. IFC stands for inside front cover.

| 1 FC | 2 IFC | 3 CONTENTS List of Figures List of Tables | 4 Section 1 Figure 1.1 Figure 1.2 |
| --- | --- | --- | --- |
| 13 Section 3 Figure 3.1. | 14 Table 3.1 | 15 IBC | 16 BC |

Traditionally, books are prepared with a number of pages that is divisible by 16.

BC stands for back cover.

**FIGURE 10.9** *Page plan for an e-book*

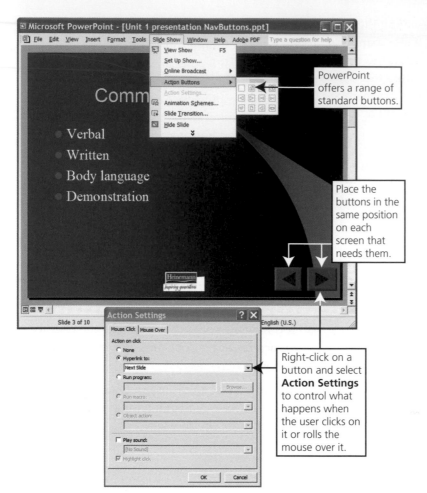

**FIGURE 10.10** *Action buttons for a slide show*

The effect of these buttons, when clicked or when the mouse moves over them, is controlled using the **Action Settings** dialogue box (Figure 10.10).

## Web-based products

If you are developing a product that is delivered via a website then, apart from the ones you would expect in a slide presentation (Next, Back, Quit), there are a variety of additional navigational aids:

* A **nav bar** can be placed on every page, allowing the visitor to jump to any of the main sections of the site.

* **Command buttons** can be used to take the visitor to a different page.

* **Hyperlinks** within the text can be used to link it to relevant text elsewhere on the site.

Figure 10.11 opposite shows these navigational devices in one web page from the Topic Training website.

### e-books

If your product is an e-book, the navigation devices will include the option to turn a page, and to refer to the contents page and jump to a particular section. You may also offer the option to jump to other sections, from within one piece of text to some related text elsewhere.

If the product is supplied as a PDF file and viewed using Adobe Acrobat Reader, the navigation devices are standard ones, used in many software products. Figure 10.8 on page 156 shows a full page with navigational aids; Figure 10.12 shows these in greater detail.

## Prototyping

Prototyping provides an opportunity to demonstrate the navigation through your product without having to develop the product completely.

Since the navigational devices should be common to all components such as slides, web pages or pages in an e-book, showing a few sample pages will illustrate exactly what you propose. This can therefore be established early on, prior to the majority of the development effort.

## User documentation

It is important that the navigation through your product is straightforward for the user. Many people avoid 'reading the manual', preferring to find out for themselves, so you have a responsibility to make the interface as intuitive as possible.

Placing the navigation aids in the same position on every slide, web page or e-book page, and using standardised buttons, or simply copying what every other software producer does, makes your product that much easier to use.

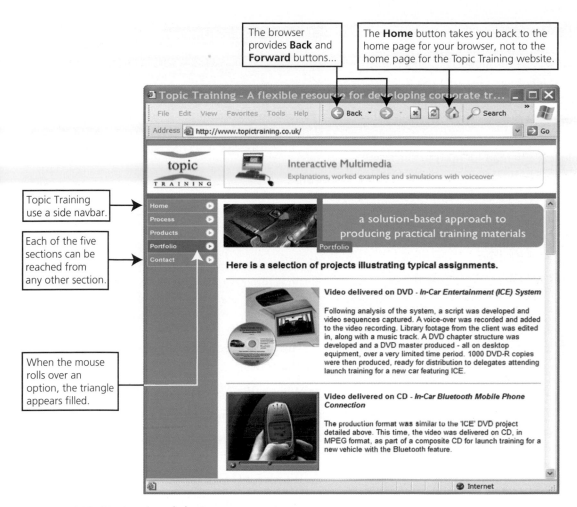

**FIGURE 10.11** *Navigational devices on a web page*

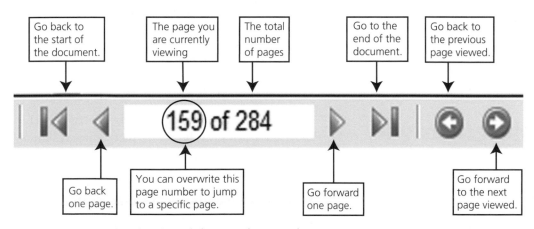

**FIGURE 10.12** *Navigation in Adobe Acrobat Reader*

However, even when you have done this, the routes available may still be complicated, especially for someone who has never used your product before. So in case the user does have to resort to the manual, you need to make the manual as easy to understand as possible.

Write some simple instructions for the user, keeping these as brief as possible, and yet as comprehensive as possible, too!

1   What is meant by navigation?

2   Explain the difference between linear and hierarchical structures.

3   How might a cross-reference be achieved within an e-book?

4   What might a site map be used to illustrate?

5   What can be shown in a page plan?

## Assessment activity

1   Review your functional specification and your design documentation. Check for any mention of navigational requirements.

2   Having established the requirements for navigation though your product, decide how you will implement this in your design. Make notes and draw diagrams to explain what you propose.

3   Develop a prototype to demonstrate the navigational devices being used and the routes available.

4   Write a user guide explaining the routes through your product.

## Assessment hint

✓ Proofread your user guide carefully. Make sure there are no spelling mistakes.

# 10.5 Graphical design

One way to make a multimedia product as user-friendly as possible is by structuring the content appropriately and making effective use of available presentation and formatting features.

By looking critically at a range of multimedia products, and by experimentation, you will learn what makes for a well designed product. In time, you will be able to incorporate some of these graphical design ideas into your own products.

**Theory into practice**

1   Select four user-friendly multimedia products. For each, list the features that make it especially user-friendly.

2   Select one multimedia product that is not user-friendly. How might it be made more user-friendly?

3   For all five multimedia products, identify any special features of the user interface.

4   Of the five multimedia products, which makes the most effective use of colour? Compare your choice with others in your group.

5   Of the five multimedia products, which one has the most easily read fonts? Note the styles, typefaces used and how emphasis is achieved.

This section considers many aspects of graphical design:

✱ What is the best design for the user interface?

✱ How can colour be used effectively?

✱ What overall effect can your chosen layout create?

✱ Which fonts will have the greatest impact?

✱ What can make your site look different?

✱ How can you achieve consistency in the presentation of a corporate image or brand?

It also considers – on page 169 – the need for some supporting documentation for a user.

## User interface

User interface is covered in detail in Section 10.11 (page 194). For now, be aware that, when designing a multimedia product, you decide how much interactivity to include:

✱ What is the purpose of your product?

✱ Are you simply presenting some information?

✱ How much input do you need from the viewers so that you present what they want to see?

✱ Are you trying to teach something?

✱ Will you need feedback from the viewers so that you can gauge the success (or otherwise) of the learning?

# CASE STUDY

The design team at Topic Training produce interactive training videos on various topics such as in-car satellite navigation, bespoke office software and induction information for motor technicians.

Figure 10.13 shows two sample screens from Topic Training's demonstration CD. The viewer is presented with questions and, to maintain interest, a variety of ways are used for the viewer to give the answer to the question: true/false, single choice, multiple choice, short-answer text entry, hot object, hotspot, and drag and drop.

1 Select five multimedia products and identify the purpose of each, and how this impacts on the extent of the user interface.

2 For one multimedia product which involves an element of learning, identify the different ways in which the user interacts with the product.

3 For a different multimedia product, check what happens if you enter incorrect information. How helpful is the interface in guiding you as to what you should input?

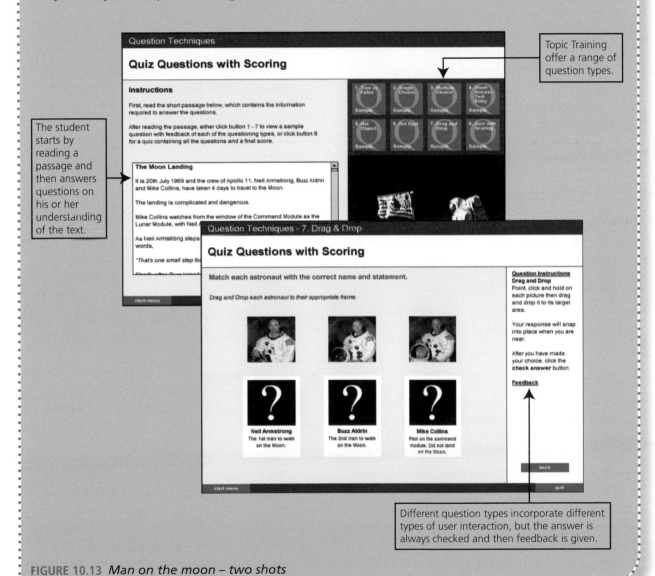

The student starts by reading a passage and then answers questions on his or her understanding of the text.

Topic Training offer a range of question types.

Different question types incorporate different types of user interaction, but the answer is always checked and then feedback is given.

FIGURE 10.13 *Man on the moon – two shots*

## Effective use of colour

Ask ten friends for their favourite colour and you will find they have differing views. Some people like bright colours and others prefer muted tones. Choice of colour is subjective!

Different colours can have a different atmospheric effect on the viewer:

* Some colours create warmth – red is seen as a passionate colour.

* Yellow is seen as cheerful and might make the viewer feel happier.

* Blue can create a peaceful ambience.

* Grey might create a sombre tone.

Which colours you decide to use could therefore be determined by your personal taste, but you should also consider the impact you are aiming to have on the viewer.

There is also a basic 'rule' that will help you to make a good choice: the 'rule of thirds' warns against using more than three colours on a printed page, a slide or a web page. Having more than three colours soon becomes distracting. And remember, you will need to reserve some colours to have a special meaning (e.g. for a hyperlink).

### Contrast

Contrasting colours can result in greater legibility, so you not only need to consider what colour the text will be, but also what colour you might use as the background:

* Dark coloured text looks best on light backgrounds – and this is the normal combination.

* Light coloured text looks best on dark backgrounds – but can be tiring to read.

Within a block of text, you could create contrast by using coloured letters. If you are careful to use different hues sparingly, you could create a jewel-like effect. However, a coloured character can 'disappear' within a text block if it is not strong enough. And too many small elements of colour can create a scattered effect.

## Pattern

**Pattern** is a repeating visual element that can be created in a number of ways. You have the option of replicating a shape, or the size of an element, or a position.

* You can duplicate – or replicate a shape to produce a pattern, as in the design of wallpaper or curtain fabric.

* You can duplicate the size used for one element, using it for other similar elements within the design. This implies that they have the same level of importance.

* You can duplicate the position so that the same things appear in the same positions on subsequent pages or slides. This creates a familiarity for the user. You can also align elements within one page or slide so that it is clear they form a group of related objects.

* You can repeat elements to create symmetry.

* You can repeat elements to create frequency – e.g. in the layout of a list of items.

### Think it over…

Discuss how else you could create pattern.

According to the theory of design, pattern is one of the second set of elements of design:

* the first set comprises shape, space (and use of white space), line and size

* the second set comprises colour, texture/ pattern, value and typography.

Notice that pattern is also referred to as **texture**.
 Both patterns and textures are used to create interest on a page or slide, and can create a mood according to the busyness of the pattern.

### Theory into practice

1 Search the Internet for examples of textures and patterns used.

2 Explore the options of your software to create textures and patterns.

## Background and borders

The **background** chosen can draw the viewer's eye to the text, so long as it is chosen carefully:

* If you keep a soft focus for the background, keeping any lines fuzzy, this will accentuate the sharpness of the text, making it more readable.

* Aim for colour gradients. Bright colours are fine, but hard lines between two colours will draw the eye away from the text and on to the colour change line. So, allow colours to blend into each other.

* You can create a 3D effect by having depth cues and distance-like colour gradients. If you make text get smaller the 'further away' it is, this has the same effect.

* The background must not compete with the foreground material, so there must be no strong focal points in the background material.

Within any layout, you could incorporate a **border** to separate one 'chunk' of material from another. Depending on the weight and colour of the border, the eye may be drawn to it, in preference to other material near by. So, deciding on border style and weight, and colour matters.

### Theory into practice

1 Search the Internet for examples of backgrounds. Notice the coloration used and any depth features.

2 Search the Internet for examples of borders. Notice the styles used and the purpose of the bordered material.

## Web-safe colours

*How many different colours can be displayed on a colour monitor?* It depends!

 If 8 bits are used to store the colour value, this means there are 256 colours ($2^8 = 256$).

 However, although there are 256, only 216 of them are included in the **web-safe palette**.

Web-safe colours are defined in terms of their **RGB** values: 0, 51, 102, 153, 204 and 255. These multiples of 51 are equal to 0%, 20%, 40%, 60%, 80% and 100% of 255, respectively.

*Why should you choose web-safe colours?*

If you don't, you can create a number of unfortunate effects:

* If you have created a web graphic with an invisible background, then you must choose a web-safe colour for the background. Otherwise, on some browsers, this may present a dithered transparency.

* If you create an image or some text that includes an invisible background colour, then try to choose a colour that is the same as your website background colour (which should also be web-safe). Otherwise, if the application is using **anti-aliasing**, there might be a fringed effect around your image.

# The impact of layout on the overall effect

Having decided the textual content of your multimedia product, you will need to decide how to lay it out on the page, slide or screen.

To make the text as readable as possible, you need to make decisions as to the **spacing** (between lines and between characters), what **emphasis** you might put on some of the text (e.g. headings or important words within running text), or how you might want to suppress other text.

There will also be other elements or objects to fit into the overall layout: images, navigational aids, command buttons and so on.

How you group all these objects is part of the graphical design process and relies on experience. You need to study other people's work – see what you like and what you don't like, and learn from this.

There are three aspects, though, that are important: composition, shape and balance.

## Composition

In the same way that an artist thinks about composition for a drawing or painting, and a photographer should think about composition for a shot, you need to consider the composition of each component of your multimedia product.

Each web page, printed page or slide needs to be composed; the music or voiceover needs composition.

The primary aim is to lead the viewer's eye to whatever is most important on the page or slide. This can be achieved by careful positioning of elements on a page or slide, as well as good use of colour and animation. Colour is discussed in this section on page 162; animation warrants its own section (see page 190).

One theory – called **proximity theory** – involves placing elements that relate to one another together. The grouped items then form a visual unit, and this provides the viewer with a visual clue as to what you are communicating. Deciding which elements belong together is the first stage of creating a **visual hierarchy**. These then form **focal points** in the composition.

To draw the eye to a particular focal point, you might consider using graphics of different sizes and colours, which will give them a **visual weight**.

### Key terms

*Visual weight* refers to the relative size and scale of an element within a design.

## Shape

Depending on your multimedia product, your basic component – a slide, a web page, a screen – has an underlying shape. The shapes you use within your basic component need to fit within the available space, although if you are designing web pages you could consider letting the viewer scroll down if necessary.

Within the basic component, you could use a variety of shapes – circles and rectangles and triangles – but using too many different shapes can result in a confusion of images for the viewer. Also, different shapes imply different moods. Soft curves – as in circles or rounded boxes – convey a more friendly tone than sharp corners on triangles or rectangles.

### Theory into practice

1　Choose a multimedia product and study the shapes that are used. What effect do the shapes have on the atmosphere of the product?

2　Look for websites that use shape poorly. Compare notes with others in your group.

## Balance

It is possible to achieve a balance using symmetry or asymmetry:

✱ If you aim for symmetry, this will involve organising elements through the alignment of graphics along a horizontal or vertical axis.

✱ If you prefer to use asymmetry, you can display an unbalanced visual weighting using elements of different sizes, colour and shape.

### Theory into practice

1　Choose a multimedia product and study the layout that is used. Make notes.

2　Look for examples of the use of proximity theory to group components.

3　Look for examples of how balance has been achieved.

4　Select a section of text that illustrates how spacing and emphasis have been used to good effect.

## How fonts can enhance or detract from readability

In the same way that you should limit the number of colours to three, a well designed page, slide or screen should contain no more than two different **typefaces**.

### Key terms

A *typeface* is a particular design of a character, such as Arial or Times New Roman.

If you stick to a single typeface, you could use a mixture of larger and smaller letters (i.e. different **point sizes**).

### Key terms

Character size is measured in *points*. Typical sizes are 10 pt or 12 pt.

When deciding on the point **size** of your text, you need to consider both the legibility requirements of the viewer and the space constraints according to how the text will be presented to the viewer:

* Larger type is easier to read but requires more space. On a web page, it can impede navigation.

* Smaller type is conveniently compact, but it can be difficult to read, especially for those with impaired eyesight.

Also important is the relative importance, and quantity, of the information:

* On a web page, information such as 'Date last updated', copyright information and captions are less important than the main text of a page. So these should appear in a smaller point size.

* Titles, chapter and section headings, and important bits of information, will warrant larger point sizes.

If you use more than one typeface, you should limit yourself to four different **fonts** – i.e. varying the type by changing the point size or the **emphasis** of the font (e.g. using bold or italic).

## Key terms

A *font* is a particular typeface in a particular point size (e.g. Arial 10 pt or Times Roman 12 pt), with or without emphasis.

Each font has its own distinct character, but they do fall into two main types:

* **Serif fonts**, such as Times Roman, have 'feet' and are considered to be easier to read. They tend to be used for large blocks of text.

* **Sans serif fonts**, such as Arial, are cleaner looking and tend to be used for headings and captions (i.e. wherever only a small amount of text is needed).

Apart from the two basic fonts (serif and sans serif), there are also script and decorative fonts, but these may not be sufficiently readable for your purposes. Also, you are best advised to choose common fonts – this will save problems later if your product is used on a computer that does not support your font.

You should avoid using all **capital letters** because text that has been set in a mix of small letters and capital letters is much easier to read. You might, however, for emphasis use all capitals for single-word headings, and perhaps brief textual links.

The combination of typeface, point size and emphasis decisions leads you to a **style** for your product.

## Key terms

A *style* is particular font with additional formatting, such as line spacing, colour of text and so on.

It is important that you apply the same style throughout your product so that it has a consistent feel. An organisation may stipulate what styles may be used for all literature that goes out under the organisation's name. This includes the use of logos (see page 168) and the contact information that has to appear – and this is called the **house style**.

## Theory into practice

1 Choose a multimedia product and study the styles that are used. Make notes.

2 Look for examples of the use of different fonts. How many are used?

3 Look for examples of different point sizes.

4 Write brief notes on the house style used.

## Consideration of presentation method

According to the nature of your multimedia product, you will need to specify how the material is to be presented to the viewer.

You have several options. You may create:

* a web-based presentation
* an e-learning package
* a slide show presentation.

Whatever the decision, it will impact on the choices you will want to make in deciding your graphical design.

### Screen size

Fitting the available material within the space available is an essential element of the graphical design.

* If the presentation is to be slide-based, you will be limited in the amount of information that will fit.
* If the presentation is to be viewed on a computer screen using browser software, you will have different limitations on the screen size.

### Nature of the audience

Apart from the age of the audience and how that should influence the terminology and way of expressing yourself, what other considerations might you need to take into account?

The purpose of the product will appeal to a particular audience:

* A game might be developed to appeal to motor-racing enthusiasts.
* An e-learning package might be developed for students interested in sailing.
* A presentation might be developed to explain the features of a new version of a popular software package.

Each of these products has a different type of audience. The tone of the content needs to match the audience, as with any communication.

### Theory into practice

1 Choose three multimedia products, designed for different audiences. In what ways has the product been designed for its audience? Compare notes with others in your group.

2 For your own product, decide how you might incorporate design features that show that you recognise the nature of your audience, and have meet their needs.

## Consistency

As with any communication, a lack of consistency creates 'noise' for the viewers and can distract them sufficiently for the message to be lost.

It is therefore important that you build in consistency at the design stage. Decide on your:

* fonts, and under what circumstances you will emphasise the text
* use of colour – for text, for backgrounds, for borders
* use of shapes and images within each basic component, so as to create balance.

### CASE STUDY

Topic Training adopts the house style of each client when producing training materials. They collect information about acceptable colour themes, and any preferences regarding layout of contact information, fonts, border, backgrounds and page sizes. Topic Training also has its own house style.

1 Imagine Topic Training is your client. Summarise the main features of its house style so that someone else could produce training materials or some other multimedia product using the Topic Training house style.

2 Consider your own house style. Document it so that anyone producing materials to match your multimedia product design can adopt the correct house style.

## Corporate branding

The product that you are developing will represent the client's organisation. Viewers will link what they see to the organisation and the impression the product gives will have an impact on their ideas about the organisation.

Feelings about an organisation can affect the buying patterns of the public, so organisations spend vast sums of money on branding themselves and promoting an image that will appeal to potential customers.

The image is conveyed via a house style, and this includes the organisation's **logo**.

> **Key terms**
>
> A *logo* is a visual sign used to represent a particular company, an idea, a special occasion or a product.

Logos are the most efficient way of creating an instant feel in the mind of the viewer for something.

In designing a logo, care will be taken to create a simple and yet memorable image:

* A logo may be similar to the product it represents.

* A logo may be created from geometrical shapes, or from natural shapes like a leaf or a tree.

* Scientific symbols may feature, or heraldic images.

* The logo may simply be the initials of a company's name, or the full name of the product.

Within the design of a logo, there needs to be contrast and tension. The space between shapes within the logo can be as important as the shapes themselves.

So, when deciding on a logo, a few 'rules' need to be considered. It must be:

* easily recognised – nothing too complex

* memorable.

Neither of these 'rules' helps you when dreaming up a new logo! But, having arrived at one that does obey the rules, it will be a success.

Logos are protected in law, so any new logo must not be too similar to one already in use.

The branding of your product needs to be decided at a very early stage. If a logo needs to appear on every page or screen or slide, space has to be made for it. It may also influence your choice of colour scheme.

### CASE STUDY

Topic Training's logo uses the two words 'topic' and 'training' and sets them in a way that gives each word weight. This carries the message that 'training' is an essential part of their product, but also that 'topic' is important to their way of working. Ian Taylor, CEO, explains:

*In any training, there are subject areas, like ICT. And within that, there are topics that the student needs to know about. For example, multimedia!*

*At Topic Training, we focus on a single topic and analyse it. What facts does the learner need to be told? What skills do they need to learn and be tested on? We then decide how best to treat*

*each facet of the topic: by hard copy, as a video, using a test – we have lots of instructional design ideas.*

*Then we explain the topic, using all our own multimedia skills, and deliver it in the most effective way for our client.*

1  For each multimedia product you have looked at, look again and consider the logos. How effective are they?

2  Cut out logos from advertisements in newspapers and magazines. Pool these with others in your group and see how many you recognise.

1  You are going to design a logo for your multimedia product. Make a few sketches of any ideas that come to mind. Share your ideas with others.

2  Pick one that looks promising and develop it further. You are unlikely to start with the finished logo in your head, so go through the process of trying out ideas and notice how new ideas occur to you and improve your design.

3  In your group, present your finished logos to each other, and discuss the merits of each one. Consider whether to make changes to your logo in response to suggestions made.

4  Present your final logo in a variety of sizes – to suit the documentation needed for your multimedia product.

## Supporting documentation

When you have completed the design of your product, you should be in a position to draft the supporting documentation.

For this qualification, you are expected to produce 'getting started with…' instructions, explaining how to install and use your multimedia product.

In the same way that your functional specification report will affect the mark band awarded, the quality of this supporting documentation will determine the marks you can be expected to gain:

* Some instructions which give an indication of how to install and use the product will put you in mark band 1.

* Giving more detail so that a competent user can install and use the product will lift your marks into band 2.

* Making your documentation comprehensive so that even a novice could use your multimedia product – i.e. making it 'foolproof' – will take you into mark band 3.

1  As your multimedia product is developed, check that your supporting material explains the kinds of things a user needs to know.

2  Test your documentation on someone who is a competent user. Use his or her feedback to improve the documentation.

3  Then try out your supporting documentation on a novice. Listen carefully to any problems the novice reports – and make sure you improve the documentation before considering it complete.

**Knowledge check**

1  What features of a multimedia product can make it more – or less – user-friendly?

2  Explain how colour can be used to create an atmosphere.

3  Why is contrast between a font colour and the background colour important? What works best?

4  What is the purpose of using patterns or texture in a graphical design?

5  Why are borders used in a graphical design?

6  What is the web-safe palette?

7  What does RGB stand for?

8  What is anti-aliasing?

9  Explain proximity theory. How can it help you to decide on the layout of a web page?

10  Explain these terms: visual hierarchy, focal point, visual weight.

11  Explain these terms: typeface, font, point size.

12  What is the difference between serif fonts and sans serif fonts? For greatest readability, which should be used in what circumstances?

13  What is house style?

14  What is the purpose of a logo?

# 10.6 Interactivity design

If you produce a multimedia product that promotes a unique kitchen gadget and your client wants this to be displayed in an endless loop, then the only interactivity needed is the option to start and end the presentation.

The display screen might be positioned at the entrance to a store's restaurant where customers queue, waiting to be allocated a table; or it may be overhead at the front of a queue, as is done in some post offices. No one is expected to watch the screen for more than a few minutes, so, provided you keep their attention for one loop, the product has met its purpose.

If you watch a cookery programme, or one on DIY or gardening, there may be similar amounts of interactivity: you turn on the programme and, at some point, turn it off. However, to maintain interest, the presenter 'talks' to the viewers and makes them feel part of what is going on.

If you are trying to teach the viewers something, you may need to provide them with stopping points at which you summarise what has gone before. In the same way that this book includes 'knowledge checks', your multimedia product might ask the viewer questions.

You might also invite responses so that you can check if they understand.

Indeed, much of the success of digital multimedia is due to its interactive capabilities, which allow users to interact with the product by responding to prompts.

## Interactive use elements

Depending on the software you use to develop the multimedia product, there will be a number of interactive use elements on offer to you. Some of these – like buttons, hotspots and rollovers – you have come across before in your AS course.

In Unit 7, Section 7.7 looks at the user interface for a database, where this is described in some detail.

## Buttons

A button is a feature that looks like a button but is activated when you click the mouse while the cursor is positioned on it.

Figure 10.10 on page 158 shows how buttons might be used to help a viewer navigate through a PowerPoint presentation.

Figure 10.10 on page 158

See the 'How to...' panel in Unit 7 (page 40)

### Theory into practice

1 See the 'How to...' panel in Unit 7 (page 40) for creating a control on a form in a database. Check that you understand the procedure.

2 For the multimedia authoring software that you are using, create a button.

3 Control the effect of this button, so that something happens if it is clicked.

4 Change its appearance in some way when the mouse is rolled over it.

## Hotspots

A hotspot is an area on a web page, like a button, except that the text or an image normally appears in a different colour, to distinguish it from other text that is not a hotspot. A hotspot, when clicked on, can provide a link to another web page. Or it may be an area that can be dragged somewhere else on the page.

### Think it over...

Discuss examples of how you could use hotspots in your multimedia products.

## Image maps

An **image map** may be used to provide a user with an intuitive way of making a selection.

### Key terms

An *image map* is an image that has been divided into regions, or hotspots.

When a user clicks a hotspot, an action occurs (e.g. a new file opens).

Client-side image maps store the hypertext link information within the HTML document. (Server-side image maps store them in a separate map file.)

When a visitor clicks on a hotspot, the URL for the link is sent directly to the server, making the process much quicker than server-side image maps.

To set up an image map, you have to define the regions for the hotspots and create the links. The web authoring software makes this as easy as possible, providing differently shaped tools for encircling each region: circles, rectangles and, for irregularly shaped hotspots, a polygon tool.

Sites like Multimap use image maps to offer a choice of place. As the cursor is moved across the map, its position is noted relative to the image. Then when you click, you are selecting the sub-area of the map.

However, image maps need not relate to maps of places. The NHS Direct website uses an image map to help the viewer to locate a part of the body that is in pain or discomfort (Figure 10.14).

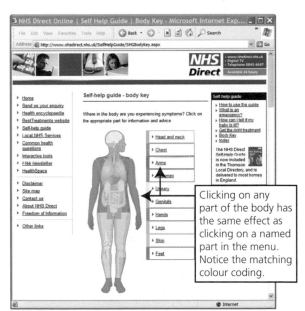

**FIGURE 10.14** *NHS body map*

### Theory into practice

1 Visit the Multimap site and try out the image map feature for yourself.

2 Visit the NHS Direct site and use the image map of the body. Notice the **Alt** tags that are used to label each area of the body as the mouse rolls over it.

3 Find out how to incorporate an image map using your multimedia authoring software.

## Text links

Although icons are user-friendly, sometimes text is better. For example, instead of a button labelled 'More information', you might display the message: 'For more information, click here'. The text 'here' can be made into a link.

The place the link leads to can be another page, screen or slide. If you are developing a web-based product, the filename for that page is the link.

Figure 10.15 shows how such a text link is created in Dreamweaver.

If you want to jump elsewhere on the same page, you would need to create an **anchor point** within the page (Figure 10.16).

## Rollovers

A rollover is an area on-screen where, when the cursor is moved across it, something happens, like the area changes colour. This helps the user know where the cursor is and can be useful when trying to locate a hotspot.

Figure 10.29 on page 188 suggests incorporating sound when the mouse is moved over a button.

## Menus

Within your multimedia product, the primary navigation system – the linking mechanism that will take the viewer from one place to another – should be kept together in a compact way, either along the top of the page or slide, or down one side, or across the bottom.

A web browser displays the web page in the browser window. Depending on how long your web page is, and what resolution the viewer is using, your web page may not fit into the browser window. Then your viewer will have to scroll up and down to see everything. In this case, you might choose

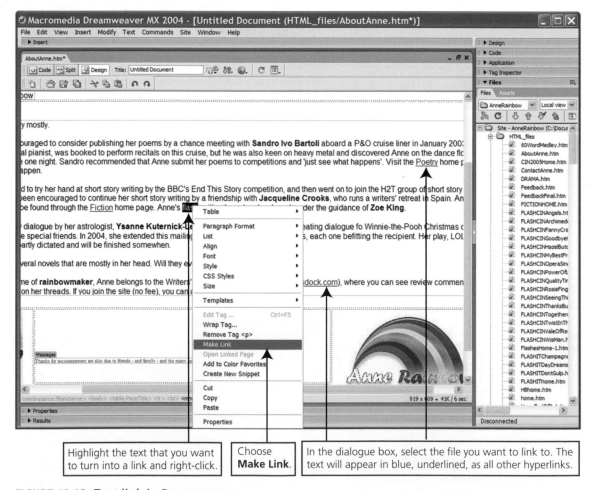

Highlight the text that you want to turn into a link and right-click.

Choose **Make Link**.

In the dialogue box, select the file you want to link to. The text will appear in blue, underlined, as all other hyperlinks.

**FIGURE 10.15** *Text link in Dreamweaver*

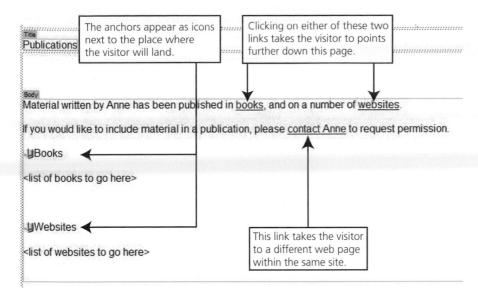

The anchors appear as icons next to the place where the visitor will land.

Clicking on either of these two links takes the visitor to points further down this page.

This link takes the visitor to a different web page within the same site.

**FIGURE 10.16** *Anchor point*

a menu bar to go across the top – and the bottom – of your web page.

It is possible to split the browser window into separate frames (Figure 10.17) so that some information, such as the menu bar, remains in place whatever is being viewed in the other areas on the screen. In this situation, even if the viewer has to scroll up and down, the main navigation options are visible at all times.

Although it is important that the menu bar is clearly visible, in line with graphical design issues discussed in Section 10.5 (page 160), it should not be over-large or more eye-catching than anything else on the page.

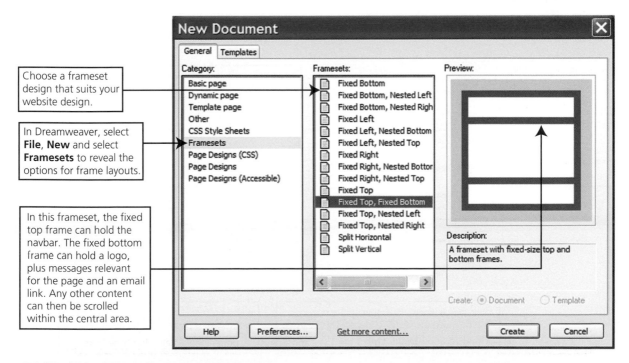

Choose a frameset design that suits your website design.

In Dreamweaver, select **File**, **New** and select **Framesets** to reveal the options for frame layouts.

In this frameset, the fixed top frame can hold the navbar. The fixed bottom frame can hold a logo, plus messages relevant for the page and an email link. Any other content can then be scrolled within the central area.

**FIGURE 10.17** *Splitting a screen into frames*

on, to start with, so that it becomes the default value.

✱ With **checkboxes**, the viewer can tick to say 'Yes'.

## User response methods

Having set up the interactivity devices, you need to allow the viewer the option to enter a response. As with form design within database software, there is a range of options available on multimedia authoring software.

Figure 10.18 shows the types of fields you might include within a form:

✱ A **text box** could be used for the viewer's name.

✱ The **list/menu** fields offer the options as a drop-down menu, which saves space on the screen.

✱ **Radio buttons** can be grouped – and given a **common group name** – so as to offer the viewer one from many choices. If you wish, you could set one of the buttons

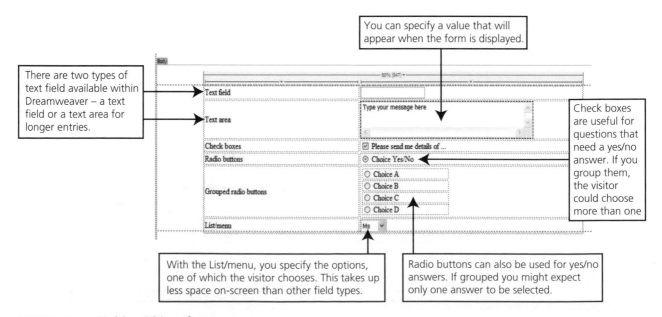

**FIGURE 10.18** *Fields within a form*

# 10.7  Image capture and manipulation

It is unlikely that your multimedia product would be devoid of images. Therefore, you need to be able to store and manipulate images so that you might incorporate them effectively.

There are two main types of graphics: **bitmap** and **vector**.

### Key terms

*Bitmap graphics* are created using painting software, such as Paint, or can be scanned in or transferred from a digital camera.

*Vector images* are created from drawing software, using objects such as lines and shapes, placed in particular positions to create the final image.

Each bitmap image is stored as a number of **pixels**, each pixel being allocated three numbers to represent its colour as a combination of red, green and blue.

### Key terms

*Pixel* is short for picture element.

The number of bits allocated for each pixel's colour value affects the range of colours available, but also the amount of storage space needed to retain this data.

Vector image data is the shape information, plus where and how these objects are grouped. This takes up far less space than a bitmap image.

For bitmap images, the **resolution** depends on how much raw data is collected when the image is captured.

### Key terms

The *resolution* of an image is a measure of the pixels or dots per inch in an image.

Bitmap images, when enlarged, can lose clarity if the resolution is not high enough – because the gaps between the pixels become too large. However, with vector graphics, there are no issues of clarity; a vector graphic can be enlarged without loss of clarity.

For any image, its resolution determines also the amount of storage space needed; the greater the resolution, the greater the file size. To reduce file sizes, images can be compressed, and this results in two main image format types:

✳   **Lossless data compression methods** involve mathematical techniques that analyse the pattern of pixels and – without loss of detail – reduce the storage space needed to store them. When the image is decompressed, the full detail is restored.

✳   **Lossy data compression methods** – as the name suggests – lose some of the data during compression, and this loss of data cannot be restored when the image is decompressed. The **JPEG** format is an example.

### Theory into practice

1   Find out what graphics software you have – and the types of images you can create using this software.

2   List some image file types (such as GIF, TIFF and JPEG), and carry out research to find more information about these files types.

3   Research the Internet to find out what image resolution is recommended for various uses (e.g. for display on a monitor or for display on a web page).

## Capturing ready-made images

Ready-made images include paper-based sources such as photographs, hand-drawn sketches and extracts from newspapers and magazines. Images may also be available digitally. These may be on a website, sent as an attachment to an email or supplied on a CD-ROM.

If you have a paper-based source, the image can be converted to an electronic form by **scanning**. You need the hardware to do this (a scanner) attached to your computer, and to install any drivers that are supplied with the hardware. You may also be provided with software that will handle the scanning process.

The photo – or whatever form your hardcopy of the image is in – has to be placed face down on the glass window of the scanner. There will be markers on the frame of the window to indicate where to position the photo, possibly with arrows pointing to where the top-left corner of the photo should be.

To start the scanning process, you may have several options:

* There may be a Scan button on your scanner. This may automatically open the scanning software – or you might open the software manually and click on the Scan option.

* You might activate a scanning process through some other software, such as PaintShopPro or Adobe PhotoShop.

The scanning process is time-consuming, and it is important to scan only that part of the scan window that interests you. For this reason, there is a Preview option, and you can specify exactly how much of the paper-based source you want to capture (Figure 10.19).

The resolution chosen (Figure 10.20) determines the number of pixels – the higher the resolution, the greater the number of pixels. Since this directly affects the storage needs for

If you are happy with the preview, click on **Accept** to start the scan/save action

FIGURE 10.19 *Preview option (source: Jon Clow)*

the image – and ultimately the time it takes to scan the photo, how long it will take to upload/download to or from any website and so on – it is important to choose an appropriate resolution.

## Creating original images

You could create your own images:

* You could use a digital camera to take photographs.

* You could, if you have artistic skills, use graphic software to produce original artwork.

### Using a digital camera

Digital cameras offer the amateur photographer a chance to capture great pictures, while still

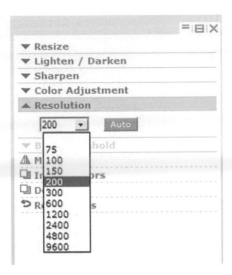

The same image scanned with resolution settings of 12, 75 and 200

**FIGURE 10.20** *Choosing the resolution*

providing the professional photographer with a sophisticated tool for taking shots.

As an amateur, you can make use of the automatic shooting features of a digital camera, or decide upon the settings manually.

If you want to use automatic settings, you must select the appropriate mode and give the camera as much information about your subject as you can.

* You may be offered choices, such as portrait, landscape, sorts (for freezing motion in rapidly moving subjects) or night-time.

* These may be specific scenarios, such as party-time, beach/snow, sunset, dusk/dawn, museum, fireworks and so on.

Each choice made will result in the automatic settings (e.g. for the **aperture** and **shutter speed**).

**Key terms**

The *aperture* is the hole through which light travels into the camera; the larger the aperture, the more light that hits the lens and is transferred to the CCD at the back of the camera.

The *shutter speed* controls the length of time the aperture is open during the shot. The faster the speed, the less time during which light can enter.

The **resolution** that you choose before you take the photo may limit the uses to which your photo can be put.

*Resolution* in a camera is measured in *ppi (pixels per inch)*. Resolution on a screen is measured in *dpi (dots per inch)*.

1 Experiment with using a digital camera to make sure you understand how to operate it and how to upload images to your computer.

2 Decide whether you need any photographs in your multimedia product and, if you do, make sure your design documentation gives full details.

* If the photo is to be printed as a print, 300 dpi should produce an image that looks good enough for the human viewer.

* If the image is to appear on-screen, the dpi could be as low as 75 dpi and still be legible.

The intended use of the photo and the print resolution you need are, therefore, factors to take into account when setting the resolution on your camera.

When you buy a camera, one of its features will be the **megapixel rating**: 2 megapixels, 3 megapixels and so on. The higher the number, in theory, the better quality photos that you can take. However, this also depends on the size of the printed photo and the quality of your printer.

Having taken the photos, you need to transfer them to your computer. There are three main methods, as illustrated in Figure 10.21. Full instructions should be supplied with the camera.

## Using graphics software

If you want to create your own images, you will need to use graphics software.

There are two main types of graphics software:

* painting software to create bitmap images

* drawing software to create vector graphics.

The basic difference between these two types of image is explained on page 175. This section focuses more on how you use graphic software to create the images (i.e. the tools you might use).

A **vector image** comprises lines, shapes and text:

* A **line** can be drawn of a particular style and thickness, and there are a variety of **pens, pencils** and **brush tools** that you can use to draw the line. The path of a line could be a simple straight line, or it could form a closed shape. The line can curve to form an **arc**, and you can make complex shapes such as a **spiral**.

* A variety of **shapes** are available: rectangles, ellipses, polygons, stars. The lines that form the shape can be styled as for any line. You can also control the inside of the shape, filling it or making it see-through.

* **Text** can be used to label an image, and you can control the type (or typeface) and attributes (bold, italic, etc.) of that text. It is also possible to distort the orientation of the characters on a path. This creates an effect similar to that of WordArt.

Bitmap images – sometimes called **raster images** – are based on **pixels** and can be created using text, brush effects and colour fill:

* **Text** is keyed into a text frame. You can control the text font (Arial, Times New Roman, etc.),

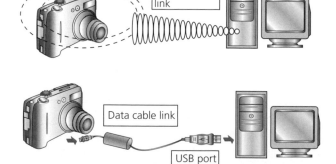

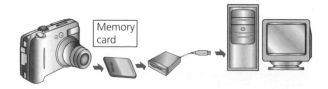

**FIGURE 10.21** *Transferring pictures to your computer*

the point size (10 pt, 12 pt etc.) and attributes such as bold, italic and underline – all from the Text toolbar within Paint.

* In the same way that an artist uses a variety of pencils or pens or **brushes**, with painting software, the toolbox includes a variety of pens and brushes, and a range of widths and effects.

* If you draw a closed shape, you may want to **fill** it with colour.

A bitmap image can be developed and manipulated, pixel by pixel. A vector image is developed component by component, but you can also convert a vector graphic into a bitmap image.

**Think it over...**

What images will you create for your multimedia product? What software might you use?

## Manipulating images

There are three particular tools that this qualification expects you to be able to use: filters; resize and crop; and colour.

    **Filtering** is achieved by creating **adjustment layers**. Each layer then has an effect on the original image, according to your requirements (e.g. to sharpen or blur the image).

**Key terms**

An *adjustment layer* is a layer of pixels, the same size as the original image, but with some effect applied to the RGB values so that, when the two layers are viewed together, an adjustment can be seen.

Figure 10.22 shows how a filter can be applied when an image is scanned in.

**Theory into practice**

1  Find out how to create a new layer in your graphics software.

2  Experiment with using filters to create different effects. Make notes.

3  Compare your findings with others in your group.

The size of an image – its **dimension** – is its height and width. This can be measured in pixels or as a length (e.g. in millimetres). **Resizing an image** can be done by dragging the grab handles until it fits into the required space. Or, if you right-click on an image, the context-sensitive menu will offer **Properties** as an option, and this leads to a dialogue box in which you can specify the size (Figure 10.23).

    **Cropping** an image involves cutting away slices from any side of the image until you are left with the part of the image that you want to retain.

    Figure 10.24 shows a photo taken at Saville Gardens, before and after it has been cropped.

Adjusting the colour here changes the RGB values that are stored after the scan. It may be better to store the original 'raw' data and adjust the colour later, using graphics software rather than the scanning software.

**FIGURE 10.22** *Using a filter when scanning an image*

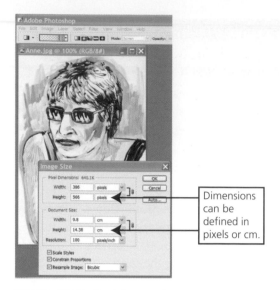

FIGURE 10.23 *Resizing an image*

Dimensions can be defined in pixels or cm.

Cropping a photo can be used to improve the composition, or to remove material that you do not want in the final image.

**Think it over...**

What other ways are there of removing unwanted parts of an image? Consider cloning and masking techniques.

**Theory into practice**

1  Find out how to resize and crop using your graphics software.

2  Experiment with these tools using some of your images. Annotate these images showing what you have done.

What is **colour**? Light is an energy source, comprising rays of different frequencies. In your eye there are colour-sensitive receptors: one sensitive to blue, another to green and another to red. Your brain interprets combinations of these to create any colour in the spectrum. There are two ways of looking at colour on a computer:

✱ The **RGB** method of adding colours is just one way of interpreting colour: the **additive method**. This method is used to produce colour on a VDU screen – there are three colour rays and the combination creates the colours you see.

The cropped version loses the buds (which detract from the main bloom) and fixes the less-than-perfect composition of the original photograph.

A small amount has also been cropped from the left-hand edge to place the image more centrally within the frame.

FIGURE 10.24 *Cropping*

✱ A second method, **CMYK** – called the **subtractive method** – uses filters to cut out colours. This method is used for printing colour on to paper – the layers are overprinted to create the full colour effect.

Figure 10.25 shows both these methods.

**Key terms**

*RGB* stands for red, green, blue; *CMYK* stands for cyan, magenta, yellow, key (black).

There are three terms that are used in graphical software to describe colour:

✱ **Hue** describes a colour – say, red or yellow. It may be shown on a colour wheel.

✱ A **tint** is a global colour with a modified intensity. So, for a colour such as red, there are many tints of red, some brighter, some lighter.

✱ **Saturation** is the vividness of a colour that results from the amount of grey in the colour. It is measured on a scale of 0 (all grey) to 255 (saturated colour). Saturated colours are bright and brilliant; desaturated colours – pastels – are subdued and appear washed out.

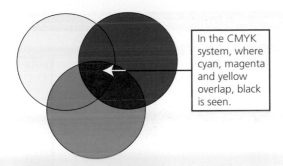

In the CMYK system, where cyan, magenta and yellow overlap, black is seen.

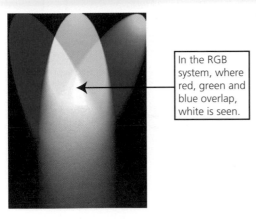

In the RGB system, where red, green and blue overlap, white is seen.

**FIGURE 10.25** *RGB and CMYK*

You can use colour in many ways in your multimedia product. Section 10.5 looks at the effective use of colour (page 162).

Here, you need to think about the tools you will use to create colour:

* The colour of the text within a text box is defined by its **foreground colour**. The background can be set as **opaque** – and then it is defined as the **background colour**. Or, the background can be **transparent**.

* You can apply a **colour wash** to an image, using a filter.

* **Colour inversion** involves replacing each colour by its colour complement. This can create interesting effects.

### Theory into practice

1 Refer to your graphical design documentation. How had you planned to use colour in your multimedia product?

2 Experiment with the colour tools in your graphical software. Annotate your images to show what you have done.

### Knowledge check

1 Explain these terms: bitmap, vector image, pixel, resolution.

2 Why is compression necessary? Distinguish between lossless and lossy data compression methods.

3 Explain these terms: aperture, shutter speed, ppi, dpi, megapixel rating.

4 Distinguish between painting software and drawing software.

5 What are the components of a vector image?

6 What is a raster image?

7 Explain filtering and how adjustment layers are used.

8 Explain two ways of resizing an image.

9 What is cropping?

10 Explain the mechanics and uses of the two colouring systems: RGB and CMYK.

11 Explain these terms: hue, tint, saturation, colour inversion, washing, foreground, background, opaque and transparent.

### Assessment activity

1 Decide what images you will need for your multimedia product. Make sure your design documentation gives full details of the images.

2 Create any images that you need. Make sure you choose an appropriate resolution to match your purpose.

3 Obtain other images (e.g. by scanning), as necessary.

4 Incorporate your images into your multimedia product to create a new prototype.

### Assessment hint

✓ Check that your client is happy with your choice of images.

# 10.8 Video

You may have used a digital camera to take still photos but, unless you plan to create an animation (Section 10.10), you need a video camera to take moving pictures, with or without an audio track.

A video camera is similar to a digital camera. However, instead of just taking still shots, a video camera takes moving pictures too, and there is the option to record a soundtrack as well. The moving picture is not actually moving – it just looks that way when you view it. Frames are taken every 1/30th of a second, so there are 30 frames per second. To the human eye, played back, this looks continuous.

**Think it over...**

Think about how you might incorporate video into your multimedia product.

## Capturing ready-made video clips

If you have a ready-made video clip, how do you incorporate it into your multimedia product?

Figure 10.26 shows how you might incorporate video into a PowerPoint presentation.

## Recording original video clips

The operation of a video camera is very similar to a digital camera: point and click the Start button, using the LCD screen to see what is being captured.

As with taking digital stills, you need to take into account the composition of the images – keeping the subject within frame. However, you also need to allow talking/walking room:

* If the video is of someone talking, he or she may look directly at the camera, but if he or she is looking to one side then the frame should allow space where a speech bubble might appear, to show what he or she is saying.

* Similarly, in an action shot, there must be room in the frame to show where the subject is going.

Choosing suitable lighting is also essential.

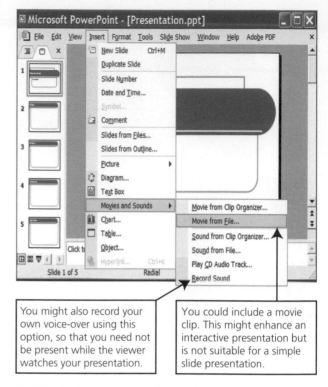

You might also record your own voice-over using this option, so that you need not be present while the viewer watches your presentation.

You could include a movie clip. This might enhance an interactive presentation but is not suitable for a simple slide presentation.

**FIGURE 10.26** *Incorporating video into a PowerPoint presentation*

If you move the video camera slowly the image will not be blurred. Quick movements are to be avoided, though – you might make the viewer giddy – unless, of course, that is your intention (e.g. a bird's-eye view of a helter-skelter ride).

There are various ways to move the video camera:

* **Panning** involves moving the video camera in the horizontal plane: from left to right or right to left.

* **Tilting** involves moving the video camera in the vertical plane: up and down (e.g. focusing on the trunk of a tree and then tilting the camera so you can see the whole tree).

* **Zooming** – as with a digital camera – appears to bring you closer to the subject. **Reverse zoom** – no surprise – is when you appear to move away from the subject.

You can also keep the video camera still and zoom in or out – focusing on a particular subject. Or, combine a zoom with a pan.

To create an interesting video sequence, you need to vary the type of shots that you take:

* A **close-up** is used to home in on the subject, perhaps to show the emotion on the face or to allow the viewer to study the face.

* A **wide shot** – also called an establishing shot or long shot – shows the whole scene. This might be used to establish the location or the people involved in the film.

* A **medium shot** shows less of the scene but more than the close-up. It acts as an intermediate image – because to jump from a wide shot to a close-up would be jarring on the viewer. You may also use this when there are two or three people to include in the shot.

How long you shoot for will depend on the subject matter. If there is lots of action, you may record for as long as 20 seconds. However, since your ultimate aim is to produce a film that holds the attention of the audience, unless it is gripping stuff, you might need to present it interspersed with **cutaway** – or 'over the shoulder' – shots. These are short clips of the presenter or interviewer looking very interested – nodding or shaking the head, smiling or frowning according to what the interviewee is saying. It is called 'over the shoulder' because the cameraman has to be positioned on the interviewee's shoulder, looking towards the interviewer.

You also need to consider using **stationary shots** – i.e. with no movement of the camera – to start and end a sequence and to use transitions between types of shots.

## Editing video clips

In the same way that you can edit images taken on your digital camera, the video can be edited. In fact, it is almost essential to edit the video. It is unlikely that the raw footage is exactly what you planned, or that it will be entertaining enough for the intended audience. However, you can delete frames (the **outtakes**) and reorder the sequence of frames, and splice parts of the video together to create a film sequence in the order you want to show it.

If you recorded on to tape, you will need another tape – a blank one – on which to copy the frames in the sequence you want them to be shown. You will need a log of what is on the raw tape – a description of the shots and how long they are. From this, you can work out the order in which to copy sequences on to the new tape. The editing equipment is attached to two VCRs – one to see the raw footage, the other to see what you have recorded on to the new tape. Then, for each tape, you need to mark where you want to start copying – the **In (insertion) point** – and on the new footage tape, where you want to stop the copying – the **Out point**. When you press Edit, the copying process will start – and you continue doing this for each sequence on the raw footage that is to end up on your final film. The bits you don't use are called **outtakes**.

Digital editing is somewhat simpler. The software provided with the digital video camera allows you to re-sequence the frames and delete frames so that the final sequence is what you want to show the audience. You can also build a film from a number of sequences by splicing them together.

### Theory into practice

1 Watch a video (e.g. of a news broadcast). The presenter may be facing the camera, but the viewer's interest may be maintained by shots being taken from more than one camera. Make notes on what types of shots are used: wide, medium and close up.

2 If you plan to incorporate video into your multimedia product, review your design documentation and make sure your plans are clear to the reader.

### Theory into practice

1 Experiment with using a video camera to record an event. What features does it have, extra to your digital camera?

2 Shoot a video, including sound, for your multimedia product.

3 Edit the video and the soundtrack. Compare your video with others prepared in your group.

# File formats

The multimedia authoring software that you are using to develop your multimedia product will support a range of file types.

When developing a video it is important that the file type is one that will be supported.

Table 10.1 lists a number of file formats.

| EXTENSION | FORMAT |
|---|---|
| .asf | Advanced Systems Format (ASF): an extensible file format that stores synchronised multimedia data. |
| .asx | Advanced Stream Redirector (ASX) files, also known as Windows media metafiles (WMM): text files that provide information about a file stream and its presentation. |
| .avi | Audio Video Interleave (AVI): a special case of RIFF, the .avi file format is the most common format for audio and video data on a computer. It is an example of a *de facto* standard. The audio content or video content that is compressed with a wide variety of codecs can be stored in an avi file. |
| .mp4 | MPEG-4 is an **ISO** specification that covers many aspects of multimedia presentation, including compression, authoring and delivery. The MPEG-4 file format, as defined by the MPEG-4 specification, contains MPEG-4-encoded video and Advanced Audio Coding (AAC)-encoded audio content. It typically uses the .mp4 extension. |
| .wax | Windows Media Audio Redirector (WAX) files: WMM that reference WMA files. |
| .wma | Windows Media Audio (WMA): ASF files that include audio compressed with the WMA codec. |
| .wmd | Windows Media Download (WMD): combines WMP skin borders, playlist information and multimedia content in a single downloadable file that uses a .wmd extension. The package can include a whole album of music videos that also displays advertising in the form of graphical branding and links to an online music retailer website. |
| .wmv | Windows Media Video (WMV): ASF files that include audio, video or both, compressed with WMA and WMV codecs. |
| .wmx | Windows Media Redirector (WMX) files: WMM that reference WMA files, WMV files or both. |
| .wms | Windows Media Player skin (WMS) definition file: an XML text document that defines the elements that are present in a skin, their relationships and their functionality. |
| .wmz | Windows Media Zip (WMZ) file: a compressed Zip archive that contains a WMP skin definition file (.wms) and associated Jscript files (.js) and its supporting graphic files. |
| .wpl | Windows Media Player Playlist (WPL) files: client-side playlists that are written in a proprietary format; .wpl format can create dynamic playlists, whereas .asx and .m3u formats cannot. |
| .wvx | Windows media video redirector (WVX) files: WMM that reference WMV files. |

**TABLE 10.1** *File formats*

The file formats available will depend on the software you are using, including the software platform (PC versus Apple). For example, an Apple computer has a QuickTime file format which lets users create, edit, publish and view multimedia files, and can contain video, animation, graphics, 3D and **VR** content.

However, only QuickTime files version 2.0 or earlier can be played in the Windows Media Player. Later versions of QuickTime require the proprietary Apple QuickTime Player.

Similarly, RealNetworks content is created by software that has been developed by RealNetworks. The content is compressed with proprietary RealVideo and RealAudio codecs, and then stored in a file format developed by RealNetworks. So to play RealNetworks content, you must first obtain the RealOne player.

Indeo Video Files (IVF) are video files that are encoded by using the Indeo codec from the Ligos Corporation; Indeo standards may change frequently so the most up-to-date Indeo package is needed to play these files.

**MPEG** files are files which adhere to an evolving set of standards for video and audio compression.

The MPEG standard permits the coding of progressive video at a transmission rate of about 1.5 million **bps**. The most common implementations of the MPEG-1 standard provide a video resolution of 352 × 240 at 30 **fps**. When you use this standard, you receive a video that is slightly lower quality than typical VCR videos.

In the Microsoft Windows XP Media Center edition, Microsoft introduced the **MDVR** (*.dvr-ms) file format for storing recorded TV content. Similar to *.asf files, *.dvr-ms file enhancements allow key **PVR** functionality, including time-shifting, live pause, and simultaneous record and playback. Video contained in a *.dvr-ms file is encoded as MPEG-2 video stream, and the audio contained in the *.dvr-ms file is encoded as MPEG-1 Layer II audio stream.

Whether you record your own video or source one, the images may be stored on a video tape (a serial medium) or on a DVD (a direct-access medium). The format of the tape is important: it may be 8 mm or VHS (240 lines of resolution), SVHS or Hi-8 (400 lines) or Beta (500 lines). The greater the number of lines, the better quality film – but it has to be compatible with the video camera so, having chosen the camera, you may be limited as to which type of tape can be used.

Videotaped images may be viewed on a video player, but not all types of tape can be viewed on all video players; compatibility is an issue here. DVDs can be viewed on a DVD player, or on your PC.

# 10.9 Sound

Silent movies were wonderful in their day and are still enjoyed by many to this day, but the introduction of sound transformed the entertainment industry.

It is unlikely that your multimedia product cannot be enhanced by including sound. If you decide to use some music and/or a voiceover, you need to be able to source it, manipulate the track, and incorporate it into your multimedia presentation.

## Recording live sound

If you are recording a soundtrack while taking a video sequence, you will need to switch the microphone on. The camera will then record pictures and sound simultaneously.

If you are simply recording a soundtrack using your computer, you need sound-recording software, such as WavePad (Figure 10.27) or, if you are using authoring software such as PowerPoint, you could use the inbuilt **Record Sound** option.

Notice that the controls are identical to those you would find on a 'normal' recorder on a tape deck or a video player.

This software lets you make and edit voice and other audio recordings. You can cut, copy and paste parts of recording and, if required, add effects like echo, amplification and noise reduction.

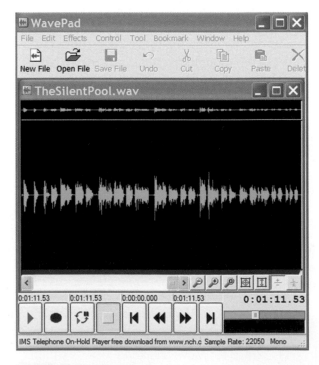

FIGURE 10.27 *WavePad*

## Hardware: microphone

To record sound, you also need some hardware: a microphone. If you are shooting a video and you need to capture what is happening, you have several choices of microphone:

* The microphone might be built into the video camera – in which case it is closer to you than it is to the subject. So, you need to avoid giving instructions to the subject – otherwise that's what will be recorded.

* A very small portable microphone, powered by a battery pack that can be hidden, might be attached to the clothing of the person who is to speak. This 'lavaliere microphone' is often used by television presenters and their guests.

* **Handheld microphones** may be attached to the camera by a long cable, giving flexibility of movement and good quality of sound recording. A handheld microphone may also be wireless – powered by a battery pack.

* The previous three types of microphone may be **omni-directional**, meaning that sound is picked up from all directions. **Shotgun microphones**, by contrast, are designed to pick up sound from a greater distance and from a limited range, so you have to point it at the subject. This type of microphone might be used to record what the referee is saying to a football player when he sends him off.

If you are recording a soundtrack on your computer, you could use the inbuilt microphone but the quality is likely to be poor. Instead, a microphone that connects to the microphone socket should provide good-enough quality.

### Theory into practice

1 Decide what sound you will incorporate into your multimedia product.

2 Investigate your options as to how you will record live sound.

3 Experiment with recording and then check the quality of the recording.

## Selecting and importing pre-recorded sound

You could use a soundtrack that has been pre-recorded. Whichever software you are using, there will be an option to import a sound track. For example, Microsoft's Movie Maker has the option to incorporate a soundtrack. Note, though, that it will not allow you to import material that is copyright protected (Figure 10.28).

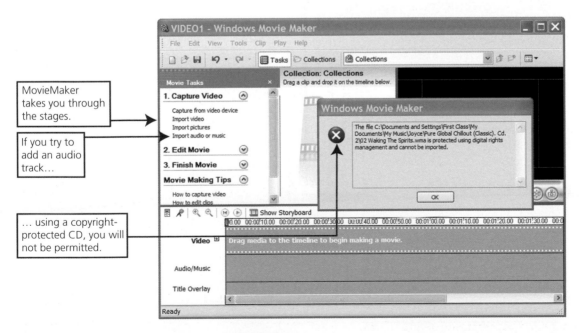

**FIGURE 10.28** *Copyright notice in Movie Maker*

## Manipulating sound

Having sourced the soundtrack, you will probably need to edit it.

### Cut and edit

The sound file is displayed as an envelope, as shown in Figure 10.27. If you click on **Play**, you can listen to the recording. A vertical bar travels across the wave so you can see where you are. If you want to cut a section, listen to see whereabouts it is in the envelope. You can then highlight the section and click on the Cut button.

WavePad allows you to record several tracks; you can copy and paste from one to another, effectively replacing sections of an original recording with new ones. If you fluff your lines you can then patch in a better version, without having to read the whole script again.

### Speed up, slow down and reverse

One of the effects on offer in WavePad is to change the speed of playback.

If you slow the pace down, the pitch of the voice drops; this could be used to disguise the speaker without loss of clarity. If you speed the pace up, the speaker sounds like he or she has gulped on helium!

You can also reverse the sound – although this would not be terribly useful for a voiceover explanation. However, you might use this to create interesting effects with other sources of sounds.

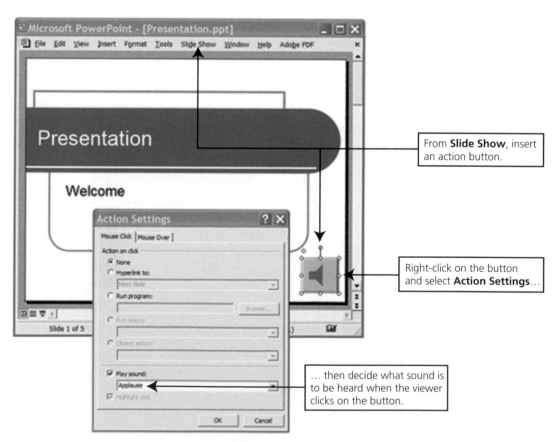

From **Slide Show**, insert an action button.

Right-click on the button and select **Action Settings**…

… then decide what sound is to be heard when the viewer clicks on the button.

FIGURE 10.29 *Assigning sound in PowerPoint*

## Assigning sound to an action or event

If you are developing a product using software like PowerPoint, you can assign a sound to an action (Figure 10.29).

## Selecting and using appropriate file formats

As with image files being compressed in a variety of formats, and video being available in different formats, sound has its own barrage of formats.

Sound is an energy that travels as a wave. When heard or captured electronically, the wave is represented by an envelope (as seen in Figure 10.27). There are a number of different formats used to record sound. It is important to check what formats are supported by the software you are using, to ensure compatibility.

### WAV

The **WAV file format** is used to store sounds as waveforms. One minute of **PCM**-encoded sound can require between 644 KB and 27 MB of storage, depending on the sampling frequency, the type of sound (mono or stereo) and the number of bits that are used for the sample.

**Key terms**

*PCM* stands for pulse code modulation.

Similar to the AVI and ASF format, WAV is only a file container. Audio content that is compressed with a wide variety of **codecs** and that is stored in a .wav file can be played back (for example, using the Windows Media Player), if the appropriate codecs are installed on your computer.

**Key terms**

A *codec* is like a printer driver; it provides information for the computer to interpret the sound files and play them through the sound card using software installed on your computer.

The most common audio codecs that are used in .wav files include **MS ADPCM** and uncompressed PCM.

**Key terms**

*MS ADPCM* stands for Microsoft Adaptive Differential PCM.

### MIDI

**MIDI** is a standard protocol for the interchange of musical information between musical instruments, synthesisers and computers.

**Key terms**

*MIDI* stands for Musical Instrument Digital Interface.

It defines the codes for a musical event: the start of a note, its pitch, length, volume and musical attributes (such as vibrato). It also defines codes for various button, dial and pedal adjustments that are used on synthesisers.

### MP3/MPEG

MPEG files are files which adhere to an evolving set of standards for video and audio compression. See Section 10.8 for more information about this standard.

## Using compression and codecs

Codecs are needed to allow your computer to unpick the sound file and to play the material back to you on your audio player.

They are similar to printer drivers and will be supplied with your hardware or software, or you may need to download them.

To see what codecs are already installed on your computer, look at the Control Panel and select Sounds and Audio Devices. This will confirm the devices that you might use to record and play back sound. Click on the Hardware tab and you will see a list of codecs and devices and drivers (Figure 10.30).

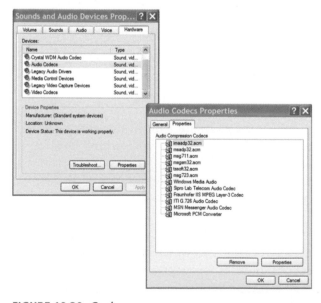

**FIGURE 10.30** *Codecs*

## 10.10 Animation

Animation is used to describe a special visual or sound effect to a text or object.

For example, in PowerPoint (Figure 10.31), you can have text bullet points flying in from one side (called **Entrance**), one word at a time, or hear a sound such as a burst of applause (called **Emphasis**) when a picture is uncovered. You can also have something special happen when one object leaves a slide (called **Exit**). The same features (Entrance, Emphasis and Exit) can be applied to objects such as a table, or elements within a table.

In PowerPoint, the animation options are grouped according to whether they are considered to be subtle, moderate or exciting. You should try these out to check they are not too subtle or too exciting – taking into account your intended audience.

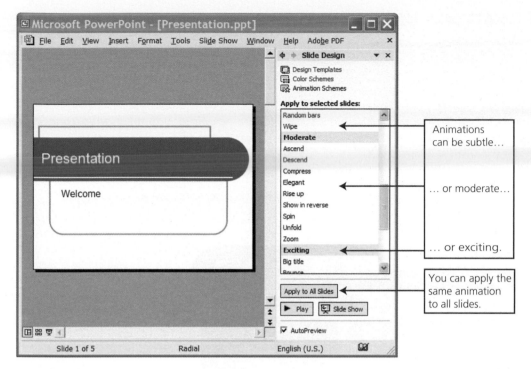

**FIGURE 10.31** *Animation in PowerPoint*

At the other end of the scale, highly sophisticated software, such as Flash, may be used to create special effects.

This section looks at three different types of animation: stop frame (below), tweened (page 193) and animated GIFs (page 193). You will learn how to create animations and use them in appropriate ways in your own multimedia products.

## Stop-motion animation

**Key terms**

*Stop-motion animation* is a series of single shots that give the impression of unaided movement of an inanimate object.

Stop-motion animation is the oldest form of animation. It involves making an inanimate object or model appear to move by taking a series of still, single-frame shots, moving the object or model a small amount between each successive pair of shots.

Stop-motion animation is a technique that has been used to very good effect in films such as the Wallace and Gromit series.

When the finished frames are run together, the illusion of continuous movement is created, and the objects appear to be able to move by themselves. (The hands of the puppeteer must not≈appear in any of the stills!)

There are a number of different stop-motion techniques:

✱ **Pixilation** involves real-life actors, not puppets or inanimate objects. Because the viewer expects continuous smooth motion, the 'moon walking' effect or the jerkiness might be exactly what you want. It was used, for example, in the video of the Peter Gabriel song 'Sledgehammer'.

✱ **Go motion** is like stop motion, except the movement of the inanimate objects is controlled by electric motors. This produces a realistic but blurred motion effect, as seen in *Robocop 2*, released in 1990.

## CASE STUDY

VPTV is an organisation offering services to those needing multimedia products.

1   Visit the VP site (Figure 10.32) and view their showcase to see what can be done (go to www.heinemann.co.uk/hotlinks, insert the express code 2156P and click on this unit).

2   Explore the animation options available in PowerPoint.

3   If you do not already have access to Flash software, visit the Macromedia website and download a trial version of Flash.

4   If you are not already familiar with using Flash, watch the training presentations offered.

5   Consider how you might incorporate animation into your multimedia product.

Editing | Audio | Multimedia | Shoot | Graphics

### MULTIMEDIA

We have experience with a range of computing tools including G4s, G5 and a network of fast PCs. They are used for websites, CD and DVD authoring and digital encoding, 3D design, morphing, PowerPoint presentations. Animation -2D, 3D and Flash. Multilayering, Scanning and output to an A2 full colour inkjet printer. We often have to convert files from one format into another.

MPEG1, MPEG2, MP3, MPEG4, AVI, WMV, Quicktime, AIFFS, WAVS, TIFFS, TARGA, PICT, PSD, GIF, JPEG, BMP, PDF, HDV, SDI, QXP.

Home | About Us | Our team | Showreel | News | Customers | Our Viewpoint | Contact Us

FIGURE 10.32  *VP site*

### Theory into practice

1   Working in pairs: one the model and one the camera operator. Use a tripod to avoid blurring. While the model walks slowly across a space, the camera person takes shots every second or so – at equal time intervals. Use each of these photos as a frame and put them together in a sequence.

2   Put an apple or some other fruit you might choose to eat on a plain surface in front of your camera. To make sure you can position the fruit in the same position for each shot, use Blu-Tac and/or pins to lock the fruit in place. Take the first shot, take a bite, reposition the fruit and take a second shot. Repeat until the fruit is totally eaten! Run the frames together and it will look as if the fruit has been eaten by the Invisible Man.

3   Combine the stop-motion technique with the blur tool in a graphics package to create the illusion of the speedy motion of an inanimate object. Choose your object: a toy car, a toothbrush or some other everyday object. Take a series of shots with the object moving a short distance in front of a fixed camera position. Add blur to some part of each image (e.g. to the wheels of the car or to the head of the toothbrush). Run the frames together and see 'real' motion blur.

4   To learn more about the history of animation and the techniques, visit the Digital Film Archive (go to www.heinemann.co.uk/hotlinks, enter the express code 2156P and click on this unit). Make notes.

## Tweened animation

The process of taking successive photos and moving objects very small distances is extremely time-consuming. If the stills are hand drawn, it is so time-consuming that a team of animators would be needed to complete a project in a sensible time frame. The main animator would draw key frames, and the rest of the team would draw the in-between frames. This led to tweening!

Flash software takes the work out of creating the frames between successive keyframes.

### Key terms

*Tweened animation* involves interpolation between keyframes of both the position and shape of an object.

*Motion tween* involves changes in object position and scale.

*Shape tween* – or *morphing* – involves changes in the object's shape.

The software offers the user options as to the speed of motion or rotation between keyframes (Figure 10.33).

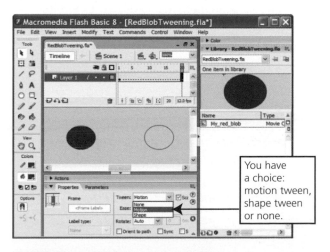

**FIGURE 10.33** *Flash tweening options*

### Theory into practice

1   Use the Internet to find simple but effective examples of tweened animations.

2   Use Flash to create a sample animation.

## Animated GIFs

Animated GIFs are ready-made animations that you can obtain, either free or for a charge, on the Internet.

### Key terms

*GIF* stands for Graphic Interchange Format.

You can download these animated GIFs and store them on your computer for later use.

You can also create your own animations using Flash and choosing GIF as your export file format.

### Theory into practice

1   Visit a website that offers free GIF animations (go to www.heinemann.co.uk/hotlinks, enter the express code 2156P and click on this unit) and explore the animations available.

2   Consider whether you could improve your multimedia product by incorporating one or more such animations.

### Knowledge check

1   Explain these terms: Entrance, Emphasis, Exit.

2   Describe how to create an animation using the stop-frame method.

3   Explain these terms: pixilation, go motion.

4   What is tweening?

5   Explain these terms: motion tween, morphing.

6   What is an animated GIF?

# 10.11  User interface

The user interface is what the user sees of your multimedia product. It is therefore essential that you focus on making the interface as user-friendly as possible for all visitors.

You should aim for accessibility and usability, since both of these factors aim to improve a visitor's experience to the site:

* accessibility focuses on making the website available to a wide user population

* usability focuses on the target audience and aims to make their visit as efficient and effective as possible.

The more you use multimedia products, the better you will understand what is good – and what is not so good – about user interfaces. Your can then incorporate the best designs into your own product. Follow these basic 'rules':

* Use a **consistent layout**. This will enable the user to feel 'at home' very quickly.

* Use **graphics** to illustrate a message. This will cut down the amount of text a user has to read.

* Add **prompts** or messages to help users find their way around. This will be useful support for newcomers to your product.

* Use **interactivity features** to allow users to initiate certain procedures. This will increase the involvement – and enjoyment – of the user.

The user interface should be high on your list of considerations at every stage of development:

* Your functional specification will have identified the intended audience (see Section 10.2, page 144).

* During the design process, you will have built in user-friendly navigation devices (as described in Section 10.4, page 155).

* Your user documentation (page 158) will further support the user, but any on-screen help will ensure your product is even more user-friendly.

* Then, in the graphical design, you will have the user in the forefront of your mind, making effective use of colour (page 162), taking care with layout (page 164) and choosing fonts carefully (page 165).

* You will have incorporated the most appropriate interactive use elements (page 170), such as buttons, hotspots and text links. You will have chosen appropriate response methods (page 174), such as text boxes, radio buttons and checkboxes.

# 10.12 Testing

Having absorbed the content of Sections 10.5–10.11, and having designed the most wonderful graphical design, planned your interactivity and then captured images, and combined them with video, sound – and added a dash of animation – you should have a vast range of options available to you in developing your multimedia product.

However, no amount of flashy graphics and interactive features is of any use if the product does not work properly. Indeed, video, sound, animation and graphics should only have been included if they have a purpose, not just because they are pretty!

How can you ensure it will work – from an early stage in the development process? Answer: prototyping. Section 10.3 introduced the idea of prototyping (page 154).

> **✳ Remember!**
>
> It is essential to involve others in the testing process. The most effective way of testing any product is to ask others to use it.

## Formative testing

Testing is a vital part of the process if you are to produce a fully working product.

One of the advantages of prototyping is that you can carry out **formative testing** as you develop your product.

> **Key terms**
>
> During development, *formative testing* is used to check that a product works; the outcomes of testing are used to decide how to improve the product.

You will need to provide evidence of how the product develops. This will include the initial design, prototypes at various stages and, of course, the finished product.

Managing your prototypes and keeping evidence of feedback from users, and what changes will be made as a result, is therefore a skill that you will need to learn.

The design of the user interface will require careful consideration, so you might focus your testing plan on this aspect of the product.

However, you should also check every component to ensure it matches your original specification. This might be in terms of graphical design, accuracy of content and the synchronisation of the various multimedia: images, sounds, animations and video.

## Summative testing

You should also undertake **summative testing** when you think you have finished.

> **Key terms**
>
> *Summative testing* looks back over what you have done. The outcomes of this testing are not used to change the end product.

Summative testing involves asking yourself questions:

✳ Does the product meet all the requirements listed in the functional specification?

✳ Do all the interactive features work correctly?

✳ Does every link go where it should with no dead ends?

✳ Is the product robust? Or can it be made to fail?

✳ Can other people use the product without help?

✳ What do people think about it in terms of design, layout, etc?

✳ How effectively do the various components that you have chosen to include in your multimedia work together? The images, sound tracks, animation and video sequences?

## Assistance

You are entitled to have assistance in producing your multimedia product. However, the level of assistance will affect the marks that can be awarded for this:

✶ If your product works, but you needed some assistance to reach this stage, your mark will fall within mark band 1.

✶ If you had occasional prompting but produced a fully working, easy-to-use product, you will raise your mark into band 2.

✶ If you worked independently and produced an attractive, fully working and easy-to-use multimedia product, your mark should be in band 3.

Therefore, the more independent you are, the better.

### Knowledge check

1  What is formative testing?
2  What is summative testing?
3  Why is feedback important when testing a product?

### Assessment activity

1  Test your multimedia product to ensure that it is fully working. Make notes of the outcomes.
2  Provide evidence of both formative and summative testing.
3  Obtain feedback and show how you have used this to improve your product.

### Assessment hint

✓ Be thorough and systematic in your testing.

# 10.13 Distribution

### CASE STUDY

Topic Training have found that, while they can produce all-singing, all-dancing multimedia products that meet the needs of their clients, few have the bandwidth capability to deliver the product on an intranet. By far the most successful way of distributing these training materials is on a CD.

1  Look again at the Topic Training website (go to www.heinemann.co.uk/hotlinks, insert the express code 2156P and click on this unit) and look at the products they create. Make notes.

2  Also look at their portfolio of typical assignments. Compare these with your own plans.

The software that you use to create your multimedia product may be specialist multimedia authoring software. You may also use a range of other software to create the individual components:

✶ For your e-portfolio materials, you will most probably have used the PDF format for paper-based publications.

✶ For images, your files may be .jpg or .png.

✶ For on-screen publications, you may have .html files.

✶ For animations, such as those created in Flash, you may have .swf files.

These file formats, while appropriate for product creation, are not suitable for viewing purposes. The user may or may not have appropriate software, and there are also issues of security to consider.

### Think it over...

In what ways do software providers protect their products?

Some software, like PowerPoint Viewer and Adobe Acrobat Reader, can be obtained free of charge. So, if you supply your product in a format that requires this software, you can also provide a link to the websites that offer a free download, just in case your user does not already have this software installed.

## Run-time software

If you use software like Microsoft PowerPoint to develop a presentation, the user needs the same software to view the **run-time version** of the product. Since PowerPoint is part of the standard package for many users, this should not cause problems.

> ### Key terms
> The *run-time version* of a product is the version the user is given.

The software that the user needs to view your product is more likely to be completely different from the software you use to develop it:

* A webmaster may use Dreamweaver to create a website. Users may access the site using a browser such as Internet Explorer.

* You may present your product as a **PDF** file, requiring the user to have Adobe's Acrobat Reader – or one of their more advanced products – to be able to view your product.

> ### Key terms
> *PDF* stands for Portable Document Format.

## Distribution medium

Once you have decided how the user will view the product, you can think about a method of distribution. If the user is expected to be able to run the program independently of the software used to create it, this will mean that you can distribute the product on a portable storage medium such as a CD or memory stick.

## Security issues

To protect your product from the user, it may be necessary to customise it so as to prevent the user changing the product. For some products, it might also be sensible to prevent the user finding out how it is produced, and thus stealing the code.

The file formats appropriate for product distribution are the read-only formats which allow the viewer to see, but not change, anything.

## Multimedia file formats

For multimedia products, there are also some special formats you should be aware of, such as **ASF**.

> ### Key terms
> *ASF* stands for Advanced Systems Format.

ASF is an extensible file format that stores synchronised multimedia data. It supports advanced multimedia capabilities, including extensible media types, component download, scalable media types, author-specified stream prioritisation, multiple language support and extensive bibliographic capabilities that include document and content management:

* ASF files that contain audio content compressed with the **WMA** codec normally use the .wma extension.

* ASF files that contain audio content, video content or both, compressed with WMA and **WMV** codecs, normally use the .wmv extension.

* Content that is compressed with any other codec normally uses the generic .asf extension.

> ### Key terms
> *WMA* stands for Windows Media Audio;
> *WMV* stands for Windows Media Video.

# 10.14  Evaluation

Evaluation falls into two distinct types: your product and how you went about developing the product.

## Evaluating a product

The starting point for any evaluation of a software development project is the functional specification. This lists what the software has to do, and the key question to answer is how well your solution meets the requirements.

For this qualification you are expected to produce a working multimedia product. The marks you earn will depend on how well it works.

If you can answer 'yes' to these questions, your mark will be in mark band 1:

∗ Does it meet *most* of the functional requirements?

∗ Does it fall short in any way?

∗ How effective is the solution?

∗ Did you make *appropriate* use of *some* of the facilities of the software?

If your product is fully working, easy to use and meets *all* the functional requirements and you have made *good* use of the facilities of the software, you could expect your marks to be higher – in band 2.

Work that bit harder so that the product meets *all* the functional requirements, communicates effectively and is easy to use – and show that you have made full and efficient use of the facilities of the software – and your marks should be in band 3.

One question you might ask yourself is 'Have I produced something that stands out from the crowd?' If your answer is 'yes', you can congratulate yourself.

## Evaluating your own performance

It is important to be able to assess your own performance on a project critically. This does not mean finding fault with everything you have done or being overly pessimistic about your abilities. Instead, you need to take a long hard look at your strengths and weaknesses, as shown up during the development of this multimedia product.

How can you judge your performance? Well, ask yourself these questions, and be as truthful as you can:

∗ What did I do well?

∗ What could I have done better?

The answers to these simple questions may help you to determine your current level of competence, and identify areas for improvement and future training needs.

## Writing up the evaluation

You are aiming for a well-rounded evaluation – incorporating feedback from others – that critically assesses your multimedia product and your own performance. Make sure that your evaluation includes meaningful evaluative comments about your solution and sensible comments about your own performance:

∗ To what extent does your final multimedia product meet the specified requirements? Fully explain any shortcomings.

∗ How effective is your solution? Include some well-thought-out suggestions for enhancements.

✱ How good was your own performance throughout the project? Include a realistic assessment of your current skill level and identify areas for improvement.

Your documentation must show that you have made some improvements to the initial design as a result of prototyping. You therefore need to provide some explanatory evaluative comments for each prototype in terms of how well it meets the specified requirements (i.e. in terms of fitness for purpose/audience).

It will add weight to your evaluation if you show clearly how feedback from test users was used to shape and refine the design.

Finally, you will need to suggest ways in which you could improve your own performance, and identify any future training needs.

## Assessment activity

1 Refer back to each of your prototypes.

2 List any shortcomings, and explain how they could be implemented.

3 Consider the effectiveness of your solution and make suggestions for improvements.

## Assessment hint

✓ Check that you have written evaluative comments for each one. Also check that you have shown how any feedback was acted upon when developing the next prototype.

## UNIT ASSESSMENT

1 Establish a set of functional requirements for a multimedia product. Write a functional specification that describes the purpose, audience and context for the product and explains what it is required to do.

2 Design and produce a product to meet these functional requirements. Make sure that your product combines multimedia components – both ready-made and original information, and include evidence of your use of prototyping to improve and refine your design.

3 Test your product to make sure that it works properly. Write supporting documentation for users, and produce evidence of formative and summative testing.

4 Evaluate the multimedia product, as well as your own performance and current skill level.

# Using spreadsheet software

Spreadsheet software provides a versatile and powerful decision-making tool. With it you can create spreadsheet models to investigate alternative options and to identify the best course of action.

In *Unit 3: The knowledge worker* you saw spreadsheets being used as a modelling tool. This unit looks again at similar spreadsheet applications, but in this unit you will learn the skills and techniques needed to design and create technically complex spreadsheets.

This optional unit contains 12 elements:

11.1    Spreadsheet applications

11.2    Functional specification

11.3    Spreadsheet design

11.4    Processing

11.5    Layout and presentation

11.6    Data entry and validation

11.7    Future-proofing

11.8    Presentation of results

11.9    Testing

11.10   Documentation

11.11   Evaluation

11.12   ICT skills

# Introduction

Unit 3 introduced spreadsheets for use as a modelling tool. This unit again considers spreadsheet applications, but here you will learn the skills and techniques required to design and create more complex spreadsheets. You will be given a scenario and brief to work from, which will enable you to demonstrate your competence in producing a spreadsheet solution.

Having established the functional requirements, you will then develop your solution, carrying out **formative evaluation and testing** throughout its development. You will seek and make use of feedback from others to help you in your work.

Your work for this unit will culminate in a spreadsheet capable of analysing, interpreting and communicating complex data.

**Key terms**

*Formative evaluation and testing:* if you learn from the evaluation and testing, and these processes then help you to improve your work, this is called formative testing. Evaluation and testing carried out during the development allow time for you to implement change and to produce a better end-product.

The **summative evaluation** of your work for this unit will include a self-assessment of your current skill levels and an indication of what else you need to know or be further able to do to enhance your ability to produce and use complex spreadsheets.

**Key terms**

*Summative evaluation* looks back over what you have done; it may help you to do better on the next project, but it is too late to make changes to this one.

This unit builds on the spreadsheet knowledge and skills you acquired in *Unit 3: The knowledge worker*. The production of a complex spreadsheet model could be used as the focus for *Unit 8: Managing ICT projects*.

The standard ways of working (see the Introduction) should be adopted in this unit, as in all other units.

## Resources required in this unit

You will need access to the Internet to carry out research (for example, to visit the Edexcel site) and to check the details of the specification for this unit.

Your e-portfolio of work must be constructed so that its contents can be accessed using fifth-generation, or equivalent, web browsers, such as Microsoft Internet Explorer version 5 or Netscape version 5, and be in a format appropriate for viewing at a resolution of 1,024 × 768 pixels.

It must submitted in one of the approved file formats specified by Edexcel and, at the end of the designated examination period, you will be expected to transfer your work to a location designated by your tutor (as instructed by Edexcel). The computer system that your centre uses will therefore need to support the formats specified and have the facility to upload folders of your work to the required location.

## How you will be assessed

This user-focused unit is internally assessed. Most of the marks available for this unit are for practical, hands-on activities, involving the design and development of a technically complex and fully working spreadsheet.

> **✱ Remember!**
>
> According to Edexcel's specification:
>
> A **complex spreadsheet** is likely to include features, such as auto-starting, a start-up screen, multiple related sheets, validated forms controls for input, look-ups, date functions, some statistical or database functions...

So, although you need to learn the terminology and understand the concepts, your final marks will depend mostly on the quality of your spreadsheet solution.

The product must have a clear purpose, and you are advised to choose one that will be sufficiently complex in nature to challenge your expertise and encourage you to develop new skills and techniques en route to producing a fully functional solution. You will be presented with a scenario – one that provides sufficient scope for you to be able to demonstrate your ability to design and produce spreadsheet solutions.

You will produce an e-portfolio as evidence of your design, development and evaluation of a spreadsheet solution. Your e-portfolio will include several sections:

* The **functional specification** will describe the purpose, audience and context for the spreadsheet solution and explain what it is required to do.

* To show the solution that you propose to develop, your e-portfolio will include an **initial design** that satisfies the functional requirements.

* To provide **evidence of prototyping**, and how you have used it to improve and refine the design, you should include selected intermediate non-working versions of the prototype, showing how the spreadsheet solution was developed and refined. You might also include notes on feedback obtained, plus your formative test results, and the changes that were made as a result of this.

* To show that you have produced a fully working spreadsheet solution, your e-portfolio will include a **final version**, with supporting **user instructions** and **technical documentation**.

* Your e-portfolio must include evidence of **formative testing** and **evaluation**, and of **summative testing**. Your evaluation will assess the spreadsheet solution and your own performance and current skills level.

## How high can you aim?

The knowledge and skills developed in this user-focused unit will be particularly relevant to those who plan to use advanced ICT skills on a daily basis. You should therefore aim to raise your skill levels to the point where you are confident in your use of ICT at work or at school/college for personal, social and work-related purposes.

It is not essential that you undertake work experience. However, you may benefit from seeing and – ideally – gaining hands-on experience of a wide range of spreadsheet applications.

## Ready to start?

This unit builds on the knowledge and skills you acquired in *Unit 3: The knowledge worker*. Before you start, read back through your notes for that unit, and refresh your knowledge.

This unit should take you 60 hours to complete. Why not keep a log of your time?

# 11.1 Spreadsheet applications

Spreadsheets are used in all sorts of contexts for tasks involving the analysis and interpretation of complex numerical data.

In this section, you will look at and – if at all possible – get hands-on experience of some real-world applications of spreadsheets.

When studying existing spreadsheet designs, to help you when designing your own, make a note of any good design features you encounter. Notice also things that you would avoid.

In particular, for each of the spreadsheets considered here, think about these issues:

* What are the inputs to the system?
* What methods are used to validate the incoming data?
* What processing takes place?
* How is information presented?

## Uses of spreadsheets

Spreadsheets can be used as models to simulate a real-life situation and to forecast what might happen in the future. As is shown in the next section, all three uses (modelling, simulation and forecasting) may be found in a particular application of a spreadsheet.

### Modelling

> **Key terms**
>
> *Modelling* involves finding parallels between the real world and some modelling tool, such as a spreadsheet.

In all the examples that follow, modelling is used in that the spreadsheet models a real-life situation.

The rows (say) can be used to list the variables that relate to a situation, and the columns (say) reflect the passing of time, for example.

The cells are allocated to contain relevant data and to show the results of any calculations.

Some values are fixed; others will change. Some will depend on other values within the spreadsheet.

The formulas that are used reflect current thinking on the 'rules' that apply in real life. For some formulas, there is no debate. The cost of a product including VAT can be calculated with a degree of certainty. The effect on future sales of a price increase, though, might be based on past experience but, at best, is an educated guess.

Having set up a model, it can then be used to simulate a situation and to forecast what might happen, given certain circumstances.

### Simulation

Spreadsheet models can be used to simulate a situation and to see what would happen if something changed in a particular way. These are sometimes called 'what if?' investigations.

Essentially, the model is set up, then particular variables are changed, just to see the knock-on effect of this on the outcomes.

> ## CASE STUDY
>
> The Teaching with Technology website explains how a teacher of economics wanted to teach economies of scale. The site offers as an example a simulation of a bakery – and the effect of baking more or fewer loaves.
>
> 1   Visit the Teaching with Technology site (go to www.heinemann.co.uk/hotlinks, insert the express code 2156P and click on this unit) and read about how the simulation was set up. Download the spreadsheet and study the formulas used.
>
> 2   Explore the Internet for more examples of using spreadsheets for simulation purposes.
>
> 3   For one particular spreadsheet, identify the inputs to the system and the methods used to validate the data.

## Forecasting

Forecasting is inherently difficult. How can you possibly tell what is going to happen in the future? The answer is: you can't. But you can make an educated guess if you have sufficient information about how things have worked out in the past, and have the tools to process this data.

You can take a measurement today and, if you have a formula that you think will work, you can calculate the values for tomorrow, the day after and so on. Then, as time passes, you can check the accuracy of your forecasts and amend your model – the formulas that you used – until they more accurately forecast the future.

A spreadsheet is useful for forecasting, not least because it will do all the calculations for you. Each new row (or column) can be used to represent the next day (or some other time interval).

### CASE STUDY

If you decide to invest in a pension, the pension company has to give you a forecast of what the pension will be worth when you eventually reach pensionable age.
The pension provider cannot forecast the interest rates for the next month, let alone the many years to come. So, they (usually) provide three forecasts. One assumes lower interest rates than the current interest rate, one the same and one higher. You can then see how much – or how little – pension you might receive.

1  Visit the Matt H. Evans website (go to www.heinemann.co.uk/hotlinks, insert the express code 2156P and click on this unit) and look for the bond valuation example. Download the spreadsheet and study how it is set up.

2  At the same site, look for the spreadsheet that analyses the lease/purchase decision for a new car. Download this spreadsheet and look at the formulas used. Notice also the layout used.

## Examples of spreadsheet applications

Spreadsheet models may be used in many different applications. Here, four are considered: statistical analysis, cost-benefit analysis, budgeting and planning.

Each one involves the setting up of a model, some simulation and forecasting.

### Statistical analysis

To make sense of a lot of numeric data, statistical analysis can provide insights into trends to arrive at **representative values**.

### Key terms

*Representative values* are single values that represent many items of data, such as means, modes and medians, and other statistical values.

To design spreadsheets for statistical analysis requires considerable knowledge of statistics, and the formulas can be complex. Using them, though, once the model has been set up, should be easy if the user interface has been well designed.

### Cost-benefit analysis

Cost-benefit analysis is a relatively simple and widely used technique for deciding whether to make a change. You simply add up the value of the benefits of a course of action and subtract the costs associated with it. If the benefits outweigh the costs you go ahead. Simple!

Costs may be one-off or may be ongoing. Benefits, however, are most often received over time. It is important to build this effect of time into any analysis by calculating a **payback period**.

### Key terms

The *payback period* is the time it takes for the benefits of a change to repay its costs.

Many companies look for payback over a specified period of time (say, five years). In its simplest form, cost-benefit analysis is carried out using only financial costs and financial benefits. For example, a simple cost-benefit analysis of a road scheme would measure the cost of building the road and would subtract this from the economic benefit of improving transport links. It would not measure either the cost of environmental damage or the benefit of quicker and easier travel to work.

A more sophisticated approach to cost-benefit analysis is to try to put a financial value on these intangible costs and benefits. This can be highly subjective:

* How, for example, do you put a price on a copse that is home to rare butterflies but lies in the way of a planned motorway (i.e. its environmental importance)?

* And for the motorist, what value can be put on stress-free travel to work?

## Budgeting

In most organisations, there are budgets for planned expenditure and each department is expected to work within the budgeted amount. There are also budgets for income, and the sales force will be given targets to meet these budgeted amounts.

Budgets are used extensively in planning. They can help an organisation to establish the most efficient use of resources. They also provide a focus and discipline for those involved:

* **Flexible budgets** take account of changing business conditions.

* **Operating budgets** are based on the everyday activities of the organisation.

* **Objective-based budgets** are driven by the objective of the organisation.

* **Capital budgets** plan the relationship between capital spending and liquidity (cash) in the organisation.

If the actual figures are different from the budgeted figures, this is called **variance**:

* positive variance is when the actual figures are less than planned

* negative variance is when the actual figures are more than planned.

Any spreadsheet used for budgeting will show budgeted income and expenditure – and the actual figures. Then management can see where the problems, if any, lie.

The calculations for a budget will be done within a spreadsheet, but the presentation of the results is more likely to be a table of data or a chart. Section 11.8 considers how best to present such information to the reader.

## CASE STUDY

Guildford Borough Council publish their budget annually and this report is available online in a section that relates to council tax. Other councils, and the government, too, publish budget information on the Internet.

1  Look on the Internet for information about your own local council's budget. Notice how the budget information is presented.

2  Create a budget for yourself. Incorporate any income and your planned expenditure over the next month. During the month, keep a record of your expenditure. Compare your actual figures against your budgeted figures and use this variance information to create a new budget for the next period of time.

## *Planning*

Planning is an essential management function:

∗ Having information about what has been promised in the way of orders can help an organisation to plan production so that customers' expectations are met.

∗ Keeping track of invoices that have been issued and knowing when they might be paid, plus what purchases have been made and when these are due to be paid, is the task of finance staff. Having this information can help the finance staff to identify cash-flow problems before they happen. This foreknowledge allows time to arrange loans, or to put surplus funds into a high-interest account.

### Knowledge check

1  What is modelling?

2  Give *two* examples of representative values that might appear in a spreadsheet providing statistical analysis.

3  Explain these terms: cost-benefit analysis, payback period.

4  Give *one* example of an intangible cost, and *one* example of an intangible benefit.

5  Give *one* example of how a spreadsheet model can be used to simulate a real-life situation.

6  What information is needed to make a forecast?

7  How can setting up a budget help an organisation?

8  In a budget, what is meant by variance?

9  Give *two* examples of how a spreadsheet can be used for planning purposes.

## Assessment activity

You will be given a scenario and brief to work from, and will be expected to design and develop a fully working spreadsheet solution to the problem presented to you.

1  Study the scenario. Identify any terms that are unfamiliar to you and find out what they mean.

2  Read the scenario many times over and try to absorb the detail. Underline or highlight what you consider to be important information.

## Assessment hint

✓ Make notes on any questions that you might need to ask, or decisions you might need to make. You do not need the answers, nor to make the decisions, right now, but it will help you later if you have recorded all your initial thoughts at this stage.

Redhouse use Microsoft Excel to keep track of orders and to plan a work schedule. Orders are recorded in a spreadsheet (Figure 11.1), with details of the customer, the item of furniture ordered, the delivery arrangements and how payment will be made. The spreadsheet can then be used to track the progress of an individual order. It can also be used to schedule work and to identify priorities for those working in the studio.

What needs to leave the studio in the next few days?

1   Visit the Redhouse website (go to www.heinemann.co.uk/hotlinks, enter the express code 2156P and click on this unit) to learn some background information about the organisation.

2   What products do Redhouse manufacture and sell?

3   In what other ways might Redhouse use spreadsheets?

The Redhouse bed-tracker spreadsheet records details of all orders.

This screenshot displays only non-confidential details. Some columns (e.g. B, C, E and F) have been hidden. Others have been made narrow so the data will not display (e.g. columns S and T).

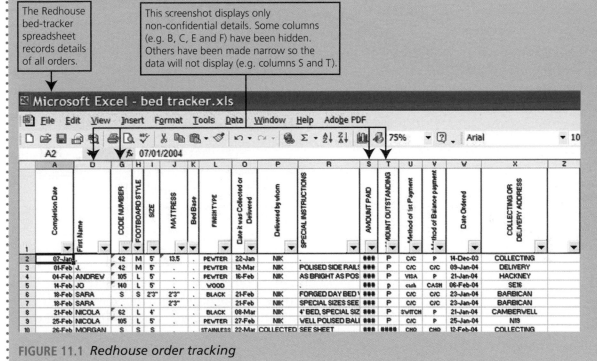

**FIGURE 11.1** *Redhouse order tracking*

# 11.2 Functional specification

A functional specification puts into writing what is needed. What is the problem and what is required by way of a solution? It explains what you are aiming to achieve:

* What is the context of the problem?
* What is the nature of the problem?
* What task(s) do you want the spreadsheet to perform?
* How you will judge the effectiveness of your solution?

For this qualification, you will be presented with a scenario and need to design and develop a technically complex fully working spreadsheet solution to meet the needs as outlined in the scenario. This section considers what you will include in the functional specification, and how you will use it during the development process.

## The functional specification report

The functional specification report presents written documentation of the proposed spreadsheet solution. Much of it will be written in a standard report style, with single paragraphs allocated to answer specific questions:

* What is the context of the problem? Background information is useful; this is considered in some detail later in this section.

* What is the nature of the problem? Understanding what is required is essential, and this is covered below.

* What task(s) do you want the spreadsheet to perform? Having identified the problem, a number of tasks can be identified, as explained later in this section.

You will produce printouts of the data in your worksheets, and also of the formulas used.

### Think it over...

What other forms of evidence might you include in your e-portfolio?

## What is the context?

The spreadsheet you are to develop will fall into one or more of the categories discussed in Section 11.1. You will be creating a model to solve a problem:

* Does your solution represent a simulation? If so, what is the real-life situation? Why is a simulation needed?

* Are you attempting to forecast something? If so, what data will be used for input? How will you process that data? And how will you present your findings?

* Will your solution involve some statistical analysis? What representative values, if any, need to be calculated?

* Will you be presenting a cost-benefit analysis? If so, identify the costs and the benefits, and the timescales involved.

* Will your solution focus on budgeting issues? If so, what time period does the budget cover? What parameters will be used to create the budget? What graphical means might you use to present your findings?

* Does you solution provide a planning tool? If so, how can you best structure the spreadsheet to incorporate the constraints?

### CASE STUDY

You might use a spreadsheet to help you to plan this project. As explained in *AS Level for Edexcel Applied ICT* (page 174), you could set up a Gantt chart (as in Figure 11.2) showing each stage of the project.

1   Check the scenario for the option to include a Gantt chart or some other planning tool within your solution.

2   Consider using a Gantt chart to keep track of the progress of your development of your spreadsheet solution.

When writing up your functional specification, make sure the context of the problem is clear. You may be able to glean much of the wording from the text of the scenario – but edit this to make it your own.

## What problem is to be solved?

The scenario will explain the situation and you will need to decide what the problem is, then write about it in your functional specification.

Problems tend to fall into distinct types:

* Data-entry errors have been made in the past and must be avoided.

* Mistakes in the calculations of formula $X$ result in inaccurate information being output.

* Accurate and reliable information is required to prevent $X$ or $Y$ happening again.

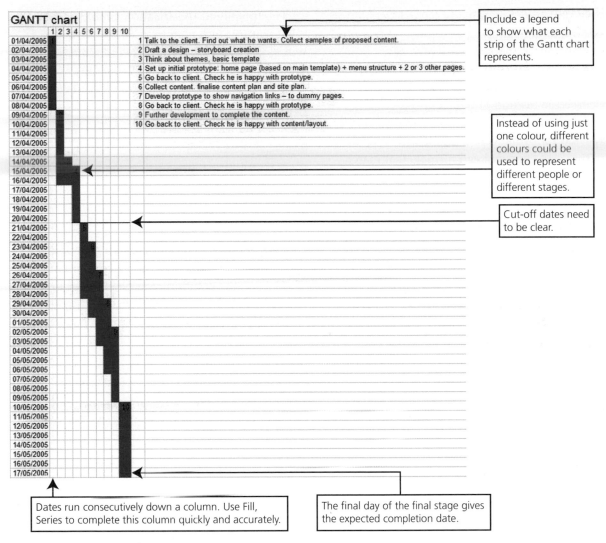

The chart shows:

| GANTT chart | 1 | 2 | 3 | 4 | 5 | 6 | 7 | 8 | 9 | 10 | | | |
|---|---|---|---|---|---|---|---|---|---|---|---|---|---|
| 01/04/2005 | | | | | | | | | | | 1 | Talk to the client. Find out what he wants. Collect samples of proposed content. |
| 02/04/2005 | | | | | | | | | | | 2 | Draft a design – storyboard creation |
| 03/04/2005 | | | | | | | | | | | 3 | Think about themes, basic template |
| 04/04/2005 | | | | | | | | | | | 4 | Set up initial prototype: home page (based on main template) + menu structure + 2 or 3 other pages. |
| 05/04/2005 | | | | | | | | | | | 5 | Go back to client. Check he is happy with prototype. |
| 06/04/2005 | | | | | | | | | | | 6 | Collect content. finalise content plan and site plan. |
| 07/04/2005 | | | | | | | | | | | 7 | Develop prototype to show navigation links – to dummy pages. |
| 08/04/2005 | | | | | | | | | | | 8 | Go back to client. Check he is happy with prototype. |
| 09/04/2005 | | | | | | | | | | | 9 | Further development to complete the content. |
| 10/04/2005 | | | | | | | | | | | 10 | Go back to client. Check he is happy with content/layout. |

Callouts:
- Include a legend to show what each strip of the Gantt chart represents.
- Instead of using just one colour, different colours could be used to represent different people or different stages.
- Cut-off dates need to be clear.
- Dates run consecutively down a column. Use Fill, Series to complete this column quickly and accurately.
- The final day of the final stage gives the expected completion date.

FIGURE 11.2 *A Gantt chart*

* Managers need to be given visual representations of the data so that they can gain an immediate impression of the trends.

* People new to the system need more guidance while using the software.

**Think it over...**

What other problems might you be faced with?

The scenario may have more than one problem that needs to be resolved. When writing up the functional specification, look at the problem from all points of views: the manager, the workers and so on.

## What tasks are needed in the solution?

Your solution will be a technically complex spreadsheet. The qualification lists the ICT skills needed (as in Table 11.2) so you can expect these skills – or a subsection of them – to be called into play.

Each of these skills is introduced in the body of this section and is covered in more depth in later sections.

You will be expected to combine complex information and link this to other applications, as described in Section 11.4. You will need to be able to organise the data – e.g. using linked sheets (Section 11.6) and LOOKUP tables (Section 11.4).

Some skills you will already have, like entering and editing data (e.g. using absolute and relative cell referencing). Others may involve new techniques, like inserting data into multiple cells simultaneously, and using multiple worksheets, as discussed in Section 11.6.

To assist the user as much as possible, you will be expected to format cells – e.g. using conditional formatting and choosing cell formats that match the data format.

You will use functions and formulas to solve complex problems. You will validate and check data, using formulas to determine valid entries for cells.

In the analysis and interpretation of data, you may use PivotTables and data maps, and may add messages to data as appropriate.

When presenting information, you will choose appropriate views and PivotTable reports, and select from a range of different types of graphs and charts – to suit the data.

You will use various means to limit access to the spreadsheet and thus protect it (e.g. hiding and protecting cells).

And, to make the spreadsheet solution as user-friendly as possible, you will customise and automate it – e.g. setting up templates, writing macros, designing forms and creating menus.

As you are working through the development of your spreadsheet solution, refer to Table 11.2 on page 255 to check your competency in each skill. Make sure also that your documentation provides evidence of these skills.

## Using the functional specification as a tool

The functional specification tends to be written at the start of a project. However, things change, so it makes sense to review it and amend it as time passes. Also, in a real-life project, as the dialogue between you and your client continues, you may understand more fully what it is that the spreadsheet must do and be able to specify these requirements more exactly.

The functional specification should identify what features you plan to develop. However, it will also – by default – specify the **scope** of your spreadsheet solution (i.e. the boundaries of the problem) and, hence, what your spreadsheet solution will not do!

### Think it over...

Look back at the notes you made about the scenario. Is it clear what your spreadsheet solution will not cover?

One important benefit of having a functional specification to refer to is that, while you are developing the solution, you need never lose sight of your goals. And when you have completed the spreadsheet, you have a yardstick to measure it against.

### Think it over...

What criteria might apply to all spreadsheets? List some that are generic. List some that apply only to certain types of spreadsheet solution.

### Knowledge check

1  Why is it important to be aware of the context of a problem?

2  List the issues that might be addressed in the functional specification.

3  What is a Gantt chart?

4  How can the functional specification be used during the development of your spreadsheet?

### Assessment activity

1  For the spreadsheet solution that you plan to develop, write the functional specification.

2  List the tasks that the spreadsheet is expected to do.

3  Write evaluative criteria that you can use when the spreadsheet has been developed, as a measure of your success in completing this project.

# 11.3 Spreadsheet design

As with any product, your spreadsheet solution can only be as good as the original design. There is almost certainly more than one way of meeting the requirements. So, the more time and thought you put into what you intend to do, the better you will be able to use your time during development, and the better your solution could be as a result of this efficient use of your resources.

Designing a solution involves making lots of decisions:

✳   How will the spreadsheet be structured? How many worksheets will there be? This is part of the data model, discussed in this section.

✳   What data entry and validation are needed? This is covered in Section 11.6.

✳   What processing is needed? What functions and formulas will be incorporated? This aspect is covered in Section 11.4.

✳   How will you lay out the data and present any results? This is covered in Section 11.5.

✳   How can you design the spreadsheet so as to future-proof the solution? This essential aspect is covered in Section 11.7.

✳   What testing will you do? This is introduced later in this section but is dealt with in more detail in Section 11.9.

This section focuses on what is expected of a designer, and it looks at some of the issues faced by a designer.

## Creating a data model

Having written your functional specification, the design stage of the spreadsheet development begins. This involves three distinct activities: analysis, design and implementation:

✳   First, using the information gleaned from the client, it is important to analyse the **data requirements** of the system. This involves identifying the inputs and outputs, and what processing is needed to turn inputs into outputs.

✳   The next step is to produce a **data model**. This is not the spreadsheet itself, but documentation that describes the design of the spreadsheet and hence how it will be built. You will most likely have more than one worksheet and need to decide the purpose of each one.

**Key terms**

A *data model* is a representation of a real-life physical process or situation.

✳   The final stage is to translate the data model into physical worksheets using appropriate spreadsheet software.

### The data requirements

It is important to study the data requirements carefully, and to model the data precisely, so that it then becomes easy to create a working spreadsheet.

Data is input; it is processed; and then the results are output in some way (Figure 11.3).

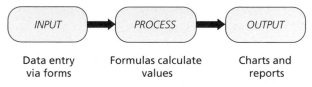

| INPUT | PROCESS | OUTPUT |
|---|---|---|
| Data entry via forms | Formulas calculate values | Charts and reports |

FIGURE 11.3 *Input–process–output*

Although the development of your solution will also include the writing of the data entry and validation functions (see Section 11.6) needed to make the spreadsheet **robust**, this may be postponed until most of the worksheets have been developed.

**Key terms**

*Robust:* a system is robust if it is difficult for the user to cause it to crash.

## The data model

A spreadsheet file comprises one or more worksheets. Within each worksheet there are rows and columns, and at the intersection of each row and column there is a cell.

The designer's job is to decide what data appears in which cell, in which row and in which column, and on which worksheet.

A sketch, like the one in Figure 11.4 showing your outline plan, will help the person who has to implement the design. If several worksheets share a common layout, you will use a template for these, and only one need be shown in the sketch.

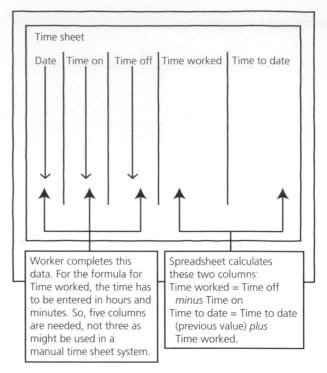

FIGURE 11.4 *Sketching the data model*

A, B, C… and each cell has a unique reference address according to its row and column (e.g. A4 and B5).

When referring to a cell on a different worksheet, the cell reference is prefixed by the worksheet name (e.g. Overview!A7). (Notice the exclamation mark.)

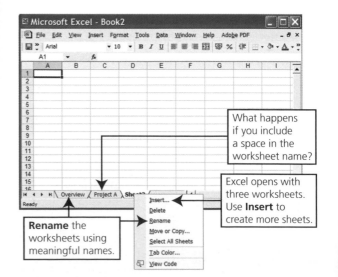

FIGURE 11.5 *Worksheets*

### CASE STUDY

The team of designers at Topic Training work on a number of projects simultaneously. Keeping track of the time spent on each project is important for billing purposes, but also for planning and scheduling of projects. Figure 11.4 shows how a spreadsheet model can be used to keep track of time.

1   Refer to the original scenario and to your functional specification to identify all the inputs to the system.

2   Identify what validation will be required.

3   Identify the processing that is required to turn the inputs into outputs.

4   Identify the output requirements. What charts and diagrams are needed?

## Worksheets

When you open a new spreadsheet, Excel creates a blank document with three worksheets. These are given the default names of Sheet1, Sheet2 and Sheet3. You should rename these (Figure 11.5) and you may insert additional worksheets according to your requirements.

Within any worksheet, the rows are numbered 1, 2, 3…, the columns are lettered

## Iterative design: prototyping

You will need to experiment with alternative designs for your spreadsheet, before finally deciding which one to choose.

The more expert you become at building spreadsheets, the better you will be at producing detailed designs. However, at this stage you will probably find it easier to use an iterative approach to software development.

Often, a **prototype** will be created which indicates the worksheet structure that is planned, the processing that will be involved and the layout and presentation of the results that are proposed.

In this context, a prototype is a working, but incomplete, spreadsheet that can be used to refine your initial design and to try out alternatives, to test that the formulas are working properly and that the underpinning logic is correct, to check for ease of use and to test for robustness.

A prototype provides a visual guide to what is planned and should be immediately understood by the prospective user. It should show the main routes for a user and how to perform the most common tasks: enter new data, amend data, display a chart or graph and so on.

Each prototype should bring you closer to a final fully functional solution. It should also help to clarify in your mind what it is you really want the spreadsheet to do.

At all stages, it is important to build in checkpoints and to go back to the functional specification to make sure you are still on track. Prototyping lets you interweave design, implementation and testing, rather than each of these being a distinct one-off stage of development.

## Testing

**Testing** (see Section 11.9) is discussed towards the end of this unit, but can start as soon as the first prototype has been developed.

## Documentation

In real-life projects, the three steps – analysis, modelling (or design) and implementation – may be undertaken by three different people or teams of people. The documentation that each person/ team produces, and the next person/team works from, then becomes quite crucial.

Section 11.10 addresses the issue of documentation, but you should avoid leaving the writing of documentation until the very end. Making notes and building documentation alongside each prototype will help you to see your progress.

## Assessment activity

1   Focusing on the data requirements of your system, identify the inputs and outputs of the system and any processing that will take place.

2   Design your data model and decide what worksheets you will need.

3   Create your first prototype to show the worksheets suitably named.

4   Test your prototype using sample input data.

5   Document your prototype, explaining what you have done so far.

## Assessment hint

✓   In your data model include measures that structure and validate data, and that consider the user interface and the presentation of results. Check that it satisfies the functional requirements as described in your functional specification.

# 11.4 Processing

Spreadsheets tend to be used to process numeric data. Part of the design stage is to specify what processing needs to happen and how this is to be achieved.

Processing numeric data includes calculating, but also many other activities that you will learn about in this section: merging data from different sources, making comparisons, sorting, grouping, filtering and pivoting data, and importing and exporting data.

## Calculating

Within every worksheet, the data within a given cell can be identified as being one of four types: a numeric value; a text (string value); a formula; or the cell could be blank.

Blank cells are like the white space on a text document – they make the worksheet more readable. How to present your data in the best possible way is considered in Section 11.5 and again in Section 11.8.

This section focuses on **formulas** – the features within a spreadsheet that do all the calculating for you.

> **Key terms**
>
> A *formula* is an expression written in terms of cell references and operators which specifies a calculation that is to be done, the result of which appears in the cell in which the formula is stored.

> **Think it over…**
>
> How can you recognise a formula in a spreadsheet? How does the software know you are entering a formula, rather than a number or a string?

You have studied spreadsheets during your AS year and should be familiar with a number of **functions** and how to use them in formulas.

> **Key terms**
>
> A *function* is a command that results in a value being returned.

> **Think it over…**
>
> What functions have you used before in a spreadsheet?

Table 11.1 lists functions that you should have met before. The triangular brackets (<>) indicate the **arguments** (shown in *italic*) of the function.

> **Key terms**
>
> An *argument* is a value of expression used within a function to specify what data is to be acted upon, or the criteria that are to be applied, or the resulting value that is required.

You need to complete the arguments within a function using cell references (such as A5 and Overview!B7), numbers, strings and expressions, as appropriate.

| FUNCTION | DESCRIPTION |
|---|---|
| AVERAGE (<cellref1>, <cellref2>, ...) | Adds up the contents of the cells and divides by the number of cells listed |
| COUNT (<value1>, <value2>, ...) | Counts the number of cells that contain the value(s) listed |
| IF (<logical_test>, <value_if_true>, <value_if_false>) | Checks the condition of the logical test and returns one of the two values accordingly |
| SUM (<cellref1>: <cellref2>) | Adds up the cells within the stated range |
| SUMIF (<cellrange1>, "<criteria>", <cellrange2>) | Tests the cells in cellrange1 against the criteria, and sums the corresponding cells within cellrange2 |

TABLE 11.1 *Functions*

If you are not sure which function you need, Excel provides help. Select **Insert Function** (Figure 11.6) and type a brief description – or look through the various lists of functions available.

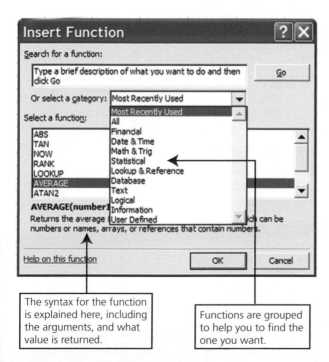

The syntax for the function is explained here, including the arguments, and what value is returned.

Functions are grouped to help you to find the one you want.

FIGURE 11.6 *Inserting a function*

### Theory into practice

1 Using sample data that you have invented, for each function listed in Table 11.1, incorporate the function into one or more formulas within a worksheet.

2 Document your examples to explain the effect of the formulas that you have created.

You will have met **relative and absolute addressing techniques** already. Absolute referencing allows you to replicate the contents of cells and yet control which parts of a formula 'move' with the rows/columns.

### CASE STUDY

Knits4U sells high-quality knitwear. Tourists may buy the jumpers without paying the VAT, provided the purchase is for export.

A stock list shows the price without VAT and, in a separate column, the price including VAT. The VAT rate is currently 17.5 per cent but may change, and so absolute addressing (see Figure 11.7) is used, rather than to embed the value in the formulas.

1 Experiment with the inclusion of the dollar symbol to check how necessary each one is, according to whether you replicate across rows or across columns.

2 Identify situations where you will use absolute addressing in your spreadsheet solution.

The VAT rate is a **parameter**. Another way of taking parameter values from fixed points rather than embed them in formulas is to use the **LOOKUP function** (as seen in Figure 11.8).

### Think it over...

Why is it best not to embed values that may change over time?

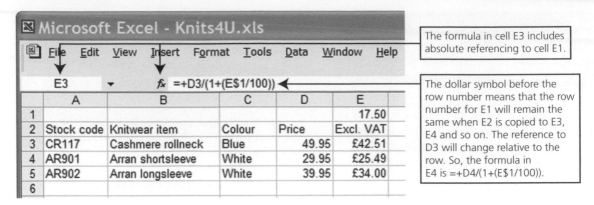

FIGURE 11.7 *Absolute addressing*

The LOOKUP function has two syntax forms: **vector** and **array**. The vector form of LOOKUP looks in a vector for a value and returns a value from the same position in a second vector.

The array form of LOOKUP looks in the first row or column of an array for the specified value and returns a value from the same position in the last row or column of the array.

The LOOKUP function is useful when you have a table of values which may change at a later date, and which you therefore do not want to embed within a formula. And the value you want depends on the contents of a cell, which also varies.

The values that you want to look up might be in the same worksheet, or in a completely different worksheet within the same spreadsheet.

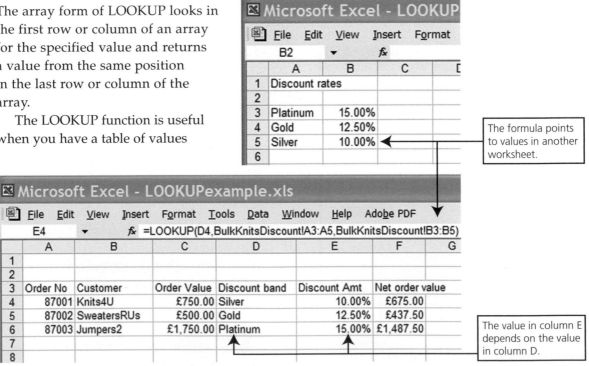

FIGURE 11.8 *A LOOKUP table*

Knits4U buys its knitwear from a manufacturer BulkKnits. BulkKnits offer discounts to wholesale customers such as Knits4U, based on the size of an individual order and on the category of client: Platinum, Gold or Silver. The discount rates are held in a spreadsheet (Figure 11.8) and are used to calculate the discount to be given on a particular order.

1   Use **Insert Function** to confirm the arguments needed for the LOOKUP function.

2   Set up some data on one worksheet that you can look up from another worksheet.

3   Write a formula that uses the LOOKUP function. Check that the formula works. If you find it does not, try extending the range of the vectors to include blank rows above and below the rows that contain the data.

4   Change the values in the table and check that the formula now displays amended accurate values.

To help future users of your spreadsheet, you should try to create as elegant a solution as possible. You will document this as explained in Section 11.10.

One example of how you can make your solution more elegant is given here. An **array formula** can be used to perform several calculations to generate a single result. This can simplify your worksheet model by replacing several different formulas with a single array formula.

For example, in a stock evaluation spreadsheet, suppose column B holds a quantity and column C a price. You could use another column (D) to hold the result of multiplying the quantity by the price. You could then sum the entries in column D to arrive at a total stock evaluation.

Alternatively, you could use an array formula (see Figure 11.9).

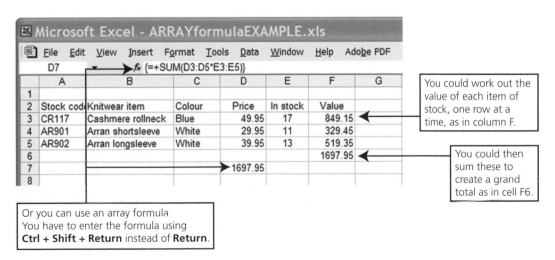

FIGURE 11.9 *An array formula*

## Selection

If you have a number of worksheets, you can control which of these worksheets are affected when you enter data by selecting the appropriate ones (Figure 11.10).

Then, when you enter data on one of the selected worksheets, the same entries appear in all other selected worksheets.

You may also select cells (Figure 11.11).

If you want to select cells according to their content as opposed to the type of content, you can apply a filter (see 'Filtering' below).

## Merging data

It is not always practical to hold all the data in one spreadsheet file. If so, there may come a time when the data may need to be merged from these different files to produce an overview of what is happening.

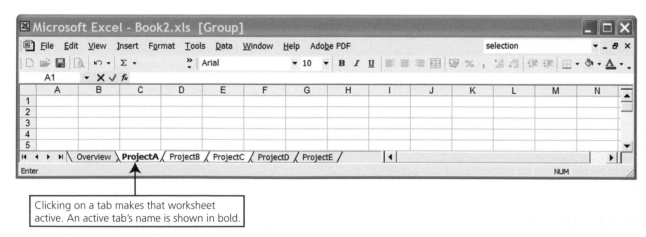

Clicking on a tab makes that worksheet active. An active tab's name is shown in bold.

FIGURE 11.10 *Selecting worksheets*

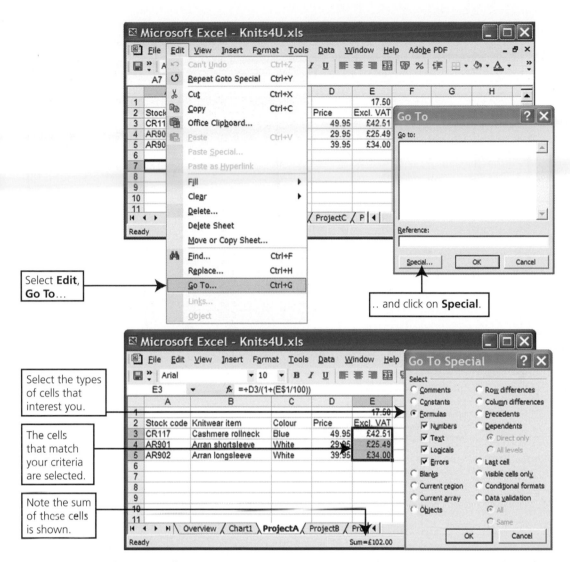

Select **Edit**, **Go To**…

.. and click on **Special**.

Select the types of cells that interest you.

The cells that match your criteria are selected.

Note the sum of these cells is shown.

**FIGURE 11.11** *Selecting cells*

## CASE STUDY

Everyone in the design team at Topic Training completes a timesheet which shows time spent on various projects. There is one spreadsheet per designer and, within that spreadsheet, one worksheet per day (Figure 11.12) plus an overview sheet (Figure 11.13). At the end of each month, the data from all overviews is merged to produce statistics for the whole team for all projects. From this data, the amounts to invoice can be calculated.

1 Why do Topic Training have one spreadsheet per designer?

2 Why does each spreadsheet need more than one worksheet?

3 Experiment with setting up a spreadsheet as a timesheet to track the time you spend on your different courses.

4 Experiment with merging your spreadsheet data with that of others in your group, to provide some analysis of how you spend your time.

The time is entered as hours and minutes in columns A–D. The time spent (in cell E3) is then calculated as +(A3*60+B3-C3*60-D3)/60.

The designer enters the project letter in column F and the time is then analysed using an IF function into columns G, H and I.

The designer only has to enter the start time at the beginning of the day, and then each time there is a change of project.

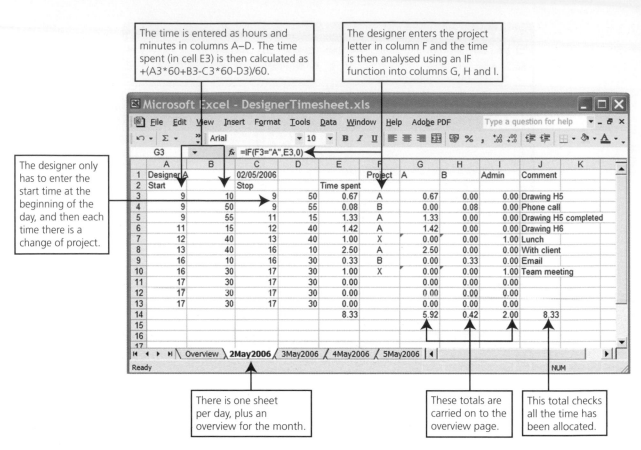

There is one sheet per day, plus an overview for the month.

These totals are carried on to the overview page.

This total checks all the time has been allocated.

FIGURE 11.12 *Individual timesheet data*

Data is taken from other worksheets within this spreadsheet.

An explanation is given for days not worked.

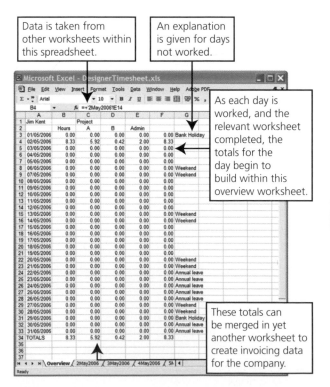

As each day is worked, and the relevant worksheet completed, the totals for the day begin to build within this overview worksheet.

These totals can be merged in yet another worksheet to create invoicing data for the company.

FIGURE 11.13 *Overview data*

## Making comparisons

Within a spreadsheet, you can compare the contents of one cell with another, using the IF function:

```
=IF (A5>A7,"Profit","Loss")
```

The > symbol in the first argument is called a **comparison operator**.

> ### Key terms
>
> *Comparison operators* (=, >, <) allow you to compare two values to give the result of either True or False.

You might also want to compare two strings to validate a data entry, and could use the EXACT function:

```
EXACT (A5,A7)
```

If lots of comparisons are needed, or data has to lie in a range, you might also use the logical function AND:

```
=IF(AND(1<A7,A7<50,A7,"Must lie
between 1 and 50")
```

## Sorting, grouping, filtering and pivoting data

Within a spreadsheet, you may need to rearrange material by sorting it; by grouping the data; by filtering the data so that only relevant material is displayed; and/or by pivoting the data.

### Sorting

It is possible to sort the data in one column of a spreadsheet while leaving the rest of the data in place. However, if each row represents a record and each column a field, then sorting in this way destroys the **integrity** (the accuracy) of the data (Figure 11.14).

It is important to expand the selection if the cells contain material that does need to be kept together in rows (or columns, depending on your design).

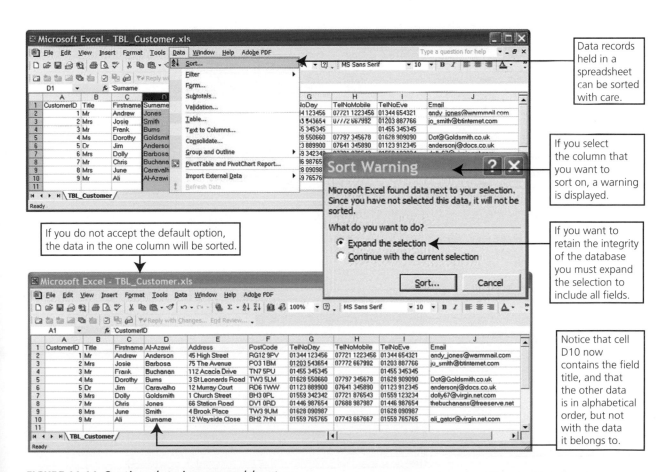

Data records held in a spreadsheet can be sorted with care.

If you select the column that you want to sort on, a warning is displayed.

If you want to retain the integrity of the database you must expand the selection to include all fields.

If you do not accept the default option, the data in the one column will be sorted.

Notice that cell D10 now contains the field title, and that the other data is in alphabetical order, but not with the data it belongs to.

**FIGURE 11.14** *Sorting data in a spreadsheet*

1  You have met the Sort command before (in *AS Level for Edexcel Applied ICT* book, page 103). Refresh your memory and check that you can sort data in both ascending and descending order.

2  Check that you can sort on more than one field.

3  Explore other features available, such as sorting without being case sensitive.

4  How would you sort on a field that contains the days of the week (Mon, Tues, Wed,…) or months of the year (January, February,…)?

## Grouping

When you set up a PivotTable (see page 226), you may need to group items (Figure 11.15):

* You might want to group numeric items. For example, you might have monthly figures but want to group them into quarters for analysis purposes.

* For dates, you might want to group by day or by weeks. For weekly grouping, the grouping is by days, but in groups of 7 (there being 7 days in a week!).

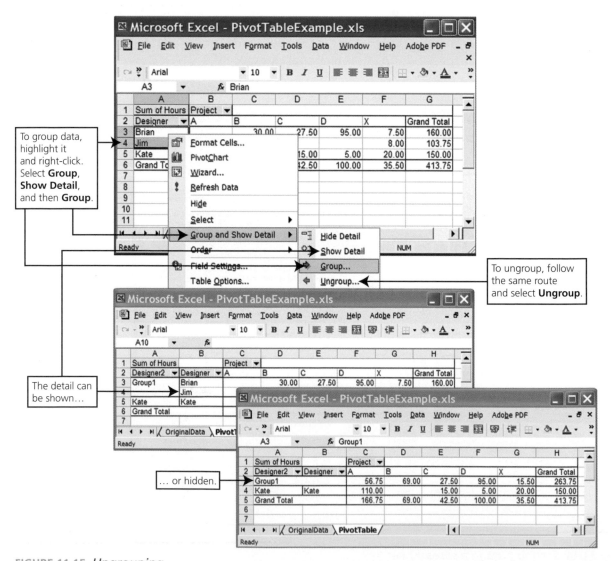

To group data, highlight it and right-click. Select **Group**, **Show Detail**, and then **Group**.

To ungroup, follow the same route and select **Ungroup**.

The detail can be shown…

… or hidden.

FIGURE 11.15 *Ungrouping*

To group items, select them (holding the Ctrl key down while you do). Then, right-click to reveal the context-sensitive menu, choose **Group** and **Show Detail**, and then **Group**. To ungroup items, right-click on the group to open the context-sensitive menu. Point to **Group** and **Show Details**, and choose **Ungroup**.

## Filtering

Filtering is one way of finding a subset of data from a **list**.

There are two filtering options:

✳ The AutoFilter creates drop-down menus for each column heading and you can click on the one you want (Figure 11.16).

✳ For more complex criteria, you need to use the Advanced Filter option (Figure 11.17).

The filtered list displays *only* those rows of the list that match the criteria that you specify for a particular column. None of the data is lost – it is just hidden from view while the filter is on.

*Note*: Filtering does not sort the data; it just displays relevant rows according to your criteria.

To remove the effect of filtering, select **Data**, **Show all**.

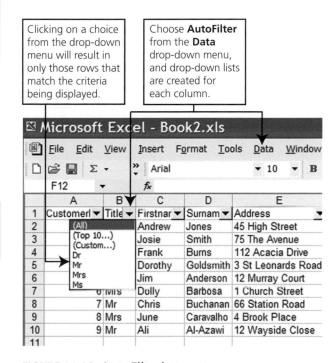

Clicking on a choice from the drop-down menu will result in only those rows that match the criteria being displayed.

Choose **AutoFilter** from the **Data** drop-down menu, and drop-down lists are created for each column.

FIGURE 11.16 *AutoFiltering*

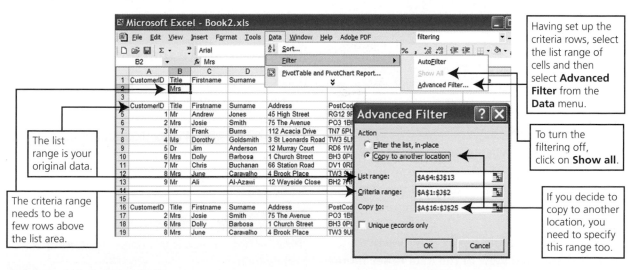

Having set up the criteria rows, select the list range of cells and then select **Advanced Filter** from the **Data** menu.

The list range is your original data.

The criteria range needs to be a few rows above the list area.

To turn the filtering off, click on **Show all**.

If you decide to copy to another location, you need to specify this range too.

FIGURE 11.17 *Advanced Filter*

## Pivoting

A PivotTable report is an interactive table that combines and compares data.

You can rotate its rows and columns to view different summaries of the source data, and display the details for areas of interest.

You might use a PivotTable report when you want to analyse related totals – for example, if you have a list of figures to sum and you want to compare several facts about each figure (Figure 11.18).

Because a PivotTable report is interactive, you can change the view of the data to see more details or to calculate different summaries,

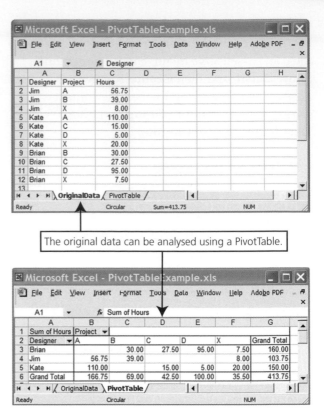

The original data can be analysed using a PivotTable.

FIGURE 11.18 *Pivoting*

such as counts or averages, as shown in Figure 11.18.

Each column or field in your source data becomes a PivotTable field that summarises multiple rows of information. For example, the Project column becomes the Project field, and each record for one value in that column (such as 'Project A') is summarised in a single 'Project A' item.

## Importing and exporting data

It is not necessary to have all your data in the one spreadsheet. If it is more convenient, you can hold data in separate spreadsheets. You can then access data that is held in another spreadsheet by **importing** it (Figure 11.20).

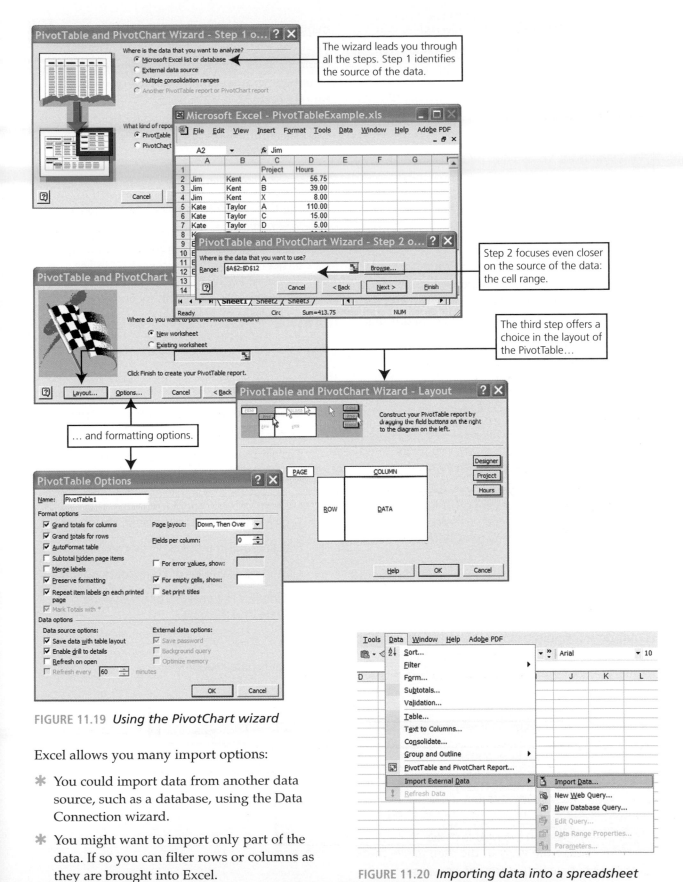

The wizard leads you through all the steps. Step 1 identifies the source of the data.

Step 2 focuses even closer on the source of the data: the cell range.

The third step offers a choice in the layout of the PivotTable…

… and formatting options.

FIGURE 11.19 *Using the PivotChart wizard*

Excel allows you many import options:

* You could import data from another data source, such as a database, using the Data Connection wizard.

* You might want to import only part of the data. If so you can filter rows or columns as they are brought into Excel.

FIGURE 11.20 *Importing data into a spreadsheet*

* If you have the necessary access rights, you can access data from the WWW.

* You might even use **VBA** to gain access to an external data source.

**Exporting** involves saving data from your spreadsheet in some format that can be imported into another application.

The Save As option provides a range of formats that are supported (Figure 11.21). Note that, for some, you may lose Excel features in the exporting process, but you will be warned if this is the case.

## Theory into practice

1 Use Excel's Help to identify the various importing options.

2 Check what importing, if any, you might need to do for your spreadsheet solution.

3 Experiment with saving a spreadsheet in a particular format. Import it into another application (such as Access) and then export it to Excel. Check that this works!

## Data mapping

A mapping program such as Microsoft MapPoint can be used with data in Excel 2002 or later to analyse data graphically, using colourful maps that let the reader identify important locations and trends across an area. The data could be sales (by volume), customers (numbers within certain regions) or product (numbers sold).

You can link or embed the data from an Excel worksheet into MapPoint.

## Theory into practice

1 Use Microsoft's Help to find out more about data mapping.

2 Many organisations use the MapPoint web service. Visit the Customer Case Studies section of Microsoft's MapPoint site to learn how Starbucks utilise this technology.

## Knowledge check

1 List the options for the contents of a cell.

2 What is the difference between a formula and a function? Give *one* example of each.

3 Explain these terms: string, argument, range.

4 Distinguish between relative and absolute addressing.

5 Explain these terms: parameter, vector, array.

6 Explain what the LOOKUP function does.

7 Give *three* examples of comparison operators.

8 Distinguish between sorting, grouping, filtering and pivoting.

9 Explain these terms: import, export.

10 What is data mapping?

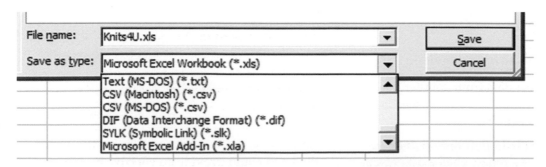

FIGURE 11.21 *Exporting options in Save As*

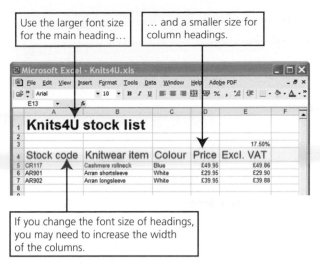

FIGURE 11.22 *Using font size*

# 11.5 Layout and presentation

A spreadsheet full of rows and rows – or columns and columns – of numeric data soon becomes tricky to read.

The spreadsheet solution that you will be designing is expected to handle complex data, and you must make sure it is easy to understand, not just for you, but for anyone else reading it.

Spreadsheets can be made more user-friendly by appropriate structuring of the content and by making effective use of the available presentation and formatting features. For maximum usability, a **start up menu** (as explained in Section 11.10) should be the first thing a user sees.

However, this section focuses on the following presentation and formatting features: font size and style, colour, borders and style, conditional formatting, headers and footers, and graphics.

## Font size and style

The legibility of a spreadsheet can be greatly improved by the appropriate choice of font size and style – as illustrated in Figure 11.22.

The control of the appearance of data within a cell is done via the formatting of the cells.

## Colours, borders and shading

To create interest in your layouts, and to draw attention to particular cells and the data displayed within them, you can add colour (Figure 11.23) for the font and/or for the background shading.

You might use an image or a photo as a background to an entire worksheet. This will be tiled and could provide an effective backdrop for your data.

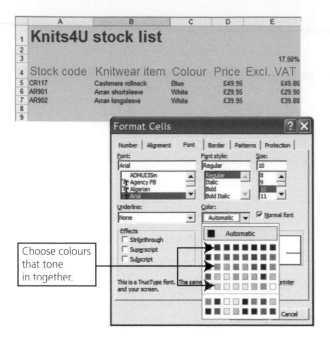

FIGURE 11.23 *Using colour*

Select **Format**, **Format Cells** and click on the **Border** tab.

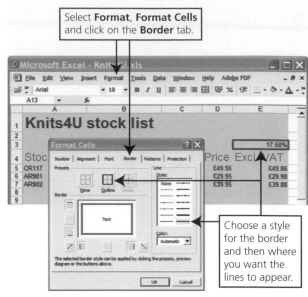

Choose a style for the border and then where you want the lines to appear.

FIGURE 11.24 *Using borders and shading*

Choose colours that tone in together.

## How to... add a background

1 Select **Format**, **Sheet**, **Background**.

2 Browse to locate the image that you want to use and click on **Insert**.

3 Review the alignment of the rows and columns to fit the edges of your background image.

4 To remove a background, select **Format**, **Sheet**, **Remove background**.

You might also outline a cell or range of cells; a border (Figure 11.24) would draw the eye to the cells and create a focal point on the screen. Similarly, shading can be used to make some cells (like headings) stand out.

## Conditional formatting

You may have used conditional formatting before (see *AS Level for Edexcel Applied ICT*, page 103, Figure 3.18).

Conditional formatting is only applied if the cell matches criteria that you set (Figure 11.25). Such formatting can be useful to draw attention to data that is on target or outside an acceptable range, or some other criterion that makes the data value more important than other values around it.

When debugging your spreadsheet, you may need to identify cells that involve conditional formatting. If so, select **Edit**, **Go To**, **Special** and click on the radio buttons for **Conditional formats** and **All Data validation**.

You can set a condition based on the cell value, or on the formula within the cell.

If the cell matches your criteria, the format can be set as specified.

You can add more conditions...

... and delete conditions.

To check which cells have conditional formatting, select **Edit**, **Go To**, **Special** and click on the radio buttons for **Conditional formats** and **All Data validation**.

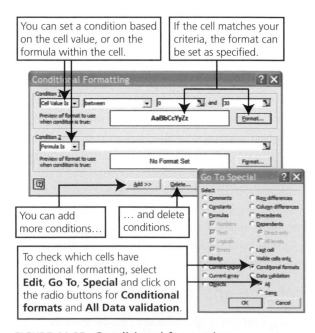

FIGURE 11.25 *Conditional formatting*

# Headers and footers

For printed output, if you have more than one page, it makes sense to repeat some information on every page and to number the pages.

This information can be placed in a header and/or footer (Figure 11.26).

You can access **Page Setup** through **View**, **Header** and **Footer**.

Click on **Custom Header** to set up your header.

Each button provides an item of data that can be placed in one of the three sections.

&[File] = filename

Text without an **&** appears exactly as you type it.

The date is today's date.

You can also access the header/footer dialogue box by previewing your spreadsheet and then clicking on **Setup**...

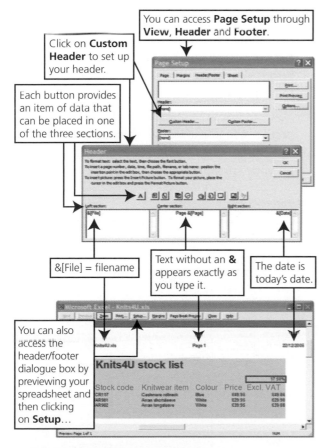

FIGURE 11.26 *Headers and footers*

# Graphics

Apart from the image that you might place as a background, you might also need to include graphics in your spreadsheet solution.

In the same way that you can insert an image into a Word document, Excel offers the same options (Figure 11.27).

Select **Insert**, **Picture**, **From File** and then browse to find the picture you want to insert.

The image 'lands' on the active cell...

... and then you can click on the image and use the grab handles to resize the image.

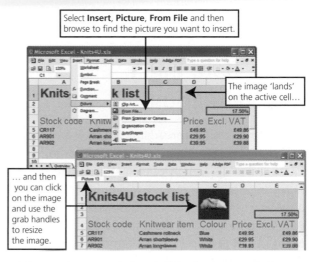

FIGURE 11.27 *Inserting graphics into a worksheet*

# 11.6 Data entry and validation

The output from a spreadsheet is only as good as the data that is entered. The 'garbage in, garbage out' maxim applies just as much to a spreadsheet as it does to any other data-processing system. In this section, you will learn how to use data validation and other techniques to reduce the potential for data entry errors. You will then apply these techniques to your spreadsheet solution.

## Validation

There are a number of techniques for validating data input and trapping errors:

* It is possible to restrict data input so that only acceptable data values can be input.

* Cells can be protected, either by hiding them from view or by locking them so that the user cannot gain access to them.

* Form controls such as list boxes and drop-down menus can force users to enter valid data.

* Rather than require data to be entered twice, you can transfer data from one spreadsheet to another.

## Restricting data input

One way of stopping the user from entering invalid data is to restrict the entry to acceptable data values.

* You can set upper and lower limits for numeric data entries.

* You can compare the entry against items in a list. You should make sure you test these boundary values.

* You can specify a time range and/or a data range. For example, in the times run for a marathon, times less than an hour would be too quick, and anything over 12 hours might be too slow to be a valid time – depending on the rules of the race.

* You can limit the number of characters accepted in a text string. This can prevent overlong strings ruining a layout elsewhere on your spreadsheet.

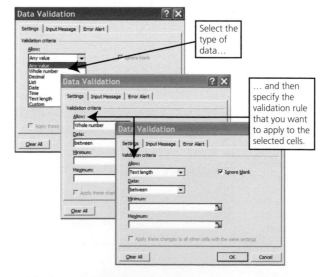

FIGURE 11.28 *Restricting data input*

* You can calculate what is allowed according to the contents of another cell. For example, if the cell contains an amount of credit available, then a loan for anything higher than that would be rejected.

* You can use a formula to calculate what is allowed. In the Formula box (Figure 11.29), the formula will have a True (valid) or False (invalid) value according to the data that is entered.

## Protecting cells

Some cells on a worksheet – and perhaps entire worksheets – may contain material that you don't want the user to access and/or change.

### Hiding cells

If a user cannot see a cell, so long as there is no option to unhide it, the cell is protected.

You can hide entire spreadsheets from the user.

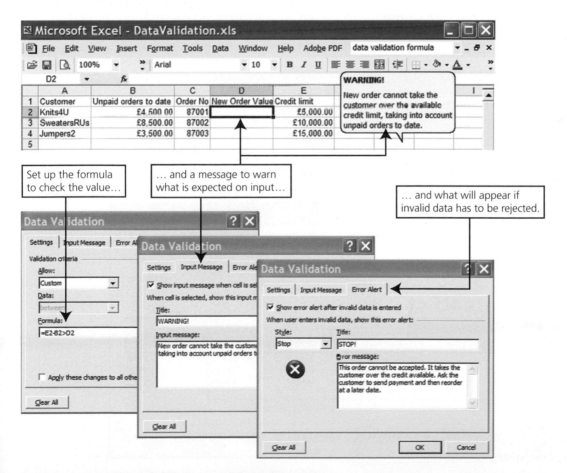

FIGURE 11.29 *Using a formula to validate data entry*

## How to... hide a spreadsheet

1. Open a worksheet within the spreadsheet.
2. Select **Window**, **Hide**. The spreadsheet disappears, but if you select **Window**, **Unhide** you will be presented with a list of hidden spreadsheets and can unhide as you wish (Figure 11.30).

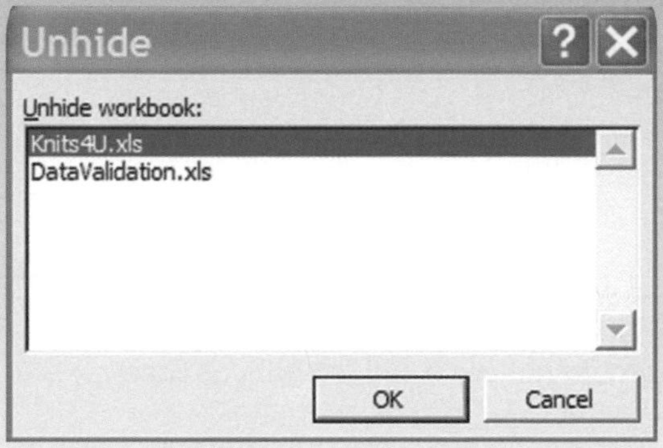

FIGURE 11.30 *Hiding a spreadsheet*

You can also hide rows and columns within a worksheet (Figure 11.31).

## How to... hide a row/column

1. Select the row(s) or column(s).
2. Select **Format**, **Row** (or **Column**).
3. Click on **Hide**. The row/column will disappear from view.
4. The row numbers (or column letters) are no longer consecutive so you can see where the hidden rows (or columns) are.
5. To unhide a row (or column), select the rows (or columns) immediately before and after, and then click on **Format**, **Row** (or **Column**). Choosing **Unhide** will result in the hidden rows (or columns) being revealed once more.

### *Locking cells*

If you need the user to see the contents of a cell but not be allowed to change them, you need to lock the cell.

The method involves unlocking cells for which you want to allow access, and then protecting the whole sheet using a password.

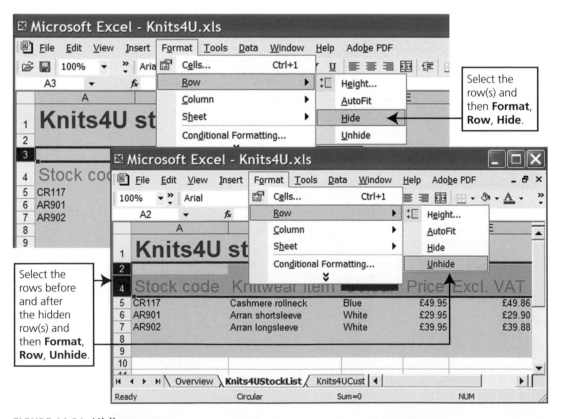

FIGURE 11.31 *Hiding a row*

1 Switch to the worksheet that you plan to protect.

2 For cells that you want the user to be able to change (e.g. data entry cells), choose **Format**, **Cells** and, on the **Protection** tab, clear the **Locked** checkbox (Figure 11.32).

3 At the same time, hide any formulas that you don't want the user to see by choosing **Format**, **Cells**, **Protection**, **Hidden** for each one.

4 Then on the **Tools** menu, choose **Protection**, **Protect Sheet**. Enter a password for this sheet. (Make sure you don't forget this!)

5 In the same dialogue box, on the **Allow all users of this worksheet to...** list, tick what you want.

6 Confirm the password, and click on **OK**.

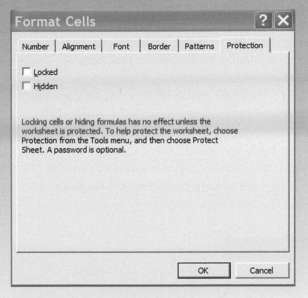

FIGURE 11.32 *Protecting cells*

What will happen if you protect a worksheet with a password and then forget the password?

1 Explore the options to lock or hide data in a spreadsheet.

2 Consider which of your cells ought to be protected from users, and which ought to be hidden from view.

3 Document your decisions and implement them.

4 Test the spreadsheet to make sure your changes have worked correctly.

## Using forms controls

In Microsoft Access, a form is like a report and, on the form, you can set up **controls** that allow the user to enter data.

A *control* is a GUI interface object such as a list box, drop-down menu or button that lets the user control the program.

Unit 7 (pages 39–41) discusses the techniques involved in setting up a form and creating controls on that form. Figure 7.43 (on page 40) shows the Access Toolbox. In Microsoft Excel, a similar set of controls is available via the **Forms** menu (Figure 11.33).

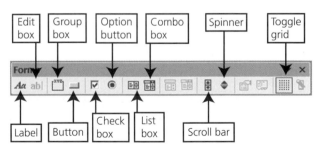

FIGURE 11.33 *Forms Menu Control Toolbox*

1 Read through Unit 7 to refresh your mind about form controls.

2 Explore the Forms toolbar in Excel to check that you understand all the controls on offer, and how to create the controls on a form.

3 Consider where you might use form controls in your spreadsheet solution.

## Automated data transfer

One of the objectives in handling data is to minimise repetition of data. So, if you already have data, for example, in an Access database, and you need to use some of that data to produce some statistics in Excel, you would not want to re-enter the data. Apart from the time this would take, it introduces the possibilities for error.

Instead, you would want a way of linking the two applications. There are a variety of ways of linking such objects, according to whether you want the data to be static or dynamic.

* If you are creating a report that is correct as at a certain date, you could take a snapshot of data from another application and, having taken that data on the right day, would not have to incorporate subsequent changes to the data. A static link would suffice here.

* If you are creating a report that needs to be up to date according to whatever data is available, you would need a dynamic link between the applications.

### Theory into practice

1 Using Microsoft's Help feature, identify the many ways of transferring data between Excel and other applications such as Access.

2 Consider situations where your spreadsheet solution needs to incorporate data from external data sources.

Within your spreadsheet solution, you might also need to transfer data from one worksheet to another:

* If you select several worksheets at once (see page 220), anything you enter into one is automatically entered into the others.

The data appears in the same cells, so you would have to plan the layout very carefully across the various worksheets.

* If, within a formula, you refer to a cell in another worksheet, any change to that cell's contents will be reflected when the formulas are recalculated.

### Theory into practice

1 Experiment with selecting more than one spreadsheet and then entering data into one.

2 Set up some data in one spreadsheet (e.g. as if it were being entered in a form) and refer to it in another, hidden worksheet.

3 Consider situations where you might enter data in one worksheet and use it in another.

## Ease of use

Most technically complex spreadsheets are used by people other than the designer or developer. One key requirement for a spreadsheet, especially because other people besides you will be using it, is to make it as easy to use as possible. In this section, you will learn how to design and create effective ways of entering data:

* You will need to create forms that guide the user to enter data with prompts as to what to do next and buttons to initiate certain procedures.

* You should limit the users to access only the parts of the spreadsheet that are relevant – not swamp them with other material that is of no importance to them.

* To help users who make incorrect data entries, you will incorporate error messages.

### Think it over...

In what other ways might you improve the ease of use of your spreadsheet?

## Using forms

In Excel, there are two ways of using forms: data forms and worksheet forms.

If you have a list of data and would like to enter the data using a form, provided at least one cell in the list is active, selecting **Data**, **Form** will present a form that could be used for data entry (Figure 11.34).

If you need a more sophisticated or specialised data entry form, you can create a worksheet or template to use as a form. For example, you might create a form on which users could report an injury, or an expense incurred, or a fault. You then need to develop a data entry application using Microsoft **VBE** to keep the data from the form in an Excel range.

In Excel, the controls you need to create your own form are available on the Forms toolbar (Figure 11.33 on page 235).

You have met data entry forms before. In the AS course, a form was used to obtain feedback from visitors to a website (see the *AS Level GCE Applied ICT for Edexcel* book, Figure 5.30, page 200).

You might decide to create a Microsoft Access form to use with Excel data. To maintain a list within your spreadsheet solution, you could use the AccessLinks add-in program to run the Access Form wizard. This will allow you to design your form in Excel, but using the capabilities of Access.

Click on a cell within the list and then select **Data**, **Form** to reveal the default form.

The form name is the same as the sheet name.

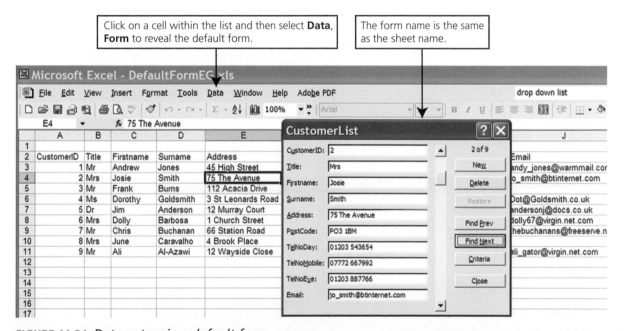

FIGURE 11.34 *Data entry via a default form*

## User views

There is no need for the user to see all the background workings of your spreadsheet solution. Indeed, you may want to keep secret how you have achieved the end result. So you may decide to limit the user's view of the spreadsheet to the parts the user can change – plus parts that display the results.

Using **Hide**, you can limit the worksheets that are visible and, within them, the cells that can be seen. You can also protect cells by locking them so that the user cannot amend the contents (e.g. of crucial formulas).

### Theory into practice

1 Review your documentation to check how you have presented the user views.

2 Check your spreadsheet solution to make sure you have taken your intended audience into account and created user views that suit the user, and yet protect the data.

## Communication with the user

While the user is using your spreadsheet solution, you are unlikely to be close by. You need to make sure that the solution includes opportunities for communication that helps the user to make the best use of your solution, unaided.

### Prompts

Adding prompts or messages to tell users what needs entering where will smooth the way for new users and provide reminders for those who have used your software before.

### Error messages

When setting up the data validation (e.g. to restrict data input as in Figure 11.28 on page 232), you can also specify the error message that you would like to appear (Figure 11.35), should the user make an incorrect entry.

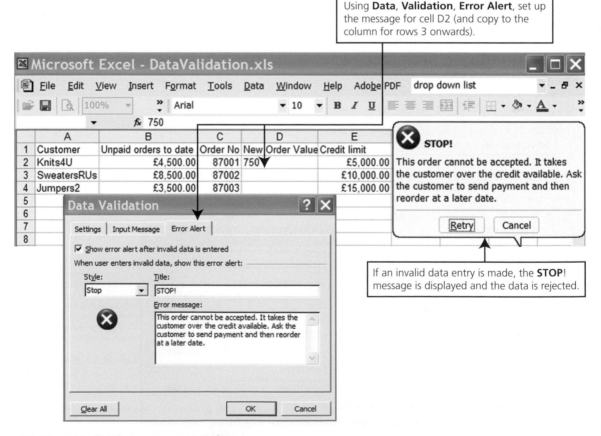

FIGURE 11.35 *Setting up an error alert*

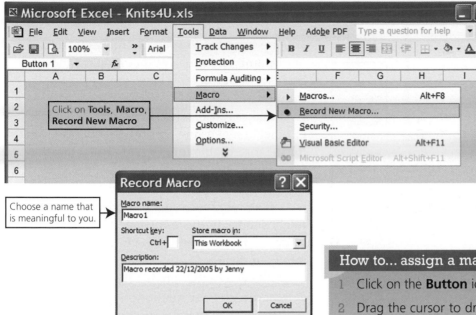

Choose a name that is meaningful to you.

**FIGURE 11.36** *Recording a macro*

## Buttons

Buttons can be provided so that users can initiate certain procedures. For the procedure to happen when the user clicks on the button, you first have to create a **macro**, and then assign the macro to the button.

The same macro could be assigned to more than one button in your spreadsheet solution, so if there are actions that are common, plan your macros carefully.

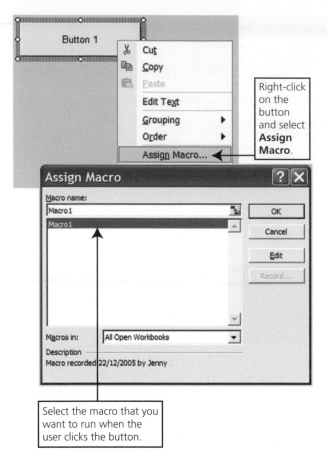

Select the macro that you want to run when the user clicks the button.

Right-click on the button and select **Assign Macro**.

FIGURE 11.37 *Assigning a macro to a button*

## Assessment activity

1 Review your design documentation. Have you given sufficient thought to the user interface? Does your solution show an awareness of the audience?

2 Develop further and refine your spreadsheet solution to create a new prototype, one that includes appropriate user interface features such as data entry forms, prompts and error messages.

3 Test your prototype and obtain feedback from others as to its ease of use.

## Assessment hint

✓ Make sure that your current prototype works as expected before you start making changes to it. This makes the testing of the next prototype easier.

# 11.7 Future-proofing

You are expected to spend roughly 60 hours on this unit and much of that time will have been spent developing your spreadsheet solution.

It makes sense, when investing such a lot of time, to make sure that the product is usable for the foreseeable future, without the need for updates and further expense of time or energy.

You should therefore be mindful of what might change in the immediate or medium-term future and try to build some future-proofing into your design.

While you cannot predict the future, you can at least design your solution so that any external changes have minimal impact on the design. This will make it much easier to implement modifications and extensions at a later date, should you need to do so.

This section considers a number of future-proofing techniques:

✱ using parameters

✱ setting up templates

✱ providing adequate documentation

✱ providing good security for your solution.

### Think it over...

In what other ways might you future-proof a spreadsheet solution?

## Parameters

Some things are bound to change. Prices rise, VAT rates change, employees resign or are made redundant, new employees join an organisation, new products are developed and so on.

### Think it over...

In the scenario of your spreadsheet solution, what things might change over time?

Some of these changes have to be accommodated on a day-to-day basis, according to the scope of the spreadsheet solution:

* when a new employee joins, a routine will create a new record (row) within a worksheet

* when a product is discontinued, data relating to that may be archived.

Some values, though, are bound to change (like VAT) and tend to be used in formulas throughout the spreadsheet.

One way to future-proof your solution is to set aside a specific area of the spreadsheet to store any values which change frequently. Formulas that rely on these parameters can incorporate them using **absolute addressing**.

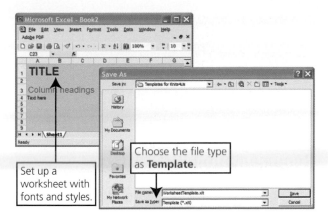

**FIGURE 11.38** *Templates*

### Think it over...

How do you apply absolute referencing to a cell in a formula?

Then the values can easily be updated – just by altering the content of one cell – without having to alter any of the formulas. (For an example of absolute referencing, see Figure 11.7 on page 218.)

### Theory into practice

1  Identify a situation in your spreadsheet solution where absolute addressing should be used.

2  Test that it works by replicating a formula that involves absolute referencing.

## Templates

If the same layout is expected to be used over and over again, you can save time by creating a **template**.

### Key terms

A *template* determines the basic structure for a document and contains settings such as fonts, key assignments, macros, page layout and styles.

Then, should there be a change to the template (e.g. to basic company contact information), only the template needs to be altered.

There are two basic types of template (Figure 11.38):

* A **workbook template** contains the sheets, default text (such as page headers and column and row labels), formulas, macros, style and other formatting you want in new workbooks based on the template.

* A **worksheet template** is one worksheet, which includes the formatting, styles, text and other information you want to appear on all new worksheets of the same type.

### How to... create a worksheet template

1  In a spreadsheet with only one blank worksheet, choose all the settings: font, style, etc.

2  Select **File**, **Save As**.

3  Choose the **Save as type** as **Template**.

4  Choose the folder where you want the template stored.

5  Enter a meaningful filename.

Microsoft Excel also includes templates that can be used to automate the common tasks of completing invoices or expenses statements.

## Documentation

One thing that may well change in the future is your availability to support the product. Hopefully, you will gain promotion or move to another organisation. Or you may just be busy developing the next spreadsheet solution.

So, the documentation that you leave for others to refer to when you are not there is important. Include explanations for the logic – or clever tricks – that you applied, and any assumptions you have made.

Section 11.10 looks at what documentation ought to be produced.

## Security

One would hope that users would not be tempted to tamper with the data and formulas in your spreadsheet. Changing them may stop the spreadsheet solution from producing the desired results. However, to maintain the integrity of the solution, you are best advised to protect these formulas.

Section 11.6 looked at protecting cells, which includes locking and password protecting cells to prevent formulas being tampered with.

# 11.8 Presentation of results

Having worked hard to develop your spreadsheet solution, using appropriate data entry and validation techniques and having established the processing necessary so that the data creates the desired results, you now need to focus on how you can best present these results.

You have a number of options:

✱ Some results may best be presented on-screen, as soon as the data entry is complete, so that the user receives immediate feedback.

✱ Some results may need to be printed in report form so that the user can study them at leisure. Such printed output provides a permanent record and is portable. This means it can be used as a discussion document (e.g. at the next management meeting).

* Some results need to be exported to another application for further processing. For example, you may want to incorporate a chart in a PowerPoint presentation. Or you may need to include some statistical information and perhaps some graphics on a website.

Having decided on the best option for output, you need to focus on how to present the results in an appropriate, easy-to-read form. This involves you making use of presentation and formatting features, such as page layout, charts and graphs, graphics, animation, colours, borders and shading.

## Page layout

The layout of each page is important. It creates an immediate impression on the reader.

Designing the page layout has similarities with planning the layout and presentation of the spreadsheet itself.

### The basic structure of the page

Each page has a basic structure (Figure 11.39) and every page should be similar enough

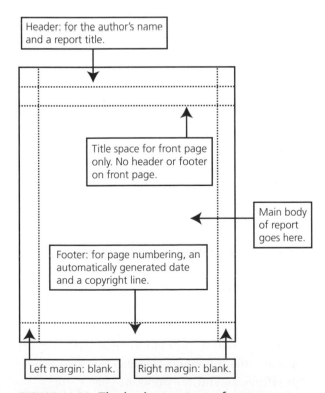

FIGURE 11.39 *The basic structure of a page*

to convey consistency to the reader. Each page should also look balanced in terms of content:

* How much space will you allocate to the text?
* How much space will you allocate to charts and graphs?
* Will you include graphics?
* Where will you leave **white space**?

You then need to consider what information you will include on each page (e.g. in a header or footer).

**\* Remember!**

A **header** appears at the top of each page. A **footer** appears at the foot of each page.

These 'rules' not only apply to the presentation of results but also to any documentation that you produce.

**Think it over…**

In your documentation, what information should appear on every page?

### Choosing fonts

Your choice of font conveys subconscious messages to the reader. Some are considered more friendly than others; some more official. And some are considered to be more legible that others:

* What fonts should you use?
* What font size is needed for headings?
* What emphasis might you put on individual words to bring them to the attention of your reader?

1  Select five different fonts and present a section of text in each font.

2  Canvass friends to find out what impression each font gives.

3  Decide what impression you want to convey and select a font that works for you. Use this as your primary font.

# Charts and graphs

Spreadsheets are invariably used to process numeric data, and the most effective way of presenting numerical results is to use charts and graphs. Charts and graphs convey a lot of information at a glance and are more easily understood by most readers.

However, you need to choose the most appropriate chart or graph – and this depends on the data that you have processed to produce the results.

## Single data series

You have several options when trying to represent a single data series:

* **Pie charts** are best for categorical data, such as the colour of a front door or the make of a car.

* **Bar/column charts** are best for discrete ordinal data, such as shoe sizes. For discrete data, the bars should not touch. If a bar chart is used for continuous data, the bars should touch, and this is then called a **histogram**.

* **Line graphs** are useful to display trends in continuous data. If a graph is used for discrete data (such as shoe sizes), the points should not really be joined because the values between the discrete values are unachievable – but they often are, to show a trend.

Excel provides a wizard to generate such graphical representations (Figure 11.40). It makes sense to use the wizard to set up a chart or graph, but then you can fine tune it so that it shows exactly what you want.

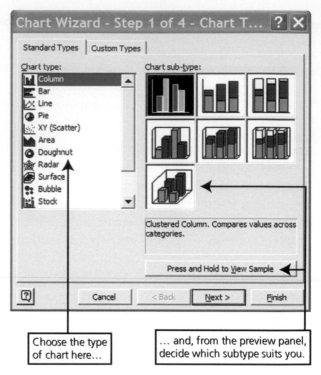

Choose the type of chart here…

… and, from the preview panel, decide which subtype suits you.

FIGURE 11.40  *Chart wizard*

*Categorical data* has separate categories, and there is no natural ordering.

*Ordinal data* may be discrete or continuous, but has a definite ordering (e.g. from smallest to largest, or oldest to newest).

*Discrete data* takes values, but not the values between them. For example, shoes sizes are 4, 4½, 5, 5½, 6, 6½, 7 and so on. There is no shoe size between a 4 and a 4½.

*Continuous data* can take a value anywhere on a number line. For example, time is a continuous variable, as are height, length and weight.

## Other data series

If you have more than one data series, more serious statistical analysis is possible:

* You may want to provide a combined bar chart to show the difference between this year's performance and the previous year's – or budgeted figures against actual figures.

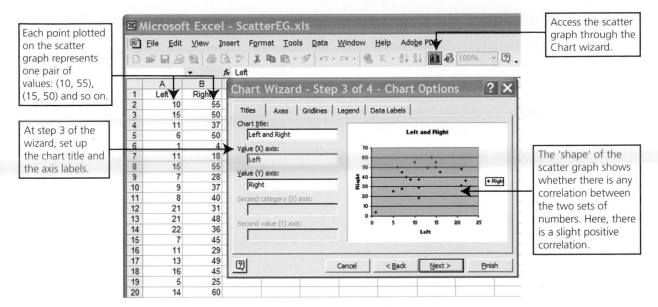

Each point plotted on the scatter graph represents one pair of values: (10, 55), (15, 50) and so on.

At step 3 of the wizard, set up the chart title and the axis labels.

Access the scatter graph through the Chart wizard.

The 'shape' of the scatter graph shows whether there is any correlation between the two sets of numbers. Here, there is a slight positive correlation.

**FIGURE 11.41** *Scatter graph*

* You may need to create a scatter graph (Figure 11.41) to show any correlation between data pairs.

**Think it over...**

What statistics might be relevant for your spreadsheet solution?

Additional analysis tools are available via the **Analysis ToolPak** box, and these are then accessed via **Tools**, **Data Analysis**. For example, you might want to:

* calculate a moving average
* sample data from a large data set
* perform statistical tests, such as the *t*-test or the *z*-test.

All these statistics, and many more, are provided by Excel.

**Theory into practice**

1 Review your design documentation to check what charts and graphics you intended to include with your spreadsheet solution.

2 Check that your choice of chart or graph is appropriate for the data.

## Graphics

You should not include graphics just for the sake of it. However, you may need to include a logo, and there may be other circumstances where a graphic would be appropriate.

**Think it over...**

When might it be relevant for you to include a graphic in your spreadsheet solution?

## Animation

If your results are presented on-screen, you may consider including some form of animation. For example, you might customise the menu options so that the user is presented with options in a more interesting way.

**How to... customise menu animation**

1 Select **View**, **Toolbars**, **Customize**.

2 On the **Options** tab, under **Menu animations**, select the menu animation of your choice: **Random**, **Unfold**, **Slide** or **Fade**.

You might also consider incorporating an animated GIF like the Office Assistant as a link to help the user. (You may have studied how to create animated GIFs in *Unit 10: Using multimedia software*.)

# Colours, borders and shading

In the same way that colours, borders and shading are important for your spreadsheet, they are also important for the presentation of your results. In creating a pie chart, for example, a set of default colours is presented to you, but you can choose your own colours – ones that will complete the general colour scheme of your presentation (Figure 11.42).

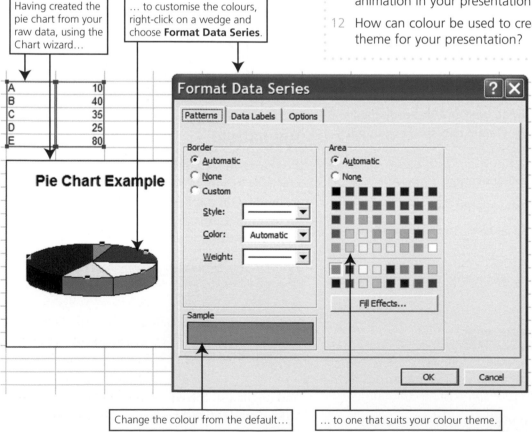

Having created the pie chart from your raw data, using the Chart wizard…

… to customise the colours, right-click on a wedge and choose **Format Data Series**.

Change the colour from the default…

… to one that suits your colour theme.

FIGURE 11.42 *Customising colours on a pie chart*

## Assessment activity

1 Review your design documentation. Check how you planned to present your results.

2 Create a prototype that demonstrates a unified and consistent approach to the presentation of results.

## Assessment hint

✓ Make sure you have paid attention to page layout, fonts, style and colours.

# 11.9 Testing

Spreadsheet output is often used to aid a decision-making process, so inaccurate or unreliable output can have devastating effects. Imagine the possible consequences if the spreadsheet used by a doctor to calculate the correct dosage of a drug has an undiscovered flaw in its logic!

Any spreadsheets that you create and use need to be relied on to provide accurate information in all circumstances. In any event, testing is an essential part of any development process.

To test the end-product, you need to know what it was you were trying to produce. The functional specification documents the aims of the spreadsheet, and it is against this that any testing should be done.

You should ask yourself these questions:

* Does the solution meet all the requirements listed in the functional specification?

* Is the underlying logic of the spreadsheet correct?

* Do all the functions and formulas work correctly?

* Do your validation checks prevent unacceptable data from being entered?

* Can the spreadsheet cope with normal, extreme and abnormal data?

* Is the spreadsheet robust? Or can it be made to fail?

* Are other people able to use it without your help?

It is essential also to involve others in the testing process. Their feedback will prove invaluable to you.

### Think it over...
Whom might you ask to test your spreadsheet solution?

## Prototyping

You do not need to wait until the database development has been completed to start the testing process. Instead, prototypes can be produced and the testing of these completed before further development work is done.

### * Remember!
Be sure to annotate the documentation created during prototyping to provide evidence for your e-portfolio.

## Test data

It is important that you select or create test data that will properly test every aspect of the spreadsheet design and implementation.

There are two ways of thinking about test data: according to whether it is valid, and according to the circumstances under which it might arise.

### Valid and invalid data

For some data items, one of a range of values is expected (Figure 11.43). The terms normal data (or valid data), extreme data (or boundary data) and abnormal data (or invalid data) describe three different types of value that might be entered, and it is important to include all three types in your test data.

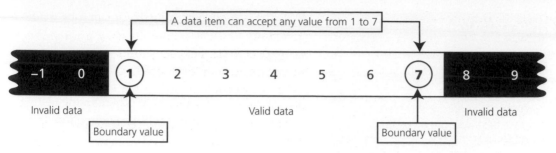

FIGURE 11.43 *Valid and invalid data – and boundary data*

The focus on individual data items and their acceptable values is an essential first stage prior to data testing. Invalid data should not be allowed into the system!

## Event data

Because the user interface allows the user to decide what to do next, there are a number of events that might happen, in any order.

It may be that, due to the way you have developed your system, the events result in the correct outcomes – but not if done in a particular order.

So, in testing your solution, you need to list the events that may happen and test combinations of these events.

## Sample data

In creating sample data, you need only create enough to test your system. If the system works for this data, it ought also to work for the complete system. Provided you include variety in your data, similar to that found in real-life data, it will be representative and will serve its purpose.

## Test plan

It is important to plan how you will test your spreadsheet solution. As well as inventing test data which tests that your validation will trap all possible errors, you must anticipate every user event.

What will happen if the user right-clicks here, or double-clicks there, or takes this route through, instead of the route you normally follow?

Writing a test plan will ensure your testing is done in a systematic way. You can list all the sequences that you need to test and tick them off as you complete the testing. You can make notes if anything untoward happens. This will help you to debug your solution.

## Auditing tools

If, having tested your spreadsheet, you find it is not working as planned, what can you do to trace the error? If you can isolate the problem to a particular worksheet or, better still, a range of cells, your workload in tracking and fixing the error will then be reduced.

So, when testing your prototypes, during the development stages, you must be sure to confirm blocks of cells as working, before moving on to develop the next section. And if you make changes to a worksheet (e.g. to incorporate a new feature), you should test that feature thoroughly before moving on to the next stage of development. In this way, you should proceed from one working prototype to another with confidence that what has gone before definitely works.

Manual checking of figures is one way to check a spreadsheet, but it is time-consuming and does not make the best use of the software. There are two software-based options which may prove useful: cross-casting and auditing tools.

**Cross-casting** involves setting up additional formulas to check other calculations (Figure 11.44). Cross-casting was an essential method in the days of manual book-keeping, and is still used today. However, it can also be used to check the logic of your formulas.

Excel also provides tools to help you to find out what is going wrong within your spreadsheet (Figure 11.45). One of the most common mistakes is to have an incorrect cell reference within a formula. For example, you may have a **circular error**.

### Key terms

If a formula includes a cell reference that leads back to itself, this is called a *circular error*.

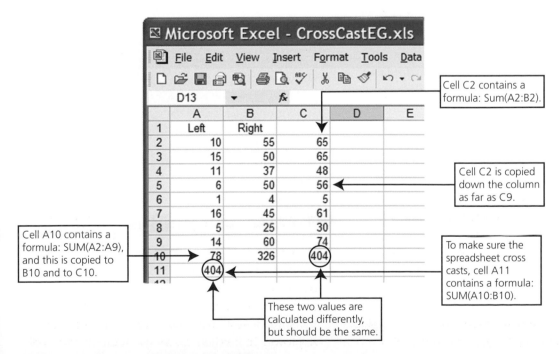

FIGURE 11.44 *Cross-casting in a spreadsheet*

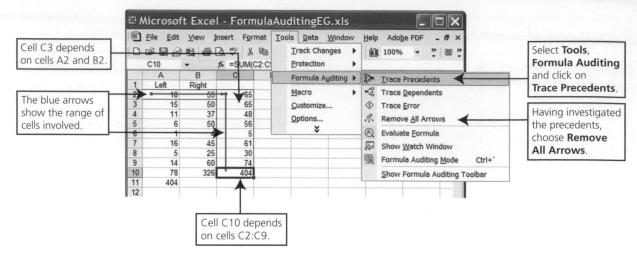

Cell C3 depends on cells A2 and B2.

The blue arrows show the range of cells involved.

Select **Tools**, **Formula Auditing** and click on **Trace Precedents**.

Having investigated the precedents, choose **Remove All Arrows**.

Cell C10 depends on cells C2:C9.

FIGURE 11.45 *Formula auditing*

Excel will trace the sources of a formula so that you can check each one and, hopefully, discover what is going wrong.

Having made one cell active – usually one holding a formula – there are various options. You can trace:

* **precedents** – the cells that are used in the formula

* **dependents** – the cells that depend on the active cell.

For any cell that is displaying an incorrect value, you can therefore trace back to see what data is being used to arrive at that value.

And if you decide to change the formula or data value in a cell, you can see what other cells this will affect.

### Knowledge check

1 How can prototypes act as an aid to testing?

2 What is boundary data?

3 Explain the difference between data testing and event testing.

4 What is sample data? In what way is it different from real data?

5 Why is important to write a test plan?

6 How can an audit trail tool help you to debug your spreadsheet solution?

## Assessment activity

1 Your spreadsheet solution needs to be fully working, so you must test it to prove it to be so.

2 Devise a test plan and follow it, documenting what works and what does not work.

3 According to how much time you have, debug your spreadsheet as best you can. Document this process.

## Assessment hint

✓ Make sure your test data includes both valid and invalid data, and boundary data. Aim also to test all eventualities. Letting someone loose on your prototype while you watch and take notes can be an effective way of event testing.

# 11.10 Documentation

If you develop a spreadsheet solely for your own use, you may feel there is no need to write any documentation. You can rely on recognising your own way of doing things to know how to operate the spreadsheet, even after a long time of not using it. However, if others are to use your spreadsheet solution, documentation becomes essential.

There are two types of documentation: user documentation and technical documentation. Both should be produced, and written, to suit the intended audience. This documentation then needs to be made available in a form that suits the intended audience.

# User documentation

Users may be skilled in developing spreadsheets like you, but you should not assume this. Instead, you need to provide enough information to enable other people to use the spreadsheet without assistance, and assuming little or no prior knowledge.

**Think it over...**

What information tends to be included in user documentation?

In this section you will consider what documentation will be most useful for end users: a 'How to' guide, including sample menus and data entry forms, an explanation of any error messages that might be met and tips for what to do if things go wrong – a troubleshooting strategy.

## How to use the application

In writing the user guide, it should help the user if you provide step-by-step instructions as to how to use the application. Try to use the same terminology as appears on-screen and keep this to a minimum. Jargon is to be avoided!

Users will become frustrated very quickly if your instructions, followed to the letter, do not lead to where they want to be. So, as with all other parts of this project, you need to test your user guide. Ideally, ask someone who is completely unaware of what your spreadsheet solution can do – and, most important, someone who is not a fellow ICT expert.

In the early days of computing, such testers, worth their weight in gold, were affectionately referred to as TOMs (thoroughly obedient morons).

## Menus and data-entry forms

Most of the user interaction will be through making choices on menus and entering data via forms.

## Menus

It is important to provide the user with a route map through your spreadsheet solution. When the spreadsheet is opened, the software defaults to the first worksheet, so this is where the main menu (Figure 11.46) should appear. (Or, perhaps you might have a 'welcome' sheet that then takes the user to the main menu.)

Every other worksheet should offer a route back to the main menu sheet – unless it is essential that the user continues on a sequence of actions without interruption.

Deciding the navigational route through your spreadsheet – and providing the features to enable to user to make relevant choices – is all part of the structure of the solution (as discussed in Section 11.3).

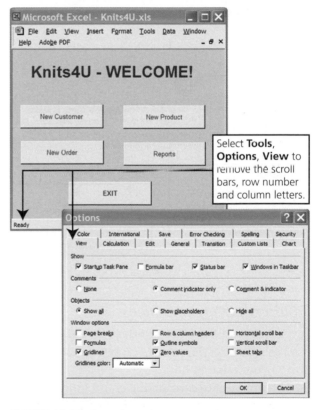

FIGURE 11.46 *A main menu*

## Entry forms

A user will enter all data through data entry forms. These forms will have been designed (as per the comments made in Section 11.6) so as to provide a user-friendly interface. Rather than relying on the intuitive value of these forms, it makes sense to provide sample forms in the user documentation, including explanations as to what is expected in every field.

The user then has no excuse for not entering error-free data!

## Error messages

If the user inadvertently enters incorrect data – or at least data that is considered invalid – then an error message might well appear (Figure 11.47).

You should (as per the guidance given on page 238) have included an error message for each field that is validated, and these should be as meaningful as possible.

However, it still helps users to have an alphabetical list of the messages that might appear, together with an explanation as to how to right the wrong – so that the user can move on.

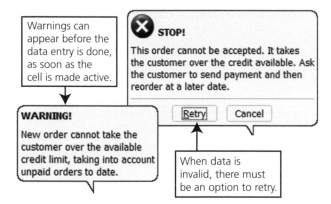

FIGURE 11.47 *An error message*

## Troubleshooting strategies

Few users read the whole guide before starting to use the software; then things go wrong and they don't know what to do.

The prospect of reading the entire guide from cover to cover hardly appeals. So, it would help if, as part of your documentation, you provide a list of **FAQs** which provide a strategy for troubleshooting.

Sometimes problems can arise if the user does not have the necessary hardware, so specifying the minimum requirements is a must.

## Technical documentation

Technical documentation is written for a different audience. This explains the innards of your system to someone who will understand and has to maintain the system long after you have gone.

You will list the formulas that you have used and explain how they fit into the overall solution. You might incorporate these as comments (Figure 11.48).

You will explain what testing has been done and why, with proof that the solution works as intended.

The level of detail will allow another competent professional to understand fully how the spreadsheet works and to be able to maintain and enhance it should you no longer be willing, able or available to do so.

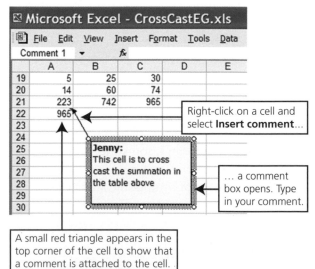

FIGURE 11.48 *Comments in a spreadsheet*

## Distribution of documentation

The documentation could be prepared for distribution in hard-copy format or electronic versions of this – e.g. as text files (Figure 11.49) or **PDF** files.

You could also include helpful documentation via Help files and online tutorials.

### Knowledge check

1  What is the purpose of documentation?

2  Compare and contrast a user guide with technical documentation.

### Assessment activity

1  Write the user guide for your spreadsheet solution.

2  Write the technical documentation.

### Assessment hint

✓ Make sure that both forms of documentation match their intended audience.

# 11.11  Evaluation

Evaluation falls into two distinct types: your spreadsheet solution and how you went about developing it.

## Evaluating your spreadsheet solution

The starting point for any evaluation of a software development project is the functional specification. This lists what the software was to do, and the key question to answer is how well your solution meets the requirements.

For this qualification, you are expected to produce a technically complex working spreadsheet. The marks you earn will depend on how well your spreadsheet solution works.

If you can answer 'yes' to these questions, your mark will be in mark band 1:

✱ Does it meet *most* of the functional requirements? What shortcomings, if any, exist?

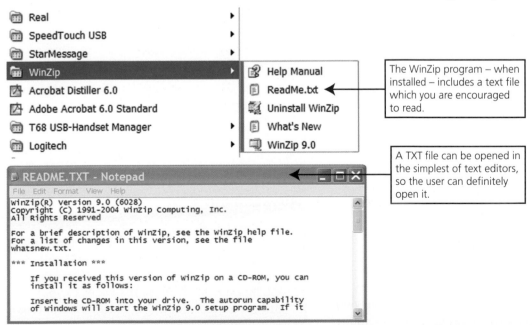

The WinZip program – when installed – includes a text file which you are encouraged to read.

A TXT file can be opened in the simplest of text editors, so the user can definitely open it.

FIGURE 11.49 *Documentation: text files*

* How effective is your solution? What suggestions can you make as to its improvement?

* Did you make *appropriate* use of *some* of the facilities of the software?

If your product is fully working, easy to use and meets *all* the functional requirements, and you have made *good* use of the facilities of the software, you could expect your marks to be higher, in band 2.

Work that bit harder so that the product meets *all* the functional requirements, communicates effectively and is easy to use, and show that you have made full and effective use of the facilities of the software, and your marks should be in band 3.

## Evaluating your own performance

It is important to be able to assess your own performance on a project critically. This does not mean finding fault with everything you have done or being overly pessimistic about your abilities.

Instead, you need to take a long hard look at your strengths and weaknesses, as shown up during the development of this spreadsheet solution.

How can you judge your performance? Well, ask yourself these questions, and be as truthful as you can:

* What did you do well?

* What could you have done better?

The answers to these simple questions may help you to determine your current level of competence:

* Are there any areas ripe for improvement or for future training needs?

* In what ways could you improve your own performance?

## Writing up your evaluation

You are aiming for a well rounded evaluation – incorporating feedback from others – critically assessing your spreadsheet solution and your own performance. Make sure your evaluation includes meaningful evaluative comments about your

solution and sensible comments about your own performance:

* To what extent does your final spreadsheet solution meets the specified requirements? Fully explain any shortcomings.

* How effective is your solution? Include some well thought-out suggestions for enhancements.

* How good was your own performance throughout the project? Include a realistic assessment of your current skill levels and identify areas for improvement.

Your documentation must show that you have made some improvements to the initial design as a result of prototyping. You therefore need to provide some explanatory evaluative comments for each prototype in terms of how well it meets the specified requirements, in terms of fitness for purpose/audience.

It will add weight to your evaluation if you show clearly how feedback from test users was used to shape and refine the design.

Finally, you will need to suggest ways in which you could improve your own performance, and identify any future training needs.

## Assessment activity

1  Refer back to each of your prototypes. Check that you have written evaluative comments for each one. Check also that you have shown how any feedback was acted upon when developing the next prototype.

2  List any shortcomings and explain how they could be implemented.

3  Consider the effectiveness of your solution and make suggestions for improvements.

## Assessment hint

✓ Be honest about how your solution has fallen short of expectations. At this stage, it is important to show the assessor that you can be critical of your own work, have vision and an understanding of the needs of your audience, even though you may not have time to implement all your ideas.

# 11.12 ICT skills

You will be using spreadsheet software to produce a solution to a problem and will need to have acquired skills in particular tasks.

Table 11.2 lists the tasks that you must be able to do, prior to completing this unit.

Some of these skills you will have learnt in Unit 3; the others you will need during the development of your solution, and should have acquired by the time you have completed this unit.

### I CAN...

| |
|---|
| Combine complex information and linking to other applications (e.g. exporting and importing data, linked objects) |
| Organise data (e.g. linked sheets, LOOKUP tables) |
| Enter and edit data (e.g. absolute and relative cell referencing, inserting data into multiple cells simultaneously, using multiple worksheets) |
| Format cells (e.g. conditional formatting, cell formats that match the data format) |
| Use functions and formulas to solve complex problems (e.g. LOOKUPS, arguments, arrays, selection) |
| Validate and check data (e.g. using formulas to determine valid entries for cells) |
| Analyse and interpret data (e.g. PivotTables, data maps, adding messages to data) |
| Present information (e.g. views, PivotTable reports, different types of graphs and charts) |
| Limit access (e.g. hide and protect cells) |
| Customise and automate (e.g. templates, macros, forms, menus) |

TABLE 11.2 *Spreadsheet tasks*

# Customising applications

PC software includes a wide range of applications to support common office data-processing tasks, such as databases, spreadsheets, word-processing and presentation applications. In this unit you are going to enhance applications using programming facilities to provide customised functions and adapt the user interface to provide a professional, easy-to-use customised application.

This optional unit contains 12 elements:

12.1 Functional specification

12.2 The need to code

12.3 Objects, control properties and events

12.4 Designing routines

12.5 Programming structures

12.6 Human computer interface

12.7 Programming and the database

12.8 Programming and the spreadsheet

12.9 Testing

12.10 Program documentation

12.11 Evaluation

12.12 Programming skills

The familiar, general-purpose applications such as word processing, spreadsheets and databases are designed to be 'Jacks of all trades' with a wide range of inbuilt facilities. However, there are times when providing additional facilities can be useful. As ICT professionals you may, in the future, be called upon to customise these applications. For example, to:

* automate a complex facility to make it easier for an inexperienced user

* build a user interface, including menus

* provide facilities which validate user input to reduce the possibility of errors.

Each of the standard office applications provides a built-in programming capability using **macros**.

Simple macros can be recorded by carrying out the action you wish the macro to perform with the Macro Recorder running. However, this unit goes beyond these basic recorded macros and looks at how to automate tasks using programming code. This unit demonstrates how to create customised applications within Microsoft Office 2003 using the built-in programming language Visual Basic for Applications (VBA for short).

## Resources required in this unit

You will need access to a computer with a customisable office software package installed such as Microsoft Office.

## How you will be assessed

For this unit you will need to design, produce, test and evaluate a working solution to a problem involving the use of a customised software application. You will need to include the following:

* A functional specification that describes the problem and explains what the customised solution will do.

* An initial design which explains how the functions described in the functional specification will work. It will need to cover the design of the forms used, data structures required and include diagrams of the structures of each function. You will also need to show how you used prototyping to develop the design.

* A fully working custom solution, including user and technical documentation.
* Evidence of the testing you have done.
* An evaluation of the solution you have created, and your own performance and skills developed in producing the solution.

## How high can you aim?

Your e-portfolio will contain all the evidence on which your performance will be judged. Some assessment activities can be used towards your e-portfolio. These contain assessment hints on what you can do to pass (✓), gain a better mark (✓✓) or achieve top marks (✓✓✓).

## Ready to start?

This unit should take around 40 hours to complete. Why not keep a log of your time? You may find it is useful to keep a record of the time you spend on this unit when you come to write your evaluation.

# 12.1 Functional specification

A functional specification does what it says: it describes the functions of the application. It explains what the application will do, but it does not go into the technical detail of how it will do it. The functional specification is an important document that needs to be agreed with the application's users. It tells the users what they are going to get, and the programmers who write the application must refer to it to ensure that what they provide meets what has been agreed.

Writing a functional specification involves investigating the problem that you are intending to solve. You will need to find out about the following:

* **The context**. What is the current situation? What software application is involved? Who are the users? What is it they are using the existing software for?

* **The nature of the problem**. You will need to look in detail at the area of the application that you plan to customise. What do the users currently do? Why is this a problem? Is there any other way the problem can be solved?

* **What the custom solution is required to do**. Having understood the problem, you next need to consider what the solution you plan to develop will need to do. You will need to consider if what you have in mind will meet the users' needs (will it really solve the problem they have?) and if it is technically feasible.

* **Measuring success**. How will you measure the success of the custom solution? The most important criterion is that the solution meets the needs of the users. You will need to consider how you can measure this. The most likely situation is that the customisation you will do will make some aspects of their use of the application easier.

Of course, in your situation, 'the users' will probably be imaginary, so you will need to try to understand the problems they might have using applications software. Your tutor should provide guidance for you as to what these imaginary users want, and agree the contents of the functional specification with you.

It is important to remember that the functional specification is not a 'write it and forget it' document. Because it should have been agreed to by the users, you must use it as your guide as to what to produce. It is all to easy, when developing customised software, to get carried

# CASE STUDY

Let's look at an example of designing a simple application. A mobile phone shop uses a spreadsheet to help customers estimate what their typical monthly bills might be with different service providers. The spreadsheet is shown in Figure 12.1.

This spreadsheet calculates the estimated bills for three different service providers (shown in E2:E4), based on the number of peak and off-peak minutes entered by the user (in E6:E7).

However, some of the salespeople in the shop are not very familiar with spreadsheets so they want a customised version of the spreadsheet.

The following is an example of a brief functional specification for the bill estimator.

## Functional specification

### The context

The mobile phone shop 'My Mobile' uses a spreadsheet to demonstrate to customers who are interested in a pay-monthly phone what the likely costs might be on different tariffs. They do this by asking the customers what their estimated number of calls per month are at peak times (usually 9 am–5 pm weekdays) and off-peak times (evening and weekends). My Mobile then enter this information into the spreadsheet.

### The problem

The problem is that some of the salespeople are not very familiar with spreadsheets and would prefer something easier to use. The company would also like to set up a 'self-service booth' where customers can check their own estimated bills. Therefore a self-contained, easy-to-use application is required.

A solution could be provided by writing a customised 'front end' to the spreadsheet.

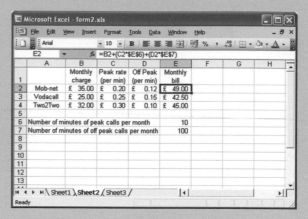

FIGURE 12.1 *Bill estimator spreadsheet*

The only other solution would be to create printed tables of tariffs, but this would not be as flexible or as easy to use as a custom application. Therefore the best option would be to write a customised front end for the existing spreadsheet.

### The solution

The customised solution will allow the user to enter the number of minutes of calls he or she estimates that he or she will make, using a form that has input boxes for these two values. Once these have been entered, the user will click a button and be taken to another form. This will display the estimated monthly cost (using the same calculation as the original spreadsheet). The user can then select different service providers from a list and can see how much his or her bill would be. A button on this form will take the user back to the previous one so that different values can be entered.

1   How could the success of the solution be measured in terms of the salespeople?

2   How could the success of the solution be measured in terms of the customers?

away with new ideas (or to find ways around problems, which means you are moving away from what you said you would do). Of course, you may come across a good idea which provides a solution that is better than what you described in the functional specification. If this is the case you need to go back to modify the specification and agree the modification with your users.

## 12.2 The need to code

Before setting out on the design and development of the customisation, you must be sure that what you have in mind cannot be provided without writing code. Modern office application suites, such as Microsoft Office, have a very sophisticated set of features as standard, and you will need to check the Help files and other documentation to ensure that you cannot meet the user's need by employing existing built-in features, such as **macros**, wizards or other ready-made functions. The reason why this is important is that writing code is not a trivial exercise, and using a built-in feature will almost always be quicker than creating a customised function.

**Key terms**

A *macro* is a short piece of programming code that can be used to automate the functions of applications software.

However, there are many situations where writing code to create a customised application is the only way to meet the users' needs adequately.

Office application suites are generalised tools designed to meet a wide range of needs. Adding customised facilities can produce a system that is closely matched to a specific user need. Examples include:

✳ making a complex function easier to use by tailoring it to a particular situation

✳ adding functionality which does not exist (or is very hard to achieve) into the standard application

✳ saving time by automating a long series of commands needed to achieve a certain task

✳ improving security

✳ facilitating data sharing between applications.

Faced with requirements like these that cannot be met in any other way, designing, writing and testing programming code are the only options.

**Assessment activity**

Research a suitable customised solution that you can produce.

**Assessment hint**

✓ You have written a functional specification for the solution you have in mind.

✓✓ You have described the problem and explained in detail what the custom solution will do.

✓✓✓ You have described specific measurable success criteria, such as '4 out 5 of the people who evaluate my solution will select the highest mark for quality on the survey they complete'.

## 12.3 Objects, control properties and events

VBA (Visual Basic for Applications) is an **event-driven**, object-orientated programming environment.

VBA is object orientated in that it deals with various 'things' within the application, such as a Document object within Word, a Worksheet object within Excel or a RecordSet object within Access. These objects have **properties** which describe the object.

Objects also have **methods**. These are the things the object can do.

These terms are important ones to understand. Imagine the list of emails you have recently received. The emails are the objects; their properties would include things like whom they were from and the date you received them. The methods that could be applied to these objects would include forwarding them to someone else and deleting them.

## Visual Basic controls

When customising applications you will often add objects such as forms, buttons and list boxes to create a user interface, although rather confusingly, Visual Basic calls these types of objects **controls**.

Button controls, for example, can be used to make something happen. When the user clicks on the button, an event occurs (known as the onClick event), and the code associated with that event runs. Buttons, like most controls, have many properties, but the ones you will use most often are their Caption property, which controls the text displayed on the button, and the Name property, which sets the name of the button. Let's look at an example.

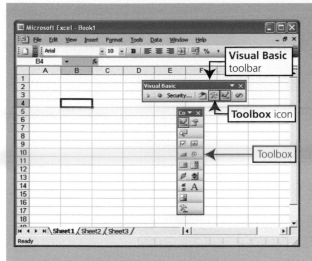

FIGURE 12.2 *The Visual Basic toolbar and toolbox*

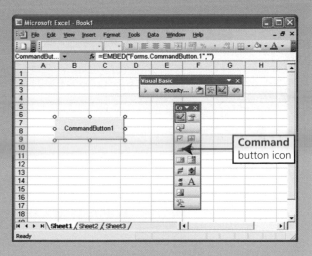

FIGURE 12.3 *A command button*

you write program code that works with the controls, you must, of course, know their names. To change the text that appears in the **Command** button, the **Caption** property must be changed. Find that property in the list and change its value to **OK**, as shown in Figure 12.4.

5 As well as setting properties using the **Properties** box, while you are designing your application, properties can be modified while the program is running. To see how this can be done, add label and text box controls, and set the **Caption** property for the label to **Enter your name**, as shown in Figure 12.5.

Note that the **Name** property of the text box is automatically set to **TextBox1** and the name of the label is set to **Label1**.

6 Now double-click on the button you have created and the **Code** box will open. An empty event procedure will already be created, called **Command1_click**. The code you enter in this procedure will run when the user clicks on the button.

You want to take the name that the user types into the text box (the **Text** property of the textbox) and add the word **Hello**, then set the **Caption** property of the label to that string. So, for example, if you enter the name Ahmed

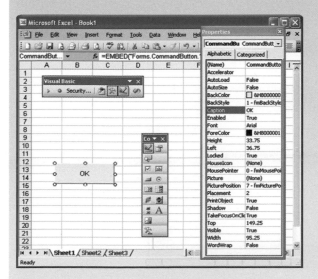

FIGURE 12.4 *Setting the Caption property*

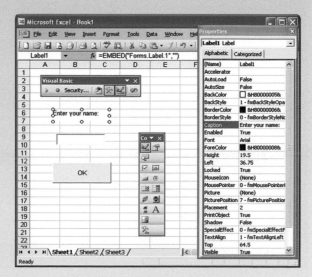

FIGURE 12.5 *Adding a label and text box*

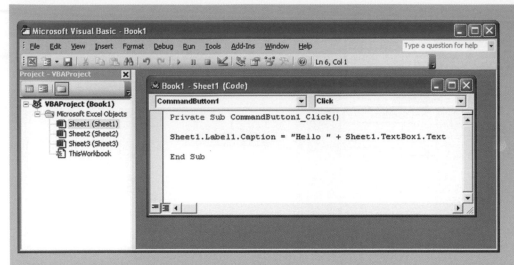

FIGURE 12.6 *Code for the button*

in the text box, the words Hello Ahmed will appear in the label. This demonstrates how to use the value of a property in a program (the **Text** property of the text box) and also how to set the property of a control within a program (the **Caption** property of the label). The required code is quite simple (only one line) and is shown in Figure 12.6.

Note that you need to specify the sheet object that the control is in when you refer to it (as in **Sheet1.TextBox1**).

7 To try out this little program you need to exit **Design** mode by clicking on the **Design Mode** button on the **Visual Basic** toolbar, then enter a name in the text box and click on the **OK** button. The result should look something like Figure 12.7.

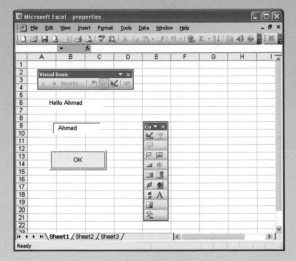

FIGURE 12.7 *The result of clicking on the OK button*

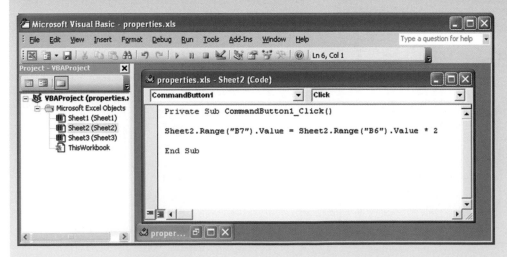

FIGURE 12.8 *Referring to a cell*

This example shows how to set the properties of controls but it does not refer to any data in the spreadsheet itself. Cells or ranges of cells within a worksheet can be referred to using the **Range** object. So to refer to the value in cell B6 on sheet2 you would use:

```
Sheet2.Range("B6").Value
```

The following code shows how this can be used. It simply takes the value from one cell, multiplies it by 2 and places the result in another cell (see Figure 12.8).

The result of running this line of code is shown in Figure 12.9.

Note that the **Value** property is the default property for the **Range** object, so if you omit it from the code it will still work. So this code:

```
Sheet2.Range("B7") =
Sheet2.Range("B6") *  2
```

will work in exactly the same way.

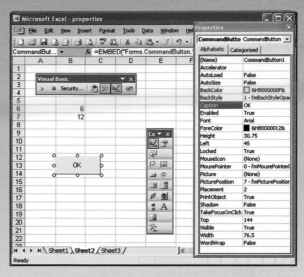

**FIGURE 12.9** *The code running*

In this section you have learnt a little about the objects and controls you can use to create applications, and about the properties which make those objects look and behave a certain way. However, before you can go any further with understanding how to create applications, we must look at how they can be designed.

## Knowledge check

1 Explain what properties and methods are.

2 Why is it important to avoid writing code in order to customise an application if possible?

3 Give some examples of situations where writing code may be necessary.

4 Explain the term 'event driven'.

5 Explain the difference between an object and a method.

6 Give some examples of Visual Basic Controls.

# 12.4  Designing routines

Creating customised applications can be a complex process, so it is important that, before you start writing any code, you produce a design for the application.

The starting point for your design will be the functional specification. This describes what the application will do, but it does not explain how it will do it. The process of producing a design involves taking a general description of what the application will do and progressively adding more detail to it.

The detailed design needs to cover the three main aspects of any application:

\* the input required

\* the output to be produced

\* the processing involved.

In addition, when designing applications which customise a spreadsheet or database, consideration needs to be given to the design of that spreadsheet or database.

## Prototyping

One problem that you will probably face when creating your designs is that you really need a good understanding of how programs are written in order to become expert at writing them. At this stage, therefore, it is probably best to use an incremental or iterative approach to software development. This involves designing and creating a simplified version of the system, which is known as a **prototype**.

Prototyping has a number of advantages:

* You may create several different prototypes to try out alternatives and investigate which approach works best.

* You can test that parts of the program within your system work properly, and that your logic is correct.

* You can show your prototype to others to obtain feedback on its ease of use and how closely it matches the user requirements.

* You can also ask others to test parts of your program to ensure it is robust and cannot easily be made to fail.

### Think it over...

Prototyping is sometimes used in commercial software development. However, for a company producing software to a fixed timescale and budget, prototyping has some disadvantages. Can you think what these might be?

Having completed a first prototype you can then add functionality to it to create further prototypes, which add more and more functionality to the system. In this way the complete system is built in an incremental way, rather that attempting the complete system all at once.

## Structure charts

Whether you are creating a design for the complete system or a prototype, the process is the same. The simplest way to start your design is to break the system down into the major components or routines (these themselves may form the basis for the prototypes in your system). Once you have done this, you can start work on the detailed designs for each routine.

The key to deciding how to break any system down into routines is a clear understanding of the functions the system will perform. Once this is understood the different routines required should become obvious.

### ✱ Remember!

Programs should not be split into routines just for the sake of it. In a well designed system, routines have a clearly defined function with as little overlap and interaction between routines as possible.

### Theory into practice

The information provided in the functional specification of the mobile phone bill estimator can be used to identify three main routines:

1 Entering the number of estimated minutes.

2 Selecting the different service providers.

3 Displaying monthly bills.

The system will still use the spreadsheet to do the calculations, but you will add a customised 'front end' (i.e. the part of the system the user interfaces with) to make it easier to use.

When designing software routines, diagrams are often used to provide a simple description of the design rather than words alone. There are a variety of diagramatic design techniques, such as structure diagrams and flow charts.

The technique described here is for structure charts. These show the way the application or routine is divided up and are developed in increasing detail.

Structure charts start with simple diagrams that show the various routines the application is split into and then move on to more complex diagrams that describe the processing steps in each routine.

The simple structure diagram showing the different routines we have identified is shown in Figure 12.10.

Once you have decided how to break the application down into modules you can proceed with the detailed design for each routine.

---

**✳ Remember!**

If you are using an incremental approach to the development of the system to start with, you may design and create one prototype routine first before moving on to the design and creation of the other routines.

---

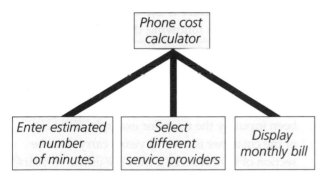

FIGURE 12.10 *Structure diagram for the phone cost calculator*

## Input design

Probably the simplest place to start the detailed design is with the required inputs. The basic information about what the user will input into the system will come from the functional specification. You need to add more detail to that information by deciding the format of the data to be input, how it will be validated and the layout of the form that will be used to collect the data. The form design must consider the user's needs and, as it is the most obvious part of the program

that the user will have experience of, the design should be neat and professional; otherwise, the user may judge the software to be of poor quality. You should also ensure the following:

✳ The fields are presented on the form in a logical order, with the most important or the one that would be completed first at the top.

✳ The fields should be clearly labelled so the user knows what should be entered in each field.

✳ The layout of the form should be neat and consistent, with the fields and the labels each aligned with the other fields and labels on the form. There should also be consistent spacing between fields.

✳ Labels and titles should be correctly spelt and, where necessary, informative titles should be added to guide the user.

The layout for each screen form should be designed by hand or by using the drawing tools in a program like Microsoft Word. You must make it clear in your design which items are labels, fields and command buttons.

The form design for the input minutes form is shown in Figure 12.11. The error message text is shown in grey because it only appears if the validation rules for the input fields are broken. The error messages are defined in the input data table, described in the next section.

Having decided on the layout for the form, the next step is to make a list of the **variables** that will be required to store the input data.

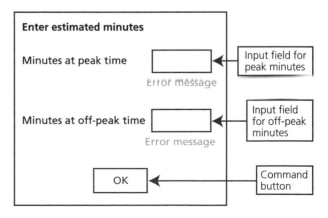

FIGURE 12.11 *Design for the input minutes form*

an @ and at least one dot. If these characters are missing, then the address must be invalid.

To check the validity of the email address, a loop is required to inspect each character of the address to see if it is one of the required characters. We also need a way to keep track of whether the required characters have been found, as they can occur anywhere in the field. One method would be to use a **flag**.

At the beginning of the loop the flag is set to zero. If either of the required characters is found, it is **incremented** by 1.

A structure diagram showing the design for this module is shown in Figure 12.16.

Above the box which describes the iteration construct, the words 'Until end of email' tell us that the loop will continue until this is the case. In the box itself an asterisk (*) is shown indicating that this is an iteration construct.

Structure diagrams are quite a useful technique for breaking the complexity of a programming problem down into initially simple steps and then adding more detail to those steps with further diagrams. However, as mentioned earlier, unless you already have some programming experience it can be difficult to work out what steps are required. Another problem can be that the diagrams don't always bear a particularly close resemblance to the code you will eventually write. These are things you may well want to comment on when you write your evaluation at the end of the unit.

## Application design

The spreadsheet and database that you will customise will also need to be included in the design work you will do. With a spreadsheet you will need to consider the following:

* What data will be stored in the spreadsheet, and how (and if) will it be split across different sheets?

* The formulas you will use to do calculations on the data.

* The layout and formatting of the spreadsheet.

Database design is a rather more complex subject and you will need to divide your raw data up into fields and tables using the techniques you have learnt in Unit 7, such as normalisation.

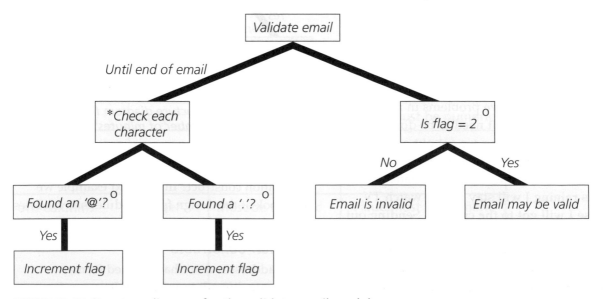

FIGURE 12.16 *Structure diagram for the validate email module*

1  What is prototyping?

2  What are the three basic types of program processing steps?

3  What is a variable?

## Assessment activity

Complete a design for the custom solution for which you previously produced the function specification.

## Assessment hint

✓  Your design satisfies most of the functional requirements and covers the data structures required, responses to events and functions to be programmed, and form layout. You have shown evidence of having completed some limited prototyping.

✓✓  Your design includes diagrams to show the structure of each function. You have made good use of prototyping, making comments on each stage.

✓✓✓  You have produced a comprehensive design that covers all aspects in detail and shows effective use of prototyping.

# 12.5 Programming structures

We mentioned the concept of different programming structures when we considered the design of the processing that a routine will carry out. We now need to look at some examples of how these structures are actually implemented using Visual Basic for applications. We will also investigate how to create sub-programs that can carry out commonly required tasks. First, let's look at selection and iteration structures.

## Selection structures

Selection structures are usually implemented using an 'if' instruction. This takes the form:

```
if (test) then
  instructions to be followed if
  test returns true
else
  instructions to be followed if
  test returns false
end if
```

As an example, you will create a simple prototype using VBA within an Excel worksheet, which will tell you if the value in a certain cell is greater or less than 10.

### How to create... selection structures

1  First, open Excel as normal, then, from the **View** menu, choose **Toolbars** and **Visual Basic**. This will bring the **Visual Basic** toolbar on to the screen.

2  Click on the **Toolbox** button on the **Visual Basic** toolbar so that the toolbox is also shown (this is the same procedure as you used in Section 12.3 when investigating objects, controls and properties).

3  Now click on the **Command** button icon in the toolbox and drag out a command button.

4  Find the **Caption** property in the **Property** box (click on the **Properties** icon in the toolbox to bring it on-screen if it is not visible), and change its value to **Check**, as shown in Figure 12.17.

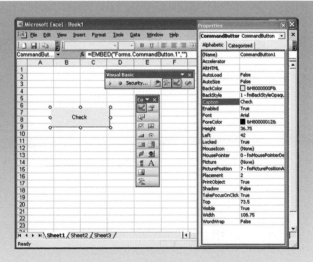

FIGURE 12.17 *Setting the Caption property*

5 In order to add the event code that will run when the user clicks on the button (which is the event), double-click on the button to open the **Visual Basic** program window. This will create an empty event procedure for you, called **CommandButton1_Click**. Figure 12.18 below shows the program window with the code added.

Note that the cell B4 is referred to in the program as 'Range("B4")', which is the way cell objects are accessed in VBA. The value property of the cell (Range("B4").value) is compared using the if statement with a value of 10. If the value in the cell is greater than or equal to 10, then the **MsgBox** function is used to pop an appropriate message on to the screen. The 'else' part of the if statement also uses the **MsgBox** function with a message telling the user that the value is less than 10.

6 To run the application, return to the Excel window (there is no need to close the VBA window), and click on the **Exit design mode** icon on the toolbox.

7 Now enter a value into cell B4 and click on the command button. A message box should appear on-screen with the correct message, as shown in Figure 12.19.

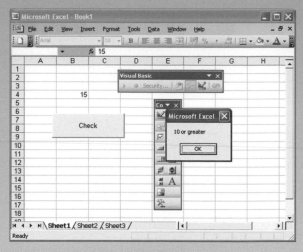

FIGURE 12.19 *The program running*

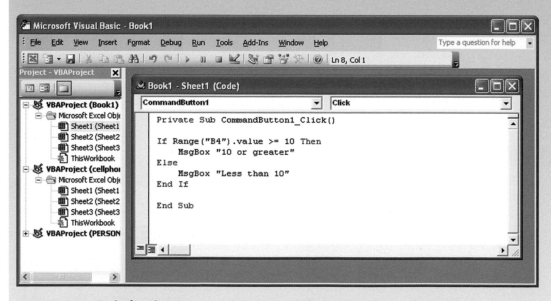

FIGURE 12.18 *Code for the CommandButton1_Click procedure*

In this example the selection structure makes a choice between two possible sections of code, each of which only contains one instruction. Of course, the sections of code can contain as many instructions as required, and there can be more than two choices. The 'ElseIf' instruction can be used to add further conditions to the selection structure (see the modified program shown in Figure 12.20).

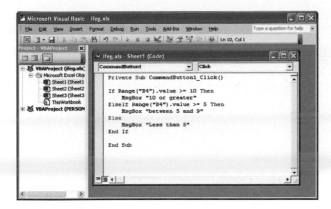

FIGURE 12.20 *Use of the ElseIf instruction*

Where there are many different conditions to be tested, selection structures using the 'if' instruction can become rather complex so, as an alternative, the 'select case' structure can be used. We will use another simple prototype to demonstrate the use of the 'select case' structure (see Theory into practice box below).

## Iteration structures

Iteration structures are used where a section of code needs to be repeated, either a certain number of times or until some condition is met.

There are three code structures used to implement iteration:

✳ for… next loops

✳ until loop

✳ while loops.

We shall look at examples of each of these in turn.

### For… next loops

A for… next loop repeats a certain number of times. It also uses a variable as a counter, which is incremented on each iteration of the loop. A for… next code structure has the general format:

```
For counter start_value to end_value
    Instructions to be executed each
    time around the loop
Next counter
```

The following example program (see page 274) takes a number entered in a cell (B4) and counts up through all the integers from 1 to the number and displays them in column D. The code for the program is shown in Figure 12.23. Here the start value for the loop is 1 and the end value is whatever number is entered in cell B4.

Theory into practice

Figure 12.21 shows a spreadsheet that could be used as part of an application in which the user is required to enter a number between 1 and 4.

The code attached to the **OK** button is shown in Figure 12.22. It uses a 'select case' structure to display a different message, depending on the value entered in cell D5. Note that the 'Case Else' instruction allows action to be taken if none of the proceeding case conditions are met.

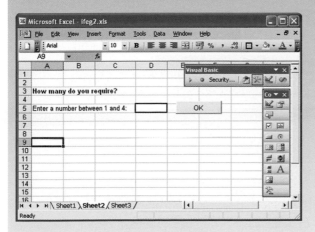

FIGURE 12.21 *Example spreadsheet*

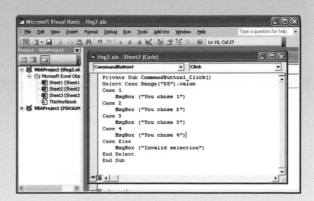

FIGURE 12.22 *Use of the 'select case' structure*

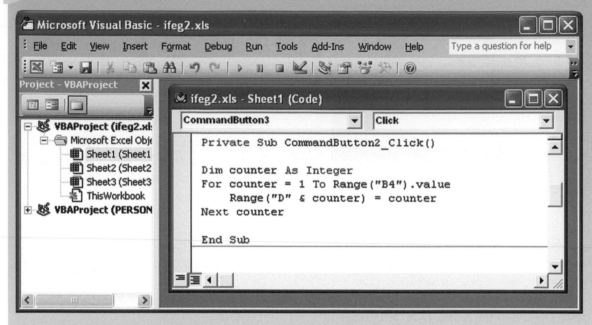

FIGURE 12.23 *For... next loop example*

Note that the row number of the cells in column D is counted through using the loop counter. The ampersand character (&) is used to join the column letter to the row number. Figure 12.24 shows an example of the program running.

## Until loops

The until loop, unlike the for... next loop, continues until some condition becomes true. It takes the general form:

```
Do Until condition
    Instructions to be carried out
    while the condition is true
Loop
```

Let's look at an example program that shows how an until loop can be used to validate user input by ensuring that it is numeric. Once again this is not a complete program. Instead, it is a fragment which demonstrates how to use this particular feature.

This program introduces the use of the **input box** function. This function displays an input dialogue box. When the user makes an entry in the box and clicks on the **OK** button, whatever he or she has entered is placed in the variable on the left side of the instruction.

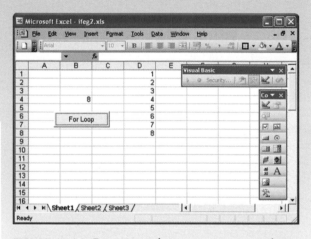

FIGURE 12.24 *For... next loop program running*

The code for the until loop example program is shown in Figure 12.25. It is, of course, the onClick event procedure for a command button.

The condition for the until loop uses another Visual Basic function called **IsNumeric( )**. This function is passed a variable. It returns True if the variable contains a numeric value and False if it does not. The loop condition therefore says, in plain English, 'loop until the user input is numeric'. Figure 12.26 shows the program running.

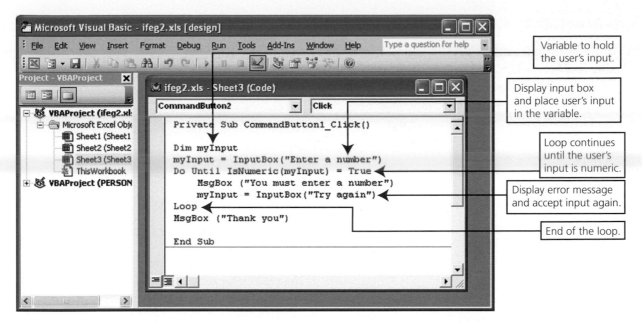

FIGURE 12.25 *Code for the until loop example*

Note that, in the program shown in Figure 12.26, if the user enters a numeric value when the input box first appears, then the code within the until loop will not be executed. This is because the condition is at the beginning of the loop (known as a **pre-condition loop**). There may be situations when you need the code within the loop to be executed at least once, in which case the condition in the loop can be moved to the end of the loop.

## While loops

An until loop continues until some condition becomes True (i.e. the loop continues while it is False); a while loop, on the other hand, continues while some condition is True. In every other respect these two types of loops are the same.

### Theory into practice

The following program will calculate the sum of the integers for any number (e.g. the sum of the integers of 8 is 8 + 7 + 6 + 5 + 4 + 3 + 2 + 1 = 36). It takes the value entered in cell A3, then uses a while loop to count down through the number (by subtracting 1 from it). As it does this it adds each value to a variable called **SumOfIntegers**. The loop ends when zero is reached and the value in the SumOfIntegers variable is inserted in cell A4. The program is shown in Figure 12.27.

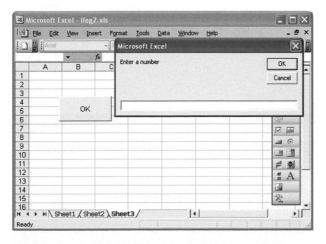

FIGURE 12.26 *The until loop program running*

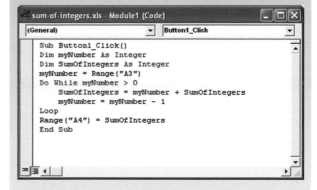

FIGURE 12.27 *Sum of Integers program*

# Sub-programs

Visual Basic supplies many built-in functions (often called **intrinsic functions**). Some functions perform common mathematical tasks, such as computing a square root. Other functions manipulate string data, such as converting text inside a string to upper case or lower case letters.

> **Key terms**
>
> A *function* is a reusable piece of code that provides some commonly required functionality.

A function's job is to save you time. For example, if you need to compute the square root of a user's entered value, you could write the code to do this calculation. The square root, however, is such a common routine that the code has already been written and stored as an intrinsic function. Now, if you want the square root of a value, you will pass the value to the square-root function, which will return the result.

You have already used a number of intrinsic functions, including MsgBox( ), InputBox( ) and IsNumeric( ). Functions are passed a value from the program that requests the function, and they return a value. The code where the InputBox function was used in the until loop example demonstrates this:

```
myInput = InputBox("Enter a number")
```

The caption for the input box "Enter a number" is the parameter that is passed to the function. The variable myInput accepts the return value from the function.

You can write your own functions and subroutines if required. Subroutines are similar to functions but cannot return values.

## How to... create a function

Suppose you were writing a system where you often needed to calculate the amount of VAT payable on a net amount (i.e. an amount to which VAT has yet to be added). Rather than duplicating the code to carry out this calculation in many parts of the system, you decide to write a function. The benefit of this approach is that it ensures the calculation is done correctly and in the same way throughout the system, and also means that if the VAT rate (currently 17.5 per cent) were ever to change, it would only need to be changed in one place in the program.

1 The first step in creating a function or subroutine is to make sure you have the Visual Basic code window displayed. Press **Alt + F11** from within Excel.

2 Click on the **View Code** button to open the **Code** window.

3 From the **Insert** menu, select the **Procedure** option. This will display the dialogue box shown in Figure 12.28.

4 Type the name of the function in the **Name** box (calcVAT), and select the type of procedure as **Function**.

5 Click on **OK**. This will create an empty function for you in the Code window. The empty brackets after the function name are where you define the values (and their data types) that are passed to the function by the calling program. In this case the function will need to be passed the net amount, which will require

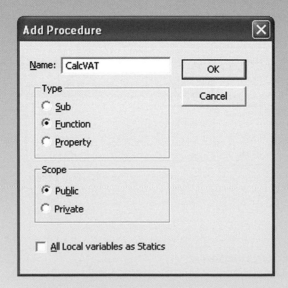

FIGURE 12.28 *The Add procedure dialogue box*

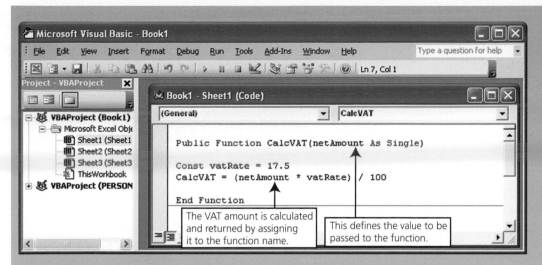

**FIGURE 12.29** *The code for the CalcVAT function*

The VAT amount is calculated and returned by assigning it to the function name.

This defines the value to be passed to the function.

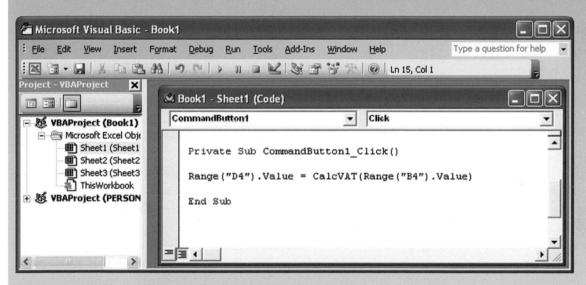

**FIGURE 12.30** *Event procedure to test the CalcVAT function*

a data type of single (so that it can accept values with a decimal part, such as 55.23).

The data that is returned by the function is specified by assigning (using the equals sign) the value to be returned to the function name. The complete code can be seen in Figure 12.29.

By itself the function does nothing, so you need to write a small prototype program to test it. This will simply pass a value from a cell in a worksheet to the function (as the net amount for which VAT is to be calculated) and display the value returned from the function in another cell. The event procedure is shown in Figure 12.30.

The working prototype is shown in Figure 12.31.

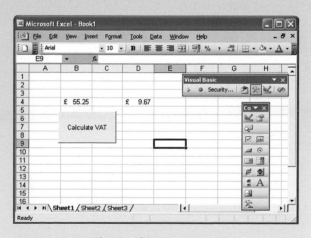

**FIGURE 12.31** *The working prototype*

There may little point in writing a function to calculate VAT as shown above – the code could have easily been included in the program but, remember, the idea of a function is it is a reusable piece of code that could be used many times within a large system.

1  Explain how a function can be used.

2  List the three different types of code used to implement iteration structures.

3  Give an example of an intrinsic function.

4  In what sort of situation might you use a 'select case' structure?

# 12.6  Human computer interface

The importance of form design has already been mentioned. You need to create forms that are easy to use and effective. In this section we shall look in more detail at how forms, and the objects on the forms (such as text boxes, labels and buttons), are created and modified.

The prototypes you have created so far to demonstrate various program features have not used forms and, while it is perfectly possible to create complete applications within Excel without using them, forms do provide a more sophisticated user interface.

**Think it over...**

Producing easy-to-use software is not as easy as you might think. Have you used any software that proved difficult to use? Why was it difficult to use, and what could the developer have done to make it easier? You may be able to use this experience to help you avoid the same problems in the software you develop.

## Creating forms

To create forms in VBA, the Forms Editor is used. Let's look at an example of how to create a form for the mobile phone cost estimator application you designed earlier (see Figure 12.11 on page 267).

The form itself – and any of the objects that can be placed on the form (command buttons, text boxes, labels, etc.) – all have a set of properties that can be adjusted to control the look and behaviour of the object. Many of these properties are beyond the scope of this unit, but there are some that you need to be aware of.

As you saw previously, every object has a **Name** property, which sets the name of the object. All objects, when created, have a default name, but this is not very meaningful and it is good practice to give objects meaningful names that give some clue as to their purpose. It is also a good idea to prefix the name to indicate what type of object it is, as this will improve the readability

**How to... create a form (1)**

1  To add a form, first make sure the VBA window is open.

2  From the **Insert** menu, choose **User form**. This will insert a blank form in the VBA window and also open the **Forms Editor** toolbar, as shown in Figure 12.32.

When editing forms it is often useful to have the **Properties** window displayed, which can be done by clicking on the **Properties button** in the toolbar.

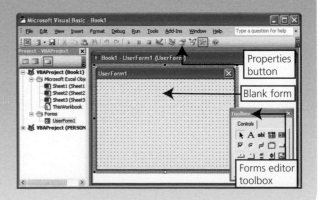

**FIGURE 12.32** *The Forms Editor*

of the code you write. Commonly used prefixes include:

* **frm** (form)
* **cmd** (command button)
* **lbl** (label)
* **txt** (text box).

The default name for the form itself is **UserForm***N*, where N is a sequential number starting at 1.

## How to... create a form (2)

For your mobile phone cost estimator application, this name could be changed to **frmInputMins** (note that object names cannot contain spaces).

The first object you will place on the frmInputMins is the title at the top. Text that the user does not need to interact with is added using a label.

1 Click on the **Label** icon in the toolbox and drag out a box for the label to appear on in the form. Initially the label's **Caption** property (which sets the text that appears in the label) is set to the default name for the label (Label1).

2 Using the **Property** window, change the value for the **Caption** property to the text you want ('Enter estimated minutes'). Also change the **Name** property to **lblTitle**.

3 Click on the **Font** property and then click on the little button that appears to the right of the current font name. This will display the **Font dialogue box** where you can set the usual range of font attributes. Make this title label 10 pt bold so that it stands out. Your form should now look like Figure 12.33.

4 Now add the other labels to the form and then the two text boxes. Remember that the two error message labels only appear if an error occurs, so setting their **Visible** property to 'false' will mean they don't appear on the form when it is first displayed.

5 Finally, add the command button.

The completed form is shown in Figure 12.34. The names given to each of the form objects are also shown.

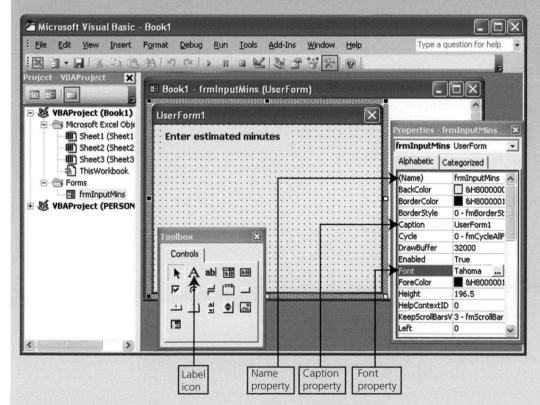

**FIGURE 12.33** *The form with a label*

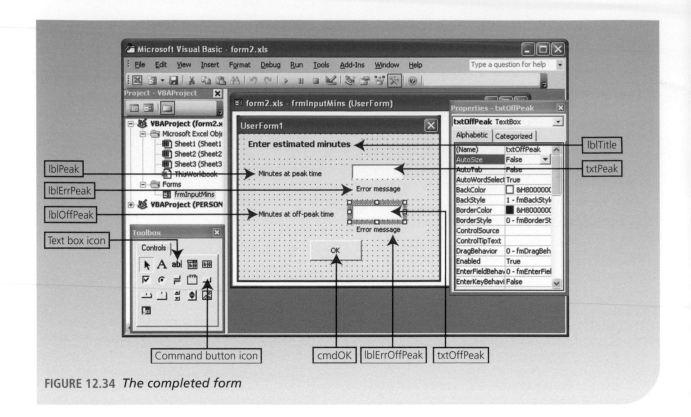

Labels pointing to the figure:
lblPeak, lblErrPeak, lblOffPeak, Text box icon, Command button icon, cmdOK, lblErrOffPeak, txtOffPeak, lblTitle, txtPeak

**FIGURE 12.34** *The completed form*

## Validation

Producing a well-laid-out, easy-to-use form is important. But it is also important to do everything you can to ensure the data entered in the form is valid. In the real world, software is used by all sorts of people, some of whom will not be computer experts – they may not have been trained properly to use the software and they may be in a hurry. All these factors can lead to mistakes when entering data into the software.

Invalid data in your program may cause the program to crash, or it may mean that the results your program produces are wrong. One way you can reduce input errors is to use list boxes for input. Rather than allowing the user to enter whatever data he or she likes into a text box, a list box presents the user with a preset list of inputs from which he or she must make a selection. Of course, list boxes can only be used in some applications where a predefined list of data inputs is possible.

You have already seen how the IsNumeric function can be used to ensure the data entered is numeric. It is important this function is used to test that a numeric entry has been made where

one is required because, if the user makes a non-numeric entry, it may cause the program to crash. You will see an example of this in Section 12.8 when you complete the mobile phone bill estimator application.

### Theory into practice

Having demonstrated how to create the input form, you should now attempt to create the output form for this application. The design for this form is shown in Figure 12.12 on page 268. The completed form should look like Figure 12.35. Use the object names as shown in the figure because these are the ones you will use when you come to write the program code. Note that a list box is used to display and select the different service providers.

### Knowledge check

1  Give an example of how to validate an entry which should be numeric.

2  Describe two effects that invalid input data may have on your program.

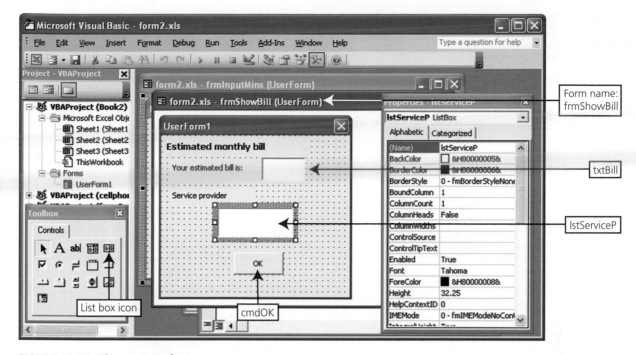

FIGURE 12.35 *The output form*

# 12.7 Programming and the database

So far we have mostly been looking at how to create applications using spreadsheet software. However, you also need to look at how applications can be customised within database software such as Microsoft Access. Fortunately, much of what you have already learnt applies to Access. Nonetheless there are some important differences.

Although it is not possible to record macros within Access, it provides a number of 'wizards' with the Access Forms Editor that allow VBA code to be created automatically, based on the choices the user makes while completing the wizard. This VBA code can, if required, be modified further to add functionality.

In this section it is assumed that you have an understanding of database concepts. If you do not, then you should work through Unit 7 first.

## How to... program the database (1)

This example shows how the look of a form can be modified to make it easier to use. The database table being used records customer details, such as name and address. Each customer also has a unique customer number, which is also the key field for the table. The form shown in Figure 12.36 has been created using the built-in forms creation wizard.

You want to combine this form with a search facility whereby the user will enter his or her customer number in a text box. Then, when the user clicks on a button, the user's details will appear.

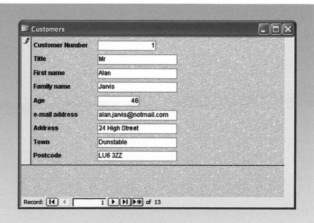

FIGURE 12.36 *Customer form*

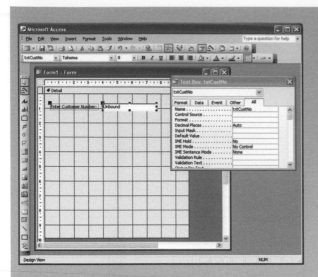

FIGURE 12.37 *Creating a text box*

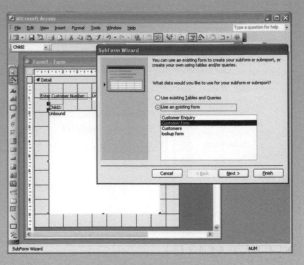

FIGURE 12.38 *The SubForm Wizard*

1  To do this, first create an unbound form (i.e. not associated with a particular database table) and add a text box where the required customer number will be entered. This is shown in Figure 12.37. This text box has been named txtCustNo.

2  Next, add a subform to this form, using the **SubForm/Report** button in the **Forms Editor** toolbar. This will start the **SubForm Wizard**. The customer form shown in Figure 12.36 is selected to be displayed in the subform, and the default name for the subform ('Customer Form', in this example) can be used (see Figure 12.38).

3  A link needs to be created between the txtCustNo box on the main form and the customer number field on the subform so that the correct customer is displayed when the customer's number is entered. Select the subform and then click on the **Properties** button to display the **Properties** box for the subform. The **Link Master Field** needs to be set to the txtCustNo field, while the **Link Child Field** needs to be set to the Customer Number on the subform (see Figure 12.39).

The subform will only show when a customer number has been entered, so also set its Visible property to 'false'.

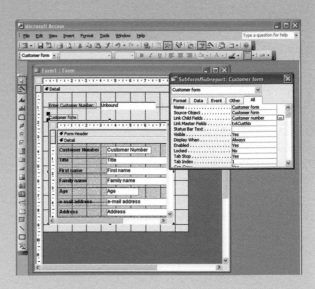

FIGURE 12.39 *Linking the main and subforms*

4  Next, add a button to the main form that will make the subform become visible when the user enters a valid customer number. Use the **Command Button** icon in the toolbox to drag out a button but, when the **Command Button Wizard** appears, click on **Cancel** because you need to enter the code for this button yourself.

5  Open the **Properties** box for this button and find the **Event** property called 'On Click' (the code attached to this property will run when the button is clicked). When you click in the

field for this property, a button with three dots in it appears to the right of the field. Click on this button and a dialogue box will appear asking you which Builder you want.

6 To add VBA code, choose the **Code Builder** and the Visual Basic code window will appear with the **Sub definition** line (and the **End Sub** line) for the command button already created for you.

7 An If statement is needed to check if the customer number entered in the txtCustNo field is a valid one. This can be done by checking if the Customer Number field on the subform contains a Null value (if it does, the customer number entered does not exist). To do this, the **IsNull** standard Visual Basic function is used. The function returns the value of True if the field it is passed contains a null value; otherwise it returns False. Since the field you need to test is on the subform, you need to precede its name with the subform name. In the situation where the field does contain a null value, a message is displayed and the subform **Visible** property is set to False. The subform will, of course, already have this set if it is the first time the button is clicked, but if other customer details have been successfully displayed the subform will be visible.

If the customer number on the subform is not a null value, then a valid number must have been entered, so the subform should be made visible. The complete code for the button is shown in Figure 12.40.

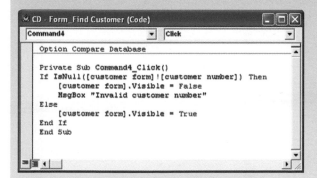

FIGURE 12.40 *The completed code*

8 The form and the button can now be tested. When a valid customer number is entered, the detail should appear in the subform, as shown in Figure 12.41.

On the other hand, if an invalid number is entered, a message will appear and the subform will not be displayed. This is shown in Figure 12.42.

FIGURE 12.41 *A valid customer number*

FIGURE 12.42 *An invalid customer number*

In this next example you will use the same customer form that you used as the subform in the previous example. However, this time you will use Visual Basic code to carry out more complex validation than can be done using the standard facilities within Access. You will add two command buttons to the form: the first will take the user to a new, empty record and the second will close the form, saving the new record as it does so.

The code for both these functions is created by the **Command Button Wizard**, but you will modify the second button so that before it closes the form it validates the customer's email address. You created a structure diagram for this module in Section 12.4.

## How to... program the database (2)

1 First, create the two command buttons using the **Command Button Wizard**.

2 Create the **Add New Record** button by choosing the **Add New Record** action under the **Record Operations** category in the wizard, as shown in Figure 12.43.

3 To create the **Close Form** button, select the **Form Operations** category and the **Close Form** action in the wizard.

4 To modify the code attached to the **Close Form** button, open its **Property** window to see the onClick event property. As shown in Figure 12.44, this contains the words 'Event procedure'.

FIGURE 12.43 *The Command Button Wizard*

When you click on the button to the right of the field, the Visual Basic code window will open and show the code the wizard created for both buttons (see Figure 12.45).

5 The code required must inspect the value entered in the email address field to see if it contains both an '@' and a dot. To do this, a standard Visual Basic function is used, called **Mid**. This function extracts a sub-string from a string, which will allow you to extract individual characters from the

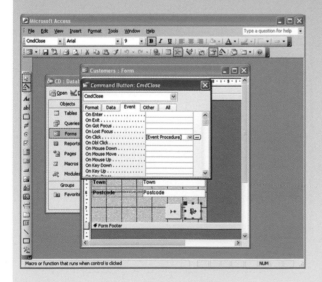

FIGURE 12.44 *The onClick property*

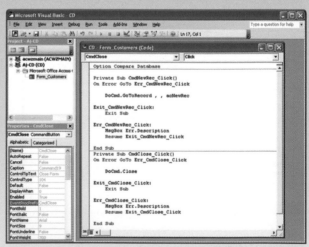

FIGURE 12.45 *Code created by the wizard*

email address and to compare them with the characters you are looking for. The Mid function takes the format:

```
Mid(String, start_char, No_of_char)
```

So, for example, if the string mystring contains "Marmalade", then

```
Mid(mystring, 3, 4)
```

will return 'rmal'.

6   Before you can use the Mid function you need to find out the number of characters the user has entered in the email field. You can then use a for… next loop to check though each character of the field. This can be done using the **Len** function, which, for example, using the same string as before, would be written as

```
Len(mystring)
```

and would return the value of 9.

Using the Mid function and an if statement inside the loop will check each character of the field, and a flag is incremented to indicate if the character is found. At the end of the loop, if the flag is set to less than 2, then the email address must be invalid because it does not contain one or other of the required characters. The code looks like this:

```
length = Len([e-mail address])
  flag = 0
  For i = 1 To length
    If Mid([e-mail address], i, 1) = "@" Then flag = flag + 1
    If Mid([e-mail address], i, 1) = "." Then flag = flag + 1
  Next i
  If flag < 2 Then
    MsgBox "Invalid e-mail"
  Else
    DoCmd.Close
```

However, before you can use the Len function, you must check that the user has entered a value in the field since, if you use the Len function on a null value, you will get an error. You can use the same **IsNull** function as in the previous example to test for this, using an If structure to display an appropriate message if the field is empty.

The complete code for the button is shown in Figure 12.46.

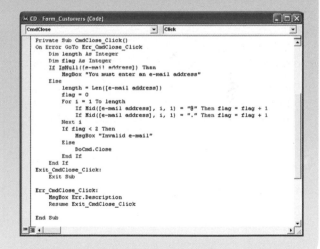

FIGURE 12.46 *The completed code*

## Theory into practice

The validation can be further improved. For example, neither the dot nor the @ sign would appear in the first or last character of a valid email address. Also, a valid email address must be more than six characters long. Modify the code shown here to take these two factors into account.

These two simple examples show how forms and buttons created by the Access wizards can be modified to add further functionality, and how data validation can be achieved. Next we shall return to spreadsheet programming and look at how a complete application can be built.

1 Describe how to use the Mid() function.

2 Explain the purpose of the Link Master and child fields in an Access subform.

# 12.8 Programming and the spreadsheet

In this section you will complete the mobile phone bill estimator application that you have been working on throughout the unit. In Section 12.6 you completed the user interface. You now need to add the code to the command buttons to make the application work. First you must create the spreadsheet that sits behind the application doing the calculations for you. You will place this on Sheet 2 of the spreadsheet as Sheet 1 will contain the button to start the application. The spreadsheet is shown in Figure 12.47.

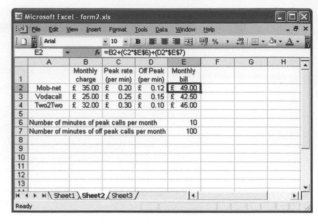

FIGURE 12.47 *Bill estimator spreadsheet*

This simple spreadsheet shows monthly charges, and off-peak and peak rates for three different service providers. As you can see from the formula in E2, the bill is estimated by multiplying the number of minutes at both peak and off-peak times by the appropriate rate and then adding in the monthly charge.

## How to... program the spreadsheet (1)

Remember to use the same spreadsheet file that you have already used to create your input and output forms.

1 The list of service providers can now be used to provide the **RowSource** property in the output form. Press **Alt + F11** to open the Visual Basic window.

2 Find the frmShowBill form and click on the list box (it should be named **lstServiceP**).

3 Click on the **Properties Window** button to display the properties (if it is not already open) and find the **RowSource** property for the list box.

4 Enter the cells which contain the service provider's name, including the sheet number (sheet2!A2:A4). The service provider names will now appear in the list box (see Figure 12.48).

5 The next step is to add a button on the first sheet of the spreadsheet which will start your application running by displaying the input form. First go to sheet 1 then, using the

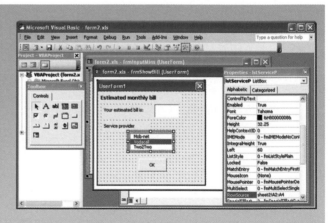

FIGURE 12.48 *Setting the RowSource for the list box*

**Command** button on the **Control** toolbox, drag out a button.

6 Double-click on the button and the Visual Basic window will be displayed with an empty code module that has been created for you. This is the click event procedure for the button. A single instruction will display the input form, as shown in Figure 12.49.

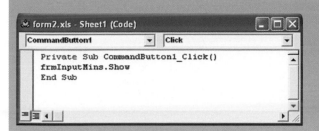

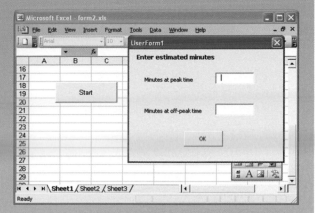

FIGURE 12.49 *The code for the command button*

7 If you now return to Excel and click on the **Exit Design Mode** button on the **Control** toolbar, you can test the button by clicking on it. If all works correctly the input form should appear (see Figure 12.50).

8 The next step is to add the code to the event procedure of the OK button on the input form. This code needs to:

a validate the user's input to ensure it is numeric

b insert the input values in the spreadsheet on to Sheet 2

c display the output form.

You should first create two variables to hold the number of peak and off-peak minutes input by the user. The names and data types of these variables were decided at design stage

FIGURE 12.50 *Displaying the input form*

(see the input data table shown in Figure 12.12 on page 268).

The code now needs to validate that the user's entry is numeric and, if it is, insert it in the correct cell in the spreadsheet. The first part (your first prototype) of this code is shown in Figure 12.51.

You might wonder why you transfer the value in the txtPeak text box to the variable first, then to the spreadsheet. Can't you just transfer it directly to the spreadsheet? You will find that, if you do this, you will get an error on the spreadsheet because the values in text boxes

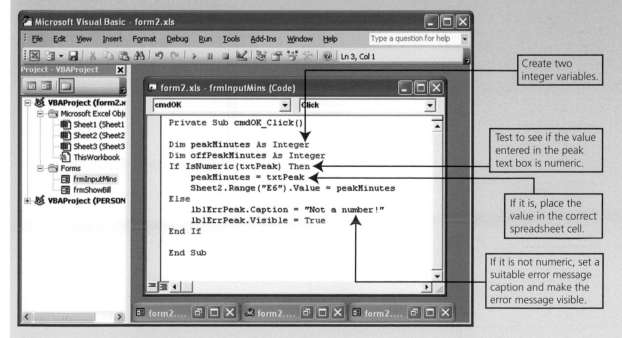

FIGURE 12.51 *First prototype of the code for the OK button*

are treated as text. Transferring the value to a integer variable converts it to a number.

Of course, this code only deals with the peak minutes value. A very similar section of code is needed to deal with the off-peak minutes value.

You also need a way to check if there has been an invalid input because, if there has, then the output form should not be displayed. A variable called **errorCode** has been added and, if the input values are non-numeric, it is set to 1.

If these two values have been validated and inserted into the spreadsheet, the output form should be displayed. The complete code for this event procedure is shown in Figure 12.52.

9   The final task this code carries out is to display the output form. If you try out the application now you should see that this happens, but the form is displayed with no total bill amount displayed. When the form is displayed, it needs to pick up the total bill for the first service provider (Mob-net) from the spreadsheet (in Sheet 2, cell E2). It needs to do this automatically without the user doing anything. To get this to happen, you must add code to the event that occurs when the form is displayed, which is called the **Activate** event.

10  To write code for the Activate event, first make sure you have the output form display in the Visual Basic window, then click on the **Code** button in the **Project Explorer**. This should

display the forms click event procedure, which is not the one you want.

11  To select the correct procedure (**Activate**), choose it from the drop-down list at the top of the **Code** window (see Figure 12.53).

A single line of code is all that is needed in this event procedure:

```
txtBill = Sheet2.Range("E2").Value
```

would work, but it would not display the values as a currency amount, with a '£' sign and two digits after the decimal point. Therefore the **Format** function should be used to show the value formatted as currency. The completed event procedure is shown in Figure 12.54.

12  The application is almost complete now, but the total bill shown in the text box needs to change if the user selects different service providers in the list box by clicking on them. When the user clicks on the list box, the list box's click event procedure will be run, so

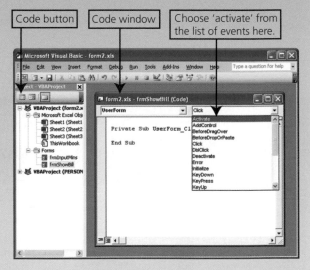

FIGURE 12.53 *Creating a Activate event procedure*

```
Private Sub cmdOK_Click()

Dim peakMinutes As Integer
Dim offPeakMinutes As Integer
Dim errorCode As Integer
errorCode = 0
If IsNumeric(txtPeak) Then
    peakMinutes = txtPeak
    Sheet2.Range("E6").Value = peakMinutes
Else
    lblErrPeak.Caption = "Not a number!"
    lblErrPeak.Visible = True
    errorCode = 1
End If
If IsNumeric(txtOffPeak) Then
    offPeakMinutes = txtOffPeak
    Sheet2.Range("E7").Value = offPeakMinutes
Else
    lblErrOffPeak.Caption = "Not a number!"
    lblErrOffPeak.Visible = True
    errorCode = 1
End If
If errorCode = 0 Then
    frmInputMins.Hide
    frmShowBill.Show
End If

End Sub
```

FIGURE 12.52 *Complete code for the OK button*

FIGURE 12.54 *The completed Activate procedure*

this is where the code to change the total bill shown needs to go. This event procedure can be accessed by double-clicking on the list box. How do you know which service provider the user has clicked on? Visual Basic provides a function, called **ListIndex**, which returns the index number of the selected item in the list box, numbering them from zero. So you can write an if construct that will find out which item in the list has been selected by the user and then display the appropriate cell in the spreadsheet to display the total bill in the text box. The completed code for this event procedure is shown in Figure 12.55.

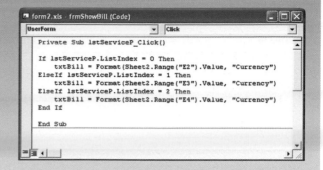

FIGURE 12.55 *The list box click event procedure*

This completes the mobile phone bill estimator, although there are a number of enhancements that could be made to the application.

## Theory into practice

You could add the following improvements to the mobile phone bill estimator:

1 No code has been added to the **OK** button on the second form, which should close the form. Add the code to carry out this task.

2 You could also add a **Try** again button to the second form which takes you back to the first form so that the user can input different values for his or her peak and off-peak minutes.

Now let's look at a different example that shows how Visual Basic code can be used to create and modify charts within an Excel worksheet. Charts are represented by a chart object, and they can be given a name so that you can refer to it. You could create a chart object called **mychart** using the following code:

```
Set MyChart = Charts.Add
```

However, to create a meaningful chart, you also need to define the data that will be used to draw the chart.

## How to... program the spreadsheet (2)

Suppose you wanted to draw a chart for the spreadsheet shown in Figure 12.56, where the data and titles to be included in the chart are in the range A2:E5.

The following code would use that range for the chart:

```
mychart.SetSourceData
Source:=Worksheets("sheet1").
Range("A2:E5")
```

We can now look at how this code can be built into a simple application that creates different charts. A command button can be added (using the **Forms** toolbar) to the spreadsheet shown in Figure 12.57, and then the code attached to the button, as shown in Figure 12.51.

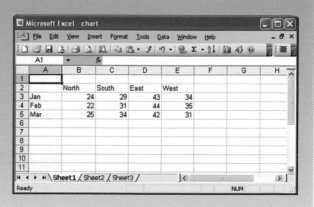

FIGURE 12.56 *Data to be included in the chart*

When the button is clicked a chart is created, but it is always the default bar chart. You can also define the type of chart to be created.

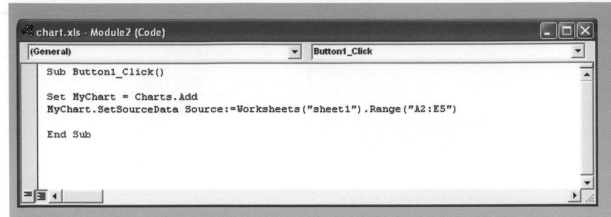

```
chart.xls - Module2 (Code)

(General)                                    Button1_Click

    Sub Button1_Click()

    Set MyChart = Charts.Add
    MyChart.SetSourceData Source:=Worksheets("sheet1").Range("A2:E5")

    End Sub
```

FIGURE 12.57 *Code for creating a chart*

For example, the following instruction will create a 3D bar chart:

`MyChart.ChartType = xl3DColumnClustered`

You might be wondering how you can find out which chart types you can choose (there are 14 basic types and many subtypes within the basic types). The answer is to use the **Object Browser**. This is a very useful Visual Basic tool that can be used to find the **members** of any of the Objects Visual Basic supports.

> **Key terms**
>
> An object's *members* include properties, that describe the object, and methods, which are things the object can do. *Classes* are templates for objects.

1  To view the **Object Browser**, go to the **View** menu and choose **Object Browser**. It will appear in a separate window.

2  In the list of classes on the left, find **Chart** and, on the right, the members of that class will be listed, as shown in Figure 12.58.

Details of the selected property are shown at the bottom of the **Object Browser** and, if you click on the class name in green (**xlChartType**), the display above will list the members of the xlChartType class (on the left), which are all the different chart types (see Figure 12.59).

You could, of course, enter the required chart type manually into the code you have already created, but it would be nicer to give the user a number of options.

3  To do this, first add a combo box to the spreadsheet (using the Visual Basic toolbar and toolbox).

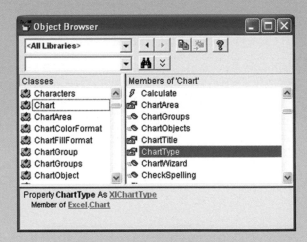

FIGURE 12.58 *The Object Browser*

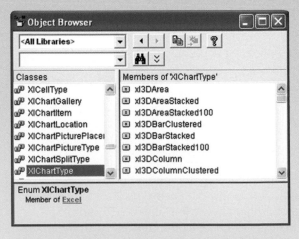

FIGURE 12.59 *The members of the xlChartType class*

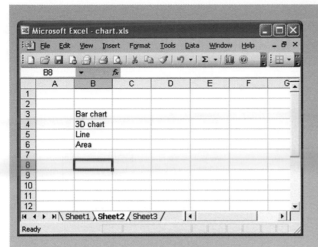

FIGURE 12.60 *List of chart types*

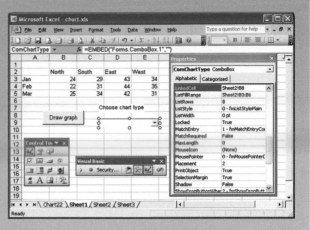

FIGURE 12.61 *Setting the properties for the combo box*

4   The combo box needs a list of chart types to appear in it when it is dropped down. Type this list into Sheet2, as shown in Figure 12.60.

5   Back on Sheet 1, modify the properties of the combo box you have added. Set the **ListFillRange** property to the cell range containing the list of chart types of sheet2 (B3:B6), and the **Linked** cell to B8 on sheet2. This will display the list in B3:B6 in the combo box and the item the user has selected from the list in B8 (see Figure 12.61).

Note that the name of the combo box has been set to **ComChartType**.

6   The code attached to the command button now needs to be modified to select the chart type based on the value selected by the user. This is collected from cell B8 in Sheet2 and

placed in a string variable called **userChoice**. This is then used within a case statement to set the chart type. The completed code is shown in Figure 12.62.

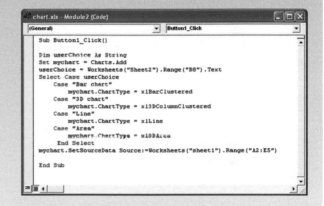

```
Sub Button1_Click()

Dim userChoice As String
Set mychart = Charts.Add
userChoice = Worksheets("Sheet2").Range("B8").Text
Select Case userChoice
    Case "Bar chart"
        mychart.ChartType = xlBarClustered
    Case "3D chart"
        mychart.ChartType = xl3DColumnClustered
    Case "Line"
        mychart.ChartType = xlLine
    Case "Area"
        mychart.ChartType = xl3DArea
    End Select
mychart.SetSourceData Source:=Worksheets("sheet1").Range("A2:E5")

End Sub
```

FIGURE 12.62 *The completed code*

The simple example application described above can be improved in a couple of ways:

1   You can add additional chart types.

2   You could give the user the option of choosing the particular region for which the chart should be drawn.

In the final example of a customised spreadsheet you will see how a sequential search can be used to locate and modify information.

## How to... program the spreadsheet (3)

The spreadsheet you are using is shown in Figure 12.63. It is used to record student grades. You are going to add a customised facility to search for a particular student and to allow his or her grade to be modified.

1   To search for a particular student, you must first ask the user what name he or she wishes to find, using a input box, then use a loop to search through the range of cells (A4:A14) to see if that name can be found. A command button has been added to the spreadsheet to start the search, and the first version of the code is shown in Figure 12.64.

FIGURE 12.63 *Unit tracking spreadsheet*

FIGURE 12.65 *The code running*

At the end of the loop, if the counter has reached 15, then the name has not been found and a message is displayed; otherwise the cell containing the match is displayed. This version is shown working in Figure 12.65.

2 However, you want to see the student's grade and be able to modify it. To do this the grade is extracted from column C and displayed as part of the message on an input box. Whatever the user enters in the input box is used as the new grade (the modified code is shown in Figure 12.66).

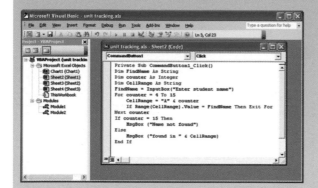

FIGURE 12.64 *Code for the Search button*

This code uses a for loop to search through the cells to find a match, but the loop needs to stop when the match is found, so the **Exit For** instruction is used to exit the for loop prematurely when this happens. When the loop is exited in this way the loop counter will be set to the row number of the matching name.

FIGURE 12.66 *The modified code*

Like the other examples, this one can be improved.

1 You could add validation so that the user can only enter a valid grade (A-D and R).

2 The way it works at the moment, even if the user does not want to change the grade, it must be retyped into the input box. Add another stage that asks the user if he or she wants to modify the grade or not.

3 You could add a more sophisticated front end to the application, using forms rather than input boxes.

These three examples show how spreadsheets can be customised to make them easier to use, completely hiding the actual spreadsheet from the user in the case of the mobile phone bill estimator. By now you should be familiar with how to handle spreadsheet objects and with how to manipulate them with programming code. You have also seen how to create and modify charts.

**Knowledge check**

1 What is the purpose of the Object Browser in VBA?

2 Explain how an Exit For statement can be used with a For loop.

3 Which property of a list box is used to identify the item in the list that the user has clicked on?

## Assessment activity

Produce a complete customised solution based on your design.

## Assessment hint

✓✓ You have done this with only occasional prompting from your tutor.

✓✓✓ You arrived at your solution completely independently.

# 12.9 Testing

Testing is an important, if often unpopular, part of the software development process. The application's users would not be very impressed if it produced the wrong answers, nor would they be happy if the application kept crashing while they were using it.

You may already have done some testing on the prototypes of your application to see if they work correctly (sometimes called **formative testing**) but, once the application is complete, it is time to subject it to formal testing.

Testing is the process of checking that all the functions of the program work as they should and give the correct results. The definition of terms like 'work as they should' and 'correct results' needs to come from the functional specification and the design documentation that you created at the beginning of the development process.

**Think it over...**

It is worth mentioning that the programmer who wrote the application is probably not the best person to test it. The programmer tends to be 'gentle' or 'forgiving' with his or her creation! It is much better to get someone else to test the program, as he or she is likely to do a more thorough job. He or she may also be able to give you advice on how easy your application is to use.

## Creating test plans

Test plans list input test data and associated actions (such as clicking buttons, etc.). For each input field a range of test data needs to be chosen that will test the working of the application as fully as possible. This involves choosing some input values and then manually working out what output the program should produce with these chosen inputs (the expected outputs).

The program is then run using these input values and the expected outputs are compared with the actual ones the program produces. If there is a difference between the expected outputs and the actual outputs, then the program has failed the test and will need to be modified so that the actual and expected values match.

The choice of input values is important. A range of values needs to be chosen in each of the following categories:

* **Normal** values are those values that would normally be expected as input values.

* **Extreme** values would, in the case of a numeric input, be unusually large or small. The design specification should state the maximum and minimum acceptable values in a numeric input filed. In the case of a text value, they might be a very large number of characters or a very small number of characters. For example, in a text field where someone's name is to be entered, two extreme values might be 'Ng' and 'Fotherington-Thomas'.

* **Abnormal** values are incorrect entries – for example, 32/10/02 for a date, 205 for someone's age or a text value where a numeric one is expected. Also in this category are null values – that is, where no entry is made in a text field. Again the design specification should state whether a particular input field may be left empty or not.

An example test plan for the mobile phone bill estimator is shown is Figure 12.67.

| Test Plan | | System: | | |
|---|---|---|---|---|
| Date: | | Tester: | | |
| Test no | Description | Input Data | Expected Outcome | Actual Outcome |
| Test run 1 (normal data) | | | | |
| 1.1 | Normal | Peak: 10<br>Off Peak: 20<br>Provider: Mob-net | £39.40 | |
| 1.2 | Normal | Peak: 50<br>Off Peak: 35<br>Provider: Voda-Call | £42.75 | |
| 1.3 | Normal | Peak: 90<br>Off Peak: 120<br>Provider: Two2Two | £71 | |
| Test run 2 (extreme data) | | | | |
| 2.1 | Extreme | Peak: 0<br>Off Peak: 0<br>Provider: Mob-net | £35 | |
| 2.2 | Extreme | Peak: 5,000<br>Off Peak: 10,000<br>Provider: Voda-call | £2,235 | |
| Test run 3 (abnormal data) | | | | |
| 3.1 | Abnormal | Peak: null<br>Off Peak: 10 | 'Not a number' error message | |
| 3.2 | Abnormal | Peak: 10<br>Off Peak: ten | 'Not a number' error message | |

**FIGURE 12.67** *Test plan for the mobile phone bill estimator*

In this example, the plan is divided up into different test runs, each test run consisting of one or more input values. Only a couple of test runs per category of input data are shown, although, in reality, many more test runs should be created in order to test the program thoroughly.

## Testing using the plan

As each test listed in the test plan is carried out, the results must be carefully recorded on the plan. If the actual outcome of the test matches the expected outcome, the software has passed the test, and 'as expected' can be written in the 'Actual outcome' column of the test plan. If, however, the actual outcome of the test does not match the expected outcome, then the program has failed that particular test and details of the actual outcome need to be completed on the test plan.

If the expected outcome and the actual outcome for a particular test differ, then the program has not passed the test and an error should be recorded in the plan.

Once the programmer has had an opportunity to correct the problems identified by the testing, the program should be tested again. You might imagine that, when the program has been corrected and is to be tested again, only those tests that it failed need to be done again. However, it is possible that the programmer, in correcting the faults identified in the first set of tests, has inadvertently introduced other faults. Therefore, to be sure the program works properly, the complete set of tests should be done again.

### Knowledge check

1 What are the three categories of input data from which test data should be selected?

2 When testing a program, what document should you use to identify the range of acceptable input values?

### Assessment activity

Produce a test plan for your solution and carry out testing.

# 12.10 Program documentation

Simply handing over a completed customised application on a disk is not sufficient. People need to know how to install the program, how to use it and how to deal with problems that may arise. The completed program must be supported by documentation. Two types of documentation need to be produced:

* **User documentation** explains to the application's users how they should use the program.

* **Program or technical documentation** describes the internal workings of the software.

Fairly obviously, the contents of these two types of documentation are rather different.

## Presentation of documentation

Although the term 'documentation' tends to suggest a printed book of some kind, it is increasingly popular to do away with the expense of producing user documentation in the form of a book. Instead, online help is provided.

The Windows operating system provides a way of producing help files in a standard format, with search and index facilities already built in. It is beyond the scope of this unit to explain how the Windows help system can be used to provide online user documentation. However, you should be aware that this is a common way for user documentation to be provided and has a number of benefits: as well as being cheaper than manuals, it is also easier to update and has more powerful search facilities.

Documentation produced in paper format should contain as many illustrations, in terms of diagrams, screenshots, etc., as possible. However, a word-processing program, such as Microsoft Word (which has built-in diagram-drawing tools), is probably sufficient for producing the material (the Word drawing tools include AutoShapes for all the flow chart symbols, making drawing flow charts simple).

Documentation should be written to certain professional standards to ensure it is consistent in appearance, structure and quality, and is therefore easy to read and understand. Typically, these standards should include the following:

* A 'house style' to govern the formatting of the titles, headings and subheadings in the document.

* Document structure, including page numbering, section numbering and headers and footers.

* A table of contents, index and glossary.

* Spelling check, grammar check and proofreading to ensure the text is error free and as understandable as possible.

Much of the material, especially for the technical documentation, will come from documents that have already been created (for example, the functional specification and the system design). If the documentation standards are applied from the beginning of the software development process, then time will be saved when it comes to completing the documentation at the end of the project.

## User documentation

User documentation is written for the program's users, and is sometimes called the **user manual** or **user guide**. There are two main approaches when writing user documentation:

* **Reference guide** – each function and feature is described, normally in some logical order.

* **Tutorial** – teaches the user how to use the program in a step-by-step fashion.

Some user manuals combine both approaches. However, whichever approach is taken to user documentation, it must be written in a way that the target audience can understand. Therefore, technical jargon needs to be avoided and the manual must be relevant to the way the application will be used in the workplace (for example, by using realistic examples). Annotated screenshots need to be used rather than long, written explanations, as these are much easier for the users to follow and the users can compare what they see on the computer when running the program with the screen dump in the manual.

The user documentation needs to contain the following:

* Details of how to start the customised application.

* Comprehensive instructions for using each of the application's customised features. This should include details of what all the buttons, text boxes, list boxes and any other objects should be used for. The instructions should also explain how to use any menus and shortcut keys.

* Explanations of any error messages that the program displays, including an explanation of what to do to correct the problem and how to avoid the error in future.

* Details of what to do if something goes wrong or if the program crashes, such as who to contact (this will generally be you!).

* How to exit the program.

* It is useful to include a section on frequently asked questions (FAQ), although you might need to use some imagination to decide what questions users may ask. Showing the program to a group of people who are unfamiliar with it and seeing what questions they come up with may help.

### Assessment activity

Write the user documentation for the customised database and spreadsheet applications you have created.

## Program documentation

Program documentation is written for support staff and programmers. Throughout the life of an application, changes or improvements may need to be made, and it may be the case that, despite careful testing, some errors only surface after many years of use. The programmers who originally wrote the software will probably have moved to new projects or perhaps different companies. Technical documentation is therefore needed so that the people who need to modify or correct the program can understand how it works.

The technical documentation for each procedure in the program should include:

* a listing of the program code

* a print of the form, including the object names

* the design specification

* details of testing carried out, and any modifications made as a result of testing.

The documentation should also include details of the operating system and version the program will work with, and the version of the application that the customisation has been designed to work with. In addition, disk space and any other hardware requirements should be listed. Instructions on how to install the software should also be included.

When improvements and/or corrections are made to the program, details of these changes should be included in the technical documentation.

# 12.11 Evaluation

There are two aspects of program writing that you can usefully evaluate. First, you can consider the process – in other words, how it was for you, the programmer. Secondly, you can evaluate the outcome – in other words, the program itself.

## Evaluating the process

Writing programs is not easy. It may well be that, if this has been your first experience of programming, it has been difficult and confusing. Evaluating your experiences can help you understand where you went wrong and where your strengths and weaknesses lie. One of the most difficult things about software development can be producing a design for a program that makes it possible to create the program relatively easily. To do this requires a good understanding of programming techniques and the way the programming language in use works. This, of course, is something that, at this stage, you probably don't have. It is worth bearing in mind that in industry, the people who produce the system design (often called system analysts) normally work for a number of years as programmers before moving on to the more senior post of system analyst.

The following are some questions you might like to ask yourself:

* Which parts of the software development process did you understand well?

* Which part of the software development process do you still not understand well? These are the areas you may need to go over again. However, developing a good understanding of the whole process will take time.

* Did the program development process go according to your plan? If not, which parts of the process took more or less time than you planned?

## Evaluating the program

As well as evaluating your experiences in developing the software, it is also important to check that the program you have produced meets its original aim. It is possible, in the excitement and relief of finally getting a program working properly, to forget the original aims of the program. You need to look at the original investigation you did and at the functional specification you wrote to see if the program you developed solves the original problem. In particular, you need to decide if the aims of the system that were originally defined in the investigation have been met. You also need to consider if the use of code was really justified. Could you have achieved the same or similar functionality using the built-in features of the software?

When evaluating a program it can be difficult to be subjective about your own work. One effective method of obtaining constructive feedback about your program is to let other people try it out and comment on it.

Some questions you might ask them to answer are as follows:

* Is the layout and labelling of the forms neat and clear?

* Does the program do what you would expect?

* Does it match the program as it was originally specified?

* Does it work properly?

* Is there anything missing from the program?

The result of the evaluation stage should be a report. In the report you need to describe your experiences in developing the software, what the other people who evaluated your program thought about it, and your views on how closely the program you wrote met the original requirements.

### Knowledge check

1   What are the two main aspects of program development that you can evaluate?

2   Who can help you evaluate your program development experiences?

### Assessment activity

Write an evaluation of the system you have developed and of your own performance in producing it.

### Assessment hint

✓✓   You have identified any weaknesses in your solution, have provided some justification of the use of coding and have described your current skills level.

✓✓✓   You have suggested improvements to your solution, fully justifying the use of coding and identifying areas where your skills could be improved.

## 12.12 Programming skills

You will need a number of programming skills to complete this unit, but most of them have already been covered.

### Constants, variables and arrays

Variables are used to store data while the program runs. The concept of a variable and how to create them was covered earlier. Constants are similar to variables except in one important way: the value of a constant is set when it is created and cannot be changed. Constants are therefore used to store fixed values, such as a conversion rate. So you might store the conversion rate from feet to metres like this:

```
Const Ft2Mts As double = 0.3048
```

Note that, if you attempt to change the value in a constant in your program code, you will get an error.

Arrays are another special type of variable. Unlike a normal variable that only holds one value, an array can hold a number of values (although they must all be of the same type). The different values can be accessed using a number, called an index. So, for example, to create an array to hold the maximum temperature for each day of the week you would use:

```
Dim MaxTemp(6) as Integer
```

Note that an array is always indexed from 0, so this gives us a seven-element array, MaxTemp(0) to MaxTemp(6). The index number can of course be a variable rather than a fixed number, so you could, for example, use a for… next loop to process all the elements of an array.

## Other programming skills

Other programming skills covered in this unit include the following:

* **Types of loops**. The different types of loops (or iteration structures) have been covered in Section 12.5.

* **Selection process**. Selection structures are covered in Section 12.5.

* **Routines and functions**. Details of how to create these can be found in Section 12.5.

* **Parameter passing** is covered in Section 12.5.

* **Input/output** is covered in Section 12.6, the human computer interface. Validating user input is also covered in the database programming examples (Section 12.7).

### Knowledge check

1 Explain the difference between variables and constants.

2 Describe what an array is and how it could be used.

3 Describe the difference between a For loop and a While loop.

# Programming

In this unit you will learn how to produce programs for modern computer systems. You will develop your programming skills, and you will write and test your own software code. You will also learn how to produce documentation for users and for other programmers.

This optional unit contains 9 sections:

# Introduction

This unit is about writing programs for modern computer systems so that they meet the needs of the users and produce accurate results. You will develop your skills in creating program specifications and in designing appropriate software, using the features and controls available to the modern programmer. You will write and test your own software code and will produce complete documentation for users and other programmers. This unit will enhance your practical ICT skills while you adhere to standard ways of working.

## What you need to learn

In completing this unit, you should achieve these learning outcomes:

* produce a program design
* program code for your solution
* implement a test plan that includes a range of planned tests and their outcomes
* produce program documentation
* produce a summative evaluation of your solution.

## Resources required for this unit

To complete this unit, you need these essential resources:

* access to computer hardware, including a printer
* access to computer software – in particular, a programming environment such as Visual Basic.Net and a word processor.

## How you will be assessed

This practitioner-focused unit is assessed internally. To meet the unit's requirements, you will produce an e-portfolio that contains program coding to implement a solution to a software user's needs. You will apply the knowledge and understanding you gain from studying this unit to produce a program design. You will demonstrate ICT problem-solving skills, will show you can evaluate your software solution and will design a program that specifies:

* the input data and validation procedures
* data structures
* forms
* printed output
* navigation routes
* events and associated processing.

You will produce program coding for your solution and a test plan that includes a range of planned tests and their outcomes, giving details of the action taken as a result of the testing. Your program documentation will include a user's guide that explains how to install, load, use and quit the program, and a technical guide for use by other programmers. You will write a summative evaluation of your solution that assesses:

* how well your solution meets the specification
* how easy it is to use
* the efficiency of the data storage and program code.

## How high can you aim?

Your e-portfolio will contain all the evidence on which your performance will be judged. Some of the assessment activities in this unit can be used towards your e-portfolio. These activities include assessment hints on what you can do to pass (✓), to gain a better mark (✓✓) or to achieve top marks (✓✓✓).

## Ready to start?

This unit should take you roughly 40 hours to complete. Why not keep a log of your time? You might devise a blank form to record the time you spend on this unit.

# 14.1  Program specification

Many programmers begin their careers producing software because they enjoy doing it. Such programs are usually written with little forward planning because the programmer knows what he or she wants to produce, so he or she sets about creating the software by producing the easy parts first and then adding the more complex features later.

Professional programmers write programs for clients as part of their jobs. In these situations, the programmer is writing to meet the needs of another person, organisation or department. If an effective software solution is to be produced, the programmer needs a thorough understanding of the client's needs. This is role of the program specification.

The program specification sets out the software's functional requirements. These requirements are contained in a document that explains exactly what the software must do to meet the client's needs. A good program specification must have no grey areas, and anything that is not clearly explained must go back to the client for further consulation. It is essential that the programmer or analyst ensures the specification is accurate and sufficiently detailed.

Clients are not expected to be programmers, but they are expected to know what they want from their software. Because of this, the program specification concentrates on the outputs, inputs and any calculations that the program may need.

It is up to the programmer to decide what processing is required to implement the calculations. This is not part of the program specification but will be in the program design. The specification, therefore, is the first stage in the program development cycle.

# 14.2  Program design

A clear program specification is needed to define the outputs and inputs required by the program, but this is not enough to start coding immediately. There are still many questions to be answered about the program design. The answers to these questions will help you explain your solution to the client and ensure that it meets the user's requirements.

Many software houses and programming departments in organisations allocate software production to teams of programmers. A detailed program design must be produced from the specification to ensure that the program's many aspects fit together to create a good solution whilst not duplicating effort.

You will produce detailed designs for programs that establish:

* the purpose of any output – both printed reports and on-screen displays

* the layout of the outputs

* the content of the outputs

* all the data that is to be input into the program

* validation procedures for input data to make it difficult to enter incorrect information

* data structures needed to store the data inside the program

* the purpose of all the forms in the program

* form layouts

* the content of forms

* the controls needed on each form for it to function correctly

* the navigation routes the user can take through the program

* the events that will occur in the program, with a description of the processing that should be done for each event.

## Output

### Purpose of output

Output is the most important function of any program – after all, this is the reason the program was written in the first place! As a programmer, you will need to understand the purpose of the output because this will influence the method, design and layout you choose to meet the user's needs.

The methods you choose will include printed reports, on-screen displays and other output devices. Recognising the purpose of an output helps the program designer to select an appropriate layout and to include only useful content.

## Layout of output

The layout of the output is an aspect of program design that is often misunderstood, resulting in too much emphasis being placed on what looks good to the programmer rather than on what meets the user's needs.

Emphasis includes the use of large font sizes, bright colours and bold text. The effect of emphasis should be to draw the user's eye to an item, so these techniques should not be overused.

Of even more importance is to recognise which items need emphasis. Many programmers routinely emphasise the static labels in a report rather than the data next to them. For example:

| Ref: DER1212 | Ref: **DER1212** |
|---|---|
| This is bad practice. The eye is drawn to the name of the field and the data is hardly noticed. | This is good practice. The eye is quickly and easily drawn to the data. The field's name is also there, should the user not recognise the item. |

Data is often **grouped** – i.e. similar items are presented together. Many techniques are available to the designer to do this, including the following:

* **White space** around grouped items of data separates areas of output.

* A **box** around a section is a powerful way of emphasising a group because the eye is naturally drawn to a rectangle on a report or form.

* **Colour** is another powerful way of showing the relationships between data. Important information should be bright and duller, darker colours should be used for the less important items. Colour can also be used to identify the scattered items of data in a large dataset that meet selection or search criteria.

* **Different** fonts can be used to separate different types of data.

Designers should be restrained in the number of colours and fonts they use on a form or report.

> **✱ Remember!**
> Less is often more!

## Content of output

The content of output is either dynamic or static. Dynamic content is data that changes from page to page or from screen to screen. Static content includes those items that are the same on every page and that are used to inform the user of the names of fields or to provide recurring instructions.

You should always limit the content to what is necessary to meet the user's needs, rather than what is available as output from the program. Again, less is often more!

Consider the following reports where data is sorted into groups:

| Homer Sampson | AS | Maths | D | Homer Sampson | AS Results |
|---|---|---|---|---|---|
| Homer Sampson | AS | English | D | Maths | D |
| Homer Sampson | AS | Health & safety | E | English | D |
| Homer Sampson | AS | Nuclear physics | F | Health & safety | E |
| Homer Sampson | AS | Parenting | F | Nuclear physics | F |
| | | | | Parenting | F |
| There is too much repeated data here. It is hard to find and understand the non-repeated data inside all the unnecessarily repeated data, especially if there are many pages in this format. | | | | Headings make the report much clearer, since the user can easily see the section heading for each group of data. Understanding the data is also made easier because only relevant, changing data is shown under the headings. | |

# CASE STUDY

Easy Runner (Figure 14.1) is a thriving independent sports clothing shop in Bristol that specialises in running and other footwear. Their website (go to www.heinemann.co.uk/hotlinks, enter the express code 2156P and click on this unit) contains pages listing and detailing many of the products they sell.

Easy Runner want to commission a program that will create the web pages for these products and upload them to their website. The program should categorise their products and should create individual pages for each product that are search-engine friendly.

The program is to run on a local PC that will allow pictures of their products to be matched to descriptions and classifications entered by an Easy Runner employee. The program will have a button that generates the HTML web pages for each product (Figure 14.2). It will also have category pages where products are grouped by manufacturer and features (Figure 14.3).

The program will need to carry out some sorting so that it can group the manufacturers into the following categories:

* Core shoes
* Off-road shoes
* Racing shoes
* Spikes
* Clothing
* Bargains.

It will also need to sort by the features in each category, such as Sprint or Long distance.

Bargains will be a page where products are discounted. Discounted products will appear on both the category and bargain pages.

Easy Runner have chosen to commission a program for this rather than using a web-authoring tool because they want the individual product pages on their website to be found with search-engine-friendly meta tags.

1  Design a form for the program which could allow an employee to enter product details.

2  Identify and list all the inputs this form will require.

FIGURE 14.1  *Easy Runner*

FIGURE 14.2  *Product web page*

FIGURE 14.3  *Manufacturer web page*

## Input

Almost every program requires data to be input. You should, however, avoid unnecessary inputs. This applies to program navigation as well as to data. A good programmer always considers the ease of use of his or her software.

It is bad practice to encumber the user with unnecessary mouse clicks or keying in. Always give high importance to getting the ease of use right. For this reason, many programmers prefer users to select from the choices a program offers so that it is easier to input valid data.

### *Validation procedures for input data*

The program design should include validation procedures for input data. As a programmer, you have a responsibility to create code that is robust and reliable and that produces accurate outputs.

Part of this responsibility is to estabish and to understand the data required by the program. Once the data is understood, you should be able to define any validation that can be applied to the data during input.

Validation offers two major benefits to a program:

* The user can be prompted if he or she enters data that is obviously wrong. This simple check allows the user to correct any typing errors so that the program will be able to process the inputs efficiently into the required outputs.
* Many programmers include internal checks on the processing in their software to detect errors before they are output, but such routines are not foolproof. Good data helps the program to produce good results.

**Key terms**

*GIGO* (garbage in, garbage out) is a term that has been used by programmers ever since the first code was produced!

Validation can be achieved using two methods: properties and code (object properties are a further validation check that can be used in

**How to... implement the LL000000L input mask and validation rules for text in an Access table**

Create an Access table using the field shown in Figure 14.4.

Set the input mask as shown: each L represents a letter which must be included and which must be in upper case; 0 represents each digit in a number which similarly must be included. Use the Access Help to find other input masks – key **Input Mask** into the Help index.

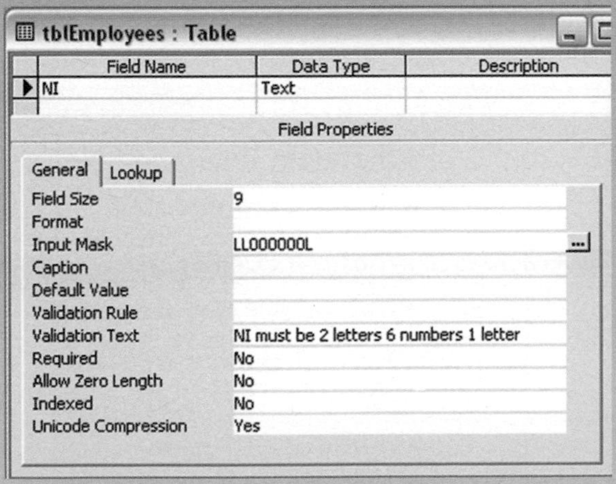


**FIGURE 14.4** *Access table field*

The validation text will be displayed if the user breaks the validation rule by entering data that does not match the mask. Such text should guide the user into making a correct data entry.

The validation rule you are creating is for a National Insurance (NI) number, which takes the form of two letters, six numbers and then one letter (e.g. YB235412A).

Use the **View** menu to see the table in **Datasheet view**. Try to enter both valid data (such as SD325578D) and invalid data (such as 234412432) to confirm your rule works as expected.

some applications). A field in a Microsoft Access table can have:

* an input mask, such as LL000000L
* a validation rule, such as ">= 65"
* validation text to prompt the user to correct the data entry.

Validation text should give positive advice to the user on what to do next: "Type a number 65 or more for your age" is a more useful validation text than "Invalid Age".

Code is usually attached to an event on the input control or when a form is submitted. Code can give you a great deal more control over how thoroughly data is validated, and it ensures that the message the user will receive if the validation rules are broken is comprehensive.

### Think it over...

Define and describe validation procedures suitable for modern UK vehicle number plates.

## Assessment activity

Identify the data needed for your program and the appropriate validation procedures. This planning work will be of use later as the basis for your data dictionary in your e-portfolio.

## Assessment hint

✓    You have identified the data to be input into each of your program forms.

✓✓   You have described the data to be input and have defined and explained the associated validation procedures.

✓✓✓ You have described the required data structures, both in the way they are used by the program (e.g. arrays) and in the way they are kept on disk so that data changes are kept between sessions.

## Data structures

Data structures store the data needed by the program. These structures range from simple variables to arrays and record structures.

### Simple variables

Simple variables hold a single value. A variable named UserScore might hold 4 when the user has answered four questions correctly, then increments to 5 when the next correct answer is input.

### Arrays

Arrays hold many values and are excellent for processing when you are using loops. An array named Questions(5) (Table 14.1) can hold six values (0–5), with the subscript (the number inside the brackets) identifying which value is current. An array with one subscript is called one dimensional.

In this example, Questions(2) holds "What is a FUNCTION?"

An array named Answers(3,5) (Table 14.2) has room for 24 values (4 times 6). This is a two-dimensional array as it has two subscripts (3 and 5). Thus Answers(0,4) holds "FOR… NEXT".

Arrays can have even more dimensions, depending upon the constraints of the language and computer memory. A three-dimensional array might be Stock(6,2000,3).

| SUBSCRIPT | DATA VALUE |
|-----------|-----------|
| 0 | What does IDE stand for? |
| 1 | What is a SUBROUTINE? |
| 2 | What is a FUNCTION? |
| 3 | What does BASIC stand for? |
| 4 | Which of these is DEFINITE LOOP? |
| 5 | What COLOUR is an ANNOTATION? |

TABLE 14.1 *A one-dimensional array*

| SUBSCRIPT | 0 | 1 | 2 | 3 |
|---|---|---|---|---|
| 0 | Inner Data Entry | Integrated Data Entry | Integrated Development Environment | Inner Development Environment |
| 1 | Part of a program that holds a value | A section of a program that can be reused | A section of a program that returns a value | A control on a form |
| 2 | Part of a program that holds a value | A section of a program that can be reused | A section of a program that returns a value | A control on a form |
| 3 | Binary All Safe In Coding | Binding All Sellotape In Celluite | Beginners All purpose Symbolic Instruction Code | Bugs All Start In Coding |
| 4 | FOR... NEXT | DO... LOOP UNTIL | WHILE... WEND | WITH... END WITH |
| 5 | Red | Blue | Black | Green |

TABLE 14.2 *A two-dimensional array*

## How to... use the VB.NET Integrated Development Environment (IDE)

The IDE environment includes form(s), tools, properties and many other aids to the programmer (Figure 14.5).

The VB.Net IDE Toolbox is used to add components, such as a text box, to the form. A form is the part of the program that shows when the program is run.

The Solution Explorer (Project Explorer in VB6) keeps track of the parts of a programming project (such as the forms) and of where they have been saved on the disk.

The **Properties** show for the object currently selected. **Properties** is used to change or set the properties of objects in **Design** view.

Code is usually attached to an event associated with an object. Most programmers double-click on an object to open the code window for that object's events.

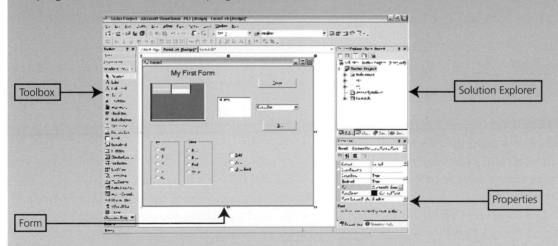

Toolbox

Solution Explorer

Properties

Form

FIGURE 14.5 *The IDE environment*

Variables are used to represent values. Most programming languages expect a variable to be declared before it is used to define the type of data (e.g. numbers, text, etc.) and the scope (which parts of the program can use the variable). VB.NET uses **Dim** statements to declare variables.

*Dim* is derived from the word 'dimension'. Early programming languages needed to know the size (dimension) of the space required by a variable in the declared memory.

A value is placed inside a variable using the assignment operator (=). Programmers often think of this operator as meaning 'becomes equal to':

```
Dim Total As Integer
Total = 3
Total = Total + 2
txtTotal.Text = Total
```

This code declares a variable Total to hold integer (whole) numbers. The number 3 is assigned to the variable that would be understood by the programmer as meaning 'Total becomes equal to 3'. From this point onwards in the code, Total represents 3.

Total becomes equal to 3 plus 2. From this point onwards, Total represents 5.

A text box named txtTotal shows 5. This is because its text property becomes equal to 5 (the number Total represents at that point in the code).

## Record structures

Record structures are used to store records (such as customer details) and are usually kept as disk files. A record structure may be implemented using an array or by defining a data type.

A defined data structure (VB.NET) or type (VB6) is a complex variable with several parts (data members) usually separated with a dot – e.g. Customer.Title, Customer.FirstName, Customer.Surname, etc.

Such structures can make code much easier to understand and therefore simpler to debug and modify during future maintenance.

When you create a data structure, code like the following is placed at the top of a form or module to define the structure:

```
Private Structure Employee
Dim Fname As String
Dim Sname As String
Dim Dept As String
Dim DoB As Date
End Structure
```

('Private' is needed if the code is behind a form because the structure only exists for that form). After the data structure has been defined, variables can be declared to that data type:

```
Dim Staff As Employee
```

After a variable has been declared to that data type, it may now be used:

```
Staff.Fname = "Steve"
lblStaff.Text = Staff.Fname
```

This code assigns the text, Steve, to the Fname data member and then assigns this to the text property of the label, lblStaff.

Compare the readability of an array:

```
Staff(0) = "Steve"
```

with a record structure:

```
Staff.Fname = "Steve"
```

The record structure makes it much easier to see what the text has been assigned to.

## Data dictionary

Every program should include a data dictionary in its documentation to record the names, data types, scopes and descriptions of the variables used.

A data dictionary is usually produced using a word-processed table, often with these column headings:

* Name
* Data type
* Scope
* Description of purpose
* Sample data.

## Assessment activity

Create a data dictionary for every variable and code module you think your program will need. You could sketch your forms and use arrows to show the data movements, with the variable's name written alongside (e.g. LastItem).

Include the scopes of the variables: all of a form? Local to the subroutine?

When your coding nears completion, you can return to this document to bring it up to date with any new variables or modules that you required, and you can identify any that were not needed, with notes to explain why.

## Assessment hint

✓ You have identified the required data structures.

✓✓ You have described the data structures fully.

# Forms

## Purpose of forms

Modern programming languages (such as Microsoft Visual Basic) use forms as the background where the controls can be placed. The IDE (Integrated Development Environment) shows a form in Design view, and it has a toolbox that contains objects that can be placed on the form.

The form has several purposes, including:

* to hold controls
* to accept inputs
* to provide outputs
* to contain code for events.

## Layout of forms

Skilled programmers pay a great deal of attention to form layout because they recognise that usability is a very important aspect of user acceptance. As a programmer, you have the responsibility to produce software with forms that are easy, quick and intuitive to use, with good ergonomics, sequencing and grouping.

The ergonomics of software are improved when designers recognise that users have three different ways to manipulate a form. These are via:

* the mouse
* the accelerator hotkeys
* the tab key.

Good form design includes all these methods, with underlines on the controls and a logical order to the tabs.

Good sequencing and grouping mean that, when the user enters data into a form, the action feels logical and sensible. For an ordering system, the name, address and telephone number would be grouped together and would probably be at the start of the sequence, with the order details in the middle and the payment at the end.

## Content of forms

Form content consists of the controls needed to accept input and to show outputs. Your form designs should show where appropriate controls will be located to enable the user to enter inputs easily and to gain information from the displayed output.

## Form controls

Controls are needed on every form if they are to function correctly. The design should therefore identify the controls to be used on the form.

The designer must ensure that each control is fit for the purpose – he or she will consider various types of controls and then select those that meet the user's needs:

* In Figure 14.6, the **label** is <u>S</u>core. The words in a label are not editable by the user. Labels are used to place words on forms, such as user instructions. **Text boxes** (**10** in Figure 14.6) are editable by the user. They are used in most situations where the user is expected to type an entry into the program.

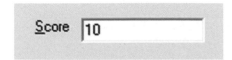

FIGURE 14.6 *Label and text boxes*

* **List boxes** (**XS**, **S**, **M**, etc., Figure 14.7) provide a choice of responses that are not editable by user. **Combo boxes** (the **XS** in Figure 14.7) present a choice of responses that are editable by user.

* **Option (radio) buttons** (**Black**, **Blue**, etc., in Figure 14.8) present a choice where only one item can be selected. **Checkboxes** (**Bold**, **Italic**, etc., in Figure 14.8) present choices where any combination can be selected.

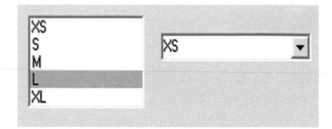

FIGURE 14.7 *List box and combo box*

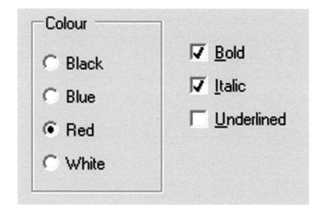

FIGURE 14.8 *Option (radio) buttons and checkboxes*

Some controls, such as a text box, may be bound to a data source, as in an Access table. This can be very powerful when you are creating applications where the program is a front end to a dataset – the programming language will handle a great many of the actions needed to update the dataset.

If you choose Access as the IDE for this unit, you will need to write code behind forms and reports to meet the grading requirements (see pages 327–9 for examples of code in a form and a report).

Nosh 4 Toffs is a new restaurant opening in Knightsbridge, London, that will target the more discerning, wealthy diner. The restaurant hopes to combine the best of traditional, quality ingredients and cooking with cutting-edge technology.

The cutting-edge technology will consist of six Centrino tablet PCs, which will allow wireless connection to the network with workstations in the kitchen, office and bar.

You have been asked to produce a suite of programs to run on the tablet PCs and other workstations.

The program for the tablet PCs will show diners the menu, which will include daily specials, photographs of the items on the menu and lists of their ingredients.

This program will allow the diners to order their meals with their cooking preferences.

The kitchen program will communicate diner choices and cooking preferences to the chef. The program running in the manager's office will edit menus, produce accounting data, summarise diner trends and update the restaurant website. The bar program will add drinks to the tab and print the diners' bills.

Produce a short report (part of the program design) identifying:

1 The inputs needed for the tablet PCs.

2 The form design for the tablet PCs' restaurant menu screen(s).

3 The outputs needed for the chef.

4 The outputs needed for the bill.

5 The report design for the bill.

## Assessment activity

Produce designs for your program outputs using form designs and mock reports. These need to be annotated to identify any features you have included, such as white space or a line round a group of data. Your designs should describe clearly when, where and how your program will work.

## Assessment hint

✓ You have briefly described the purpose, layout and content of the forms and printed output.

✓✓ You have described the purpose, layout and content of the forms and printed output.

✓✓✓ You have fully described the purpose, layout and content of the forms and printed output.

## Navigation routes

A navigation route is a sequence the program can run through. Most programs can run in many ways, depending on the choices the user makes, the data that is entered and the selection statements inside the code.

These routes through the program must be identified and documented to aid communication and testing. Communication is important to both the programmer and the user. The programmer must understand how a program is expected to work – which includes during the design process, when undertaking the coding and when carrying out any maintenance. The users must know the routes through a program so that they can use it more effectively.

Program testing should be as thorough as possible so that any bugs are found and fixed before delivery to the user. The progammer should identify and test all the navigation routes to ensure that they all work as expected.

The techniques for documenting navigation routes include form links and structure diagrams.

## Form links

The form links can be shown easily using sketches or diagrams of the planned forms linked together with arrows (Figure 14.9).

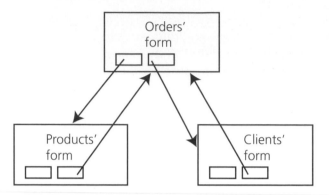

FIGURE 14.9 *Form links*

## Structure diagrams

Structure diagrams can be very effective for showing how the forms fit together in a program design (Figure 14.10).

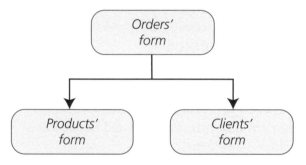

FIGURE 14.10 *Structure diagrams*

The programmer should choose which type of diagram best explains the design.

# Events

The various events that will occur in a program and the processing that results as a consequence of these events must be documented. This documentation will help the user to understand and approve the proposed design before the programmer begins the time-consuming and costly coding phase.

The programmer should clarify which events are expected and which actions the code behind the events should achieve. Many events are available to the modern programmer.

It is therefore important that appropriate events are chosen so that the code starts at the correct times and by the correct controls.

The desired outcomes of the code for events are identified as narrative (written descriptions) or **pseudo-code**. For example:

```
Initialise arrays
Accept user password
Show main form
```

## Assessment activity

Continue to plan your assessment program. Add to your technical documentation all the events and modules requiring coding that you can identify, such as command buttons and any other objects (e.g. a text box that responds to the **Enter** key being pressed).

Produce diagrams to show the navigation routes through these program modules and events. You may choose form link diagrams, structure diagrams or any other method. Use the method that you feel best explains your plans for the coding.

## Assessment hint

✓ You have included at least one diagram giving an indication of the navigation for the program. You have listed the events to be handled.

✓✓ The diagram(s) you have included showing the navigation for the program are accurate. The list of events includes brief descriptions of the processing associated with each.

✓✓✓ The diagram(s) you have included showing the navigation for the program are both accurate and clear. The list of events includes full descriptions of the processing associated with each.

1. What is validation?
2. Identify 4 uses of forms.
3. Identify the differences between these form controls:
   a. Label and textbox
   b. List and combo boxes
   c. Option buttons and checkboxes.

# 14.3 Coding

You must produce a design for your program before you start the coding. Coding without a design often results in a program that does not work properly or that takes much longer to write because sections need to be rewritten or are found to be unnecessary.

You will use an IDE or text editor to write the **high-level code** in your chosen language. The language will have a compiler to translate the high-level code you write into the machine code the computer can run.

**Key terms**

*Low-level code* is the machine code understood and executed (run) by the processor.
*High-level code* is the program written by the programmer. The programming language translates the English-like high-level code into the binary code that actually runs on the computer.

Modern programming languages provide an IDE where you can write, compile, run and debug programs. Most programming concepts are available in every language, but different languages often use different key words or **syntax**.

**Key terms**

*Syntax* is the sequence and structure of the statements in a language. 'A style has programmer' is an example of an English statement with bad syntax. Every programming language has its own syntax which defines how the sequence and key words must be arranged if a statement is to work.

Programming concepts include:

* declaring variables
* declaring constants
* data types
* the scope of variables (local or global)
* operators (assignment, arithmetic, relational, logical)
* selection (if statement, select case statement)
* repetition (for loop, while loops)
* data structures (arrays, records)
* built-in functions.

You will use a range of form controls, set their **properties** and use **methods** and events as appropriate.

**Key terms**

*Properties* are used to define the colour, position, size, etc., of an object. Many programmers think of properties as being similar to adjectives, which describe objects (nouns).

**Key terms**

*Methods* are actions that can be carried out on objects, such as 'move'. These may be thought of as verbs – 'doing words'.

**How to... use BNF**

Most programming languages provide syntax diagrams of the key words based on BNF (Backus-Naur Form). These diagrams explain how the key word is used.

BNF uses ┆ to show where a choice must be made and [ ] to show the optional parts of a statement. Thus:

```
<object>.Visible = True | False
```

shows that the Visible property of an object can be set to True or False.

Similarly:

```
Dim <variable> [ As TypeName ]
```

shows that a variable declared with a Dim statement has an optional typename.

The controls you will learn about include:

* labels
* text boxes
* buttons
* combo boxes
* list boxes
* option (radio) buttons
* checkboxes.

The IDE you use may provide other controls which you can use, if appropriate.

Event-driven languages stucture code into subroutines that handle the **events** of controls on forms.

You will write your own subroutines and will learn how to pass parameters by value and by reference to these subroutines.

Good code should be easy to read and understand. You will therefore need to:

* write comments in code explaining the purposes of sections of code
* use meaningful identifiers (names) for variables
* indent code in consistent, acceptable ways to identify such structures as an iteration (loop) or a selection.

## Assessment activity

You should have completed the planning for your assessment program, so you can now create the program. The program must work, so adopt a methodical approach, starting with the basic requirements and leaving the cosmetic enhancements for later.

Include your coding **annotations** or documentation that show how your program meets the grading requirements.

## Assessment hint

✓ You have produced a working program that meets some of the requirements of the functional specification. You have made some appropriate use of form controls, event procedures, and selection and repetition.

✓✓ You have produced a fully working program that meets most of the requirements of the specification. You have made appropriate use of form controls, event procedures, selection and repetition, and local and global variables. Your program demonstrates some use of general procedures.

✓✓✓ You have produced a fully working program that meets all the requirements of the specification. You have made effective use of form controls, event procedures, selection and repetition, local and global variables, general procedures and parameter passing. You have demonstrated careful consideration of program design principles, including the user interface.

## Programming concepts

### Variables and constants

Programming languages need variables and constants as these represent the data in a program. Variables hold data that changes (varies) as the program runs. Constants hold data that is always the same (constant) each time the program runs.

A variable, UserName, could be set when the program starts. Its function could be to set a label on each form which welcomes the user by name.

A constant, VAT, could be used to hold the VAT rate for a program. Its function could be to calculate the final totals for quotations. This rate would be the same every time the program runs. To change the VAT rate, the program would need to be re-compiled.

Variables and constants should be **declared** in a program to reduce errors and to state their scope and type.

## Scope of variables

The scope of variables (Figure 14.11) depends upon where the declaration is in the program. It could be local, form or global.

A declaration inside a subroutine produces a local variable with the scope of that subroutine only. A local variable does not exist for any other part of the program.

A declaration at the top of the code behind a form produces a form variable with the scope of that form only. A form variable does not exist for other forms in the program.

A global declaration at the top of a module (VB6) or in the Globals Object (VB.NET) produces a variable which will exist throughout the program. A value given to it will be available to every subroutine that runs after the value is assigned.

A variable's type defines the range of data that can be held.

## Data types

Some programming languages accept variables that have not been declared as to their type. Not to declare a variable is bad practice because the programmer will have less control over the program, which may result in errors that are

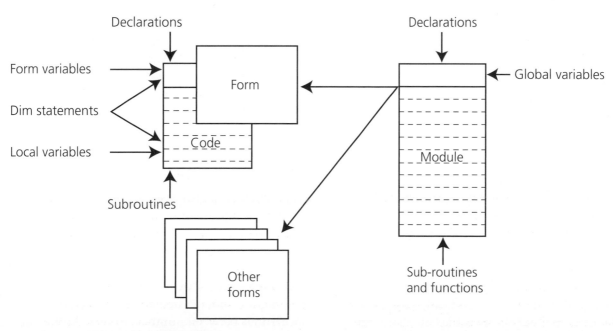

FIGURE 14.11 *The scope of variables*

difficult to spot during the testing phase and that are still in the code when it is released to the end users.

Variables that have not been declared with a type take on the default variant (VB6) or object (VB.NET) type, which adapts itself to whatever data is assigned to it. Undeclared variables take up a considerable amount of **overhead** in the programming environment, and they reduce the response time and place extra demands on the computer's resources.

Reducing errors is always a priority for programmers. The more errors that are recognised and debugged during the testing phase, the fewer errors that are left in the code the end-user receives.

Declaring data types for variables is a simple and effective method of reducing errors because, if there is any code which tries to place data of a type that is not expected into a variable, then it will be identified quickly. Structure and readability are improved by variable and constant declarations because they will be grouped together in the code with comments that assist in understanding their planned purpose.

Each variable has a data type, such as string or number. The default variable type in VB.NET is a variant which adapts to whatever type of data is first assigned to it. As we have seen, professional programmers always assign a data type to a variable when it is declared. This is to make the code more reliable, as an error will be generated if an unexpected type of data is entered into the variable. Bugs are thus detected early in the testing.

Declaring data types to variables also makes the code work better because variant data types need a great deal of extra overhead to cope with all the potential variations in the data that might have been assigned.

A string is also known as text. This data type is the most flexible of all because it can accept virtually any combination of characters, numbers and punctuation.

Number data types accept numerical data. There are many numerical data types, including the following:

* **Date**, which also has time information. The whole part of a number in this format is the date, with the decimal part the time. Thus 06:00 on 12 January would be stored as 12.25 in a date variable.

* **Decimal**, for numbers with fixed decimal places.

* **Double**, for real numbers – i.e. with a decimal part which may vary. These are also known as floating point (real) numbers.

* **Integer**, for signed whole numbers stored in 32 bits (up to $4.29 \times 10^9$).

* **Long**, for large integer numbers stored in 64 bits (up to $1.84 \times 10^{19}$).

* **Short**, for small integer numbers stored in 16 bits giving a range of +65535 to –65536.

* **Single**, for smaller real numbers.

* **Boolean** data types can only take one of two values, True or False (which may be shown as Yes or No).

## Assignment of operators

Operators are used to produce a result – usually a calculation or comparison.

The syntax for the assignment of operators statement is as follows:

```
<var> = <value> <operator> <value>
```

where <var> represents a variable or control, <value> is a variable or control containing data suitable for the operator, and where <operator> is the action to be carried out between the values and then assigned to the variable.

### Arithmetic operators

Arithmetic (numeric) operators are used for calculations between numbers or text. Arithmetic operators are listed in Table 14.3.

| OPERATOR | SYMBOL | FUNCTION | EXAMPLE | RESULT |
|---|---|---|---|---|
| Addition | + | Adds two or more values together | `Ans = 2 + 3` | The variable, Ans, is set to 5 |
| Subtraction | – | Takes a value from another value | `Ans = 12 − 3` | The variable, Ans, is set to 9 |
| Division | / | Divides a value by another value giving a real-number (floating point) result | `Ans = 9 / 2` | The variable, Ans, is set to 4.5 |
| Division | \ | Divides a value by another value giving a whole-number (integer) result | `Ans = 9 \ 2` | The variable, Ans, is set to 4 |
| Division | Mod | Divides a value by another value giving the remainder as the result | `Ans = 9 Mod 2` | The variable, Ans, is set to 1 |
| Multiplication | * | Multiplies two or more values together | `Ans = 2 * 3` | The variable, Ans, is set to 6 |
| Raising a power | ^ | Calculates a result using a value as the superscript to another value | `Ans = 2 ^ 3` | The variable, Ans, is set to 8 |

TABLE 14.3 *Arithmetic operators*

## Truth tables

Truth tables (Figure 14.12) are used to predict the outcomes of logical operations. Each truth table has every possible combination of inputs, with the output for each combination. The inputs are arranged in order as binary numbers.

## Text (string) operators

Text (string) operators are listed in Table 14.4.

## Relational (comparison) operators

Relational (comparison) operators are very similar to logical operators as they produce the result True or False. Relational operators are listed in Table 14.5.

## Logical operators

Logical operators are very similar to relational operators because they may produce a result of True or False if the operation is between **Boolean values**.

*Boolean values* are either True or False (yes or no).

| Inputs | | Output |
|---|---|---|
| A | B | Q |
| 0 | 0 | 0 |
| 0 | 1 | 0 |
| 1 | 0 | 0 |
| 1 | 1 | 1 |

**AND truth table**

| Inputs | | Output |
|---|---|---|
| A | B | Q |
| 0 | 0 | 0 |
| 0 | 1 | 1 |
| 1 | 0 | 1 |
| 1 | 1 | 1 |

**OR truth table**

| Inputs | | Output |
|---|---|---|
| A | B | Q |
| 0 | 0 | 0 |
| 0 | 1 | 1 |
| 1 | 0 | 1 |
| 1 | 1 | 0 |

**XOR (exclusive OR) truth table**

| Input | Output |
|---|---|
| A | Q |
| 0 | 1 |
| 1 | 0 |

**NOT truth table**

FIGURE 14.12 *Truth tables*

| OPERATOR | SYMBOL | FUNCTION | EXAMPLE | RESULT |
|---|---|---|---|---|
| Concatenation | + | Concatenates (combines) two string values | Ans = "Hi " + "there" | The variable, Ans, is set to "Hi there" |
| Concatenate to string | & | Joins two values (including different data types) into a string | Ans = 5 + " correct" | The variable, Ans, is set to "5 correct" |

TABLE 14.4 *Text operators*

| OPERATOR | SYMBOL | FUNCTION | EXAMPLE | RESULT |
|---|---|---|---|---|
| Less than | < | Compares two values of the same data type to produce a True if the first is less than the second | Ans = 2 < 4 | The variable, Ans, is set to True |
| | | | Ans = 4 < 4 | The variable, Ans, is set to False |
| Less than or equal to | >= | Compares two values of the same data type to produce a True if the first is less than or the same as the second | Ans = 2 <= 4 | The variable, Ans, is set to True |
| | | | Ans = 4 <= 4 | The variable, Ans, is set to True |
| Greater than | > | Compares two values of the same data type to produce a True if the first is larger than the second | Ans = 2 > 4 | The variable, Ans, is set to False |
| Greater than or equal to | >= | Compares two values of the same data type to produce a True if the first is larger than or the same as the second | Ans = 2 >= 2 | The variable, Ans, is set to True |
| Equal to | = | Compares two values of the same data type to produce a True if the first is the same as the second | Ans = 2 = 4 | The variable, Ans, is set to False |
| Not equal to | <> | Compares two values of the same data type to produce a True if they are different | Ans = 2 <> 4 | The variable, Ans, is set to True |

*Note:* In some of these examples, two equals signs can make the statements confusing. Another way to write these, therefore, is to use brackets to separate out the part of statement making the comparison:

    Ans = ( 4 <= 4 )

Care is needed with these operations as mistakes can occur at the boundaries (e.g. <5 will not include 5).

TABLE 14.5 *Relational operators*

## How to... use Boolean values

Boolean values may be used in Boolean expressions where the terms have logical operations, such as OR performed to produce an overall Boolean result:

    Valid = Warranty AND InDate

If the variables contained these values:

    Warranty = True
    InDate = False

the result would be that the variable, Valid, is set to false.

If logical operations are applied to numeric values, the result will be a number. Each of the numeric values is converted to a binary number. The logical operation is then carried out between each pair of bits from the numbers to calculate the result. The result is usually shown in the form taken by the original numeric values:

```
Ans = 65 AND 223
```

The variable, Ans, is set to 65. This is how the calculation works:

```
 65      0 1 0 0 0 0 0 1
223      1 1 0 1 1 1 1 1
AND      0 1 0 0 0 0 0 1
Ans = 97 AND 223
```

The variable, Ans, is set to 65. This is how the calculation works:

```
 97      0 1 1 0 0 0 0 1
223      1 1 0 1 1 1 1 1
AND      0 1 0 0 0 0 0 1
```

Logical operators may be applied to Boolean or numerical terms. Table 14.6 lists the Boolean logical operators.

These logical operators used on numerics are shown in Table 14.7.

Such calculations are used in, for example, the Ucase() function, which converts text to upper case. The character code for **A** is 65 and the character code for **a** is 97, so ANDing

| OPERATOR | FUNCTION | EXAMPLE | RESULT |
|---|---|---|---|
| AND | Carries out a logical operation on two Booleans to produce a Boolean result | Ans = True AND False | The variable, Ans, is set to False |
| NOT | Carries out a logical operation on a Boolean to produce a Boolean result | Ans = NOT False | The variable, Ans, is set to True |
| OR | Carries out a logical operation on two Booleans to produce a Boolean result | Ans = True OR False | The variable, Ans, is set to True |
| XOR (exclusive OR) | Carries out a logical operation on two Booleans to produce a Boolean result | Ans = True XOR True | The variable, Ans, is set to False |

TABLE 14.6 *Boolean logical operators*

| OPERATOR | FUNCTION | EXAMPLE | RESULT |
|---|---|---|---|
| AND | Carries out a logical operation on two numerics to produce a numerical result | Ans = 2 AND 4 | The variable, Ans, is set to 0 |
| NOT | Carries out a logical operation on a numeric to produce a numerical result | Ans = NOT 97 | The variable, Ans, is set to −98 |
| OR | Carries out a logical operation on two numerics to produce a numerical result | Ans = 2 OR 4 | The variable, Ans, is set to 6 |
| XOR | Carries out a logical operation on two numerics to produce a numerical result | Ans = 2 AND 5 | The variable, Ans, is set to 6 |

TABLE 14.7 *Logical operators used on numerics*

a character code with 223 will result in the character code for the equivalent upper-case character:

```
  97     0 1 1 0 0 0 0 1
 223     1 1 0 1 1 1 1 1
 AND     0 1 0 0 0 0 0 1
```

In this example, 223 is called a bitmask as it forces bit 32 to a definite value (0).

## Flow charts

Flow charts are used to show the navigation routes through a program. They are very useful when you are looking in detail at specific modules.

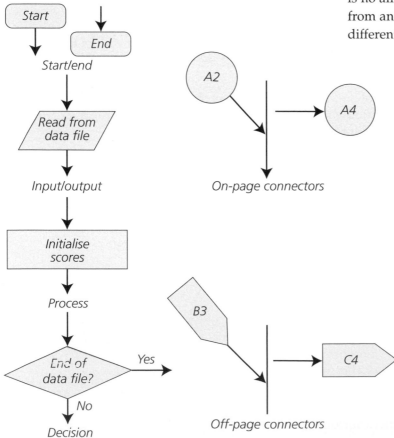

FIGURE 14.13 *Flow chart symbols*

Flow charts use a number of standard symbols (see Figure 14.13), but many writers simply choose the shapes they feel best represent the structure they are describing:

* **Start/end**: this symbol shows the starting and finishing points in the flow chart. There may be several of these.

* **Input/output**: this indicates any point in the program where something goes in (mouse/keyboard) or out (screen/printer).

* **Process**: any part of, or module in, the program.

* **Decision**: any point where the program can take two directions. Directions should be annotated with the conditions that enabled them.

* **On-page connectors**: used to connect two parts of the flow chart as an alternative to drawing a line. It is usual to have the same reference inside each symbol (e.g. A2) so that there is no ambiguity. In Figure 14.13, A2 returns from another part of the page. A4 sends to a different part of page.

* **Off-page connectors**: used to connect two parts of the flow chart that are on different pages. It is usual to have the same reference inside each symbol (e.g. B3) so that there is no ambiguity. In Figure 14.13, B3 returns from another page. C4 sends to different page.

## If statements

An if statement is a selection statement that is used when a program needs to be able to navigate through a choice of two routes, depending on a condition that results in True or False.

In the following code, the Boolean variable Discount is used to test whether the numeric variables DiscountRate and SubTotal are to be multiplied and shown in a label, lblDiscount, on a VB.NET form:

```
If Discount Then
lblDiscount.Text = DiscountRate
* SubTotal
Else
lblDiscount.Text = 0
End If
```

Figure 14.14 shows a flow chart for this code.

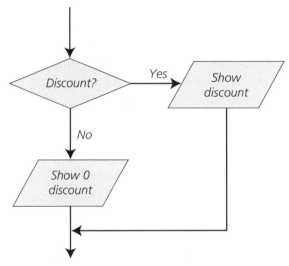

FIGURE 14.14 *An if statement*

## Case statements

A case statement is used when a program must be able to navigate through a choice of many routes, depending on a condition that results in any of several values.

In the following example, the numeric variable HeadSize is used to determine which crash helmet size is shown in the label lblHelmetSize on a VB.NET form:

```
Select Case HeadSize
  Case Is < 53
    lblSize.Text = "XXS"
  Case Is < 55
    lblSize.Text = "XS"
  Case Is < 57
    lblSize.Text = "S"
  Case Is < 59
    lblSize.Text = "M"
```

```
  Case Is < 61
    lblSize.Text = "L"
  Case Is < 63
    lblSize.Text = "XL"
  Case Else
    lblSize.Text = "XXL"
End Select
```

Notice how, as the structure tests each case statement in turn, the first condition to be met runs its code then program jumps to the End Select statement (Figure 14.15). Only one segment of code in the structure will be executed. In this code, 59 in HeadSize will show L on the form in lblHelmetSize.

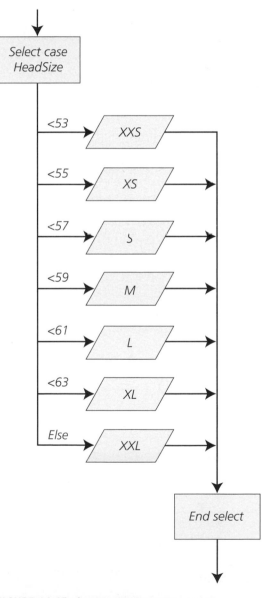

FIGURE 14.15 *A case statement*

## For loops

The for… next structure is a definite loop used for iteration (repetition). Definite loops repeat for a known number of iterations.

The following code saves an array called Scores() to disk, using a numeric variable LastScore to control how many values are sent to disk (Figure 14.16):

```
FileOpen(1, "c:\rjm.txt",
OpenMode.Output)
For Y = 1 To LastScore
   Print(1, Scores(Y))
Next
FileClose(1)
```

A program that saves data to a disk file usually knows how many records are to be saved – hence the use of a definite loop.

## While loops

A while loop is an indefinite loop that is used for repetition (iteration). It repeats until a condition is met:

```
FileOpen(1, "c:\rjm.txt",
OpenMode.Input)
LastScore = 0
```

```
While Not EOF(1)
   LastScore = LastScore + 1
   Input(1, Scores(LastScore))
End While
FileClose(1)
```

This code loads a file from disk into an array called Scores(), using a numeric variable LastScore to count how many values are loaded from disk (Figure 14.17).

Programs that load data from a disk file do not usually know how many records are to be input – hence an indefinite loop is used to keep reading the records until the end of file is reached.

The above is an example of a precondition loop because the condition () is at start of the loop. A post-condition loop has the condition at the end of the loop structure. The following is how the code would be written using a post-condition loop:

```
FileOpen(1, "c:\rjm.txt",
OpenMode.Input)
LastScore = 0
```

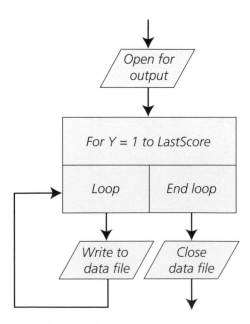

FIGURE 14.16 *A for loop*

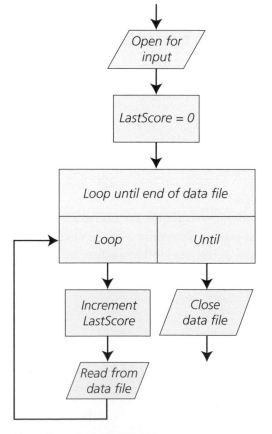

FIGURE 14.17 *A while loop*

```
Do
   LastScore = LastScore + 1
   Input(1, Scores(LastScore))
Loop Until EOF(1)
FileClose(1)
```

The position of the loop condition is shown through the use of **Until** in the loop description box, rather than **Wend**. This position is shown more clearly using standard flow chart symbols (see Figure 14.18).

Flow charting often permits you to use different ways to show a structure, so always use the way which is most to your liking.

In many programming situations it makes little difference whether an indefinite loop is pre- or post-condition. The choice of which to use often depends on whether the loop code has to run at least once (as in the post-condition in Figure 14.18) or if the loop code must not run if the condition is not met (use a pre-condition).

## Data structures

Data structures are used when a collection of values must be held in a single variable. Data structures include arrays and records.

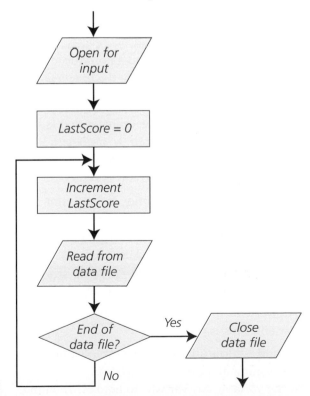

FIGURE 14.18 *While loop with flow chart symbols*

## Arrays

An array is a variable that can hold many values with one or more subscripts. The subscript is an index number that indicates which of the values in the array are current.

A three-dimensional array (Figure 14.19) has three subscripts and may be thought of as a collection of pages or as a 3D grid. The array represents (4,3,2), which can be visualised as (X,Y,Z), with the X axis declared as 4 (it actually has 5 values when zero is included (0–4)).

Arrays work very well with for… next loops which can easily process members of the array. The following sample code shows how a 2D array named Stock() can be copied to a flexgrid control named grdStock:

```
grdStock.Rows = LastStock + 1
For Y = 1 To LastStock
   grdStock.Row = Y
   For X = 0 To 2
      grdStock.Col = X
      grdStock.Text = Stock(X, Y)
   Next
Next
```

The rows and columns in a flexgrid control are numbered from zero. In Figure 14.20, row zero is used for the column headings, with the text (e.g. Ref) assigned in code not shown here.

The number of rows in the column is set according to the number of records from the variable LastStock. This needs to have one added to cater for row zero (there are three columns: 0, 1 and 2).

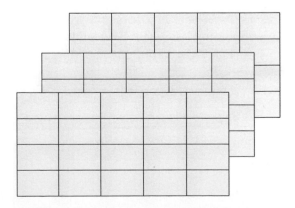

FIGURE 14.19 *A three-dimensional array*

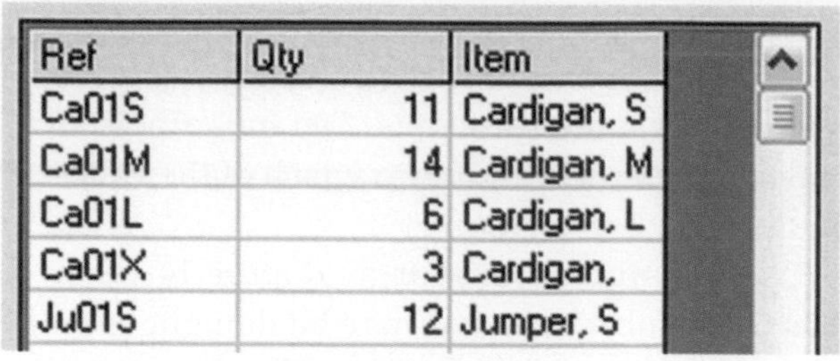

| Ref | Qty | Item |
|---|---|---|
| Ca01S | 11 | Cardigan, S |
| Ca01M | 14 | Cardigan, M |
| Ca01L | 6 | Cardigan, L |
| Ca01X | 3 | Cardigan, |
| Ju01S | 12 | Jumper, S |

FIGURE 14.20 *A flexigrid control*

### Records

Many programs need to manipulate data structures. The programmer has a choice of methods that include user-defined records and arrays.

**User-defined records**: these records are variables with attributes that are used in a similar way to object properties. A type is defined, then a variable is declared to that data type. In the following example a data type StockRecord is defined:

```
Type StockRecord
   Ref As String * 5
   Qty As Integer
   Item As String * 30
End Type
```

In this example, Ref is allowed five characters. An array Stock() is declared to this data type:

```
Dim Stock(500) As StockRecord
```

12 can be allocated to Qty element of Stock():

```
Stock(1).Qty = 12
```

**Arrays**: arrays have been covered elsewhere in this unit. They are particularly powerful when combined with loop structures.

## *Built-in functions*

Many programming languages have built-in functions, such as **Now** to pull the date off the computer clock.

Functions may be categorised as:

* date and time
* formatting
* number
* string
* user-defined.

### Date and time

Date and time functions use the computer's inbuilt calendar and clock to show a date or time:

```
lblDate.Text = Now()
```

shows:

```
21/02/2005  18:15:21
```

For more control over the appearance of these functions, use **Format function** to define the formatting.

### Formatting

Formatting functions give you control over the way data, such as a number, is displayed:

```
lblPrice.Text = Format(2, "£0.00")
```

shows:

£2.00

To show dates in a particular form:

```
lblDate.Text = Format(Now, "long
date")
```

shows:

12 October 2005

### Number

Number functions return numbers produced from the argument (the number inside the brackets). Number functions include the following:

* **Ceiling** returns the smallest integer that is not less than the argument: `Ans = Ceiling ( ArgVar )`. If the variable ArgVar was to hold 3.7, then the variable Ans is set to 4.
* **Floor** returns the largest integer that is not greater than the argument: `Ans = Floor ( ArgVar )`. If the variable ArgVar was to hold 3.7 then the variable Ans is set to 3.
* **Number** converts the argument to a number: `Ans = Number( ArgVar )`. If the variable ArgVar was to hold "3.7" (as a string) then the variable Ans is set to 3.7.
* **Round** returns an integer closest in value to the argument: `Ans = Round( ArgVar )`. If the variable ArgVar was to hold 3.7 then the variable Ans is set to 4.

## String

String functions are used with text (strings):

* **Contains** returns True if the first argument string contains the second argument string; otherwise it returns False: Ans = Contains ( FirstArg, SecondArg ). If the variable FirstArg holds "Paper" and SecondArg holds "ape", then the variable Ans is set to True.

* **Normalise-space** returns the argument string with the white space stripped: Ans = Normalize-space ( ArgVar ). If the variable ArgVar was to hold "No way", then the variable Ans is set to "Noway".

* **Starts-with** returns True if the first argument string starts with the second argument string; otherwise it returns False: Ans = Starts-with (FirstArg, SecondArg ). If the variable FirstArg holds "Paper" and SecondArg holds "Pap", then the variable Ans is set to True.

* **String** converts an object to a string: Ans = String( ArgVar ). If the variable ArgVar was to hold 3.7, then the variable Ans is set to "3.7".

* **String-length** returns the number of characters in the string: Ans = String-length ( ArgVar ). If the variable ArgVar was to hold "seven", then the variable Ans is set to 5.

### Theory into practice

The following is code for an Access form behind the click event for a combo box named cboAssignments:

```
Private Sub cboAssignments_Click()
Dim SQLtext As String

SQLtext = "SELECT tblStAssGrading.[Student ID], tblStAssGrading.AssignmentRef, "
SQLtext = SQLtext + "tblStAssGrading.GradeRef , tblStAssGrading.Grade,
   tblStudents.st_group "
SQLtext = SQLtext + "FROM tblStAssGrading INNER JOIN tblStudents ON "
SQLtext = SQLtext + "tblStAssGrading.[Student ID] = tblStudents.st_id "
SQLtext = SQLtext + "WHERE (((tblStAssGrading.AssignmentRef)=
   '" & cboAssignments & "'));"
MsgBox SQLtext

Screen.ActiveForm.RecordSource = SQLtext
Me.Refresh
End Sub
```

The string variable SQLText was built over five lines of code to hold as valid SQL. This was done to define the record source of the form to those records that match the assignment ref in cboAssignments.

The SQL was created in a query. When it worked, the SQL view was copied and pasted into this code, then edited into the SQLText lines above.

When a line was added to SQLText, each SQLText line (except the last) was given a space before the last double quotes to separate the new SQL from the previous one. Double quotes inside a line that has been edited to single quotes start and end the text.

The message box (Figure 14.21) in the code is for debugging. This shows the current state of SQLText so that the programmer can check that the SQL was built correctly from the code and combo box.

The form's record source is set to the SQL in SQLText, and the view is then refreshed.

FIGURE 14.21 *Message box in the code for debugging*

## Theory into practice

The code for an Access report about students' assignments is placed behind a group header band that prints out the grades for the assignments.

The module creates the dataset shown in Figure 14.22 from the table in Figure 14.23:

| Outcome | Unit |
|---------|------|
| P6 | Unit 10 |
| P5 | Unit 10 |
| P4 | Unit 10 |
| P3 | Unit 10 |

| | OutcomeRef | Unit | Outcome |
|---|-----------|------|---------|
| + | ASDp3 | Unit 10 | Customise the user interface with the application by making good use of features such as menus, dropdown menus, toolbars, dialogue boxes and tool buttons as appropriate |
| + | ASDp4 | Unit 10 | Install the application making suitable provision for system controls and starting the application, eg icon on desktop, button in a tool bar, entry in start list |
| + | ASDp5 | Unit 10 | Identify and correct any errors which are encountered and produce an executable version of the program |

FIGURE 14.22 *Dataset*   FIGURE 14.23 *Table*

The dataset is used to print the unit grading outcomes row, ringed below in Figure 14.24:

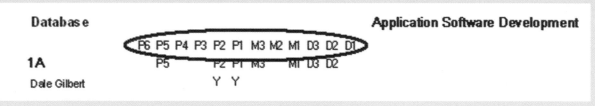

FIGURE 14.24 *Student results row*

```
Private Sub GroupHeader1_Format(Cancel As Integer, FormatCount As
Integer)
Me.ScaleMode = 6
Me.FontSize = 7
XTab = 30

SQLText = "SELECT DISTINCT UCase(Right$([OutcomeRef],2)) AS Outcome,
   tbl_Outcomes.Unit "
SQLText = SQLText + "FROM tbl_Outcomes WHERE (((tbl_Outcomes.Unit) =
   '" & Unit & "')) "
SQLText = SQLText + "ORDER BY UCase(Right$([OutcomeRef],2)) DESC;"

Set MyWorkspace = DBEngine.Workspaces(0)
Set dbsTemp = MyWorkspace.Databases(0)
Set rstGrades = dbsTemp.OpenRecordset(SQLText)

rstGrades.MoveLast
rstGrades.MoveFirst
```

```
For X = 0 To rstGrades.RecordCount - 1
    Me.CurrentY = 8
    Me.CurrentX = XTab
    Set fldQueryDef = rstGrades.Fields(0)
    Print fldQueryDef.Value
    XTab = XTab + 5
    rstGrades.MoveNext
Next
End Sub
```

Me refers to the current report. The scalemode statement sets the numbering system to mm. The font size is then set to 7 pt. The SQLText variable holds an SQL statement that uses the Unit field in the report to find records for that unit's assignments. The recordset is opened for use by this code. A Right$() function pulls out the rightmost 2 characters from the OutcomeRef field, e.g. P3 which the SQL statement names as Outcome. The MoveLast and MoveFirst statements ensure that the number of records is known and the first record is current.

The for... next loop iterates through the fields brought back from the SQL. Inside this loop, CurrentY and CurrentX are used to define the location of the next text. fldQueryDef represents the current field. The value of this is the data inside the field. XTab is a variable that is used to keep distance from the left margin for the next text. MoveNext is used to move to the next record for the next loop iteration.

## Basic form controls

### Labels

Labels are simple objects that are used to show text on a form for user prompts and to describe controls, such as text boxes.

Labels cannot be edited in a running program, so they are not used for data entry. A label cannot take the focus but they can be used to provide an accelerator key for an object such as a text box, providing the text box is the next object in the form's tab order.

### Buttons

Command buttons are used in virtually every form. Users press command buttons to accept choices and to carry out other actions, such as showing another form.

Most programmers make sure a letter is underlined in the caption (VB6) or text (VB.NET) on a command button to indicate the accelerator key. As a result, users can activate the button by pressing **Alt** and the underlined letter.

This formatting is accomplished by inserting an & before the letter that is to be underlined (Figure 14.25).

FIGURE 14.25 *Underlining a letter*

This action produces the button shown in Figure 14.26.

**Alt + Q** will therefore operate the button.

FIGURE 14.26 *The Quit button*

## Text boxes

Text boxes are used for free-form data entry because they allow users to enter any text. Some programmers build data validation into text boxes – they add code for key-press events so that every character keyed in can be checked to make sure it is valid. The following code:

```
Private Sub
txtNumber_KeyPress1(ByVal
sender As Object, ByVal e As
System.Windows.Forms.KeyPress
EventArgs) Handles
txtNumber.KeyPress
        Dim KeyAscii As
        Short KeyAscii =
        Asc(e.KeyChar)
        MsgBox(KeyAscii)
        If KeyAscii = 13
        Then
<code>
        End If
    End Sub
```

will run <code>, when the **Enter** key is pressed during typing into txtNumer.

## Combo boxes

Combo box controls allow users to choose from the options the program presents them with. The following code, which is inside the load event for the form, adds items to a combo box named cboSize:

```
cboSize.Items.Add("XS")
cboSize.Items.Add("S")
cboSize.Items.Add("M")
cboSize.Items.Add("L")
cboSize.Items.Add("XL")
cboSize.SelectedIndex = 0
```

The result of this code is shown in Figure 14.27.

Notice how the default item is set with the SelectedIndex property.

Combo boxes are economical in the space they use on a form as the choices offered to the user close up when one is chosen.

Users can key into combo boxes, but code must be attached to the combo box's control in

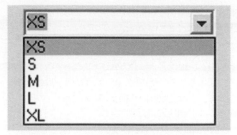

FIGURE 14.27 *The cboSize combo box*

case a user types in something that might be added to the items in the box.

## List boxes

List box controls similarly allow the user to choose from the options presented by the program. The following code, which is again inside the load event for the form, adds items to a list box named lstSize:

```
lstSizes.Items.Add("XS")
lstSizes.Items.Add("S")
lstSizes.Items.Add("M")
lstSizes.Items.Add("L")
lstSizes.Items.Add("XL")
lstSizes.SelectedIndex = 3
```

The result of this code is shown in Figure 14.28.

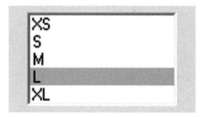

FIGURE 14.28 *The 1stSize list box*

Notice how the default item is set with the SelectedIndex property. As the list starts with item 0 (XS), the example above shows the fourth item (L) (the SelectedIndex = 3 is the number of the item, not the position).

A list box takes up more space than a combo box, and users cannot type into a list box.

## Option (radio) buttons

Option (radio) buttons are handy when you want to offer the user a choice where only one option is possible. When an option button is

This exercise will add an item to a combo box when the user presses **Enter**.

**Create** a combo box on a VB.NET form and name it **cboSizes**.

Double left-click on a blank area of the form to start the code for the form load event. Add the following code to the event:

```
cboSize.Items.Add("XS")
cboSize.Items.Add("S")
cboSize.Items.Add("M")
cboSize.Items.Add("L")
cboSize.Items.Add("XL")
cboSize.SelectedIndex = 0
```

**Run** the program to ensure the combo box is filled with sizes.

Type a new entry into the combo box and press the ↵ key. Select another item in the combo box to see how the typed entry has not been kept.

**Close** the program, return to **Design** view and double left-click on the combo box to start a code event.

The code for the default SelectedIndexChanged event is started by VB.NET. Use the combo box in the code window shown in Figure 14.29 to create a key-press event for cboSize (Figure 14.30).

**FIGURE 14.29** *Code window*

**FIGURE 14.30** *Key-press event*

Type the following code between the Private sub and End sub lines in the code window of this event:

```
If e.KeyChar = Microsoft.VisualBasic.ChrW(13) Then
  e.Handled = True
  cboSize.Items.Add(cboSize.Text)
End If
```

**Run** the program, type a new entry into the combo box and press the ↵ key. Select another item in the combo box to see how the typed entry has now been kept.

selected, another option in the group is deselected (Figure 14.31).

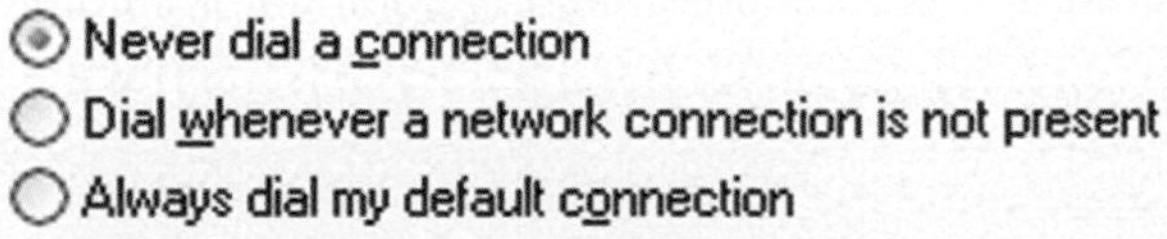

**FIGURE 14.31** *Option (radio) buttons*

Frames (VB6) or group boxes (VB.NET) are often used to group option buttons so that selecting one does not affect the option buttons in another group (Figure 14.32).

Coding an option button is easy as it has only two values (VB6) or checked states (VB.NET) – True or False. Any code in an option button's click event will run when it is checked.

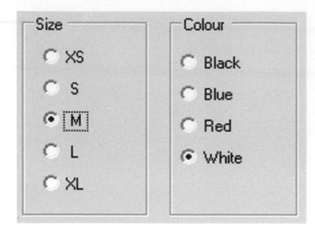

FIGURE 14.32 *Grouped option buttons*

FIGURE 14.33 *Checkboxes*

## *Checkboxes*

Checkboxes are useful when any combination of options is possible. When a checkbox is selected, this has no effect on any other checkbox (Figure 14.33).

The coding for an option button should be done carefully because option buttons have up to three values: checked, unchecked or greyed out.

The code behind a checkbox should be tested for CheckState (VB.NET) or value (VB6).

## Writing good code

To write good code, you should first establish how the sections of a program will work together. This is the program structure.

The techniques for documenting program structures include:

* flow charts
* JSPs
* decision tables.

## *Flow charts*

A flow chart (Figure 14.34) uses symbol shapes to represent parts of a program, with lines connecting the symbols.

Flow charts are especially useful when small, complex sections of code are being designed because

### How to... use a checkbox to set a label to italic

The following code uses a variable named NF, which is set to a new font based on the font already in the label, lblStaff. The new font is set to italic or regular, according to whether the checkbox, chkItalic, has a tick in it:

```
Private Sub chkItalic_Click(ByVal sender As Object, ByVal e As _
    System.EventArgs) Handles chkItalic.Click
        Dim NF
        If chkItalic.CheckState = CheckState.Checked Then
            NF = New System.Drawing.Font(lblStaff.Font, FontStyle.
    Italic)
            lblStaff.Font = NF
        Else
            NF = New System.Drawing.Font(lblStaff.Font, FontStyle.
    Regular)
            lblStaff.Font = NF
        End If
    End Sub
```

Similar code could be used to set the font to bold:

```
NF = New System.Drawing.Font(lblStaff.Font, FontStyle.Bold)
```

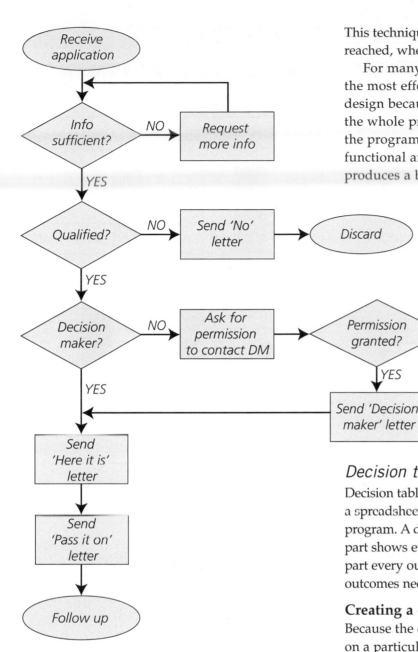

FIGURE 14.34  *A flow chart*

This technique is repeated until module level is reached, when the coding can begin.

For many years JSP has been considered the most effective methodology for program design because it forces the designer to study the whole program before he or she decides how the program can be divided into the appropriate functional areas. This approach, therefore, produces a balanced, effective design.

## Decision tables

Decision tables (Figure 14.36) are often created using a spreadsheet or a table in a word-processing program. A decision table is in two parts. The upper part shows every input possibility, and the lower part every outcome. Each column identifies the outcomes needed for each combination of inputs.

### Creating a decision table

Because the content of a decision table depends on a particular input or combination of inputs, the inputs and their linked outputs must be identified. All the expected inputs and outputs are listed as row names in a table or spreadsheet. Some of the inputs can be grouped – such as when a range of numbers can be simplified as less than a value, inside a range, above a value, etc.

Once the inputs are defined, all the combinations are entered as Y/N. The Y/Ns should be structured in the ways they are distributed, as shown in Figure 14.37.

Inputs are cancelled out when a combination of column pairs is found to be invalid, as highlighted in Figure 14.38 (paying with cheque and plastic).

they provide an accurate, easily understood diagram that shows selections and routes through the code.

## JSPs

JSPs are structure diagrams that show the program design according to the Jackson Structured Programming (JSP) methodology (Figure 14.35).

This methodology is top down – it considers the program as a whole and then divides the program into functional areas. Each of the functional areas is then divided into sections.

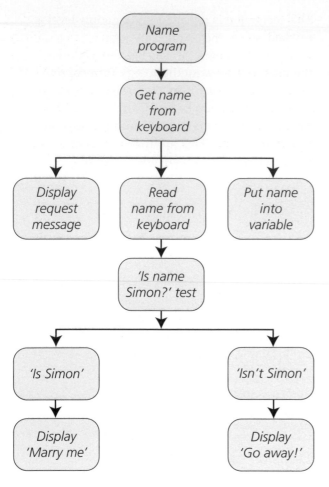

FIGURE 14.35  *A JSP*

| | | | | | | | | |
|---|---|---|---|---|---|---|---|---|
| <£50 | Y | Y | Y | Y | N | N | N | N |
| Cheque | Y | Y | N | N | Y | Y | N | N |
| Plastic | Y | N | Y | N | Y | N | Y | N |

FIGURE 14.37  *The structured Y/Ns*

| | | | | | | | | |
|---|---|---|---|---|---|---|---|---|
| <£50 | Y | Y | Y | Y | N | N | N | N |
| Cheque | Y | Y | N | N | Y | Y | N | N |
| Plastic | Y | N | Y | N | Y | N | Y | N |

FIGURE 14.38  *Inputs cancelled out*

| | | | | | | |
|---|---|---|---|---|---|---|
| <£50 | Y | Y | Y | N | N | N |
| Cheque | Y | N | N | Y | N | N |
| Plastic | N | Y | N | N | Y | N |

FIGURE 14.39  *Column pair deleted and other invalid pairs identified*

The column pair can be deleted and other invalid pairs identified (Figure 14.39). The invalid column pair is then deleted (Figure 14.40).

| | | | | |
|---|---|---|---|---|
| <£50 | Y | Y | N | N |
| Cheque | Y | N | Y | N |
| Plastic | N | Y | N | Y |

FIGURE 14.40  *Invalid column pair deleted*

Finally, the outputs are identified for each combination of inputs (Figure 14.41).

| Under £50 | Y | Y | N | N |
|---|---|---|---|---|
| Pays by cheque | Y | N | Y | N |
| Unknown customer | N | N | - | - |
| | | | | |
| Ring up sale | X | | | |
| Check from local database | | X | | |
| Call Supervisor | | | X | |
| Check credit card database | | | | X |

FIGURE 14.36  *A decision table*

| <£50 | Y | Y | N | N |
|---|---|---|---|---|
| Cheque with £50 card | Y | N | Y | N |
| Plastic | N | Y | N | Y |
| | | | | |
| Ring up sale | X | | | |
| Credit card sale | | X | | X |
| Call supervisor | | | X | |

FIGURE 14.41  *Outputs identified*

## Subroutines

In the early days of programming, many programmers wrote their code as one module. This code started at the beginning and finished at the end. This lead to the term 'spaghetti programming' – the code jumped from place to place, which made it difficult to follow (to trace), debug and maintain.

Structured programming has since evolved, where code is divided into subroutines: each subroutine contains code for one part of the program.

A subroutine can be called from a line of code. The subroutine would then run and, when a return or end substatement was met, the program would return to the line of code *after* the place where the subroutine was called. Subroutines can therefore be called from many places, which reduces the need to duplicate code (the dotted lines in Figure 14.42 show where a subroutine has been called from different places).

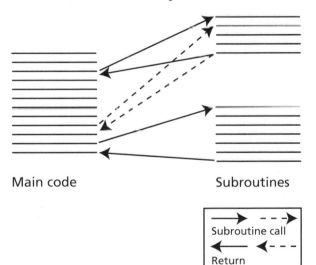

Main code                    Subroutines

Subroutine call

Return

FIGURE 14.42 *A subroutine*

Subroutines have made programs much easier to follow, debug and maintain. They have also made code much easier to understand because the structure can be readily seen from the meaningful names allocated to subroutines or comments. For example:

```
Call Initialise()
Call LoadArrays()
Call SortArrays()
```

Modern programming languages are event-driven, which means that code is now naturally divided into modules or subroutines.

A subroutine can be run on a form by the event handlers of a control, the code being attached when the event occurs. An event could be a mouse click, a key press or similar.

Some subroutines require one or more values to run. These values should be passed into the subroutine as a parameter (also known as an argument).

The following code shows a variable, UserName, set to a value (Richard), then passed as an argument to the subroutine ShowName:

```
UserName = "Richard"
Call ShowName(UserName)
```

This code shows how the subroutine, ShowName, is declared with the parameter SName inside brackets after the subroutine name:

```
Sub ShowName(ByVal SName)
    MsgBox(SName)
End Sub
```

This subroutine uses a message box (Figure 14.43) to show the contents of the parameter SName. In this example, the parameter is passed by value. This means that a copy of UserName is used in the subroutine, but this copy cannot directly change the contents of UserName.

If the parameter had been passed by reference, then SName would represent UserName inside the subroutine. Any changes to SName would therefore also institute the same changes to UserName.

## User-defined functions

It is possible to write your own functions. A function looks very similar to a subroutine

FIGURE 14.43 *Subroutine message box*

in code, except that it has the following structure:

```
Function MyFunction()
    <code>
 MyFunction = <value>
End Function
```

rather than this structure:

```
Sub MySubroutine()
    <code>
End Sub
```

*Note*: <code> represents program code.

## How to... use a ByVal parameter

ByVal is used to declare a parameter that uses a copy of the value passed to it in a subroutine. If this subroutine:

```
Sub ShowName(ByVal SName)
  SName = SName + "ski"
End Sub
```

is called from this code:

```
UserName = "Richard"
  Call ShowName(UserName)
MsgBox(UserName)
```

this is shown as in Figure 14.44.

FIGURE 14.44 *Using a ByVal parameter*

This occurs because the variable UserName is not affected by the subroutine ShowName. SName is a parameter that receives its value from the variable UserName.

ByVal ensures that only a copy of the value in UserName is in SName.

A function returns a value, so the syntax for calling it has to be:

```
<var> = MyFunction(<parameters>)
```

where <var> is a variable or control that takes a value; MyFunction is the name of the function you have created; and <parameters> are the values passed into that function.

## How to... use a ByRef parameter

ByRef is used to declare a parameter that acts as the variable passed to it in a subroutine. If this subroutine:

```
Sub ShowName(ByRef SName)
  SName = SName + "ski"
End Sub
```

is called from this code:

```
UserName = "Richard"
  Call ShowName(UserName)
MsgBox(UserName)
```

this is shown as in Figure 14.45 because the variable UserName is affected by the subroutine ShowName.

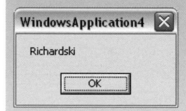

FIGURE 14.45 *Using a ByRef parameter*

ByRef ensures that SName is a parameter that points to the value held in the variable UserName. Any changes to SName change UserName because both these variables use the same part of the memory.

## Comments

As a programmer, you should produce code that not only performs and delivers the user's requirements but that is also easy to debug and maintain.

Experienced programmers always write comments (annotations) in code to explain the purpose of event handlers, variables, loop controls, etc. They recognise that it is often very obvious how a program works when it is being written, but that this is quickly forgotten. Comments help to make code self-documented so that it is much easier to read and so that complex sections are explained.

While comments are useful to the original programmer, they are essential for any programmer who must maintain the code. This is because they make it much simpler to understand how the code works and they help subsequent progammers to recognise features in the code that are not readily apparent.

Comments, however, should complement the code, not just repeat it. Effective commenting explains sections of code rather than individual lines.

## Meaningful identifiers

An identifier is the name given to a variable. Meaningful identifiers should be used so that the code becomes self-documenting. For example, a variable named UserName probably holds the user's name. This is good practice, whereas a variable named A$ gives no indication of its use – so this is an example of bad practice.

## Indentations

Indentations (or indents) are used to show coding structures, such as loops and selections. Good programmers indent code in a consistent and acceptable way. The following code has an indentation that shows clearly which code is repeated inside the for... next loop structure:

```
FileOpen(1, "c:\Tester.txt",
OpenMode.Output)
For Y = 1 To 12
   PrintLine(1, Y * 2)
Next
FileClose(1)
```

In some programming languages, such as VB6, the programmer has to indent lines using the Tab key. New lines are automatically indented to the same amount as the previous line. VB.NET indents lines automatically, so the programmer does not need to do this.

# 14.4 Debugging

A bug is a problem with the code that may prevent the program from running properly. Many bugs do not stop the program running but do affect the accuracy of outputs.

Debugging is the process by which the programmer finds and corrects errors. There are three main types of errors:

* **syntax** errors are caused by the incorrect use of the programming language

* **run-time** errors stop the program running

* **logic** errors arise from mistakes made when the code was first planned.

## Syntax errors

A syntax error occurs when a statement is in the wrong sequence, is misspelt or lacks a vital part of code.

The compiler usually finds any syntax errors when it runs the program. The compiler will usually refuse to continue attempting to run the code. It will display a message and highlight the offending code to assist the programmer in recognising and correcting the error.

### Problems

Syntax errors cause very few problems because they are found early in the programming cycle – the IDE usually refuses to run the code until these errors have been resolved. This means that such errors are corrected before the main testing begins, so the user is unlikely to experience them.

### Detection

Because the IDE understands the requirements of the key words used by the programming language, it continually checks the code as it is being typed and again when the code is run. Hence, any syntax errors are detected.

### Removal

The programmer re-examines the code highlighted by the IDE and rewrites the line so that it meets the syntax's requirements. The Help files are a useful source of examples of how the code should be written.

## Run-time errors

A run-time error will show itself when the code is run. The lines of code meet the program's syntax but they lack something the program requires if it is to run. Run-time errors may be found by the IDE but they usually result in the program crashing because of a system error. The offending line of code may be pinpointed by the IDE to assist in debugging.

Such errors often occur because the wrong type of data enters a control or variable. Data may also present problems if it has empty or null values. For example, the contents of a text box that should hold a number used in a calculation might have been deleted. This will cause an error because the null value will be used instead of the number.

Run-time errors are also caused when the expected is unavailable – for example, a program tries to open a data file that is not found.

### Problems

Run-time errors can cause serious problems if any remain in the code when the program is released to the users. No one is impressed if his or her software crashes.

### Detection

Many run-time errors are detected and resolved the first time the program is run. Most other run-time errors are discovered during the program's formal testing. Some run-time errors, however, may still remain after this testing if all the testing is done on the same PC. The program should therefore be tested on another PC to confirm that all the run-time errors have been resolved.

### Removal

Run-time errors are removed by carefully testing the program, especially on other PCs.

## Logic errors

Logic errors do not cause the program to malfunction but, instead, mistakes occur in the way the program runs or makes calculations. The results are incorrect calulations or wrong decisions. Logic errors usually give rise to incorrect output.

Logic errors are found during the testing phase of program development – this is why a structured and thorough testing plan is an essential requirement for any program. Such mistakes do not show themselves as error messages but as inaccurate outputs or events (such as the incorrect screen being displayed) – neither of which is acceptable to the end-users.

Logic errors arise from mistakes in the logic of the code. Whereas syntax errors are usually found by the compiler and run-time errors by the IDE, logic errors do not cause the program to stop running. A purpose of debugging, therefore, is to find and correct logic errors.

There are two main causes of logical errors:

* inadequate planning

* typing errors.

Inadequate planning may result in such errors because the programmer has not fully understood the user's requirements. The programmer's calculations may be wrong or may depend on incorrect assumptions, such as the post and packaging charge being the same for all items of stock.

Typing errors might have been made when the programmer entered the code (e.g. keying in + instead of − can make a real difference to the outcome of a calculation).

### Problems

Logic errors will produce output that is unreliable, which will reduce the user's confidence in the program, perhaps to the extent where it is not used at all. Undetected logic errors may therefore result in incorrect information.

### Detection

Logic errors are removed thorough program testing.

When VB encounters a problem running code, it will display an error message. These messages help to identify the problem but they need interpreting.

### Sub or function not defined

This message means an object's name has been misspelt. The names of like objects must be spelt in the same way.

### Invalid method or property

This message indicates that an object has been assigned a full stop when the word that follows it is not a method or property. This can happen when typing in code. Use the Help provided by the IDE if this happens.

When an object's name is typed in, the full stop brings up the methods or properties available to that object. The first letter of the required method is typed in and the arrow keys are used to select it. The Tab key is then employed to copy the section to the code (Figure 14.46).

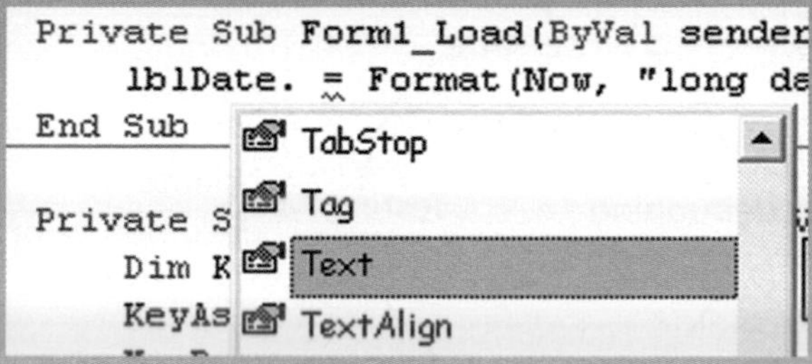

**FIGURE 14.46** *Copying a section to code*

This approach is quick and it reduces the possibilities of misspelt code.

### Variable not defined

This message indicates that a variable does not have a Dim statement to declare it. It is also caused by code that refers to an object that does not exist or that has a different (misspelt?) name.

### Type mismatch

This message occurs when an operation is attempted on objects or variables that represent different types of data – usually string (text) and numeric data e.g. "5" + 6.

## *Removal*

Logic errors are removed by careful testing: the route the program took to get to the point where the error occurred should be examined.

## Debugging tools

To meet the requirements of this unit, you will need to know how to use basic debugging tools, including the following:

* Putting **breakpoints** into your code to force the program to pause when it reaches the breakpoint (Figure 14.47). Breakpoints are useful when you want to confirm an event that is expected to run a section of code does actually run it. It is also useful to be able to inspect the contents of variables and other run-time values.

* Placing **watches** on variables allows you to have a prearranged view of the relevant variables when the program pauses (Figure 14.48).

* **Stepping-through code** is used when a program is paused. This allows you to see and examine the effect of each line of code.

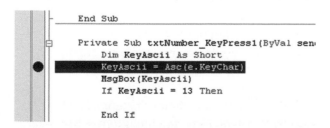

**FIGURE 14.47** *A breakpoint*

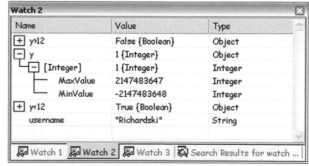

**FIGURE 14.48** *A watch*

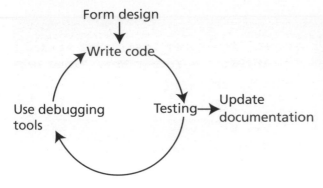

FIGURE 14.49 *Debugging code*

## Breakpoints

Breakpoints are a very effective debugging tool because the program will run up to the line of code with the breakpoint and then pause.

### How to... use breakpoints

To insert a breakpoint in VB, position the cursor on the relevant line, then use the **F9** key or single left-click in the left margin of the code window. The line will now be highlighted in brown.

To remove the breakpoint, carry out the same action to toggle it off and to clear the brown highlight.

Because the program has paused rather than ended, you may inspect the values inside the variables and other objects. You can also undertake more complex explorations to establish the state of the program or to change the values inside the variables and properties of other objects.

Breakpoints can also be used to confirm that an expected event will run as a result of a particular section of code. They similarly allow you to inspect the contents of variables and other run-time values at the moment the program pauses.

## Watches

Watches on variables show a view of the relevant variables when the program pauses at a breakpoint or as a result of pressing **Ctrl** + **Esc**.

The Watch window available in VB allows you to inspect how the variables and expressions' values change as the program runs.

In VB.NET, the Watch window is only available when a running program has been paused to break mode using **Ctrl** + **Alt** + **Break** or the **Break all** button.

There are four watch windows that can be accessed via the **Debug**, **Windows**, **Watch** menu option or via **Ctrl** + **Alt** + **W** and then a number (1–4). Thus you can create up to four windows containing collections of variables and expressions that are appropriate for debugging different sections of the program.

### How to... debug using a watch

To enter a new variable or expression in a watch window, click in the Name column and then type it in (Figure 14.50).

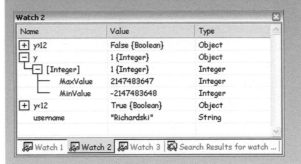

FIGURE 14.50 *Putting watches on variables and expressions*

In this example, Y had a value of 1 when the watch window screenshot was taken. The Y>12 expression shows false because 1 is not larger than 12. The Y value is shown as 1. This row was expanded by clicking on [+] to show that Y is an integer data type with maximum and minimum values. The Y<12 expression will now show True as 1 is smaller than 12. The variable username will be shown with its current value of Richardski.

## Stepping-through code

Stepping-through code allows you to run the code statement by statement. This tool can be very useful when you have inserted a breakpoint to pause the program at a place where you suspect a problem lies.

In VB you have a choice of stepping into (F11) or over (F10) the next statement to run the code line by line.

## How to... step into and over code

Try this example to explore how to step into and over code. Use a new or existing project. Create the folllowing subroutine in the code window:

```
Sub Tester()
  MsgBox("Message during",,"Tester")
End Sub
```

Return to **Design** view. Place a new button on the form and name it **btnTester**. Set the caption to **&Tester** (the caption will show on the form as **Tester**). Double left-click on the button and then type the following into the button's click event code:

```
MsgBox("Message before",,"Tester")
Call Tester()
MsgBox("Message after",,"Tester")
```

Position the cursor on the "Message before" line and use **F9** or the mouse to create a breakpoint. The line will be highlighted brown. Run the program (use **Alt** + **t** or another method to press the button). The program will pause on the "Message before" line, which is highlighted in yellow. Tap **F10** to step over and you will see the message displayed in Figure 14.51.

The yellow highlight will now be on the next statement where the Tester subroutine is called. Tap **F10** again and you will see the message displayed in Figure 14.52.

This message box came from the Tester subroutine. Tap the **F10** key again and you will see the message displayed in Figure 14.53.

This message box indicates that the program has returned from the Tester subroutine. The yellow highlight will now be on the End Sub line of code. Tap the **F5** key to continue running the code normally. You will be returned to the form.

Press the **Tester** button. The program will pause on the "Message before" line, which will be highlighted yellow. Repeat the previous actions but using the **F11** key (step into) instead of the **F10** key (step over). This time you will see each line of code in the Tester subroutine highlighted in yellow, together with the code behind the button.

FIGURE 14.51 *Message before*

FIGURE 14.52 *Message during*

FIGURE 14.53 *Message after*

When you employ stepping over and the statement calls a subroutine or function, you will not see the code in the called routine line by line. The program instead simply shows the next line in the main code (but the subroutine or function does run).

Stepping-through code is used when a program is paused because it permits the effect of each line of code to be seen and examined.

Each line of code may be stepped into or over. In both these tools the line of code will run. The difference is, however, that if the code calls a subroutine or function, then step into shows each line of the called routine. Step over, on the other hand, calls the subroutine but does not show it.

### Knowledge check

1  Describe examples of these types of errors:

   a. Syntax

   b. Run-time

   c. Logic.

2  How does declaring a variable type help a program become robust?

# 14.5 Testing

Testing is vital to demonstrate that the coded solution fulfils all the requirements of the program specification and design. You should identify the various paths through a piece of code and test each with acceptable, extreme and erroneous sample data.

Testing actually begins with the coding because the IDE identifies many syntax and typing errors as the code is typed and run. The real skill in testing is to identify and eradicate any logic errors in the code, which can only be achieved through a logical and thorough test plan.

## The test plan

To meet the requirements of this unit, you will design a test plan and produce documentary evidence to show that you have carried it out. Your test plan should include details of the actions you have taken as a result of your testing to ensure that the program is robust.

## Test plan evidence

Your test plan evidence should consist of written documentation and screenshots of the outcomes of the tests. These should be cross-referenced with the test plan itself.

## Designing the test plan

You will design a test plan and provide documentary evidence that you have carried it out. Each test in a test plan should include:

* the test number
* the purpose of the test
* which subroutine the test relates to (if appropriate)
* the data used for the test
* the expected outcome of the test
* the actual outcome of the test
* actions taken to resolve failed tests.

## White-box testing

This is the name given to a series of tests designed to ensure that the program works as expected. White-box testing requires knowledge of the inner workings of the program (see Figure 14.54).

Every route through the software must be tested. Tests are devised to confirm that every selection works as expected, with alternative coding routes correctly selected.

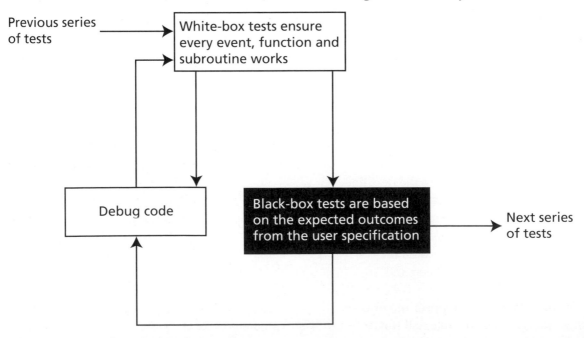

FIGURE 14.54 *Black and white-box testing*

## How to... design test data

The example in Table 14.8 accepts three data items: Quantity (integer 1–49), Item code (single letter then three digits) and Payment code ('P', 'C' or 'H').

First, identify the valid and invalid classes of data that might enter the program. Give each a class number.

| INPUT CONDITION | VALID | | Class number | INVALID | Class number |
|---|---|---|---|---|---|
| Quantity | | | | | |
| Value | 1–49 | | 1 | <1 | 8 |
| | | | | >49 | 9 |
| | | | | Non-numeric | 10 |
| | | | | Non-integer | 11 |
| Item code | | | | | |
| 1st character | Alphabetic | | 2 | Non-alphabetic | 12 |
| Size | 4 characters | | 3 | <4 characters | 13 |
| | | | | >4 characters | 14 |
| Last 3 characters | Numeric | | 4 | Non-numeric | 15 |
| Payment code | | | | | |
| Value | 'P' | | 5 | | 16 |
| | 'C' | | 6 | | |
| | 'H' | | 7 | | |

TABLE 14.8 *Designing test data*

Now create the test cases shown in Table 14.9.

| TEST CASE | INPUTS | | | CLASSES COVERED | TYPE |
|---|---|---|---|---|---|
| | Quantity | Item | Payment | | |
| 1 | 25 | r123 | 'P' | 1, 2, 3, 4, 5 | Valid |
| 2 | 33 | X345 | 'C' | 1, 2, 3, 4, 6 | Valid |
| 3 | 44 | G786 | 'H' | 1, 2, 3, 4, 7 | Valid |
| 4 | 0 | h123 | 'H' | 8 | Invalid |
| 5 | 123 | D123 | 'C' | 9 | Invalid |
| 6 | 1ab | S123 | 'P' | 10 | Invalid |
| 7 | 1.26 | f123 | 'P' | 11 | Invalid |
| 8 | 25 | 0123 | 'P' | 12 | Invalid |
| 9 | 36 | e1 | 'P' | 13 | Invalid |
| 10 | 23 | a12345 | 'C' | 14 | Invalid |
| 11 | 33 | abcd | 'H' | 15 | Invalid |
| 12 | 10 | v123 | 'B' | 16 | Invalid |

TABLE 14.9 *Test cases*

This approach makes for very effective, targeted test data.

Error trapping (if present) is tested, and expected errors are duplicated and program reponses checked. Some of the calculations will also be tested, especially any with an internal error checking, to ensure these checks are actioned and work.

## Black-box testing

This testing technique regards the program as a black box – nothing is known of the program's workings, only that it is there to do a job (see Figure 14.54). The test data is therefore based on the job the code is expected to do – in other words, the data employed reflects the user's requirements.

Data for black-box testing is therefore the normal, erroneous and extreme data that will be entering the program:

* **normal** data includes examples of entries that could be accepted

* **erroneous** data includes examples of entries that should be rejected

* **extreme** data tests the boundaries – good data (biggest/smallest; confirm, accepted) and bad data (biggest/smallest; confirm, rejected).

# 14.6 User documentation

Because the user documentation is written for the end-users, you must assume they have only basic computing skills and do not understand technical language.

Users need instructions to show them how to operate programs in such a way that they get the most out of them. User guides (Figure 14.55) should be clearly written and well illustrated, with a contents page and page numbering. The simple, non-technical language it contains will provide such information as:

* the system requirements needed to run the program. This will include the hardware

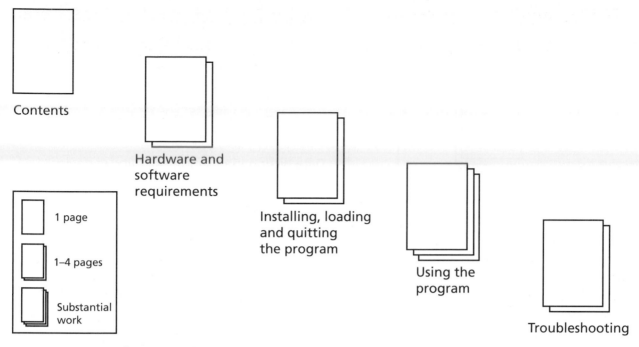

**Contents**

**Hardware and software requirements**

1 page

1–4 pages

Substantial work

**Installing, loading and quitting the program**

**Using the program**

**Troubleshooting**

FIGURE 14.55 *User documentation*

and the operating system, plus any other software the system may require

* the installation, with how to load and quit the program

* how to use the program

* troubleshooting and known errors.

# 14.7 Technical documentation

The technical documentation (Figure 14.56) is for yourself and other programmers because program code often needs to be modified and extended over time as the users' needs change. The programmers who write the new code are not always the same as those who wrote the original code. They therefore need accurate, detailed documentation to help them understand how the program works.

Technical documentation can also be useful to the original programmers if it is these people who are to maintain the code, as many

details are soon forgotten, especially when programmers are engrossed in writing other projects.

Some aspects of the technical documentation are in the program code itself. These are the features that make the code as easy to understand as possible, as well as self-documenting:

* meaningful identifiers

* correct and consistent indentation

* useful comments.

The other information that should be included in the technical documentation is as follows:

* a **data dictionary**, listing all the variables used and their purpose

* the **events** and the **task(s)** performed by each

* **user-defined subroutines**, stating their purpose and any required parameters

* **explanations** of how particularly complex parts of the program work (if this is not covered by comments in the code).

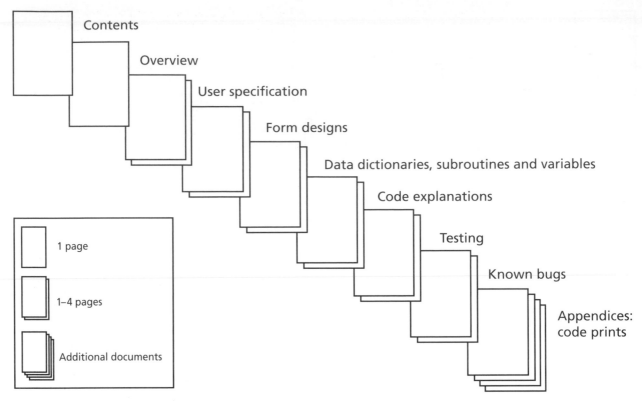

FIGURE 14.56 *Technical documentation*

## Assessment activity

Your assessment program has passed the test plan – the bugs identified during testing have been resolved. You should now produce user and technical documentation.

A starting point for your technical documentation could be the planning you undertook before

you started the coding. You must keep a copy of this planning information in its original form for your earlier assessment evidence, but you should also copy it to your technical documentation and edit it to meet the technical guide's requirements.

## Assessment hint

✓ Your user guide uses non-technical language, with some useful information for a non-specialist user. You have produced a basic technical guide for use by others, giving an indication of how the program works.

✓✓ Your user guide uses non-technical language and identifies the hardware and software needed to run the program, and it explains how to install, load, use and quit. Your technical guide is detailed enough to get an overview of how the program works.

✓✓✓ Your user guide is easy to use and contains non-technical language that identifies the hardware and software needed to run the program. Your guide explains clearly how to install, load, use and quit. Your guide is comprehensive enough for use by other programmers, with sufficient information to enable another competent programmer to understand fully how it works and to maintain it without assistance.

# 14.8 Evaluation

You should evaluate your programming from the viewpoints of both the end-user and the programmer. For the user, consider:

* how well the program meets the original program specification
* ease of use
* how the interface could be improved.

For the programmer, consider:

* how well the code was written (e.g. the use of structures for selection and repetition, local and global variable declarations and the parameters used with subroutines)
* data storage efficiency (e.g. how accurately the data types were declared and array sizes)
* any coding that did not work as intended.

# 14.9 ICT skills

In order to produce efficient program code you must be able to use a range of tools and

techniques, such as the programming concepts described in Section 14.3 and the features for debugging code described in Section 14.4.

## Assessment activity

Your assessment program project is complete. All that remains is for you to evaluate your documentation and to produce the program.

## Assessment hint

✓ You have included some evaluative comments that consider the extent to which the program meets the specification. You have also indicated how easy it is to use.

✓✓ Your evaluation assesses how well the program meets the specification, identifying any weaknesses. You have also indicated the efficiency of the solution and how easy it is to use.

✓✓✓ Your evaluation incorporates feedback from others, critically assessing how well the program meets the specification, identifying any weaknesses and suggesting some improvements. You have also indicated the efficiency of the solution and how easy it is to use, making some suggestions for improving the interface.

## UNIT ASSESSMENT

You must first decide on a programming need you could use for this project. There are many possibilities – try asking the people around you.

The best projects are often based on others' software needs.

Project ideas include the following:

1 A system to catalogue a large music collection held on your own and your friends' different computer systems.

2 A builder wants a program to help him produce estimates for new work.

3 An animated window display.

To fulfil the requirements for this unit you must:

A01  Produce program coding to implement your solution (assessment evidence b)

A02  Apply your knowledge and understanding to produce a program design (assessment evidence a)

A03  Exercise ICT problem-solving (assessment evidence a, b, c and d)

A04  Evaluate your solution (assessment evidence c, d and e).

Your program design should specify:

* the data input needs

* the validation procedures

* the data structures

* the form designs with their purpose, layout and content

* the printed outputs with their purpose, layout and content

* the navigation routes

* the events and any other processing

* assessment evidence a.

You must produce program coding that implements the solution (assessment evidence b).

Your test plan should include a range of tests and their outcomes, with details of the action taken as a result of the testing (assessment evidence c).

Your program documentation should include a user guide and a technical guide (assessment evidence d).

Your evaluation should assess:

* how well the specification was met

* how easy users found the program

* how well the data storage and program code were utilised (assessment evidence e).

# Glossary

**1NF** A table with no repeating groups – i.e. every attribute has precisely one value (called atomic).

**2NF** A table that is already in 1NF, and every non-key attribute is *fully* dependent on the primary key.

**3NF** A table already in 2NF, and no non-key attribute is dependent on another.

**Adjustment layer** A layer of pixels, the same size as the original image, but with some effect applied to the RGB values so that, when the two layers are viewed together, an adjustment can be seen.

**Alt** Short for 'alternative text'.

**Anchor tag** Can act either as a bookmark or as a hyperlink, depending on its attributes.

**Annotations** Written comments which help to explain sections of code. In VB.NET, each annotation starts with a single quote and is green.

**Anti-aliasing** A process which mends the edges of images into the background.

**Aperture** The hole through which light travels into the camera; the larger the aperture, the more light hits the lens and is transferred to the CCD at the back of the camera.

**Argument** A value of expression used within a function to specify what data is to be acted upon, or the criteria that are to be applied, or the resulting value that is required.

**Array** A range of cells that covers more than one row and more than one column (e.g. A5:D9).

**ASF** Stands for Advanced Systems Format.

**ASP** Stands for Active Server Pages.

**Asynchronous communication** Occurs when data is sent from one device to another device at irregular intervals, often in bursts. The receiving device does not know when the next piece of data will be sent nor how long it will take to receive the data.

**Attribute** A data item that describes an entity that is considered important enough to be stored in a database.

**Baseline plan** The plan fixed and agreed at a key point in a project – often at the start of a phase.

**Bitmap graphics** Created using painting software, such as Paint, or can be scanned in or transferred from a digital camera.

**Boolean values** Either True or False (yes or no).

**bps** Stands for bits per second.

**Browser** Interprets the HTML code of your website and displays it on the visitor's screen.

**Business case** In the business world, if a project is to gain senior management approval, a viable business case must be provided for the project. This business case will set out the advantages the company will gain from the project, over and above how much it will cost the company to undertake it.

**Cancellation** When a signal travels down a conductor an electric field is created, this interferes with any wires close by. Twisting pairs of wires, to an extent, cancels this effect.

**Categorical data** Has separate categories, and there is no natural ordering.

**CFML** Stands for Cold Fusion Mark-up Language.

**CGI** Stands for Common Gateway Interface. The CGI is an agreed standard for sending data collected on a form on a web page to a database.

**Circular error** A formula includes a cell reference that leads back to itself.

**Click-stream analysis** Involves the automated data collection of each click made by an individual, monitored over an extended period of time, and then the statistical analysis of this data to establish patterns of behaviour.

**Client-side code** Used for static pages. Each .htm or .html file is developed by the client, stored on the host's server and displayed via the browser.

**CMYK** Stands for cyan, magenta, yellow, key (black).

**Codec** Like a printer driver; it provides information for the computer to interpret the sound files and play them through the sound card using software installed on your computer.

**Command button** A control on a form or slide that is linked to a macro so that, if clicked (triggered by an event), an action happens.

**Comparison operators** (=, >, <) Allow you to compare two values to give the result of either True or False.

**Contingency** An activity you add to a plan to allow for as yet unknown work.

**Continuous data** Can take a value anywhere on a number line. For example, time is a continuous variable, as are height, length and weight.

**Control** A GUI interface object such as a list box, drop-down menu or button that lets the user control the program.

**CSMA/CD** Stands for Carrier Sense Multiple Access/Collision Detection.

**css** Stands for 'cascading style sheet'.

**CSV** Stands for comma separated variable. This format of file can be imported into most database management software packages.

**Customer deliverables** Those things the project creates that are useful to the customer.

**Data model** A representation of a real-life physical process or situation.

**Data type** Determines how many bytes of storage are to be allocated to each attribute and the kinds of functions that can be carried out on that data. For example, calculations can only be carried out on numeric data.

**Datagram** A special message that transports data from one device on a network to another.

**Declaration** Occurs when a program encounters a variable or constant for the first time. The declaration establishes the name and scope of the variable and should define the type of data that can be held in the variable.

**Definition** A document that explains clearly a project's scope: who will be involved, the benefits that should arise from undertaking the project, its success criteria and so on.

**Deliverable** A product or service that a project endeavours to produce.

**Dependency** Something that must be done before a phase in a project can be completed.

**Desirable** Things the project should do if to achieve these features does not overstrain the available resources.

**DHTML** Stands for Dynamic HTML.

**Dim** Derived from the word 'dimension'. Early programming languages needed to know the size (dimension) of the space required by a variable in the declared memory.

**Discrete data** Takes values, but not the values between them. For example, shoes sizes are 4, 4½, 5, 5½, 6, 6½, 7 and so on. There is no shoe size between a 4 and a 4½.

**Dithering** A process which produces a smooth transition between colours.

**DLL** A Dynamic Link Library. A set of commands that controls a device or service.

**DMBS** Stands for database management software.

**DNS** Stands for Domain Name System – and Domain Name Service.

**DPA** Stands for Data Protection Act.

**Dynamic data** Data that is updated.

**E-marketing**  Involves collecting data about potential customers and contacting them with information about products and services.

**Encapsulate**  To wrap in or to enclose.

**Entity**  Something (a person, a thing, a concept) in the real world that is to be represented in a database.

**ERD**  Stands for entity-relationship diagram.

**Ergonomics**  Involves fitting the interface to the worker, not the worker to the interface. It is the science of adapting workstations so that they are compatible with individual workers rather than forcing workers to endure awkward program designs.

**Event**  An action by the user (e.g. clicking on the mouse).

**Event driven**  Means that the program code modules you write run in response to user events, such as a mouse click. Code modules are therefore associated with particular events.

**Extent** (of a book)  The number of pages – including prelims (at the start of the book) and endmatter (at the end of the book).

**FAQs**  Stands for Frequently Asked Questions.

**File lookup check**  Matches the data entered to a record within a file and presents that information to the data entry clerk for verification.

**Financial year**  All companies must prepare their accounts on a yearly basis ready for inspection by the tax authorities. The yearly basis a company uses may not run from 1 January to 31 December but may run, for example, from the date the company was founded. Whatever the dates a company chooses to start and end its accounting period, this period is known as the company's financial year.

**Flag**  An indicator that shows the state of something within a program. It is implemented using a variable.

**Font**  A particular typeface in a particular point size (e.g. Arial 10 pt or Times Roman 12 pt), with or without emphasis.

**Footer**  A space at the bottom of each page – and the data that appears there.

**Foreign key**  A field (or field combination) in one table whose value is required to match those of the primary key in another table.

**Form**  Provides the user with a guided route to data entry.

**Form handler**  Translates the data that is input through the fields within a form into a code that can be input to a database or processed in some other way.

**Form variable**  Will have the Dim statement at the start of the code, behind the form where it will be used.

**Format (picture) check**  Checks the characters entered against a mask that specifies the data type of individual characters within a data item.

**Formative evaluation**  If you learn from the evaluation and it then helps you to improve your work, it is called formative. Evaluation carried out during the development allows time for you to implement change and produce a better end product.

**Formative testing**  Used during development to check that a product works; the outcomes of testing are used to decide how to improve the product.

**Formula**  An expression written in terms of cell references and operators which specifies a calculation that is to be done, the result of which appears in the cell in which the formula is stored.

**fps**  Stands for frames per second.

**Frame relay**  An efficient data transmission technique using a relay of frames to one or many destinations from one or many end-points. A cheaper 'always on' connection than DSL or cable.

**FTP**  Stands for File Transfer Protocol.

**Function**  A command that results in a value being returned.

**Functional relationships** (in a network)  The means by which the different components in a system fit together so that the entire network functions efficiently and effectively.

**Functional requirements** (in a software project) Those tasks the customer specifies the software must be able to perform.

**Functionality** Refers to what the website does, or the options it offers the user.

**GIF** stands for Graphic Interchange Format.

**Global variable** Can be used anywhere in the program.

**HCI** Stands for human computer interface.

**Header** A space at the top of each page – and the data that appears there.

**High-level code** The program written by the programmer. The programming language translates the English-like high-level code into the binary code that actually runs on the computer.

**Hit list** A list of website addresses that match a criterion used with a search engine.

**Host** A company that offers services to clients who want to publish a website on the Internet.

**House style** Specifies any requirements of documents which represent an organisation. This includes sizing and positioning of logos, static information that needs to be included (like company registration details), which font is to be used, acceptable colours and so on.

**HTML** Stands for HyperText Mark-up Language.

**Hyperlink** An icon or piece of text which, when clicked on, results in an object such as another web page being loaded. The hyperlink is the URL of the resource to which the viewer wants to jump.

**IEEE** The Institute of Electrical and Electronics Engineers. This is an American organisation that sets standards in the fields of electrical and electronic engineering.

**Image map** An image that has been divided into regions, or hotspots.

**Import** (data) To bring data in from some other source.

**Important** Things the project should do, if at all possible.

**Increment** Means to add 1 to a value.

**Integrated Development Environment (IDE)** The name given to a modern programming language.

**Integrated Services Digital Network (ISDN)** A digital telephone line that can share voice and data communications.

**Integrity** Refers to the accuracy of the data.

**Interim deliverables** Those things that appear part way through a project.

**Internal hyperlink** Takes the visitor to a different place within the same site. An external hyperlink leads to a new site altogether.

**International Standards Organisation (ISO)** Sets standards for a wide range of areas, not just computing.

**IP** Stands for Internet Protocol.

**ISDN** Stands for Integrated Services Digital Network. This is a network designed to transmit both voice messages and data.

**Iterative approach** Repeats a cycle of activities, all the time moving closer to some target solution.

**JPEG** Stands for Joint Photographic Expert Group.

**Landing page** The first page that a visitor sees on your website. This may not be the home page – it is the page the browser defaults to if a visitor presents an incomplete URL.

**Layout** The process of arranging the text on the page.

**Length of data check** Limits the number of characters that can be entered.

**List** A series of worksheet rows that contain related data. The first row contains labels for the columns.

**List server** Manages one or more mailing lists for groups of users.

**Local variable** Will have the Dim statement at the start of the subroutine (or function) that uses it.

**Log analysis tools** Provide feedback to a site manager about traffic on the site, such as visitor activity, most requested pages, downloads and referrals on search engines.

**Logical topology** The 'network on paper' – the design and planning phase. This is often shown by a simple diagram.

**Logo** A visual sign used to represent a particular company, an idea, a special occasion or a product.

**Low-level code** The machine code understood and executed (run) by the processor.

**MAC** Stands for Media Access Control.

**Macro** A short piece of code that results in a specific action taking place.

**Mandatory** Things the project must do.

**Mask** A string of characters that is used to specify the format of a data entry item.

**Mbps** Stands for million bits per second.

**MDVR** Stands for Microsoft Digital Video Recording.

**Metadata** Data about the data.

**Methods** Actions that can be carried out on objects, such as 'move'. These may be thought of as verbs – 'doing words'.

**Micron** A thousandth of a millimetre.

**MIDI** Stands for Musical Instrument Digital Interface.

**Milestone** A date, external to the project, by which certain activities must be finished.

**Modelling** Involves finding parallels between the real world and some modelling tool, such as a spreadsheet.

**Motion tween** Involves changes in object position and scale.

**MPEG** Stands for Moving Pictures Expert Group.

**MS ADPCM** Stands for Microsoft Adaptive Differential PCM.

**MV** Stands for Windows Media Video.

**Mystery meat navigation** Involves unmarked links and navigational buttons that rely on JavaScript to describe their function when you accidentally roll the mouse over the link.

**Narrowband signals** Have a limited frequency range.

**Nav bar** Short for navigation bar.

**Navigation** The way in which the user can move around/through the product.

**Network operating system** Provides the same services as an operating system but to users or computers spread across a network.

**Normalisation** Involves checking that there is no unnecessary duplicated data; it maximises the efficiency of a database.

**OLE object** Something like a Microsoft Excel spreadsheet, a Microsoft Word document, graphics, sounds or other binary data which is linked to or embedded in an Access table.

**Operating system** The software installed on the computer that enables the user to access and manage the computer's system (e.g. start-up, logon procedures and so on).

**Ordinal data** May be discrete or continuous, but has a definite ordering (e.g. from smallest to largest, or oldest to newest).

**OUI** Stands for Organisationally Unique Identifier. This is the part of the MAC address that identifies the device's manufacturer.

**Page counter** A record that someone has used a browser to access a page on your site. A link tracker counts the number of times a link is clicked. A download counter keeps track of the number of times a file is downloaded.

**Payback period** The time it takes for the benefits of a change to repay its costs.

**PCM** Stands for pulse code modulation.

**PDA** Stands for Personal Digital Assistant. PDAs are handheld computers that often include a Bluetooth or WiFi connection, and some incorporate mobile phone.

**PDF** Stands for Portable Data Format.

**Peer** Something that, in nearly all respects, is equal to something else. For example, you and your fellow students are peers – you are about the same age, are studying the same course, have a similar educational background and so on.

**Person-hour** The amount of work a person can be expected to do during one clock hour.

**Person-month** The amount of time a person can be expected to work during one calendar month. Unlike a calendar month, therefore, a person-month does not include weekends, bank holidays and nights.

**Phase** A subproject within a project. Phases make projects easier to manage.

**Physical topology** The finalised structure of a computer network: the wiring, the devices that will be used, the software that will be installed and so on.

**Pivot** To rotate about a point. In a spreadsheet, the point is a cell, and the rows and columns become interchanged.

**Pixel** Short for picture element.

**Points** A measurement of font size. Typical sizes are 10 pt or 12 pt.

**POP** Stands for point of presence. This is the room where the network will connect to the Internet and to the company's other sites.

**Port** A socket or connection on a computer.

**Presence check** Checks the data that is being input by comparing it with data that is already held in the database.

**Primary key** A field (or group of fields) that uniquely identifies a data record (i.e. one row in a database table).

**Productivity** A measure of how efficiently a company or organisation operates. A commercial company's productivity, for example, will be measured in terms of how much it costs to produce a product or service in comparison with how much it sells that product or service for.

The higher the production costs, the lower the productivity. The lower the production costs, the higher the productivity.

**Properties** Used to define the colour, position, size, etc., of an object. Many programmers think of properties as being similar to adjectives, which describe objects (nouns).

**Protocol** A predefined way that someone or, more likely, something – like a web browser – who wants to use a service talks with that service.

**Prototype** A model or mock-up built, quickly and cheaply, to resemble the finished product. This is usually done so that the proposed system can be tested and so that the customer can have an idea of what the final system will look like.

**Pseudo-code** A mixture of code and normal writing. It is used to explain how a section of code works. Key words from the programming language are included, but detail is omitted.

**PVR** Stands for Personal Video Recorder.

**QBE** Stands for query by example.

**Quality criteria** The predetermined standards a deliverable must conform to.

**RAID** Stands for Redundant Array of Integrated Drives. A RAID is used to connect many hard drives together so that, should one fail, the data on that drive can be recovered from the other hard drives.

**Range check** Rejects data outside a valid range of values.

**RDBMS** Stands for relational DBMS.

**Referrer** The URL of the web page from whence your visitor came.

**Relationship** Links two entities, via their attributes.

**Representative values** Single values that represent many items of data, such as means, modes and medians, and other statistical values.

**Required functionality** What the network will be required to do.

**Resolution** (image)  A measure of the pixels or dots per inch in an image.

**Resolution** (in a camera)  Measured in ppi (point per inch). Resolution on a screen is measure in dpi (dots per inch).

**RFC**  Stands for 'request for comment'.

**RGB**  Stands for red, green, blue.

**Risk**  Any event – either foreseen or unforeseen – that *may* happen and that puts the success of a project in jeopardy.

**RJ**  Stands for registered jack. This is the American term for a plug that has been recognised as acceptable by a computer standards organisation.

**Robust**  A system is robust if it is difficult for the user to cause it to crash.

**Run-time version** (of a product)  The version the user is given.

**Scalable network**  A network that can be extended easily or that is capable of growth.

**Scope** (of a project)  What the project aims to achieve.

**Scope creep**  Where the size and, hence, the cost and time of a project grow greatly as a result of many minor extensions.

**Search engine**  A website that provides a 'lookup' service to Internet users. It keeps an index of key words found on websites and allows users to look for particular sites using these key words.

**Self-documented code**  Has sensibly named objects. The objects are named in such a way that the code can almost be read like a book.

**Shape tween** (or **morphing**)  Involves changes in the object's shape.

**Shutter speed**  Controls the length of time the aperture is open during the shot. The faster the speed, the less time light can enter.

**Site map**  Lists all the pages in a website diagrammatically and shows how they are interlinked.

**Spam**  Unsolicited mail.

**Spider**  A type of software that scans websites to collect information about the sites.

**Spread-spectrum signals**  These use a wide range of frequencies and broadcasting techniques.

**Stakeholder**  A person or organisation who is actively involved in a project or whose interests the project may affect.

**Static data**  Data that does not change.

**Static pages**  Web pages that display the same content each time you view them. Dynamic pages display content that is affected by a changing data source. Such pages may be customised (e.g. to show the current time/situation and to address the viewer personally).

**Stop-frame animation**  A series of single shots that give the impression of unaided movement of an inanimate object.

**Storyboard**  A sequence of diagrams showing the stages through which a game or film will go. They are like the stills of a movie.

**Style**  A particular font with additional formatting, such as line spacing, colour of text and so on.

**Summative evaluation**  Looks back over what you have done; it may help you to do better on the next project, but it is too late to make changes to this one.

**Summative testing**  Looks back over what you have done. The outcomes of this testing are not used to change the end product.

**Synchronous communication**  Occurs when data is sent at regular intervals and when the receiving device is aware of how long it will take for the data to arrive.

**Syntax**  The sequence and structure of the statements in a language. 'A style has programmer' is an example of an English statement with bad syntax. Every programming language has its own syntax which defines how the sequence and key words must be arranged if a statement is to work.

**Tabbed order**  The data entry fields on a form are presented in an order, and if the user presses the

Tab key (rather than Return), the cursor jumps to the next logical field for data entry.

**Tag** One or more characters written within triangular brackets.

**T-commerce** Commerce via your TV.

**TCP** Stands for Transmission Control Protocol.

**Telegraphics** What makes people take action – what motivates them.

**Template** Determines the basic structure for a document and contains settings such as fonts, key assignments, macros, page layout and styles.

**TLD** Stands for 'top-level domain', the broadest categories of computer host on the Internet.

**Topology** Describes the way a network has been structured. This will include such things as the connections between the different hardware devices, the networking software employed, the measures in place to keep the system secure and so on.

**Trojan** A malicious piece of code contained inside seemingly harmless programming or data. Once inside a computer system, it will take control and do its damage.

**Tweened animation** Involves interpolation between keyframes of both the position and shape of an object.

**Typeface** A particular design of a character, such as Arial or Times Roman.

**Unique visitor** A unique IP address that has made at least one hit on one page of the website during a given period.

**Uploading** The process of transferring files from a client computer to a web server.

**URL** Stands for Uniform Resource Locator: the unique file address of a resource such as a web page, an image or a sound file.

**User interface** The link between the computer and the user: what the user sees, how the user tells the computer what is required and how the results are displayed.

**Validation** Checks should trap data that is invalid. They may not trap data that is incorrect.

**Validity-checking features** Features built into a system to ensure that it functions as expected.

**Variables** Used by programs to store data. Essentially, they are named memory locations. They can be used, for example, to store data input by the user or to store the results of calculations. To refer to the variable, the programmer gives it a name and also defines its data type. The data type controls the type of data that can be stored in the variable. Common data types used in Visual Basic include integer for storing whole numbers and string for storing text.

**VB** Stands for Visual Basic.

**VBA** Stands for Visual Basic for Applications.

**VBE** Stands for Visual Basic Editor – an environment in which you can edit macros and write new ones.

**Vector** A one-row or one-column range.

**Vector images** Created from drawing software, using objects such as lines and shapes, placed in particular positions to create the final image.

**Verification** Checks that data is correct. It involves comparing the data with another source.

**Virus** A malicious file created to damage a computer when it gains access to it. Once on a computer, viruses often reproduce, causing further damage.

**Visual weight** Refers to the relative size and scale of an element within a design.

**VLAN** Stands for Virtual Local Area Network. A VLAN is created when a LAN is divided into smaller areas, often for security reasons.

**VoIP** Voice over Internet Protocol. Allows the user to make telephone calls using a broadband Internet connection instead of a regular phone line.

**VR** Stands for virtual reality.

**VRML** Stands for Virtual Reality Mark-up Language.

**W3C** Stands for World Wide Web Consortium. This forum for information, commerce, communication and collective understanding develops material – such as specifications, guidelines, software and tools – to lead the Web to its full potential.

**Web manager** The person who is responsible for the smooth running of a website.

**Web server** Used to store the files making up a website and to deliver them, on request, to web browsers.

**Web-safe palette** Consists of the 216 colours that will display as solid and non-dithered, consistently on any computer monitor or web browser which is capable of displaying at least 8-bit colour.

**White space** An area on a printed page that is left intentionally blank so as to create overall balance on the page and to draw the eye to other features on the page.

**WiFi** Short for wireless fidelity. WiFi devices connect over distances of up to 30 m (98 ft) using radio signals.

**Wire frame** A flowchart that shows the interaction between a user and the computer, supported by sample screens showing the layout of the interface.

**WMA** Stands for Windows Media Audio.

**Worm** A program that can move around a computer system. Somewhere on its travels it will leave its payload – a virus or Trojan.

# Index

All entries in *italic* refer to Unit 13 which is available from the Heinemann website. Go to www.heinemann.co.uk/vocational, click on **IT & Office Technology**, click on **GCE** and select **Free Resources**.